Acknowledgments

I have not been able to write this book without some considerable help from other people. In particular I would like to acknowledge the help of the following people: Christopher Berry of 11 Stone Buildings Lincoln's Inn, Dr. Timothy Denison, Andrew Griffin at CLT Professional Publishing Ltd., Nicola Hacking of 11 Stone Buildings Lincoln's Inn, Lawrence Harrison of Harrison Curtis, Leonard Lipton, Tim Penny of 11 Stone Buildings Lincoln's Inn, Trevor Tayleur of The College of Law.

Dedication

I would like to dedicate this book to two people: to my late mother Sheila Elizabeth Lipton, and to my father and best friend Leonard Lipton. It was easy to find the words to write this book but impossible for me to find the words to write this dedication. All I can say is thank you, but this does not adequately convey my real feelings.

Music:
The Law and
Music Contracts

Nigel Lipton
Solicitor, Liptons. Proprietor of London Legal Training,
Visiting Lecturer, The College of Law

CLT Professional Publishing Ltd
A CLT Group Company

© Nigel Lipton 2000

Published by
CLT Professional Publishing Ltd
Part of the Central Law Group
31-33 Stonehills House
Welwyn Garden City
Hertfordshire
AL8 6PU

ISBN 1 85811 215 X

Typeset by Saxon Graphics Ltd, Derby
Printed in Great Britain by Antony Rowe Ltd

Contents

Foreword

Like so many people I have always dreamt of being a famous musician or footballer. Like the majority of people I have not been blessed with the talent or luck to be either. I think I knew this from a very early age because my other ambition from about the age of 8 or 9 was to be a barrister or a solicitor. Sadly like so many people I will not know what it feels like to have a number 1 hit nor will I know what it must feel like to score a goal for Leeds United. I would be a liar if I were to say that being a solicitor has more than made up for such serious deficiencies in my life! However being a solicitor has rewards of its own which help to some extent to compensate for my lack of talent in music and football. It was whilst I was at university that I hit upon the idea of trying at some stage to combine my love of music and football with the law. Hence a book on music, the law and music contracts. A book on football and the law will have to follow next!

I am aware that throughout the book I refer to an artist or a performer as "he". I am equally aware that for every successful male musician there is an equally successful female musician. Before writing the book I looked at several other legal texts to see how they dealt with the third person singular. All referred to "he" and not "she". Whether this is right or wrong is for you to decide. My defence if it bothers you is to say I am a sheep and am following what other writers have done and ask you to accept that I have acknowledged the situation here and to please feel free to substitute the word "she" for "he" when you see it.

Throughout the book I have tried as far as possible to follow the exact wording of the Copyright Designs And Patents Act 1988. There are quite a few places where I have not slavishly used the exact wording of the Act because I felt it was easier to slightly alter the wording purely for the sake of clarity. In addition I must point out that there is one deliberate omission from my copying of the wording of the Act. I have not referred to any references which occur throughout the act to "dramatic works" as such works do not fall within the scope of this book.

I am aware that there is some repetition of information throughout the chapters. This was a deliberate decision because I wanted to reduce the amount of cross-referencing from chapter to chapter down to a minimum. Having said that there is no getting away from the fact that the book does ask you to cross-refer at times. Hopefully this does not impede the ease with which each chapter can be read.

I have on occasions had to make decisions about whether certain information should be included in the book or whether it should be left out. I would have liked to have included more information in the book but I have to accept that there has to be a cut off point. The length of the book is in fact in the region of 3 to 4 times what was originally envisaged by the publishers.

I feel that I must make a point here which I repeat again in Chapter 1. In no way is this book to be taken as replacing the need for a thorough detailed understanding of the music industry and the law. It is meant as an introduction to aid the understanding of this complex and fascinating business. No book can replace experience in business and this book is no exception to this maxim. If you are not a lawyer and are reading this book and are about to negotiate any music business contracts you must take specialist legal advice.

Table of Cases

Table of Statutes

Chapter 1

Art Versus Money

The music business is regarded by most people with an air of mystique. There is no career path which will guarantee success. What works for one artist may not work for another. There are certainly massive financial rewards for the lucky few artists who succeed in the music business, but for every Elton John, Spice Girls or Pavarotti there are thousands of very talented artists who will struggle or who will never see their ability and hard work turned into the success they desire.

A record company may believe an artist has a great future and will use all their efforts to convert their belief into record sales and profits, but no amount of artist talent or record company finance will guarantee that the buying public will rush out to buy the finished article. It is often forgotten by an artist that for every successful profit-making record released by a record company there may easily be 50 to 100 equally good records released by the record company which are loss-makers.

It is true that many artists are impoverished when first signed to a music publisher or record company, and are delighted to have been spotted, taken out of the unsigned talent pool and given a chance to build a huge career. Invariably they will sign any contract to secure their chance of stardom whether or not the contractual terms are fair. What is also equally true is that for the few artists who achieve great success, some may turn round when they achieve superstar status and complain that they are not now, nor ever were paid sufficient for their work and seek legal redress. Whatever the legal merits of a superstar feeling so aggrieved the company will always take the attitude when first signing an unknown artist that at the outset the artist is unproven, has no commercial track record and is a financial risk to the company. They will only pay the artist what they believe to be the market rate, which is largely based upon the company's belief that the artist might eventually become a commercial success. It has to be remembered that publishing and record companies are in business to make a profit not for any altruistic reason. They will make substantial losses on many artists who do not suceed in commercial terms, and these losses are offset against the company's few big successes. The company will pay the artist a royalty figure which they believe is fair and reasonable. The figure the company will pay is negotiable, but the company will want to ensure that they can make a profit exploiting the artist's talents.

Successful artists do indirectly subsidise those starting out, but they themselves were indirectly subsidised by other successful artists when they were at the start of their career. At the end of the day a compromise must be found between the company who wants to make as much profit as possible, and the artist who wants to be paid as much as he can achieve for his talents. The compromise will depend on whether the artist is being courted by other interested companies, in which case the artist has a good negotiating stance ("leverage" in America), and is able to play one company off against the other to get the best deal, upon how much the company want the artist, and very importantly upon the abililty of the lawyers involved to get the best deal for their client.

Tales are rife in the music industry of artists achieving national or international status and receiving little or no money for their success. Certainly, many well known artists have felt, or indeed actually have been exploited by either their manager, their publisher or record company, and in some cases by all of them. Some artists have had to pursue expensive legal action to try and recover what was rightfully due to them. The history of the music business is full of tales which defy belief about how artists have been taken advantage of, and sadly in many case these tales are true. Artists were often easily taken advantage of once they became a success due to the contracts they had signed. To some extent this may still go on today, but hopefully it is nowhere near as prevalent as in the past. The music industry is now largely run by huge conglomerates, public quoted companies, and the "Arthur Daleys" who often acquired substantial power within the business in the past have largely, although sadly by no means totally, been consigned to history. That is not to say that household names are no longer prone to sign unreasonable deals, or that they may not fall out with their manager, publisher or record company over contractual matters. Nowdays the music industry is well aware of the need to be seen to treat artists correctly in their contracts. They are kept in check, if they need to be, by the fear of possible expensive litigation by high profile artists.

The business is now run largely by professional businesmen advised by well qualified industry accountants and lawyers. Artists are more likely to consult a lawyer before signing any contract, although sadly there are still many artists who do not feel they need to seek legal advice before signing and will only do so later when they have a contactual dispute. The industry is well aware of this problem, and in light of high profile cases a clause is now inserted in contracts stating that not only has the artist taken legal advice, but has taken it from a lawyer with experience of music contracts. It is to be hoped that the frequency of artist versus industry disputes may now largely diminish.

Artists tend to regard their work as works of art that should be treated with love and care. The music industry invariably regards the work of an artist as product to be exploited in the most advantageous way to generate consumer purchase. There is certainly a tendency by a few artists to claim that they "are not in the business for the money" and "they only want to get their music heard by the people". It is hard to believe any such altruistic claim. There is yet to be an artist who has refused to accept an advance or royalty cheques from their publisher or record company for the commercial exploitation of his work. The majority of artists are in the business because they are creative, want people to hear what they produce and they most certainly do want to make money. They want to make money by their works being marketed sensitively. The industry usually does not regard the work of an artist as something that is sacrosanct. Indeed, the industry terminology for an artist's songs or recordings is called "product", which is to be "exploited" as much as possible to achieve profit maximisation.

There is no such thing as a standard music industry contract. Each company has its own in-house contracts which are negotiated and amended from transaction to transaction. The extent to which a company will be prepared to negotiate depends on the factors mentioned above. The aim of this book is to look at the key clauses in music industry contracts and, where appropriate, suggest how they may be dealt with by the artist's solicitor. This book is aimed at lawyers and other interested people who need an understanding of the music business. It must be stressed that each final form contract is peculiar to those contracting parties' negotiating strengths and weaknesses. In no way is this book to be taken as replacing the need for a thorough detailed understanding of the music industry and the law. It is meant as an introduction to aid understanding of this complex and fascinating business. No book can replace experience in business and this book is no exception to this maxim. If you are not a lawyer and are reading this book and are about to negotiate any music business contracts you must take professional legal advice. It might be said that as a solicitor the author would be bound to say that. That may be true, but the statement itself is still nevertheless true.

The book will examine the main music industry contracts and the key terms in these contracts. Before these can be understood it will be necessary to look at copyright, moral rights and performer's rights, as detailed in the Copyright Designs and Patents Act 1988 ("CDPA"), at some important areas of contract law, and at music industry associations and collecting societies. After these topics have been examined the book will look at how a band might run their business affairs, and at management, publishing, recording, touring, sponsorship and merchandising contracts. The book will conclude with a brief look at music and the internet.

It should be noted that there is no room in a book of this size to examine the weighty and complex subject of taxation, nor is there room to explain in detail the basics of contract law.

The book will assume that any prerequisites which are needed to qualify for copyright protection under the CDPA, as detailed in Chapter 2, have been met.

Copyright Law and the Copyright, Designs and Patents Act 1988

Introduction

If you hold a George Michael compact disc, mini disc or cassette in your hands you are holding not just the software which, with the appropriate hardware, will enable you to play music, but you are also holding a bundle of intellectual property rights. Each song on the compact disc will usually consist of words and music, and both the words and the music will have their own separate copyright. The sound recording which contains the words and music on the compact disc will be copyright. The artwork on the cover of the compact disc will be copyright as will the information and acknowledgements contained in the compact disc booklet. The artist/group name and logo may have protection as a trade mark. The name and logo of the record company on the record sleeve will usually be protected as a trade mark. The performers on the record and the record company will have performers' rights. The composer of the words and the composer of the music will have moral rights in the compositions.

What follows below is a detailed examination of the Copyright, Designs and Patents Act 1988 (CDPA) in relation to copyright, moral rights and performer's rights. In relation to copyright the following will be looked at, namely, copyright relating to:

- a composition consisting of words and music,
- a sound recording of the composition,
- a radio or television or cable broadcast,
- a film or video,
- the artwork for the record cover.

(It should be noted that an examination of trade mark law is beyond the scope of the book. Readers are advised to refer to specialist books on trade marks for details.)

Copyright, Designs and Patents Act 1988

The CDPA came into force on 1 August 1989 and is now the primary Act governing copyright in the United Kingdom. The CDPA protects rights in "property".

What is capable of copyright protection?

Section 1(1) of the CDPA states that copyright can subsist in *inter alia*:

"(a) original literary, musical or artistic works,
(b) sound recordings, films, broadcasts, cable programmes."

If a work falls within the ambit of section 1(1) of the CDPA, then subject to other criteria being satisfied (for which see below), the work will attract copyright protection.

It should be noted that section 1(1)(a) requires the literary, musical or artistic work to be "original". The case of *Ladbroke (Football) Ltd* v *William Hill (Football) Ltd* [1964] 1 WLR 273 dealt with the concept of "original". The court held that for the work to be "original" it "should not be copied but should originate from the author". The cases of *University of London Press Ltd* v *University Tutorial Press Ltd* [1916] 2 Ch 601 and *Interlego AG* v *Tyco Industries Inc* [1988] 3 WLR 678 also dealt with the concept of "original". The cases held that the author of the work did not have to express any original ideas in the work, but that the author had to use his own skill and effort to produce the work. It is therefore possible for an author to use, for example, the same 17th Century archive documents in a library as another author to produce his work, but he must use his own skill and effort to produce his work and not copy from the other author.

It is possible for a songwriter to come up with the the same or substantially the same melody line as another songwriter without knowing of the second songwriter's melody. If this situation were to arise then both songwriters would have copyright in their own work. It is possible, as happened to George Harrison, for an artist to write a song and not have copyright in the words and music, not because he intentionally copied the other work, but because he heard the other work and may have subconsciously retained the information and used it to create the new work.

Section 3(2) provides that copyright will not exist in a literary or musical work "unless and until it is recorded, in writing or otherwise".

Writing is defined in section 178 as "any form of notation or code, whether by hand or otherwise". The criteria for recording in writing or otherwise will be satisfied for a piece of music if it is written down in proper musical notation or if it is recorded onto a cassette tape or onto a computer, provided it is permanently stored and capable of replaying the work when required. Section 3(3) further provides that it is immaterial whether the work was recorded by the author or with the permission of the author.

The situation can arise where a musician composes a new song in his head and fails to record it. The musician may decide to try out the new song live in concert to see if it is worth going into the studio to record. The new song which is played live in concert is not at this stage capable of qualifying for copyright protection as it has not satisfied the section 3(2) requirement. The concert promoter may decide without the consent of the musician to make a recording of the concert. The recording by the concert promoter of the new song for the first time without the consent of the musician is not an infringement of any copyright in the new song because copyright cannot exist until the new song has been recorded. The concert promoter will not be regarded under the CDPA as the author or owner of the new song (*see below for* The Author and the Owner of a Copyright Work). (The concert promoter can only have a possible claim to be the author and owner of the sound recording.) The unauthorised recording of the new song will now satisfy the section 3(2) recording requirement and enable the musician and not the concert promoter to claim copyright protection for the new song.

There is no requirement in the CDPA for a copyright work to be registered for it to attract copyright protection. Occasionally disputes may arise over the work, for example as to whether the work was original and not copied from another work or as to who is the author or owner of the work. (*See below for* Author and Owner of a Copyright Work, for Copying, *and above for* what is meant by original). To help establish when the work was actually created it would be advisable for the person who created the work to either send a copy of the work to himself by recorded delivery post and not open it when it is delivered, or send a sealed copy of the work to his solicitor or accountant to hold in safe custody and get the solicitor or accountant to give him a dated receipt for its deposit, or deposit a copy of the work at Stationers' Hall in London. Stationers' Hall keeps a register of copyright works and will for a fee register a work for 7 years, and will at the end of the 7 year period re-register the work for a further fee.

Definitions

Literary Work

Section 3(1) of the CDPA defines a "literary work" as "any work, other than a dramatic or musical work which is written, spoken or sung". The literary work must be original (see section 1(1)(a) above). There is no requirement for it to be a scholarly work, although to qualify for copyright protection as a literary work the author should have used some skill and effort producing the work. Works which the courts have held to be literary works include letters from one person to another, examination papers and football fixture lists. The courts have held that certain works do not qualify as a literary work because, for example, little or no skill and effort was used in producing the work, or because the work is too brief, or because the work does not give any information, or because it does not provide any instruction or provide any pleasure. (Where a work does not qualify as a literary work it may be possible to register it as a trade mark.) Works which the courts have refused to give copyright protection to include, the title of a song: see *Francis Day & Hunter* v *Twentieth Century Fox Corporation Ltd* [1940] AC 112, and names: see *Exxon Corporation* v *Exxon Insurance Consultants Ltd* (1982).

Musical work

Section 3(1) defines a "musical work" as "a work consisting of music, exclusive of any words or action intended to be sung, spoken or performed with the music".

Artistic work

Section 4(1) defines an "artistic work". An artistic work includes *inter alia* under section 4(1)(a), a graphic work or a photograph, irrespective of artistic quality. Section 4(2) defines a "graphic work" and includes *inter alia* under section 4(2)(a) any painting or drawing. Section 4(2) defines a "photograph" and means "a recording of light or other radiation on any medium on which an image is produced or from which an image may by any means be produced, and which is not a film". This means that the design for the album sleeve and the photographs for the album sleeve/inner booklet will be copyright protected as an artistic work. Also a performer's/group's logo may possibly qualify for copyright protection as an artistic work. If a performer's/group's logo does not qualify for copyright protection as an artistic work it may be possible to register the logo as a trade mark.

Sound recording

Section 5A(1)(a) and (b) defines a "sound recording" as "a recording of sounds, from which the sounds may be reproduced, or a recording of the whole or any part of a literary, dramatic or musical work, from which sounds reproducing the work or part may be produced, regardless of the medium on which the recording is made or the method by which the sounds are reproduced", *e.g.* compact disc, DAT, mini disc or any other format which when played will reproduce the sounds. Section 5A(2) states there is no copyright in a copy of a previous recording.

Broadcast

Section 6(1) defines a "broadcast" as "a transmission by wireless telegraphy of visual images, sounds or other information" which (a) is "capable of being lawfully received by members of the public", or (b) is "transmitted for presentation to members of the public". Section 6(6) states that there is no copyright in a broadcast which infringes the copyright in another broadcast or cable programme.

Film

Section 5B(1) defines a "film" as "a recording on any medium from which a moving image may by any means be produced". Section 5B(2) provides that the film soundtrack forms part of the film. This means that Digital Versatile Discs, Video Films, and CD-ROMs fall within the definition of "film". Section 5B(4) provides that there is no copyright in a copy of an existing film.

To sum up the CDPA, (subject to other criteria being satisfied), gives copyright protection to *inter alia*, the original words of a song (section 3(1)), to the original music of a song (section 3(1)), to the design for the album sleeve and to the photographs for the album sleeve/inner booklet (section 4(1)), to the sound recording containing the words and music (section 5A(1)), and to any video of the song performance (section 5B(1)). The requirement for the work to be "original" does not apply to a film, sound recording, or broadcast copyright, although the provisions of the CDPA do not enable copyright to subsist in a copy of an existing film, or of a previous sound recording, nor in a broadcast which infringes the copyright in another broadcast.

Having seen what work is capable of attracting copyright protection, it is necessary to look at the other criteria which have to be satisfied before the work will actually qualify for protection.

Other requirements for copyright protection

Section 1(3) states that copyright will not subsist in a work unless certain qualifying requirements have been satisfied. The requirements to be satisfied before copyright protection will be afforded to a work are detailed in section 153 *et seq* and relate to either a) the author (detailed in section 154), or b) to the country in which the work was first published (detailed in section 155), or c) in the case of a broadcast or cable programme the country from which the broadcast was made or the cable programme was sent (detailed in section 156).

Author requirement (s 154)

An author qualifies if he was a "qualifying person" at the "material time". Section 9(1) provides that the "author" of a work is the person who creates it. (There are cases in the CDPA where this assumption does not apply. This is dealt with in more detail later in the chapter.) A "qualifying person" is defined under section 154(1) as any of the following:

> "(a) a British citizen, a British Dependent Territories citizen, a British National (Overseas), a British Overseas citizen, a British subject or a British protected person within the meaning of the British Nationality Act 1981, or
> (b) an individual domiciled or resident in the United Kingdom or another country to which the relevant copyright provisions extend, or
> (c) a body incorporated under the law of a part of the United Kingdom or of another country to which the relevant copyright provisions extend."

Section 154(2) also provides that a work also qualifies for copyright protection:

> "if at the material time the author was a citizen or subject of, an individual domiciled or resident in, or a body incorporated under the law of a country to which the relevant provisions of the CDPA have been extended."

As mentioned above the author must be a "qualifying person" at the "material time". The "material time" is detailed in section 154(4) and (5) as:

(a) In relation to a literary, musical or artistic work :
(i) if the work is unpublished, it is when the work was made or, if the making of the work extended over a period, a substantial part of that period (Section 154 (4) (a))
(ii) if the work has been published, it is when the work was first published or, if the author had died before that time, immediately before his death (Section 154 (4)(b))

(b) In relation to other types of work the material time is:
(i) for a sound recording or film when the work was made (Section 154 (5) (a))
(ii) for a broadcast when the broadcast was made (Section 154 (5) (b))
(iii) for a cable programme when the programme was included in a cable programme service (Section 154 (5)(c)).

Publication requirement (s 155)

As opposed to qualifying for copyright protection as an author it is possible for the work to qualify by reference to the place of first publication. Section 155(1) provides that a literary, musical or artistic work, a sound recording or film will qualify for copyright protection if it is first published in:

(a) the United Kingdom, or
(b) any country to which to which the relevant provisions of the CDPA have been extended.

The question arises as to what is meant by the word "publication"? The CDPA defines publication in section 175(1)(a) as issuing copies to the public, and (b) for literary, musical or artistic works it includes making them available to the public by way of an electronic retrieval system. Section 175(4) also states that certain acts do not constitute publication, *inter alia*:

In the case of literary, or musical works:
(i) performing the work, or
(ii) broadcasting the work, or
(iii) including the work in a cable programme service. (Section 175 (4) (a) (i) and (ii))."

In the case of a sound recording or a film: -
(i) playing or showing the work in public, or

(ii) broadcasting the work, or
(iii) including it in a cable programme service. (Section 175 (4) (c) (i) and (ii)).

The case of *Francis Day Hunter v Feldman* [1914] 2 Ch 728 examined the question of whether sufficient numbers of the work were made available to satisfy the requirement of "publication". The case concerned the sheet music to the song "You Made Me Love You (I Didn't Want To Do It)". The court looked at the number of copies available on sale and held that the work had been published in the United Kingdom because it had satisfied the small anticipated demand for the sheet music. The work must therefore be available "to satisfy the reasonable requirements of the public" before it will be regarded as published under the CDPA. Indeed, section 175(5) specifically states that the requirement for publication is not satisfied if the publication is "merely colourable and not intended to satisfy the reasonable requirements of the public". What is "merely colourable" depends on the facts of each case.

Programme transmission requirement (s 156)

Apart from satisfying the author requirement under section 154 it is also possible for a broadcast or a cable programme to qualify for copyright protection if it has been sent from a place in:

(a) the United Kingdom, or
(b) any country to which to which the relevant provisions of the CDPA have been extended.

Joint authors

It is very common for a work to be created by more than one person. Where this happens the question arises do all or some of the joint authors have to satisfy the qualifying requirements before copyright protection will exist? This common situation is dealt with in section 154(3). The section states that a work of joint authorship will qualify for copyright protection if at the material time any of the authors satisfies the section 154 author qualification requirements. However, even if the work qualifies for copyright protection, only those authors who satisfy the author requirement under section 154 will be taken into account when considering matters such as who is the first owner of the copyright and the duration of copyright. (These matters will be looked at later in this chapter.)

Where does the CDPA apply?

The CDPA applies to England and Wales, Scotland and Northern Ireland. In addition it applies to the Isle of Man, Hong Kong and Guernsey.

The CDPA also provides that the Act can be applied to another Member State of the EU or to other countries which are Convention countries. A Convention country is a country which has signed a copyright convention to which the United Kingdom is also a signatory. There are several copyright conventions in existence, the most significant being the Berne Convention of 1886 (as subsequently revised) (which is more formally known as the Convention for the Protection of Literary and Artistic Works) and the Universal Copyright Convention of Geneva, 1952 (as subsequently revised). The United Kingdom has adopted both the Berne Convention and the Universal Copyright Convention. Most of the countries in the world are signatories to either the Berne Convention and/or the Universal Copyright Convention. The signatories to these conventions will, as well as providing copyright protection to the works of their own nationals, provide copyright protection to the works of nationals from the other signatory countries. In order to secure protection under the Universal Copyright Convention a copyright work must contain the copyright symbol © followed by the name of the copyright owner followed by the year in which the work was first published. It should be noted that the © symbol and subsequent details are not required for copyright protection under the CDPA but are required only for international protection under the Universal Copyright Convention.

Under the Rome Convention of 1961 (which is more formally known as the International Convention for the Protection of Performers, Producers of Phonograms and Broadcasting Organisations) international protection is given to performers, producers of sound recordings and broadcasters. As well as the Rome Convention, the Phonogram Convention of 1971 (more formally known as the Convention for the Protection of Producers of Phonograms against Unauthorised Duplication of their Phonograms (Geneva Convention)) exists to protect sound recordings against piracy. For a sound recording to qualify for protection under these conventions the sound recording or the packaging should contain the symbol ℗ followed by the year of first publication, followed by the name of the owner of the sound recording. To protect the performers' rights the performers' names should be included on the sound recording or the packaging. The use of the © symbol with the required accompanying details will put people on notice, for example, that the artistic work, namely the design for the album sleeve, is copyright. The use of the ℗ symbol with the required accompanying details will do likewise with reference to the sound recording. The use of the © and ℗ symbols with the required accompanying details will bring about the section 104 and 105 copyright presumptions. (*See below*, Copyright Presumptions, for sections 104 and 105.)

In addition, under section 159(3), the CDPA may also apply to other countries which have made, or will make provision under their law to protect adequately copyright works for copyright owners.

The author and owner of a copyright work

The CDPA distinguishes between the concepts of authors and owners. The person who is the author of a piece of music which is capable of copyright protection may not always be the owner of the copyright. The author, even if he is not the copyright owner, may be entitled to moral rights in the work. Moral rights will be examined later in this chapter, but it should be noted at this stage that if the author is entitled to moral rights, he has these rights notwithstanding somebody else being the owner of the copyright in the work.

There is a difference between ownership of the copyright and ownership of the item which contains the copyright work(s), *e.g.* if A writes a letter to B, A owns the copyright in the words as a literary work whereas B owns the paper on which the copyright work was written. B cannot therefore exploit the literary copyright in the letter which was sent to him. Likewise, if C buys a record, C does not own the copyright in the literary and musical works (which will be owned by the composer or his publisher) nor will C own the sound recording copyright (which will usually be owned by the record company). All C owns is the record which he purchased.

The author of the work

As mentioned above, section 9(1) provides that the "author" of a work is "the person who creates it". Usually it is clear who actually created the work. For example, a composer of a classical work would under section 9(1) be regarded as the "author".

In the case of sound recordings the "author" under section 9(2)(aa) is the producer. The producer is defined in section 178 and means the person who makes the necessary arrangements for the creation of the sound recording.

In the case of a broadcast, section 9(2)(b) provides that the "author" is "the person making the broadcast". Section 6(3)(a) and (b) provides that the person making the broadcast is (a) "the person transmitting the programme, if he has responsibility to any extent for its contents", and (b) any person who makes the necessary arrangements for the transmission of the programme. (Section 10(2) provides that a broadcast is a work of joint authorship where more than one person has made the broadcast.)

For a cable programme section 9(2)(c) provides that the "author" is the person providing the cable programme service.

For a film made on or after 1 July 1994 section 9(2)(ab) provides that the "author" is "the producer and the principal director". Section 10(1A) provides that a film is to be "treated as a work of joint authorship unless the producer and the principal director are the same person". The producer has the same meaning as the producer of a sound recording (see above). The CDPA does not define who is the principal director.

The CDPA deals with works that have been generated by computer. Section 9(3) provides that where a computer has generated a literary, musical or artistic work, the author is the person who made the necessary arrangements for the creation of the work. Section 178 defines a computer-generated work as a work "generated by computer in circumstances where there has been no human author of the work". It is important to note that a computer-generated work is different to a work created by a person using a computer. In the field of music, computers in the form of synthesisers are being used all the time. If an artist uses a computer like a musical instrument and programmes his tune into it, this is not a computer-generated work. A computer-generated work is one where the computer itself randomly creates the work and the author in this instance will under section 9(3) be the person who made the necessary arrangements for the creation of the work.

Quite frequently a piece of work is created by more than one person. In such a case the work is regarded under section 10 as a work of joint authorship. A work of joint authorship is defined in section 10 (1) as a work produced by the collaboration of two or more authors where the contribution of each author is not distinct from that of the other author(s). Taking an example of an Elton John and Bernie Taupin composition, if Elton John wrote the tune on his own without Bernie Taupin, and Bernie Taupin wrote the words on his own without Elton John, this is not a work of joint authorship. Elton John in this example would be the author of the musical work and Bernie Taupin would be the author of the literary work. If, however, Elton John and Bernie Taupin collaborated with each other so that each contributed to the tune and to the words, this would be a work of joint authorship if their respective contributions were not distinct from each other, in which case Elton John and Bernie Taupin would be the joint authors in the two copyright works, namely the musical copyright and the literary copyright. If, however, Elton John and Bernie Taupin collaborated with each other so that each contributed to the tune and to the words but in this example Elton John wrote all the words to the chorus and Bernie Taupin wrote all the words to all the verses this is not a joint authorship of the literary work as their contributions are distinct from each other.

If one person contributes before (*Donoghue* v *Allied Newspapers Ltd* [1937] 3 All ER 503) or after (*Wiseman* v *George Weidenfeld & Nicolson Ltd* [1985] FSR 525) the work has been created, this will not create a work of joint authorship. Suggesting ideas rather than being directly responsible for the copyright work will not create a work of joint authorship (*Robin Ray* v *Classic FM*, *The Times* 8 April 1998.)

To save any argument later, where artists plan to write music and lyrics together, before starting work they should enter an agreement making it clear whether or not they are joint authors of the music and lyrics.

In the case of a broadcast section 10(2) provides that it will be treated as a work of joint authorship where more than one person is making the broadcast. (Section 6(3)(a) and (b) referred to earlier deals with who is the person making the broadcast.)

The owner of the work

As seen earlier, the general rule set out in section 9(1) is that the author of the work is the person who created it. The general rule regarding copyright ownership is stated in section 11(1) and provides that the author of the work is the first owner of the copyright.

Employees

The employer/employee situation (a contract of service, rather than a contract for services which is self-employment) is dealt with in section 11(2). This provides that where a literary work, musical work, artistic work, or film is made by an employee in the course of his employment, his employer is the first owner of any copyright in the work unless there is any agreement between the parties to the contrary. A sensible employment contract should specifically deal with this matter. An employer/employee relationship is quite common in the music business. Often for tax planning reasons an artist might set up his own limited company(ies) and will be employed by the company(ies) to provide specific services for the company(ies). So, for example, a composer might set up a limited company which will employ him to compose. The company as the employer will, unless the employment contract provides otherwise, be the first owner of the copyright in the compositions written by the composer in the course of his employment.

The producer of a sound recording

As mentioned above, the author of a sound recording under section 9(2)(aa) is the producer. The producer is defined in section 178 and means the person who makes the necessary arrangements for the creation of the sound recording. Also, the general rule regarding copyright ownership is stated in section 11(1) which provides that the author of the work is the first owner of the copyight. The general rule will therefore mean that the producer is the first owner of the copyright in the sound recording.

The performer will either produce his own recordings or a third party who is usually not a record company employee will be brought in to produce the recordings. To avoid the application of the general rule under section 11(1), the performer's recording agreement will contain a clause which provides that where the performer produces his own recordings, he will assign the ownership of the copyright in the sound recording to the record company. Similarly, where a third party produces the performer's recordings the producer's agreement will contain a clause which provides that the producer will assign the ownership of the copyright in the sound recording to the record company. (*See also* Chapter 8 Recording Agreements, Introduction *below*.)

Commissioned works

It is quite common in the music business for a work to be commissioned by somebody to use in a television programme, a film or an advertisement. The author of the work is the person who created it (section 9(1)). The CDPA does not deal with who is the first owner where a work has been commissioned. In this situation the first owner is the author, in other words the composer of the music unless, which will usually be the case, there is a contract between the commissioner and the author specifically dealing with who owns the copyright.

Usually the commissioner will seek an assignment of the copyright in the work from the author.

Joint ownership

If the creators of the work are joint authors as defined in section 10(1) the creators will also be joint owners of the work. (Where the joint authors are employees and the literary, musical, artistic work or film was made by employees in the course of their employment, the employer will be the first owner of any copyright in the work unless there is any agreement between the parties to the contrary. (*See* Employees above).) Section 173(2) provides that where there is joint ownership any licence to use the copyright work requires a licence from all the joint authors.

Joint authors can hold the ownership as either joint tenants or as tenants in common. If the ownership of the work is held as joint tenants when one joint tenant dies, his share in the work passes automatically to the remaining living joint tenants. If the ownership of the work is held as tenants in common when one tenant in common dies, his share in the work does not pass to the surviving living tenants in common but it passes under his estate to the beneficiaries under his will or where there is no will it passes under the intestacy rules. A joint tenancy can be converted into a tenancy in common by a joint tenant severing the joint tenancy during his lifetime, *e.g.* by giving written notice to the other joint tenants.

Where two or more people intend to create a work together, there should be a written agreement between the parties as to whether the ownership of the work will be held as joint tenants or as tenants in common. In the absence of any agreement between the parties the law will usually assume that the ownership of the copyright will be held as tenants in common.

Anonymous works

The CDPA in section 104(4) deals with the situation where a literary, musical or artistic work exists but the author of the work is not known.

This situation may be rare but can arise. For example, (and this is a variation of a true story), imagine there is a top music industry party and one of the waiters at the party persuades a guest who is a publisher to listen to his songs which he has written and recorded onto tape, which by chance he happened to have on his person. The publisher takes the tape and a few days later listens to it in his car. The publisher realises the songs are commercially viable and wants to publish them. The publisher looks at the tape but there are no details about the waiter on the tape. The waiter had forgotten to give the publisher his name and address at the party, and the company that hired the waiting staff for the party cannot find any details on their records about the waiter. The publisher decides to publish the songs on the tape, and being an honest person puts all royalties accruing to the exploitation of those songs into a separate bank account on trust for the waiter. By virtue of section 104(4) where there is no name purporting to be the author on copies of the work but:

> "(a) the work qualifies for copyright protection by virtue of section 155 [The publication requirement. See earlier for details], and
> (b) a name purporting to be that of the publisher appeared on copies of the work as first published,
>> the person whose name appeared [the publisher] shall be presumed, until the contrary is proved, to have been the owner of the copyright at the time of publication."

In our example the publisher will by section 104(4) be deemed to be the owner of the works until the true owner, the waiter, comes forward to claim the ownership of the copyright in the works.

How can the copyright owner exploit the copyright work?

Having seen what type of work can be afforded copyright protection, how a work qualifies for copyright protection, who is the author of the copyright work and who owns the copyright work, the next matter to consider is how the copyright owner can exploit, or in other words make money out of the ownership of his work.

Section 90(1) of the CDPA provides that copyright owners can deal with their work in the same way as with their personal or moveable property. This means that a copyright work can be transferred by assignment, by will, or by operation of the law. A copyright owner can make money from his copyright work by exploiting the work himself, or by permitting others to exploit it.

A copyright owner can permit others to exploit his work by granting either:

(a) a licence, or
(b) an assignment of the copyright work.

Copyright licences

A licence is a contractual right, a permission, given by the licensor (the copyright owner), to the licensee. A licence should grant specific rights to the licensee and reserve everything else to the licensor. A licence does not pass any title in the work to the licensee. It is a permission from the licensor to use the work in accordance with the licence agreement. An example of where a licence is often used is where the owner of the sound recording, which is usually the record company, agrees to license the sound recording for use in a television advertisement.

A licence can be either:

(a) exclusive, or
(b) non-exclusive.

Section 92(1) of the CDPA provides that an exclusive license is a licence in writing, signed by or on behalf of the copyright owner, authorising the licensee, to the exclusion of everybody else including the licensor, to exercise the rights granted which would otherwise be exercisable exclusively by the copyright owner. Section 101(1) provides that an exclusive licensee has except against the copyright owner the same rights as if he had been given an assignment (see below for assignees' rights). Section 101(2) provides that the rights and remedies of an exclusive licensee are concurrent with the rights and remedies of the copyright owner.

A non-exclusive licence will be granted where the licensor wants to grant the same rights to more than one licensee. A non-exclusive licence does not have to be in writing although it usually would be. If there is any infringement of copyright a non-exclusive licensee cannot take legal proceedings for the infringement. A non-exclusive licensee must require the copyright owner to bring proceedings for infringement.

Section 90(4) provides that where a licence is granted by the copyright owner it will bind not only the copyright owner but also every successor in title to his copyright, except for a purchaser for value acting in good faith and without notice of the licence. In addition, anybody who derives title to the copyright from such a purchaser for value who acted in good faith and without notice of the licence will also not be bound by the licence.

Copyright assignment

Section 90(3) states that

> an assignment of copyright is not effective unless it is in writing signed by or on behalf of the assignor.

Where there is an assignment of copyright, section 176(1) provides that for a limited company " the requirement … that the instrument be signed by or on behalf of a person is also satisfied in the case of [a limited company] by the affixing of its seal". If the assignment is by the original copyright owner it will be known as a grant of copyright, whereas subsequent dealings are known as assignments of copyright.

Section 91(1) allows for the copyright in works which have yet to be created to be assigned, *e.g.* a publishing agreement will provide that the composer will assign the copyright in all the compositions which he writes during the term of the agreement to the publisher. Once the work has been created and can be afforded copyright protection the purchaser of the future copyright (or a purchaser from him) is entitled to require the copyright in the work to be vested in him.

An assignment is an actual transfer of ownership of rights in the work. The assignee becomes the owner of rights in the work which have been assigned to him. This means that the assignor of the work can be prevented from doing anything which infringes the rights given to the assignee.

Using an assignment or licence

As stated earlier, a copyright owner can make money from his copyright works by selling copies of the work himself, or by permitting others to sell copies. If he permits others to sell copies he will do so by giving another person(s) either an assignment or an exclusive or non-exclusive licence to use the work.

Section 90(2) provides that an assignment, licence, or any other permitted way of dealing with copyright does not have to be of the whole of the copyright work. It can be limited so that it can apply:

"(a) to one or more, but not all, of the things the copyright owner has the exclusive right to do"

(see below for what are the exclusive rights of the copyright owner),

"(b) to part, but not the whole, of the period for which the copyright is to subsist."

(See below for how long copyright subsists.)

In summary, the copyright owner can exploit his work by giving a third party an assignment or licence of either:

(a) all his rights in the copyright work for either:
    (i) the whole period for which copyright subsists, or
    (ii) part of the period for which copyright subsists,

or
(b) some of his rights in the copyright work for either:
   (i)   the whole period for which copyright subsists, or
   (ii) part of the period for which copyright subsists.

Dealing with rights

It is common for an artist to want to limit the rights he has granted to specified territories. Many small record companies are established in England and have no ability to market the artists' records abroad, and yet they may seek to secure rights from the recording artist not only for the the territory in which they operate but also for the rest of the world. The recording artist may well try and resist the record company having world rights and seek to limit rights to the territory in which the record company presently operates. The CDPA allows rights to be limited to geographical areas but if there is a purported assignment of rights which is limited to certain territories, this will be taken to be a licence and not an assignment of the copyright.

There can often be a problem deciding whether a document is an assignment or an exclusive licence. The document should state whether it is intended to be an assignment or an exclusive licence. However, stating what the document is intended to be does not necessarily turn the document into its title. It will only suggest what the document may be. If the document is described as an assignment but the rights granted are limited to certain territories the document will in fact be a licence. A licence rather than an assigmnent may be presumed if the assignee has ongoing obligations to comply with under the terms of the agreement. The most common ongoing obligation for a publisher or record company is to pay royalties to the composer/artist. An assignment containing a provision for royalty payments which is standard in publishing and recording agreements in some cases may be regarded not as an assigment but a licence.

The copyright owner with his solicitor will need to decide whether he wants to grant an assignment or a licence to the third party. He will also need to consider in detail exactly what rights he intends to grant to the third party and ensure that he grants only those rights and retains all the other rights.

The rights clause must be very tightly drafted so that there can be no dispute as to whether the right to exploit the work using future technology has been granted to the third party or reserved to the copyright owner. If we go back to the 1960s nobody could then have foreseen the development of CD, DAT, Mini-Disc or DVD. The value of having the rights to exploit in these formats is huge. Future technology should therefore be thought about very carefully when considering the drafting of the rights clause. If the agreement is not clear as to whether the right to exploit a work via a new form of technology has or has not been given, disputes between the parties could easily arise and it could be left to the courts to decide the construction of the agreement.

The copyright owner will need to consider very carefully the length of the term he is prepared to give and the territory for which he is granting the rights. Many other contractual terms will also have to be considered by the copyright owner. The relevant contractual terms will be looked at in later chapters of this book.

It should be noted that copyright can be left by a will. It will vest in the personal representatives of the estate who will pass it on to the beneficiary entitled under the will, or if the deceased did not leave a will, it passes by the rules of intestacy.

If the copyright owner becomes bankrupt, the copyright in his works will vest in his trustee in bankruptcy.

Other relevant rights, *e.g.* moral rights, will be dealt with where the relevant rights are discussed.

Duration of copyright

Copyright does not last in perpetuity. The CDPA as amended by the Duration of Copyright and Rights in Performances Regulations 1995 (SI 1995/3297) which came into force on 1 January 1996 sets out the duration of copyright for the various types of copyright works in the United Kingdom. The duration of copyright protection under the CDPA was for the most part for a period of 50 years. However, the Duration of Copyright and Rights in Performances Regulations 1995 has altered the duration of copyright in some cases. The section below sets out the copyright duration as amended by these Regulations.

Literary, musical or artistic works

Section 12(2) of the CDPA provides that for literary, musical or artistic works, copyright expires 70 years "from the end of the calendar year in which the author dies".

Section 12(8)(a)(i) provides that for section 12(2) if the work is one of joint authorship (see above for joint authorship), if the identity of all the authors is known, the period will expire 70 years from the end of the calendar year of the death of the last author to die. Section 12(8)(a)(ii) covers the situation where the identity of only some of the joint authors is known and provides that the period will expire 70 years from the end of the calendar year of the death of the last identifiable author.

Section 12(3) provides that if the work is of unknown authorship copyright expires:

> "(a) 70 years from the end of the calendar year in which the work was made, or
> (b) if the work had been made available to the public during that period it will expire 70 years from the end of the calendar year in which it was first made available to the public."

Section 12(5)(a)(i) and (ii) provides that for a literary, or musical work making the work available to the public includes, performing it in public, or broadcasting or including it in a cable programme.

Section 12(7) provides that if the work is a computer-generated work (see above for the definition of a computer-generated work), that copyright expires "50 years from the end of the calendar year in which the work was made."

Sound recordings

For sound recordings made after 1 August 1989 section 13A(2)(a) and (b) provides that copyright in a sound recording expires:

(a) 50 years form the end of the calendar year in which it is made, or (b) if it is released during the 50 year period referred to in (a), it will expire 50 years from the end of the calendar year in which it is released. Section 13A(3) provides that "released" means when it is first published, (i.e. defined in section 175(1)(a) as issuing copies to the public), played in public, broadcast or included included in a cable programme. Section 13A(3) specifically states that in determining if a sound recording has been released no account will be taken of any unauthorised acts.

(The duration of a sound recording copyright made before 1 August 1989 is outside the scope of this book.)

Films

Section 13B(2) provides that for a film, copyright will expire 70 years from the end of the calendar year from the death of the last to survive of:

"(a) the principal director.
(b)   the author of the screenplay,
(c)   the author of the dialogue, or
(d)   the composer of music specially created for and used in the film."

(There are provisions in section 13B(3) for calculating 70 years from the last person to die where the identity of one or more of the people listed in section 13B(2)(a)–(d) is known and the identity of one or more of them is not known. Section 13B(4) deals with the period of copyright where the identity of all the people in section 13B(2)(a)–(d) is not known. Section 13B(9) deals with the duration of copyright where there is no person who falls within the category of persons listed in section 13B(2)(a)–(d.) The details fall outside the scope of the book, and the reader is referred to the CDPA for these details.)

(The duration of film copyright made before 1 August 1989 is also outside the scope of this book.)

Broadcasts and cable programmes

Section 14(2) provides that the duration of copyright in a broadcast or cable programme service is 50 years "from the end of the calendar year in which the broadcast was made or the programme was included in a cable programme service".

It should be noted that section 14(5) provides that

"copyright in a repeat broadcast or cable programme expires at the same time as the copyright in the original broadcast or cable programme."

Extended and revived copyrights

As mentioned earlier, the duration of copyright under the CDPA has been altered in some cases by the Duration of Copyright and Rights in Performances Regulations 1995 (SI 1995/3297).

The effect of these Regulations is that the duration of some types of copyright work has increased to 70 years, and some works which had fallen out of copyright have come back within copyright protection.

Among the detailed provisions of the Regulations are provisions for the ownership of any extended or revived copyright.

The previous section "Duration of Copyright" sets out the copyright duration as amended by the Copyright and Rights In Performances

Regulations 1995. Any other effects of the Duration of Copyright and Rights in Performances Regulations 1995 (save as detailed earlier) are outside the scope of this book.

It should be noted that it is common in agreements assigning copyright for the full period of copyright for the duration clause to be drafted to provide that copyright is assigned for the full period of copyright and for all renewals and extensions of copyright.

Exclusive rights of copyright owner

Section 16(1) provides that the owner of the copyright in a work has the exclusive right to do the following acts in the United Kingdom:

> "(a) to copy the work (section 16(1)(a)).
> (b) to issue copies of the work to the public (section 16(1)(b)).
> (c) to rent or lend the work to the public (section 16(1)(ba).
> (d) to perform, show or play the work in public (section 16(1)(c)).
> (e) to broadcast the work or include it in a cable programme service (section 16(1)(d)).
> (f) to make an adaptation of or do any of the above in relation to an adaptation (section 16(1)(e))."

These acts are restricted acts, or as section 16(1) calls them, "acts restricted by copyright". Section 16(2) provides that

> "copyright in a work is infringed by a person who without the licence of the copyright owner does, or authorises another to do, any of the acts restricted by the copyright."

By virtue of section 16(3) (a) copyright infringement can occur where a section 16(1) restricted act is done "in relation to the whole or any substantial part" of the copyright work by, for example, a person who does not have permission to do so from the copyright owner. There is no definition in the CDPA of the word "substantial". As in *Ladbroke (Football) Ltd* v *William Hill (Football) Ltd* [1964] 1 WLR 273, in deciding whether a "substantial part" of a work has been used, the courts will look at the quality of what was taken rather than the quantity of what was taken.

The case of *Warwick Film Productions v Eisenger* [1969] 1 Ch 508 looked at the situation where A had prepared a work which was part original and part copied from another source and B copied from A's work the part that A had copied from another source. The court found that A's work was a copyright work but that B had not copied a substantial part of A's work as A had himself copied that part from another source.

In *Hawkes & Son (London) Ltd v Paramount Film Service Ltd* [1934] Ch 593 the court considered that a defendent who used 20 seconds from a four-minute tune had used a "substantial" part of the work and so infringed copyright. It is not possible to say that x number of seconds or minutes will be regarded as "substantial" for the purposes of infringement. Obviously, the more of the work used, the more likely the court will say that a "substantial" part has been taken. However, taking the example of Beethoven's Symphony Number 5 in C minor, assuming it was a copyright work and protected under the CDPA, if somebody used the opening four notes from the symphony, which are the most commonly known part of the work, a court would probably say that was a "substantial" part of the work judged on a qualitative basis. If somone used a different set of four notes from the symphony the court might possibly not regard this as a "substantial" part of the work judged on a qualitative basis. The court will when considering alleged infringement of a musical work hear evidence from musicologists representing each side. Expert evidence in such cases can be very important in determining if there has been any infringement.

Having discussed the exclusive rights of the copyright owner, these rights must be examined in more detail. Sections 17–21 of the CDPA go into more detail about each exclusive right.

Copying

Section 17 deals with copying and provides that this is a restricted act.

Section 17(2) provides that copying for a literary, musical or artistic work means reproducing the work in any material form, including storing the work in any medium by electronic means.

Section 17(4) provides that copying in relation to a film, television broadcast or cable programme includes making a photograph of the whole or any substantial part of any image which forms part of the film, television broadcast or cable programme.

Section 17(6) also states that a work is copied where the copies which are made are transient or incidental to some other use of the work.

It is frequently easy to establish whether a work has been copied. Making a recording of a Sting CD to a mini-disc, DAT, recordable CD or any other format will constitute copying.

Sometimes it is not easy to determine at first glance if the work has been copied. The case of *Francis Day & Hunter Ltd v Bron* [1963]

Ch 587 dealt with the similarity between two songs. The court held that it was possible for there to be subconscious copying of a work, where, for example, the defendant heard a song on the radio and many years later wrote a song which, without consciously meaning to do so turned out to be a copy of the original song heard many years ago on the radio. The fact that it was in the subconscious mind of the defendant when he wrote his song may cause the defendant to copy a work without realisation. (The defendant in the *Francis Day & Hunter Ltd* case was found not to have copied as there was not enough evidence before the court for them to establish copying. However, the case did establish the principle of subconscious copying.) A famous example of subconscious copying is the case of George Harrison whose "My Sweet Lord" was held to have been copied subconsciously from the song "He's So Fine". It is an easy trap for a songwriter to fall into innocently, and this is the reason why some record and music publishing companies will refuse to listen to unsolicited material, and some companies will not even open a package if they are aware or suspect that it contains an unsolicited tape recording.

Sampling is another area of copying that is rife in the music industry. Sampling is the taking of part of a recorded work, perhaps a bit of the drum beat, or a bit of the bass line or perhaps a bit of the vocal, and using it in a new recorded work. The use of the sample may possibly be very obvious in the new tune. The sample may be high up in the record mix so it can be heard and related to the previous recorded work by even the most untrained ear, or it can be mixed down in such a way that only experts would know that it was taken from, say, a James Brown track.

Sampling is used in all types of popular music, and it has to be remembered that if the sample used is the whole or a substantial part of another work that constitues copying. Artists using samples have frequently and wrongly felt that if they were only taking a couple of seconds of a previously recorded work that they were doing nothing wrong, or in some cases the artist knew what he was doing was wrong but did not care. What should happen before an artist uses a sample on his record is that permission should be obtained to use that sample. This is called obtaining "clearance". If, for example, the sample that the artist wants to use on his record is the chorus of a well-known record, there will need to be three clearances obtained: to use the words (the literary copyright), the music (the musical copyright) and the sound recording (the sound recording copyright). The cost of clearance(s), if the owner(s) is willing to allow the sample to be used, could be anything from a small sum to a share in or all the rights in the music publishing of the new work.

Record companies are so concerned about the dangers of an artist using samples on records that they now require the artist to tell them what samples he intends to use before he uses them on the recording and the record company will want the rights cleared before the sample is used. This will save litigation, damages and an injunction which would mean the record company would have to withdraw the record using the sample from the record shops.

Another way a work may be copied is by parody. A parody which by definition is a play upon an existing work may amount to being a copy of an existing work. The rules for parody are the same as mentioned earlier, in other words, has the whole or a substantial part of a work been copied? Parody records are rare but do exist. See, for example, the 1984 comedy parody hit record by Weird Al Yankovic "Eat It" which was a play on Michael Jackson's 1983 hit "Beat It".

It is wrongly thought that if you buy, say, a Spice Girls CD you can make a copy onto tape for your own personal use on your cassette walkman. Section 17 does not allow this to be done. Copying even for private domestic use is an act of infringement.

Issuing copies

Section 18 deals with issuing copies of the work to the public. Section 18(1) provides that this is a restricted act.

Section 18(2)(a) and (b) deals with what is meant by issuing copies of a work to the public, whilst section 18(3) deals with what does not constitute issuing copies of a work to the public.

Section 18(2) provides that issuing copies of a work to the public means:

"(a) putting into circulation in the EEA [European Economic Area] copies not previously put into circulation in the EEA by or with the consent of the copyright owner, or
(b) putting into circulation outside the EEA copies not previously put into circulation in the EEA or elsewhere."

Section 18(3) provides that issuing copies of a work to the public does not include:

"(a) any subsequent distribution, sale, hiring or loan of those copies previously put into circulation (subject to the section 18A rental or lending right.)"

(*See below* for section 18A), or

"(b) any subsequent importation of such copies into the United Kingdom or another EEA state,
except so far as section 18(2)(a) applies to putting into circulation in the EEA copies previously put into circulation outside the EEA."

One effect of section 18 is that if, for example, a record company issues, say, 1,000 copies of a record in the EEA the record company cannot under section 18 stop any subsequent distribution or sale of those 1,000 copies, nor can the record company stop the subsequent importation of those 1,000 records into the United Kingdom or another EEA state. It should be noted that although the record company in the example cannot stop the subsequent distribution, sale, hiring, lending or importation of those records, it can stop the subsequent rental of those records due to the fact that section 18(3)(b) is subject to the section 18A restricted act of renting and lending. (See below for section 18A rental or lending of copies of the work.)

Renting or lending copies to the public

Section 18A deals with renting or lending copies of the work to the public. Subsection (1) provides that this is a restricted act in:

    (a) a literary or musical work, (section 18A(1)(a)),

    (b) an artistic work, other than:

        (i) a work of architecture in the form of a building or model for a building, or

        (ii) a work of applied art (section 18A(1)(b)), or

    (c) a film or sound recording, (section 18A(1)(c))

Section 18A(2)(a) and (b) defines what constitutes "rental" and "lending".

Section 18A(2)(a) provides that "rental" means

"making a copy of the work available for use, on terms that it will or may be returned, for direct or indirect economic or commercial advantage".

Rental therefore means hiring out the work, usually for money.

Section 18A(2)(b) provides that "lending" means

"making a copy of the work available for use, on terms that it will or may be returned, otherwise than for direct or indirect economic or commercial advantage, through an establishment which is accessible to the public."

Lending therefore means loaning a work out for free. The lending must be done by an establishment which is accessible to the public, *e.g.* a public library. (Section 18A(5) states that if a charge is made purely to cover the establishment's operating costs the establishment will still be "lending" under the definition.)

Section 18A(3) provides that "rental" and "lending" does not include:

"(a) making available for the purpose of public performance, playing or showing in public, broadcasting or inclusion in a cable programme service,
(b) making available for the purpose of exhibition in public, or
(c) making available for on-the spot reference use."

Section 18A(4) also provides that "lending"

"does not include making available between establishments which are accessible to the public."

Any references in section 18A to the rental or lending of copies of a work include by virtue of section 18A(6) the rental or lending of the original work.

(It should be noted that the wording of section 18A is almost identical to the wording of section 182C. For the wording of section 182C *see* Rights in Performances, the Performer's Rights below.)

Rental and the right to equitable remuneration

Section 93B(1) provides that where an author has transferred his rental right concerning a sound recording or a film to the producer of the sound recording or film, he retains the right to equitable remuneration for the rental.

The authors to whom section 93B applies include:

(a) the author of a literary, musical or artistic work and
(b) the principal director of a film.

Section 93B(2) provides that the right to equitable remuneration cannot be assigned by the author except to a collecting society for the purpose of enabling it to enforce the right on his behalf. (*See* Chapter 4 Collecting Societies and Music Industry Associations). (Section 93B(2) does allow for the right to receive equitable remuneration to be transmissible by testamentary disposition or by operation of the law as personal or moveable property, and that the right to receive equitable remuneration may be assigned or further transmitted by any person into whose hands it passes.)

The person who is liable to pay the equitable remuneration is stated in section 93B(3) to be the person who is currently entitled to the rental right. Section 93B(4) provides that the amount payable for equitable remuneration is the amount agreed by the parties, or, in default of such agreement, then by virtue of section 93C either party can ask the

Copyright Tribunal to determine the amount payable. Section 93B (5) provides that any clause in an agreement purporting to exclude or restrict the right to equitable remuneration will have no effect.

There are also provisions in section 93C(2)(a) and (b) where equitable remuneration is payable, for either party to the agreement to apply to the Copyright Tribunal to:

(a) vary any agreement as to the amount payable, or
(b) vary any previous determination of the Copyright Tribunal.

Any clause in an agreement purporting to prevent a party questioning the amount of equitable remuneration before the Copyright Tribunal will by virtue of section 93C(5) have no effect.

Section 93C(4) provides that the remuneration will not be considered inequitable merely because it was paid by way of a single payment or at the time of the transfer of the rental right.

(*See* Chapter 4 Collecting Societies and Music Industry Associations for the Copyright Tribunal.)

(Section 93A(1) provides that

> "where an agreement concerning film production is concluded between an author and a film producer, the author shall be presumed, unless the agreement provides to the contrary, to have transferred to the film producer any rental right in relation to the film arising by virtue of the inclusion of a copy of the author's work in the film."

Section 93A does have relevance to a composer of music because section 93A(2) provides *inter alia* that an author means an author, or prospective author of a literary or musical work. In addition, section 93A(3) provides that section 93A(1) does not apply to any rental right in relation to the film arising by virtue of the inclusion in the film of, *inter alia*, music specifically created for and used in the film.)

Performing, showing or playing the work in public

Section 19(1) provides that the performance in public of a literary or musical work is a restricted act.

Section 19(2)(a) and (b) provides that a performance in relation to a literary or musical work:

(a) includes, *inter alia*, the delivery of lectures, and
(b) any visual or acoustic presentation, including presentation by means of a sound recording, film, broadcast or cable programme of the work.

Section 19(1) provides that the performance in public of *inter alia*, a literary or musical work is a restricted act. Section 19(3) provides that the playing or showing in public of a sound recording, film, broadcast or cable programme is a restricted act.

Where, for example, CDs are played by a café on a CD player and on a jukebox, permission to do this should be obtained by the café from the owners of the literary and musical copyrights and from the owners of the sound recording copyrights. If the CDs are played by the café without the relevant permissions, the café will be infringing the copyrights in the literary and musical works and in the sound recordings. It will be impossible for the café to contact all the relevant copyright owners to obtain the necessary permissions. To secure the relevant permissions the café should apply to the Performing Rights Society and to the Phonographic Performance Ltd for blanket licences to play CDs on a CD player and on a jukebox. (*See* Chapter 4 Collecting Societies and Music Industry Associations for the Performing Rights Society and for Phonographic Performance Ltd.)

The infringement occurs when performing, playing or showing the work in public. There is no infringement if the work is played in private. There is no definition of what constitutes in public. There have been several cases which have dealt with what "in public" means. The general attitude taken by the courts in these cases is that if the performance takes place in a situation where people have to pay money to attend, or in a commercial environment, *e.g.* a football match or a hotel, this suggests the performance is in public. A private performance is essentially of a domestic nature, *i.e.* in the presence of family and friends.

Broadcasting or including the work in a cable programme

Section 20 provides that broadcasting or including in a cable programme service:

    (a) a literary, musical or artistic work,
    (b) a sound recording or film, or
    (c) a broadcast or cable programme
is a restricted act.

Consent must therefore be obtained from the copyright owner of any of the works in (a)–(c) above to include such a work in a broadcast or a cable programme.

Making an adaptation

Section 21(1) provides that it is a restricted act to make an adaptation of a literary or musical work. The adaptation is deemed to have been made when it has been recorded, for example, in writing. Writing here means under section 178 "any form of notation or code, whether written by hand or otherwise and regardless of the method by which, or medium in or on which, it is recorded."

Section 21(2) provides that doing any of the acts specified in sections 17–20 or in section 21(1) in relation to an adaptation of the work is also an act restricted by the copyright in a literary or musical work. Section 21(2) provides that it is immaterial whether the adaptation has been recorded in writing or otherwise at the time the act is done. So, for example, if a musical work is adapted and the adaptation is subsequently copied, the copying of the adaptation is an infringement of the copyright in the musical work.

Section 21(3) defines what is an adaptation. For a literary work an adaptation includes, *inter alia*, a translation of the work. For a musical work an adaptation means an arrangement or transcription of the work.

Primary infringement

Where somebody without a licence from the copyright owner does, or authorises somebody else to do any of the exclusive section 16 restricted acts he will be committing an act of primary infringement. There is no need for any *mens rea* by the infringer. Doing or authorising somebody else to do any of the section 16 restricted acts is sufficient to be liable for an act of primary infringement.

Secondary infringement

Sections 22–26 deal with five other infringing acts called secondary infringement. These acts are usually carried out by the infringers for monetary gain.

Before any secondary infringement can exist there needs to be some element of knowledge of infringement by the alleged infringer. The act specifically states that there will be secondary infringement if the person commits the infringing act, and either (i) knew, or (ii) had reason to believe, (using an objective test), that he had an infringing copy of the work.

Importing Infringing Copies

Section 22 provides that it is an infringing act if someone without a licence from the copyright owner imports into the United Kingdom, except for his private and domestic use, an article which he knows or has reason to believe is an infringing copy of the work.

An article is an infringing copy:

(a) if its making constituted an infringement of copyright in the work, (section 27(2)), or

(b) it has been or is proposed to be imported into the United Kingdom (section 27(3)(a)), and its making in the United Kingdom would have constituted an infringement of the copyright in the work, or a breach of an exclusive licence agreement relating to that work (section 27(3)(b)).

The CDPA makes it perfectly clear in section 27(5) that an article is not an infringing copy if it can be legally imported into the United Kingdom due to any enforceable EU provisions within the meaning of section 2(1) of the European Communities Act 1972. Article 28 of the Treaty of Amsterdam (formerly Article 30 of the Treaty of Rome) makes provisions for the free movement of goods within Member States. The effect of Article 28 is that once goods have been put on sale in a Member State (*e.g.* France) with the consent of the copyright owner a third party can take these goods and import them into the United Kingdom for re-sale without committing any section 22 act of secondary infringement. It should be noted that although Article 28 allows such goods to be imported for re-sale, Article 30 provides a limited exception to Article 28. Article 30 will stop the free movement of goods within Member States if the restriction can be justified by showing that it is for "the protection of industrial and commercial property". It should also be noted that as well as Articles 28 and 30 of the Treaty of Amsterdam there is also the European Court of Justice's doctrine of exhaustion of rights. The doctrine of exhaustion of rights means that where goods have been lawfully put on sale in a Member State that the copyright owner cannot stop these goods being imported into other Member States.

(For further details about Articles 28 and 30 of the Treaty of Amsterdam readers are advised to refer to specialist books on the subject.)

Possessing or dealing with infringing copies

Section 23 provides that it is an infringing act if someone without a licence from the copyright owner either:

(a) possesses in the course of a business,
(b) sells or lets for hire, or offers or exposes for sale or hire,
(c) in the course of a business exhibits in public or distributes, or
(d) distributes otherwise than in the course of a business to such an extent as to affect prejudicially the owner of the copyright,

an article which is, and which he knows or has reason to believe is, an infringing copy of the work.

Section 23 will therefore catch people who trade in pirate cassettes and CDs. Section 23(d) will also catch people who are not in business but who, for example, are fans who have pirate live tapes of their favourite band and let other fans of the band have copies of the recording for free or for a nominal charge to cover the cost of a blank tape and postage.

Providing the means for making infringing copies

Section 24 provides that it is an infringing act if someone without a licence from the copyright owner either:

(a) makes,
(b) imports into the United Kingdom,
(c) possesses in the course of a business, or
(d) sells or lets for hire, or offers or exposes for sale or hire,

an article specifically designed or adapted for making copies of that work, knowing or having reason to believe that it is to be used to make infringing copies.

Section 24(2) provides that

> "Copyright in a work is infringed by a person who without the licence of the copyright owner transmits the work by means of a telecommunications system (otherwise than by broadcasting or inclusion in a cable programme service), knowing or having reason to believe that infringing copies of the work will be made by means of the reception of the transmission in the United Kingdom or otherwise."

(A telecommunications system is defined in section 178 as a system to convey visual images, sounds or other information by electronic means.)

This section covers the machinery used to make copies of the work. For example, it will cover CD pressing plants. The pressing plant will have to make enquiries of their customers before pressing up the CDs to ensure that they are not pressing up infringing CDs.

Permitting use of premises for infringing performances

Section 25(1) provides that where the copyright in a literary or musical work is infringed by a performance at a place of public entertainment, any person who gave permission for that place to be used for the performance is also liable for the infringement, unless when he gave permission he believed on reasonable grounds that the performance would not infringe copyright.

Section 25(2) provides that a place of public entertainment

"includes premises which are occupied mainly for other purposes but are from time to time made available for hire for the purposes of public entertainment."

Section 25 can possibly catch the owner of the venue where the musical work is performed in concert. It does not apply to venue owners playing a record on a jukebox or on a hi-fi as the section does not deal with sound recordings.

Providing apparatus for infringing performances

Section 26(1) provides that where copyright is infringed by a public performance of the work, or by the playing or showing of the work in public, by means of apparatus for:

(a) playing sound recordings,
(b) showing films, or
(c) receiving visual images or sounds conveyed by electronic means,

the following persons are also liable for the infringement:

(a) "a person who supplied the apparatus, or any substantial part of it, is liable for the infringement if when he supplied the apparatus or part–he knew or had reason to believe that the apparatus was likely to be so used as to infringe copyright," (section 26(2)(a)) or, "in the case of apparatus whose normal use involves a public performance, playing or showing, he did not believe on reasonable grounds that it would not be so used as to infringe copyright" (section 26(2)(b))
(b) "an occupier of premises who gave permission for the apparatus to be brought onto the premises is liable if when he gave permission he knew or had reason to believe that the apparatus was likely to be so used as to infringe copyright" (section 26(3))
(c) "a person who supplied a copy of a sound recording or film used to infringe copyright is liable if when he supplied it he

knew or had reason to believe that what he supplied, or a copy made directly or indirectly from it, was likely to be used to infringe copyright" (section 26(4)).

Permitted acts/defences

It is not possible for a solicitor to decide if there has been any copyright infringement without first asking several questions. The checklist of questions he should work through include:

(a) Is the work which has been allegedly infringed one that is capable of copyright protection? If so,
(b) Who is the author of the work?
(c) Is the author the owner of the work? If not, who is the owner?
(d) Is the work still within the relevant copyright protection period?
(e) Has there been an act of primary infringement?
(f) Has there been an act of secondary infringement?
(g) Are there any any valid defences available to the alleged infringer?

It is this last question that we now examine.

The CDPA in sections 28-76 sets out the "permitted acts" which can be done with a work by a third party even though copyright exists in the work. These permitted acts control to some considerable extent the rights of the copyright owner. There may well have been a prima facie infringement of one or more of the copyright owner's exclusive rights, but the prospective defendant may be able to use one or more of the CDPA permitted acts as a defence which, if established, would mean that there has been no infringement of copyright.

What follows below is a discussion of the most likely permitted acts which could be used as a defence in a copyright infringement action.

Fair dealing

The permitted act of fair dealing is available in two circumstances:

(a) fair dealing for research and private study (section 29), and
(b) fair dealing for the purpose of criticism, review and news reporting (section 30).

There is no definition of fair dealing in the CDPA. There has been some considerable case law on this matter. Lord Denning in *Hubbard* v *Vosper* [1972] 2 QB 84 set out criteria for deciding what is fair dealing.

His criteria and other case law has shown that what constitutes fair dealing depends on the facts of each case. There are many factors that the courts will take into account including, how much of the work was copied or used, and the purpose behind the use of the work.

Research and private study

Section 29(1) provides, *inter alia*, that fair dealing with a literary or musical work for research or private study does not infringe copyright in the work. It should be noted that the fair dealing defence for research and private study does not apply to dealing with a sound recording, broadcast or film.

Section 29(3) deals with copying by a person other than the researcher or student himself.

Section 29(3)(b) provides that with the exception of a librarian (who is dealt with in section 29(3)(a) and which is beyond the scope of this book), copying by a person other than the researcher or student himself is not fair dealing if:

> "the person doing the copying knows or has reason to believe that it will result in copies of substantially the same material being provided to more than one person at substantially the same time and for substantially the same purpose."

This will stop a teacher copying an extract from a book of song lyrics for a class of 40 students. The teacher may possibly be able to make one copy of the extract for one student but that is still subject to the requirement that the copy is used for research or private study and that its use constitutes a fair dealing with the work.

(It should be noted that copyright also exists in the typographical arrangement of a published work for a period of 25 years from the end of the calendar year in which the edition was first published (section 15). Section 29 also allows for the possibility of fair dealing with the typographical arrangement of a published work.)

Criticism, review and news reporting

Section 30(1) provides that:

> "Fair dealing with a work for the purpose of criticism or review, of that or another work or of a performance of a work, does not infringe any copyright in the work provided that it is accompanied by a sufficient acknowledgement."

Section 30(2) provides that:

> "Fair dealing with a work (other than a photograph) for the purpose of reporting current events does not infringe any copyright in the work provided that (subject to subsection (3)) it is accompanied by a sufficient acknowledgement."

Section 30(3) provides that:

> "No acknowledgement is required in connection with the reporting of current events by means of a sound recording, film, broadcast or cable programme."

Section 178 defines "sufficient acknowledgement" as:

> "an acknowledgement identifying the work in question by its title or other description, and identifying the author unless-
> (a) in the case of a published work, it is published anonymously;
> (b) in the case of an unpublished work, it is not possible for a person to ascertain the identity of the author by reasonable inquiry.

Section 30(1) will enable a magazine music reviewer to review a CD for a magazine and to use extracts of the lyrics in the review to show, for example, the incisiviness or otherwise of the lyricist's style. If the reviewer wants to quote from the lyrics in his review he must ensure that he acknowledges in the review who the copyright owner of the lyrics is and the work from which the lyrics were taken.

If the remaining Beatles decided to reform for a one off reunion concert in England this would be a worldwide news story. The BBC on the news could review the concert and may decide that the review would benefit from using extracts from some Lennon and McCartney lyrics. The BBC could do so as it is reporting current events and under section 30(3) they do not have to give any copyright acknowledgement.

If a national newspaper reviewed the concert and used the same extracts from the Lennon and McCartney lyrics in the newspaper which the BBC had used on the news, the newspaper could do so as it is reporting current affairs, but under section 30(2) the newspaper would have to acknowledge who are the copyright owners of the lyrics and the works from which the lyrics were taken.

The three examples above are again subject to the requirement that the use constitutes a fair dealing with the copyright work.

Incidental inclusion of copyright material.

Section 31(1) provides that:

> "Copyright in a work is not infringed by its incidental inclusion in an artistic work, sound recording, film, broadcast or cable programme."

Section 31(2) goes on to say:

> "Nor is copyright infringed by the issue to the public of copies, or the playing, showing broadcasting or inclusion in a cable programme service, of anything whose making was, by virtue of subsection (1), not an infringement of the copyright."

Section 31(3) further provides that:

> "A musical work, words spoken or sung with music, or so much of a sound recording, broadcast or cable programme as includes a musical work or such words, shall not be regarded as incidentally included in another work if it is deliberately included."

Section 31 is easier to understand by way of an illustration. If, for example, whilst an MP is being interviewed live outside the House of Commons for the TV news, music from the open window of a car driving past was picked up on the broadcast, the broadcast company could probably use the defence of incidental inclusion under section 31(1) and (2) as the broadcast company was not able to control the car driving by at the time of the interview. (If however, the interview with the MP was recorded for broadcast, the defence of incidental inclusion may very possibly not be available due to the fact that the interview could have been re-recorded.)

If, however, there is a closed film set, the director will have control of all the events going on. The defence of incidental inclusion will not be available where, for example, the director films a scene in which the actors are listening to a song on the radio. This is because the song has been deliberately included by the director. The director controls what he films. To use the song in the film, the director should have obtained a licence from the copyright owner of the words and music of the song and a licence from the copyright owner of the sound recording.

Education

Sections 32-36A deals with permitted acts for educational purposes.

Instruction or examination

Section 32 deals with doing things with the work for the purpose of instruction or examination. Section 32(1) provides that:

> Copyright in a literary, musical or artistic work is not infringed by being copied in the course of instruction or of preparation for instruction, provided the copying: -
> (a) is done by a person giving or receiving instruction, and
> (b) is not done by means of a reprographic process.

Section 178 defines a "reprographic process" as a process:

"(a) for making facsimile copies, or
(b) involving the use of an appliance for making multiple copies,
and includes, in relation to a work held in electronic form, any
copying by electronic means, but does not include the making of a
film or sound recording."

A music lecturer can therefore write a music score on a whiteboard
and the students can copy it down. However, photocopies of a music
score cannot be made by the music lecturer and given to the students.

Section 32(2) contains similar provisions to section 32(1) in relation
to copying a sound recording, film, broadcast or cable programme.
The subsection states that they can be copied:

"by making a film or film soundtrack in the course of instruction, or of
preparation for instruction, in the making of films or film sound-tracks,
provided the copying is done by a person giving or receiving instruction."

Section 32(3) allows the use of copyright material in setting or
answering exam questions, but section 32(4) specifically states that
this does not extend to making a reprographic copy of a musical work
for use by an examination candidate performing the work.

Performing, playing, showing a work in course of activities of educational establishment

Section 34 deals with performing, playing or showing a work in the
course of the activities of the educational establishment. Section 34(1)
provides that:

The performance of a literary or musical work before an audience
consisting of teachers and pupils at an educational establishment and
other persons directly connected with the activities of the establishment–
(a) by a teacher or pupil in the course of the activities of the establishment,
or
(b) at the establishment by any person for the purposes of instruction, is
not a public performance for the purposes of copyright infringement.

Section 34(2) deals with the playing or showing of a sound recording,
film, broadcast or cable programme. If it is done at an educational
establishment for the purposes of instruction before the audience
referred to in section 34(1), it will not constitute a playing or showing
of the work in public for the purposes of copyright infringement.

It should be noted that section 34(3) specifically states that a person
is not directly connected with the activities of the educational establishment simply because he is a parent of the pupil.

Other educational uses

Other permitted uses for education include the right for educational establishments to record broadcasts and cable programmes for educational purposes (section 35), and the right to reprographically copy passages from published literary or musical works for the purpose of instruction (section 36). Section 35(2) provides that if there is a licensing scheme in place under the CDPA to grant educational establishments a licence to record broadcasts or cable programmes, the section 35 permitted act will not apply. There is a similar provision in section 36(3) which provides that the section 36 permitted act does not apply if licences to copy were available and the person making the copies knew or ought to have known of this. Also, for the section 36 permitted act to apply there is a limit to the amount of the work that can be copied. The amount is specified in section 36(2) as allowing no more than 1% of the work to be copied in any quarter of the year, namely 1 January to 31 March, 1 April to 30 June, 1 July to 30 September, 1 October to 31 December.

Libraries

Sections 37-44 deal with the permitted acts for libraries.

Copying parts of published works by a librarian

Section 39(1) allows a librarian under certain circumstances to copy part of a literary or musical work without infringing copyright. Part of a work is not defined in the act and it will depend on the facts of each case. The circumstances when this can be done are set out in section 39(2). These include that:

(a) The librarian is satisfied that the person requiring the copies wants them only for research or private study, and
(b) No person is given more than one copy of the material or with a copy of more than a reasonable proportion of the work, and
(c) The person wanting the copies pays for them. The charge must not be less than the cost (including a contribution to the general expenses of the library) attributable to their production.

The librarian will require the person who wants the copying done to sign a declaration confirming that he wants it for his research or private study. Under the CDPA the librarian can rely upon the declaration to show that he had checked and was satisfied that the copying was validly requested. This declaration cannot be relied upon by the librarian if he knew that its content was false.

Anonymous or pseudonymous works

Section 57(1) provides that copyright in a literary, musical or artistic work is not infringed when:

"(a) it is not possible by reasonable enquiry to ascertain the identity of the author, and

(b) it is reasonable to assume

(i) that copyright has expired, or

(ii) that the author died 70 years or more before the beginning of the calendar year in which the act is done or the arrangements are made."

If the work is one of joint authorship section 57(3) provides that:

(a) the reference in section 57(1) to it being possible to ascertain the identity of the author shall be construed as a reference to it being possible to ascertain the identity of any of the authors, and

(b) the reference in section 57(1)(b)(ii) to the author having died shall be construed as a reference to all the authors having died.

Recordings of folksongs

Section 61 deals with folksongs.

Section 61(1) allows a sound recording of a performance of a song to be made to be included in an archive which is maintained by a designated body. The designated archives are listed in the Copyright Recordings of Folk Songs for Archives (Designated Bodies) Order 1989 (SI 1989/1012) and include the North West Sound Archive and the Centre for English Cultural Tradition and Language. Copyright will not be infringed in the words or the music if the conditions in section 61(2) are met. The conditions are that:

"(a) the words are unpublished and of unknown authorship at the time the recording is made,

(b) the making of the recording does not infringe any other copyright, and

(c) its making is not prohibited by any performer."

If a sound recording is made under section 61(1) copies of that sound recording may be made by the archivist without infringing any copyright under section 61(3) provided that:

(a) copies are only supplied to people who satisfy the archivist that they require them only for research or private study (section 61(4)(a)), and

(b) no person will be given more than one copy of the same recording (section 61(4)(b)).

Clubs and societies

Section 67 deals with playing a sound recording as part of the activities of a club, society or other institution. Playing a sound recording will not be an infringing act if under section 67(2):

> (a) the organisation is not established or conducted for profit and its main objects are charitable or are otherwise concerned with the advancement of religion, education or social welfare, and
>
> (b) the proceeds of any charge for admission to the place where the recording is to be heard are applied solely for the purposes of the organisation.

Recording for purposes of time shifting

Section 70 provides that:

> "The making for private and domestic use of a recording of a broadcast or cable programme solely for the purpose of enabling it to be viewed or listened to at a more convenient time does not infringe any copyright in the broadcast or cable programme or any film included in it."

This section will enable somebody to videotape "Top of the Pops" to watch at a more convenient time.

Other defences

It should be noted that although the CDPA has created these permitted acts, there are common law defences available as well. These include the defence that the work is not protected on the grounds of public policy, *e.g.* the original work is obscene. There is also the possibility of using the EU defences under the Treaty of Amsterdam such as Article 28 dealing with the free movement of goods. It should, however, be remembered that the EU defences are unlikely to succeed in the English courts in a case of copyright infringement.

Remedies for infringement

Civil and criminal remedies are available for the copyright owner where infringement has occurred.

Civil remedies

Section 96(1) provides that copyright infringement is actionable by the copyright owner, and under section 96(2) the copyright owner can seek damages, injunctions, an account of profits, or any other remedy which is available for the owner of a property right.

Damages

Damages are available as a remedy for the copyright owner but section 97 can control the amount of damages awarded.

Section 97(1) provides that if the defendant did not know, nor had any reason to believe at the time of the infringement that copyright existed in the work, the claimant owner is not entitled to damages. This does not preclude the claimant pursuing other legal remedies.

By contrast section 97(2) allows the court to take account of all the circumstances surrounding the infringement, and in particular to see if the defendant flagrantly infringed copyright and to look at any benefit the defendant may have acquired from infringing copyright. Having looked at all the cicumstances the court may then award the claimant additional damages. The courts can use section 97(2) as an additional punishment against the defendant for their behaviour in using the copyright work.

Delivery up of infringing articles

Section 99(1) covers the situation where the defendant:

> "(a) has an infringing copy in his possession, custody or control in the course of a business, or
> (b) has in his possession, custody or control an article specifically designed or adapted for making copies of a copyright work, knowing or having reason to believe that it has been or is to be used to make infringing copies."

In such a situation the copyright owner can apply to court for an order that the infringing copy or article is delivered up to him or to any other person whom the court directs.

Right to seize infringing copies and other articles

Section 100 is aimed at trying to catch street traders who sell pirate CDs and tapes of the latest hit albums. If the copyright owner who is entitled to seek a court order under section 99 (for delivery up) finds that infringing copies are actually on sale or for hire, the copyright owner, or anybody authorised by him, may seize and detain the infringing copies. The right to seize and detain is subject to section 114 (see below) and to the following conditions:

> (a) before seizing anything notice of the time and place of the proposed seizure should be given to the local police (section 100(2)),

(b) the seizer of the goods may enter premises to which the public have access but may not seize anything in the possession, custody or control of a person at that person's permanent or regular place of business (section 100(3)),

(c) no force can be used (section 100(3)),

(d) when the goods are seized a prescribed form of notice must be left at the premises where the goods are seized stating who is seizing the goods or upon whose authority the seizure is made, and the grounds upon which the seizure is made (section 100(4)).

As already mentioned this section is aimed at catching street traders. Because section 100(3) precludes the use of force, it would be sensible when informing the police of the proposed seizure under section 100(2) to request them to actually attend at the seizure.

Customs and excise treatment of infringing copies

Section 111(1) enables the copyright owner of a published literary or musical work to give notice in writing to Customs and Excise:

(a)   that he is the copyright owner, and

(b)   that he requests Customs and Excise for a period specified in the notice (which under section 111(2) cannot exceed five years and can not extend beyond the period for which copyright can subsist), to treat as prohibited goods printed copies of the work which are infringing copies.

Section 111(3) enables the copyright owner of a sound recording or film to give notice in writing to Customs and Excise that:

(a)   he is the copyright owner, and

(b)   infringing copies of the work are expected to arrive in the United Kingdom at a time and place stated in the notice, and

(c)   he wants Customs and Excise to treat the copies as prohibited goods.

Under section 111(3A) Customs and Excise can then treat as prohibited goods only those infringing copies which arrive in the United Kingdom

(a) from outside the EEA, or

(b) from within the EEA but not those goods which have entered the UK under the doctrine of exhaustion of rights.

Section 111(3B) provides that:

"This section does not apply to goods entered, or expected to be entered, for free circulation, export, re-export or for a suspensive procedure in respect of which an application may be made under

Article 3(1) of Council Regulation (EC) No. 3295/94 laying down measures to prohibit the release for free circulation, export, re-export or entry for a suspensive procedure of counterfeit and pirated goods."

Section 111(4) provides that when a notice is in force under section 111 that:

"the importation of goods to which the notice relates, otherwise than by a person for his private and domestic use, subject to subsections (3A) and (3B), is prohibited; but a person is not by reason of the prohibition liable to any penalty other than forfeiture of the goods."

Order to dispose of infringing copies

Section 114 provides that an application may be made to the court for an order that an infringing copy or other article which has been delivered up pursuant to section 99 or 108 (see criminal remedies below for section 108), or seized and detained pursuant to section 100 shall be:

(a) forfeited to the copyright owner, or
(b) destroyed or dealt with as the court thinks fit, or
(c) for a decision that no order should be made.

This section allows the copyright owner once he has made a seizure from a street trader under section 100 to go to court to have the pirate CDs and tapes destroyed.

Other civil remedies

It should be remembered that other civil remedies, such as the equitable remedy of an account of profits, a search order, or an interlocutory injunction should be considered as remedies that may be of use to the copyright owner as well as the remedies set out in the CDPA.

Presumptions in civil litigation

Section 104(1) and (2) creates a rebuttable presumption in relation to proceedings concerning a literary, musical or artistic work. Under section 104(2), where a name purporting to be that of the author appears on copies of the published work or on the work when it was made, the person whose name appears is presumed, until the contrary is proven, to be

(a) the author of the work and
(b) *inter alia* not to have made it in the course of his employment.

Section 105(1) creates a rebuttable presumption in relation to proceedings concerning a sound recording. Where copies of a sound recording issued to the public bear a label or other mark stating that:

  (a) a named person was the copyright owner in the recording at the date of issue of the copies (section 105(a)), or
  (b) that the recording was first published in a specified year or in a specified country (section 105(b),

the label or mark is admissible as evidence of the facts stated and presumed correct until the contrary is proved.

Criminal remedies

Criminal liability for making or dealing with infringing articles etc

Section 107(1) creates an offence where someone without a licence:

  (a) makes for sale or hire, or
  (b) imports into the UK other than for his private and domestic use, or
  (c) possesses in the course of a business with a view to committing any act infringing copyright, or
  (d) in the course of a business–
    (i)   sells or lets for hire, or
    (ii) offers or exposes for sale or hire, or
    (iii) exhibits in public, or
    (iv   distributes, or
  (e) distributes other than in the course of a business to such an extent as to affect prejudicially the copyright owner,

an article which is, and which he knows or has reason to believe is, an infringing copy of a copyright work.

Section 107(2) provides that a person commits an offence who:

"(a) makes an article specially designed or adapted for making copies of a particular copyright work, or
(b) has such an article in his possession,
knowing or having reason to believe that it is to be used to make infringing copies for sale or hire or for use in the course of a business."

Section 107(3) provides that where copyright is infringed (other than by reception of a broadcast or cable programme):

  (a) by the public performance of a literary or musical work, or
  (b) by the playing or showing in public of a sound recording or film,
  any person who caused the work to be performed, played or shown is guilty of an offence if he knew or had reason to believe that copyright would be infringed.

Section 107(4) states that a person guilty of an offence under subsection (1)(a), (b), (d)(iv) or (e) is liable:

"(a) on summary conviction to imprisonment for a term not exceeding 6 months or a fine not exceeding the statutory maximum, or both;

(b) on conviction on indictment to a fine or imprisonment for a term not exceeding 2 years, or both."

Section 107(5) states that

"a person guilty of any other offence under this section is liable on summary conviction to imprisonment for a term not exceeding six months or a fine not exceeding level 5 on the standard scale, or both."

The presumptions in sections 104 and 105 which apply in civil cases do not apply in criminal proceedings under section 107.

The *mens rea* for criminal infringement under section 107 is of an objective standard.

As well as the above criminal remedies there are provisions in section 108 for the court when hearing a section 107 offence to order the delivery up of an infringing copy or article, and for the police under section 109 to obtain a search warrant to look for infringing material relating to offences under section 107(1)(a),(b),(d)(iv) or (e).

There are other offences which may apply, *inter alia*, section 110 relating to the liability of officers of a company, the Trades Descriptions Act 1968, and under the Trade Marks Act 1994. These and any other offences are beyond the scope of this work.

Moral rights

Prior to the CDPA the law did not recognise the European concept of moral rights. Moral rights are rights which belong to the author of the work. The ideology behind the concept of moral rights is to protect the creativity of the author.

As we have seen earlier the author, if he is the owner, can license or assign the copyright in the work. Section 94 provides that moral rights cannot be assigned by the author. They can only be waived by him.

What are moral rights?

There are four moral rights, of which only three have relevence in the music business. These are:

(a) A paternity right. This is the right to be identified as the author. (Section 77.)
(b) An integrity right. This is the right to object to derogatory treatment of a work. (Section 80.)
(c) A right for a person not to have a work falsely attributed to him as the author. (Section 84.)

The fourth moral right which is not relevant in the music business is the right to privacy of certain photographs and films. (Section 85).

Section 86 deals with the duration of moral rights. The paternity right and the integrity right last for as long as copyright exists in the work. The right to object to false attribution lasts for 20 years after a person's death.

Right to be identified as the author (s 77)

Section 77(1) provides that the author of a copyright literary, musical or artistic work, and the director of a copyright film, has the right to be identified as the author or director of the work.

Section 77(3) provides that

"the author of a musical work, or a literary work consisting of words intended to be sung or spoken with music, has the right to be identified when:
(a) the work is commercially published,
(b) copies of a sound recording of the work are issued to the public, or
(c) a film of which the sound-track includes the work is shown in public or copies of such a film are issued to the public."

By section 77(7) the author has the right to be identified on every copy of the work which is commercially published or issued to the public. If that is not appropriate then the identification must be made in such a way as to bring the identity of the author to the notice of the person acquiring or seeing a copy of the work. The identification has to be both clear and reasonably prominent.

Some songwriters write under a pseudonym or initials. In such a case section 77(8) provides that the identification of the author will be the pseudonym, initials or other form of identification the songwriter uses. If he is not identified in this way the subsection allows for any other reasonable form of identification to be used to show he is the author. Examples of where songwriters have writen and also performed under different names are Elvis Costello who wrote and performed a single in 1983 under the name The Imposter, and Prince, or The Artist Formerly Known As Prince who has also written and recorded under a symbol.

It is important to note that sections 77(1) and 78(1) provide that although there is a paternity right it is only infringed where the author has asserted his right. Assertion can be done by inserting a clause into the document assigning copyright. If such a clause is inserted into the assignment, section 78(4)(a) provides that the assignee and anyone claiming through him is bound by it, whether or not he knew of the assertion. It is possible to make the assertion by letter from the author to the person permitted to deal with the work. If a letter is written asserting the paternity right, section 78(4)(b) provides that the persons bound by it are anybody to whose notice the assertion is brought.

A sensible songwriter will always want to assert his paternity right and will in addition request that a note of it is inserted into every copy of the work.

The paternity right does not apply or is not infringed in certain cases listed in section 79. These include:

(a) where anything is done with the authority of the copyright owner where the copyright originally vested in the author's employer by virtue of section 11(2)(a work produced by an employee during the course of his employment) (section 79(3)(a)),

(b) where copyright would not be infringed by virtue of:
   (i) section 30, fair dealing so far as it relates to reporting current events by means of a sound recording, film, broadcast, or cable programme, (section 79(4)(a)),
   (ii) section 31, incidental inclusion of a work in an artistic work, sound recording, film, broadcast or cable programme, (section 79(4)(b)).

Right to object to derogatory treatment (s 80)

Section 80(1) provides that the author of a copyright literary, musical or artistic work, and the director of a copyright fim, has the right, in certain circumstances, not to have his work subjected to derogatory treatment.

Such "treatment" is defined in section 80(2)(a) as any addition to, deletion from or alteration to or adaptation of the work other than:

(a) a translation of a literary work, or

(b) an arrangement or transcription of a musical work involving no more than a change of key or register.

Under section 80(2)(b) a treatment of a work is derogatory if it amounts to "distortion or mutilation of the work or is otherwise prejudicial to the honour or reputation of the author or director."

Section 80(3) provides that in the case of a literary, or musical work the right is infringed by someone who:

"(a) publishes commercially, performs in public, broadcasts or includes in a cable programme service a derogatory treatment of the work, or
(b) issues to the public copies of a film or sound recording of, or including, a derogatory treatment of the work."

In the case of a film, under section 80(6) the right is infringed by a person who:

"(a) shows in public, broadcasts or includes in a cable programme service a derogatory treatment of the film, or
(b) issues to the public copies of a derogatory treatment of the film."

Section 83 provides that the right is also infringed by a person who:

"(a) possesses in the course of business, or
(b) sells or lets for hire, or offers or exposes for sale or hire, or
(c) in the course of a business exhibits in public or distributes, or
(d) distributes other than in the course of business so as to affect prejudicially the honour or reputation of the author or director,
an article which is, and which he knows or has reason to believe is, an infringing article."

The integrity right does not apply in certain cases listed in section 81 and includes instances where any work is made for reporting current events. In addition, section 82(1)(a) and (2) makes it clear that where a work was created by an employee in the course of his employment and the copyright originally vested in his employer, the right to object to derogatory treatment of the work does not apply to anything done in relation to such a work by or with the authority of the copyright owner unless the author:

(a) is identified at the time of the relevant act, or
(b) has previously been identified in or on published copies of the work,
and where in such a case the right does apply, it is not infringed if there is a sufficient disclaimer.

In the case of *Morrison Leahy Music Ltd & Another v Lightband Ltd* [1992] 1 Ent LR George Michael obtained an injunction to prevent the release of a megamix of some of his songs. He argued that as the author of the songs he had suffered derogatory treatment in the megamix. The case did not get to trial although at an interlocutory hearing the judge agreed that George Michael had an arguable case that his work had been subject to derogatory treatment.

Right to object to false attribution (s 84)

Section 84(1) provides that a person has the right not to have a literary, musical or artistic work falsely attributed to him as the author.

Under section 84(2)(a) the right is infringed by a person who issues to the public copies of such a work in which there is a false attribution.

Under section 84(3) the right is also infringed in a literary or musical work, by a person who performs it in public, broadcasts it or includes it in a cable programme as being the work of a person, knowing or having reason to believe the attribution to be false.

Section 84(4) provides it is an infringement to issue to the public or display to the public material containing a false attribution.

Section 84(5) states that the right is infringed by a person who, in the course of a business, possesses or deals with a copy of such a work in which there is a false attribution, knowing or having reason to believe that there is such an attribution and that it is false.

Duration of moral rights (s 86)

The paternity and integrity right will last for as long as copyright exists in the work. The right to prevent false attribution lasts until 20 years after a person's death.

Consent and waiver (s 87)

There is no infringement of moral rights where the author has given his consent. The author may waive any of his moral rights. Section 87(2) allows a waiver to be in writing. Section 87(4) allows for the possibility of an informal waiver, in which case the general law of contract or estoppel will apply. Notwithstanding section 87(4), for the sake of clarity any waiver should be recorded in writing and signed by the person waiving the rights. Indeed, waivers will be negotiated and, if agreed, included in any copyright assignment.

Section 87(3)(a) permits a waiver to relate to a specific work or to general works. It may also relate to existing works or to works created in the future. Section 87(3)(b) permits a waiver to be conditional or unconditional and allows it to be revocable. If the waiver is made in favour of the copyright owner it is presumed, unless the contrary intention is indicated, to apply to the copyright owner, his licensees and his successors in title.

Joint authors (s 88)

Section 88 deals with joint authors and moral rights.

Where there are joint authors the paternity right is a right for each joint author to be identified as a joint author. Each joint author must assert the right to be identified in relation to himself (section 88(1)).

Where there are joint authors the integrity right is a right of each author. An author's integrity right is satisfied if he consents to the treatment of the work (section 88(2)).

The right of false attribution is infringed:

(a) by any false statement about the authorship of a work of joint authorship, and
(b) by the false attribution of joint authorship in relation to a work of sole authorship,

and such a false description infringes the right of every person to whom authorship of any description is, whether rightly or wrongly attributed (section 88(4)(a) and (b)).

Section 88(3) provides that a waiver under section 87 of the rights of one joint author does not affect the rights of the other joint authors.

Part of a work (s 89)

The paternity right applies to the whole or a substantial part of a work.

The integrity right and the right not be falsely attributed as the author applies to the whole or to any part of a work.

Remedies

The remedies available for infinging moral rights are set out in section 103(1) and (2).

Under section 103(1) an infringement of a moral right is actionable as a breach of a statutory duty owed to the person entitled to that right. An infringement will enable the author to seek damages and an injunction.

Section 103(2) deals with the integrity right and provides that the court may, if it thinks it is an adequate remedy, grant a prohibitory injunction unless a disclaimer is made in terms approved by the court disassociating the author from the treatment of the work.

Moral rights on death of author (s 95)

Section 95 deals with what happens to the paternity and integrity rights on the author's death. Section 95(1)(a) allows the author to leave these rights as a specific bequest under his will. If there is no such bequest of these rights then, under section 95(1)(b) if the copyright in the work forms part of his estate, these rights belong to the person to whom the copyright passes. Where these rights do not pass under section 95(1)(a) or (b) then, by virtue of section 95(1)(c) they are exerciseable by the author's PRs.

Any consent or waiver given by the author binds any person to whom a right passes under section 95(1). This is provided for in section 95(4).

Any infringement after a person's death relating to a false attribution of a work is actionable by the deceased's PRs. This is provided for in section 95(5).

Any damages recovered by the PRs for infringement of moral rights after a person's death will pass as part of his estate as if the right of action had subsisted and been rested in him immediately before his death. This is provided for in section 95(6).

Conclusion

Moral rights are a valuable protection for the author. They give him the right to let the world know that he is the author of a work and protect him from being labelled as the author of another work with which he had no association. The integrity right also protects the author's work from being denigrated by others.

In any contractual negotiations for a licence or assignment of copyright, the author will want to assert his paternity right and will not want to waive his other moral rights. The licensee or assignee will often be prepared for the author to assert his paternity right (or will require the author to waive his statutory paternity right and replace it with a similar contractual right), but will usually require the author to waive his other moral rights.

Rights in performances

Introduction

So far we have seen that the CDPA protects a copyright work, such as a composition consisting of words and music and the sound recording of the composition. We have also seen that the CDPA gives the author of the work moral rights. The CDPA also protects:

(i) the musicians who actually perform on the record, and
(ii) the person, who has an exclusive recording contract with a performer, by giving that person rights in the performer's performances. (The person who has an exclusive recording contract with a performer is usually a record company.)

Section 180(1)(a) provides that the consent of the performer is needed to exploit his performances.

Sections 182, 182A, 182B, 182C, 183 and 184 detail the different ways in which a performance can be exploited, each of which requires the performer's consent. (See below for sections 182, 182A, 182B, 182C, 183 and 184.) The necessary consents required under these sections will be given by the performer in the recording contract with his record company, or where a session musician appears on a record the necessary consents will be given by the session musician in the session musician contract with the record company. (The session musician contract that will generally be used will be the standard session musician contract which was agreed between the Musicians's Union and the British Phonographic Industry Ltd.) (*See* Chapter 4 Collecting Societies and Music Industry Associations for the Musicians' Union and the British Phonographic Industry Limited.)

Section 180(1)(b) provides that the person who has recording rights in relation to a performance, *e.g.* a record company, has rights in relation to recordings made without his consent or the consent of the performer. To be entitled to such rights the person who has recording rights in relation to a performance must have an exclusive recording contract with the performer. Sections 185–188 deal with the rights of the person having recording rights. (*See* Exclusive Recording Contracts below for details.)

A "performance" is defined in section 180(2) and includes under section 180(2)(b) a musical performance which is given live by one or more individuals. The word "live" is used in the widest sense and includes a performance in concert before an audience or it could be performed in private in the confines of a recording studio. There is no definition of "performer" in the Act, but anybody who gives a performance under section 180(2) will be regarded as a performer, *e.g.* a singer, session musicians and musicians in a group.

Section 180(2) provides that a "recording" of a performance means a film or sound recording:

> "(a) made directly from the live performance, or
> (b) made from a broadcast of, or cable programme including, the performance, or
> (c) made, directly or indirectly, from another recording of the performance."

Section 180(4) provides that the rights in a performance are independent of any copyright or moral rights that may exist.

Performer's rights

Section 181 provides that a performance is a qualifying performance in relation to performer's rights if it is given by a qualifying individual or takes place in a qualifying country.

A qualifying country is defined in section 206(1) and includes:

(a) the United Kingdom, or
(b) another Member State of the EU, or
(c) a country where an Order in Council is made under section 208 acknowledging reciprocal protection of performers' rights.

This will include:

(i) a country which is a party to a convention relating to performers' rights to which the United Kingdom is also a party, and
(ii) a country which has, or will under its law give adequate protection for British performances. (Section 208(3)(a) and (b) defines a British performance as a performance given by an individual who is a British citizen or resident in the UK, or which takes place in the UK.)

A qualifying individual is defined in section 206(1) as "a citizen or subject of, or an individual resident in, a qualifying country".

Section 206(1) also contains a definition of a qualifying person. This is

"a qualifying individual or a body corporate or other body which has a legal personality which:

(a) is formed under the law of a part of the United Kingdom or another qualifying country, and

(b) has in any qualifying country a place of business at which substantial business activity is carried on."

A performer's rights are infringed by a person who, without the consent of the performer:

"(a) makes a recording of the whole or any substantial part of a qualifying performance directly from the live performance, (section 182(1)(a)).

(b) broadcasts live, or includes live in a cable programme service, the whole or any substantial part of a qualifying performance, (section 182(1)(b)).

(c) makes a recording of the whole or any substantial part of a qualifying performance directly from a broadcast of, or cable programme including, the live performance, (section 182(1)(c))."

Section 182(2) provides that the section 182(1)(a), (b) and (c) rights are not infringed by a person making a recording for their own private and domestic use.

Section 182(3) provides that damages for infringement under section 182(1)(a), (b) and (c) will not be awarded where the defendant can show that at the time of the infringement he believed on reasonable grounds that consent had been given.

A performer's rights are also infringed by a person who, without the consent of the performer:

"(d) makes, other than for his private and domestic use, a copy of a recording of the whole or any substantial part of a qualifying performance (section 182A(1)). This is referred to as the "reproduction right".

(e) issues to the public copies of a recording of the whole or any substantial part of a qualifying performance (section 182B(1)). This is referred to as the "distribution right".

(f) rents or lends to the public copies of a recording of the whole or any substantial part of a qualifying performance (section 182C(1)). (This includes renting or lending the original recording of the live performance (section 182C (6)). This is referred to as the "rental right" and the "lending right"."

Section 182C(2)(a) provides that "rental" means

> "making a copy of a recording available for use, on terms that it will or may be returned, for direct or indirect economic or commercial advantage."

Rental therefore means hiring out the work, usually for money.
Section 182C(2)(b) provides that "lending" means

> "making a copy of a recording available for use, on terms that it will or may be returned, otherwise than for direct or indirect economic or commercial advantage, through an establishment which is accessible to the public."

Lending therefore means loaning out a work for free. The lending must be done by an establishment which is accessible to the public. (If a charge is is made to cover the establishment's operating costs, the establishment will still be "lending" under the definition. This is by virtue of section 182C(5).)

Section 182C(3) provides that "rental" and "lending" does not include:

> "(a) making available for the purpose of public performance, playing or showing in public, broadcasting or inclusion in a cable programme service,
> (b)   making available for the purpose of exhibition in public, or
> (c)   making available for on-the-spot reference use."

Section 182C(4) also provides that "lending" "does not include making available between establishments which are accessible to the public."

(It should be noted that the wording of section 182C is almost identical to the wording of section 18A. For section 18A *see* Exclusive Rights of the Copyright Owner, Issuing Copies, above.)

> (g) either:
>   (i)   "shows or plays in public the whole or any substantial part of a qualifying performance," (section 183(a)), or
>   (ii) "broadcasts or includes in a cable programme service the whole or any substantial part of a qualifying performance," (section 183(b)),
>   by means of a recording which was, and which that person knows or has reason to believe was, made without the performer's consent.

(h) either:
  (i) "imports into the United Kingdom other than for his private and domestic use," (section 184(1)(a)), or
  (ii) "in the course of a business possesses, sells or lets for hire, offers or exposes for sale or hire, or distributes," (section 184(1)(b)),
  a recording of a qualifying performance which is, and which that person knows or has reason to believe is, an illicit recording.

Section 184(2) provides that where an infringement action is brought under section 184, if the defendant can show the illicit recording was innocently acquired by him, or a predecessor in title of his, the only remedy available for the infringement will be damages which cannot exceed a reasonable amount.

Section 197(2) defines an illicit recording as a recording of the whole or any substantial part of a performance made other than for private purposes without the consent of the performer.

Section 184(3) states that "innocently acquired" under section 184(2) means "that the person acquiring the recording did not know and had no reason to believe that it was an illicit recording."

The word "substantial"

Sections 182, 182A, 182B, 182C, 182D, and 183 refer to a "substantial" part of a qualifying performance. There is no definition in the Act of the word "substantial". It is likely that "substantial" will have the same meaning as has been applied by the courts to the word "substantial" in copyright infringement cases. (*See* Exclusive Rights of the Copyright Owner, section 16 (3) above.)

Duration of performer's rights

Section 191(2) provides that the performer's rights expire:

  (a) 50 years from the end of the calendar year in which the performance takes place, or
  (b) if during the 50-year period in (a) above a recording of the performance is released, the period is 50 years from the end of the calendar year in which it is released.

By section 191(3) a recording is released

"when it is first published, played or shown in public, broadcast or included in a cable programme service".

Any unauthorised act will not constitute a release of a recording.

Performer's property rights and non-property rights

Section 191A(1) states that the rights of the performer under sections 182A, 182B, and 182C are property rights. (See above for sections 182A, 182B and182C.)

Section 192A(1) states that the rights of the performer under sections 182, 183, and 184 are non-property rights. (See above for sections 182, 183 and 184.)

Property rights

Section 191B(1) provides that

"a performer's property rights are transmissable by assignment, by testamentary disposition or by operation of the law, as personal or moveable property."

Section 191B(2) allows for any assignment or any transmission of a performer's property rights to be limited. Therefore an assignment can be limited to:

(a) one or more of the things which require the consent of the rights owner

(b) part of the period for which the rights subsist.

Section 191B(3) states that

"an assignment of a performer's property rights is not effective unless it is in writing signed by or on behalf of the assignor."

By virtue of section 191B(4) a licence granted by the owner of a performer's property rights binds every successor in title to his interest in the rights, except for a purchaser in good faith for valuable consideration and without notice of the licence or a person deriving title from such a person.

Section 191C allows for there to be an assignment in the whole or in part of a performer's property rights relating to the future recording of a performance. Such assignment should be signed by or on behalf of the performer. Where there has been such an assignment, once these property rights come into existence they will vest in the assignee or in any successor in title of the assignee.

Section 191D allows for an exclusive licence of a performer's property rights to be granted.

Non-property rights

Section 192A(1) provides that a performer's non-property rights cannot be assigned nor are they transmissible. However, under section 192A(2) on the death of a person entitled to non-property rights, the rights can pass by will to any chosen beneficiary, (section 192A(2)(a)), or if there is no such direction in the will, the rights are exercisable by his PRs (section 192A(2)(b).)

Section 193 deals with the issue of consent. The performer's non-property rights are infringed where acts are done without the performer's consent. Section 193(1) provides that consent for non-property rights can be given for a specific performance, a specified description of performances or for performances in general. It is also possible under section 193(1) for consent to relate to past or future performances.

Consent does not have to be given in writing. As with any permission it is better for it to be recorded in writing so the parties are clear what can and cannot be done. Indeed, consent may have been impliedly given due to the conduct or actions of the performer. To avoid disputes any consents which are required by a record company from a performer should be dealt with in a recording agreement. A recording agreement should make it clear that the performer agrees to his performance being recorded by the record company, that he consents to copies of these recorded performances being made, and that he consents to the sale of copies of the recorded performances.

The question of whether consent has or has not been given can be contrasted by two cases. In *Mad Hat Music* v *Pulse 8 Records Ltd* [1993] EMLR 172 it was held that consent given by a performer to make a recording of a performance meant that there was no need for consent to be given by the performer to make records of that performance. In *Bassey* v *Icon Entertainment* [1995] EMLR 596 it was held that consent to make records of a performance was required, notwithstanding the fact that consent had been given to the recording of the performance. These cases were decided before the insertion into the Act of section 182A which now makes it clear that the performer's consent is needed to copy (other than for private and domestic use) a recording of a performance. These cases illustrate the point that disputes can arise over whether a performer has given the necessary consent(s) and that a written agreement should specifically detail to what the performer is consenting.

Right for performers to receive equitable remuneration

For the exploitation of a sound recording

Under section 182D a performer has the right to equitable remuneration where his performance is exploited by way of a sound recording. Section 182D(1) provides that where a

> "commercially published sound recording of the whole or any substantial part of a qualifying performance is:
> (a)   played in public, or
> (b)   included in a broadcast or cable programme service,
> the performer is entitled to equitable remuneration from the owner of the copyright in the sound recording."

Therefore, the record company as the copyright owner in the sound recording will have to pay equitable remuneration to all the performers on the record. (*See* Chapter 4 Collecting Societies and Music Industry Associations below for Phonographic Performance Limited, the Performing Artists' Media Rights Association and the Association of United Recording Artists for the mechanics of how equitable remuneration is paid by the record company to performers where a sound recording is played in public or included in a broadcast or cable programme service.)

Section 182D(2) makes it clear that the right to receive equitable remuneration cannot be assigned by the performer, although it may be assigned to a collecting society which will enforce the right on the performer's behalf. (Section 182D(2) does allow for the right to receive equitable remuneration to be transmissible by testamentary disposition or by operation of the law as personal or moveable property, and that the right to receive equitable remuneration may be assigned or further transmitted by any person into whose hands it passes.) (*See* Chapter 4 Collecting Societies and Music Industry Associations below for Collecting Societies.)

Section 182D(3) provides that the amount of equitable remuneration is to be determined between the parties. The Act does not set out any guidelines as to what constitutes equitable remuneration, although the following sections provide some help to the contracting parties:

(a) Section 182D(4) which provides that if the parties cannot agree the amount of equitable remuneration that should be paid either party can apply to the Copyright Tribunal to determine the amount that should be paid.

(b) Section 182D(5) which provides that where equitable remuneration is payable either party can apply to the Copyright Tribunal to vary any agreement as to the amount payable. There is also a provision in section 182D(5) to apply to the Copyright Tribunal to vary any previous decision made by them.

(*See* Chapter 4 Collecting Societies and Music Industry Associations below for the Copyright Tribunal.)

There is provision in section 182D(7) that any clause in an agreement between the parties excluding or restricting the right to equitable remuneration (section 182D(7)(a)), or preventing a person questioning the amount of equitable remuneration or restricting the powers of the Copyright Tribunal (section 182D(7)(b)) will have no effect. Any clause attempting to exclude or restrict such rights will therefore have no effect.

Where the section 182C rental right in the sound recording has been transferred

Section 191G(1) provides that where a performer has transferred his rental right in a sound recording to the producer of the sound recording, the performer retains the right to receive equitable remuneration for the rental. Section 191G(2) specifically provides that the right to equitable remuneration cannot be assigned by the performer except to a collecting society which can enforce the right on his behalf. (Section 191G(2) does allow for the right to receive equitable remuneration to be transmissible by testamentary disposition or by operation of the law as personal or moveable property, and that the right to receive equitable remuneration may be assigned or further transmitted by any person into whose hands it passes.) (*See* Chapter 4 Collecting Societies and Music Industry Associations below for Collecting Societies.) The person who is liable to pay the equitable remuneration is stated in section 191G(3) to be the person who is currently entitled to the rental right namely the person to whom the right was transferred or any successor in title of his. Section 191G(4) provides that the amount payable for equitable remuneration is the amount agreed by the parties, or in default of such agreement then by virtue of section

191H(1) either party can ask the Copyright Tribunal to determine the amount payable. Section 191G(5) provides that any clause in an agreement purporting to exclude or restrict the right to equitable remuneration will have no effect.

There are also provisions in section 191H(2)(a) and (b) where equitable remuneration is payable, for either party to the agreement to apply to the Copyright Tribunal to:

(a) vary any agreement as to the amount payable, or

(b) vary any previous determination of the Copyright Tribunal.

Any clause in an agreement purporting to prevent a party questioning the amount of equitable remuneration before the Copyright Tribunal will by virtue of section 191H(5) have no effect. Section 191H (4) provides that the remuneration will not be considered inequitable merely because it was paid by way of a single payment or at the time of the transfer of the rental right. (*See* Chapter 4 Collecting Societies and Music Industry Associations below for the Copyright Tribunal.)

Exclusive Recording Contacts

As mentioned earlier, the CDPA gives rights to people who have the benefit of an exclusive recording contract with a performer(s), *e.g.* a record company or a production company which signs artists to record exclusively for them.

Section 185(1) defines an "exclusive recording contract" as

> "a contract between a performer and another person under which that person is entitled to the exclusion of all other persons (including the performer) to make recordings of one or more of his performances with a view to their commercial exploitation."

Section 185(4) provides that "with a view to commercial exploitation" means "with a view to the recordings being sold or let for hire, or shown or played in public."

Section 185(2) provides that

> " "the person having recording rights" in relation to a performance are (subject to subsection (3)) to a person:
> (a)   who is a party to and has the benefit of an exclusive recording contract to which the performance is subject, (section 185(2)(a)), or
> (b)   to whom the benefit of such a contract has been assigned, (section 185(2)(b)),
> and who is a qualifying person."

A qualifying person is defined in section 206 and means

> "a qualifying individual or a body corporate or other body which has a
> legal personality which:
> (a) is formed under the law of a part of the United Kingdom or
> another qualifying country, and
> (b) has in any qualifying country a place of business at which
> substantial business activity is carried on."

(*See* the Performer's Rights above for the definition of a qualifying
individual and qualifying country.)

Section 185(3) provides that if a performance is subject to an
exclusive recording contract but the person mentioned in section 185(2)
is not a qualifying person that the references in the Act to "a person
having recording rights" in relation to a performance are to any person:

> "(a) who is licensed by such a person to make recordings of the
> performance with a view to their commercial exploitation, or
> (b) to whom the benefit of such a licence has been assigned,
> and who is a qualifying person."

By virtue of section 185(3)(a) if, for example, record company A is not
a qualifying person under the Act and has the benefit of an exclusive
recording contract with a performer and licenses record company B to
make recordings of the performer, record company B will be entitled
to the rights conferred by the CDPA, provided record company B is a
qualifying person. Using the same scenario, by virtue of section
185(3), where the benefit of the licence has been assigned by record
company B to record company C, record company C will be entitled
to the rights conferred by the CDPA, provided record company C is a
qualifying person.

Section 192B(1) provides that the rights of "a person having
recording rights are not asssignable or transmissible". However, section
192B(2) does provide that the provisions of section 192B(1) do not
affect section 185(2)(b) or (3)(b), so far as section 185(2)(b) or (3)(b)
confers rights on a person to whom the benefit of a contract or licence
is assigned. The effect of section 192B(2) is, for example, that an
assignee who is a qualified person who has the benefit of an exclusive
recording contract will be entitled to the rights conferred by the CDPA.

Rights of person having recording rights

The rights of a person having recording rights in a performance are
infringed where a person does any of the following acts:

(a) makes a recording of the whole or any substantial part of the performance, other than for private and domestic use, without the consent of the person having recording rights in a performance or the consent of the performer (section 186 (1)).

It is provided in section 186(2) that where there is an action for infringement under section 186(1) damages will not be awarded where a defendant can show that at the time of the infringement he believed on reasonable grounds that consent had been given.

(b) without the consent of the person having recording rights in a performance, or in the case of a qualifying performance, without the consent of the performer:
  (i) "shows or plays in public the whole or any substantial part of the performance" (section 187(1)(a)), or
  (ii) "broadcasts or includes in a cable programme service the whole or any substantial part of the performance" (section 187(1)(b)),
  by means of a recording which was, and which that person knows or has reason to believe was made without the appropriate consent.

(c) without the consent of the person having recording rights in a performance, or in the case of a qualifying performance, without the consent of the performer:
  (i) "imports into the United Kingdom other than for his private and domestic use" (section 188(1)(a)), or
  (ii) "in the course of a business possesses, sells or lets for hire, offers or exposes for sale or hire, or distributes (section 188(1)(b)",
  a recording of the performance which is, and which that person knows or has reason to believe is, an illicit recording.

For the purposes of the rights of a person having recording rights, an 'illicit recording' is defined under section 197(3) as a recording of the whole or any substantial part of a performance which is subject to an exclusive recording contract, and made other than for private purposes, without the consent of the person having recording rights in a performance, or the consent of the performer.

Section 188(2) provides that where a defendant can show that the illicit recording was innocently acquired by him or a predecessor in title of his, the only remedy available will be damages not exceeding a reasonable sum in respect of the act complained of. "Innocently acquired" means under section 188(3) that the "person acquiring the recording did not know and had no reason to believe it to be an illicit recording."

As mentioned earlier when dealing with non-property rights, section 193 deals with the issue of consent. The rights of a person who has recording rights are infringed where acts are done without the consent of the person who has recording rights or are done without the consent of the performer. Section 193(1) provides that consent can be given for a specific performance, a specified description of performances or for performances generally. It is also possible under section 193(1) for consent to relate to past or future performances.

It should be noted that sections 186, 187 and 188 require the consent to be given by either the record company or the performer. This means that where the performer gives his consent to the recording of a performance by a third party when he is bound by an exclusive recording contract, the record company will be bound by the consent given by the performer. The record company could, however, sue the performer for breaching his record contract, and might possibly be able to sue the third party for inducing a breach of contract.

Sections 186 and 187 refer to any "substantial" part of the performance. There is no definition in the Act of the word "substantial". It is likely that "substantial" will have the same meaning as has been applied by the courts to the word "substantial" in copyright infringement cases. (*See* Exclusive Rights of the Copyright Owner, section 16(3) above.)

Permitted acts/defences

As with copyright, by virtue of section 189 performers' rights are subject to various permitted acts. Where a permitted act is done this will mean that the performer's rights have not been infringed. The permitted acts are set out in detail in Schedule 2 to the CDPA. The permitted acts correspond broadly, but not exactly to the copyright permitted acts.

The permitted acts in Schedule 2 include:

(a) fair dealing with a performance or recording for criticism or review,
(b) incidental inclusion of a performance or recording,
(c) recording a performance of a folksong for the purpose of including it in a designated archive,
(d) playing a sound recording as part of the activities of, or for the benefit of a club, society or other organisation,

(e) playing or showing a sound recording, film, broadcast or cable programme at an educational establishment for the purposes of instruction before an audience consisting of teachers and pupils at the establishment and other persons directly connected with the activities of the establishment.

Section 190(1) allows the Copyright Tribunal to give consent to someone who wants to make a copy of a recording where:

(a) the identity or whereabouts of the performer cannot be ascertained by reasonable inquiry (section 190(1)(a)), or
(b) a performer unreasonably withholds consent (section 190(1)(b)).

If the Copyright Tribunal gives consent it will have effect as if the consent had been given by the performer. The Copyright Tribunal may by virtue of section 190(2) attach conditions to the consent being given. (*See* Chapter 4 Collecting Societies and Music Industry Associations below for the Copyright Tribunal.)

Section 190(4) provides that the Copyright Tribunal shall not give consent under section 190(1)(b) "unless satisfied that the performer's reasons for withholding consent protect a legitimate interest of his." It is for the performer to show the reasons why he is refusing to give his consent. If the performer does not give evidence why he is refusing to give consent, the Copyright Tribunal may draw such inferences as it thinks fit from this.

Section 190(5) requires the Copyright Tribunal to take into account the following factors:

(a) "whether the original recording was made with the performer's consent and is lawfully in the possession or control of the person who wants to make the further recording" (section 190(5)(a)),
(b) "whether the making of the further recording is consistent with the obligations of the parties to the arrangements under which, or is otherwise consistent with the purposes for which, the original recording was made" (section 190(5)(b)).

If the Copyright Tribunal give consent it shall under section 190(6), in default of agreement between the parties, make such order as it thinks fit as to the payment that should be made to the performer in consideration of such consent being given.

Remedies for infringing performers' rights

Civil and criminal remedies are available where there has been an infringement of a performer's rights.

Civil remedies

Section 194 provides that an infringement of a performer's non-property rights, or of any right of a person having recording rights, is actionable by the person entitled to the right as a breach of statutory duty. An infringement will enable the person entitled to the right to seek damages and an injunction. An order for delivery up under section 195 and the right to seize illicit recordings under section 196 are also available. (See below for sections 195 and 196.)

As mentioned earlier section 182(3) provides that damages for infringing the section 182(1)(a) (b) and (c) rights will not be awarded where the defendant can show that at the time of the infringement he believed on reasonable grounds that consent had been given. Also as mentioned earlier, section 184(2) provides that where an infringement action is brought under section 184, if the defendant can show that an illicit recording was innocently acquired by him, or by a predecessor in title of his, the only remedy available for the infringement will be damages which cannot exceed a reasonable amount.

Section 191I(1) makes it clear that an infringement of a performer's property rights (namely, the rights under sections 182A, 182B, 182C) is actionable by the rights' owner. Section 191I(2) provides that in an action for infringement of a performer's property rights the remedies available to the claimant are the same as those for infringing any other property right. The remedies available for infringement include damages, injunctions and an account of profits.

Section 191J(1) provides that in an action for infringement of a performer's property rights, if it is shown that at the time of the infringement the defendant did not know, and had no reason to believe, that the rights subsisted in the recording to which the action relates, the claimant is not entitled to damages. This does not prevent the claimant from pursuing any other available remedy.

By contrast, section 191J(2) allows the court in an action for infringement of a performer's property rights to take account of all the circumstances, and in particular to look:

"(a) at the flagrancy of the infringement, and
(b)   at any benefit the defendant may have acquired from infringing."

Having looked at all the circumstances the court may award the claimant additional damages. The courts can use section 191J(2) as an additional punishment against the defendant for infringing the performer's property rights.

Section 191L(1) provides that

"an exclusive licensee has, except against the owner of a performer's property rights, the same rights and remedies in respect of matters occurring after the grant of the licence as if the licence had been an assignment."

Section 191L(2) provides that the exclusive licensee's

"rights and remedies are concurrent with those of the rights' owner."

Section 191M(1) provides that where an action for infringement of a performer's property rights brought by the rights' owner or an exclusive licensee relates (wholly or partly) to an infringement in respect of which they have concurrent rights of action, the rights-owner, or as the case may be, the exclusive licensee may not, without leave of the court, proceed with the action unless the other is joined as a claimant or added as a defendant. Section 191M(3) provides that section 191M(1) does "not affect the granting of inter-locutory relief on an application by the rights' owner or exclusive licensee alone".

Section 191M(4) provides that

"where an action for infringement of a performer's property rights is brought which relates (wholly or partly) to an infringement in respect of which the rights owner and an exclusive licensee have or had concurrent rights of action:

(a)   the court shall in assessing damages take into account:
   (i)   the terms of the licence, and
   (ii) any pecuniary remedy already awarded or available to either of them in respect of the infringement;

(b)   no account of profits shall be directed if an award of damages has been made, or an account of profits has been directed, in favour of the other of them in respect of the infringement; and

(c)   the court shall if an account of profits is directed apportion the profits between them as the court considers just, subject to any agreement between them;

and these provisions apply whether or not the rights owner and the exclusive licensee are both parties to the action."

Section 191M(5) provides that

"the owner of a performer's property rights shall notify any exclusive licensee having concurrent rights before applying for an order under section 195 (order for delivery up) or exercising the right conferred by section 196 (right of seizure); and the court may on the application of the licensee make such order under section 195 or, as the case may be, prohibiting or permitting the exercise by the rights-owner of the right conferred by section 196, as it thinks fit having regard to the terms of the licence."

Delivery up

Section 195(1) provides that where a person in the course of business has in his possession, custody or control an illicit recording of a performance, the person who has performer's rights or the person who has recording rights in relation to the performance, may apply to the court for an order that the recording is delivered up to him or to such other person as the court directs. An order by the court to deliver up does not affect any other power the court has (section 195(4)).

Right to seize illicit recordings

Under section 196(1) where a person is entitled to seek a court order for delivery up, he, or someone authorised by him, may, if an illicit recording of a performance is exposed or is immediately available for sale or hire, seize and detain the recording. This section is aimed (like section 100 which is a similar remedy available for copyright infringement) at trying to catch street traders who sell pirate CDs and tapes of the latest hit albums.

There are conditions which have to be complied with before any illicit recordings can be seized. These are the same as the conditions which apply to seizing illicit copyright material under section 100. (For section 100 *see* Right to Seize Infringing Copies and other Articles above).

An illicit recording is defined in section 197(2) and (3) as:

(a) for the purposes of a performer's rights, it is a recording of the whole or any substantial part of a performance, if it is made other than for private purposes, without the consent of the performer (section 197(2)),

(b) for the purposes of the rights of a person with recording rights, it is a recording of the whole or any substantial part of a performance which is subject to an exclusive recording contract, if it is made, other than for private purposes, without the consent of the person with recording rights or the consent of the performer (section 197(3)).

Criminal remedies

The CDPA provides that in some cases a criminal offence is committed where there is an infringement of the performer's rights. The criminal offences in the Act are similar to those which exist for copyright infringement. The criminal offences are:

(a) Under section 198(1), which provides that an offence is committed where a person 'without sufficient consent:
  (i) makes for sale or hire (section 198(1)(a)), or
  (ii) imports into the United Kingdom other than for his private and domestic use (section 198(1)(b)), or
  (iii) possesses in the course of a business with a view to committing any act infringing the rights conferred by the act (section 198(1)(c)), or
  (iv) in the course of a business:
    (aa) sells or lets for hire, or
    (bb) offers or exposes for sale or hire, or
    (cc) distributes (section 198(1)(d)(i)(ii)(iii))
a recording which is and which he has reason to believe is, an illicit recording'.
(An illicit recording is defined in section 197(2) and (3) above).
(b) Under section 198(2), which provides that an offence is committed where a person 'causes a recording of a performance made without sufficient consent to be:
  (i) shown or played in public, (section 198(2)(a)), or
  (ii) broadcast or included in a cable programme service, (section 198(2)(b)), thereby infringing any rights conferred by the act, if he knows or has reason to believe that those rights are thereby infringed'.

(Section 198(3) defines 'sufficient consent'. In the case of a qualifying performance it means the consent of the performer (section 198(3)(a)).

Section 198(5)(a) and (b) provides that a person who is guilty of an offence under section 198(1) (a), (b) or (d) (iii) is liable:

(a) upon summary conviction to imprisonment for a term not exceeding six months or a fine not exceeding the statutory maximum, or both,
(b) if convicted on indictment a person will be liable to a fine or imprisonment not exceeding two years, or both.

Section 198(6) provides that for any other offence under section 198 a person will be liable upon summary conviction to a fine not exceeding level 5 on the standard scale or imprisonment for a term not exceeding six months, or both.

(c) Under section 201(1), which provides that "it is an offence for a person to represent falsely that he is authorised by any person to give consent for the purposes of the act in relation to a performance, unless he believes on reasonable grounds that he is so authorised".

Section 201(2) provides that a person guilty of this offence is

"liable on summary conviction to imprisonment for a term not exceeding six months or a fine not exceeding level 5 on the standard scale or both".

The CDPA also has provisions for the court to order delivery up where criminal proceedings are brought under section 198 (section 199), for the police to obtain a search warrant (section 200), for the possible liability of the officers of a body corporate where the company has committed an offence (section 202), and for the court to order the disposal of an illicit recording of a performance (section 204).

Chapter 3

Music Industry Contracts

Before we can examine the key clauses in specific music contracts it is necessary to consider briefly a few matters which can affect any contract.

Minors

There are many solo artists or groups whom the law regards as minors. A minor is someone who is under the age of 18. The pop music industry has produced many successful artists who have made hit records whilst they were minors. Jimmy Osmond, Hanson, Billie, Britney Spears in pop music, Charlotte Church and Aled Jones in classical music are just a few of the many hundreds of artists who have had hit records as minors. Minors are regarded in law as a group needing special protection. They need protection from unscrupulous adults who may seek to take unfair advantage of them. There are controls over when and for how long they may work. This therefore places restrictions on their ability to promote their recordings. In addition, the law places great concern over any contract which a minor has entered into with a third party. Contracts with minors are valid if they are beneficial for the minor. If the contract is beneficial for the minor it is enforceable as if it had been entered into with an adult. A contract is regarded as beneficial if it gives the minor a genuine training or education. Education does not just mean a school education. The courts can interpret it in a wider way. The contractual terms must be fair and reasonable and give the minor a reasonable payment for their services. If the contract does not satisfy these requirements then the minor may be able to challenge it in court and have the contract declared voidable. The courts will not declare a contract to be voidable because the record company or the concert promoter will make a reasonable profit out of utililising the artist's services. Nor will the courts declare a contract to be voidable because some clauses are more beneficial to the third party than to the minor. The court will look at the whole of the contract and decide if it is fair and reasonable for the minor to be bound by it. In addition, the courts will examine whether the contractual terms were explained at the time to the minor and to his parents, if they were understood by the minor, and if the minor received independent legal advice from a solicitor with experience of music contracts.

If the minor disputes the contract it is by no means certain that the courts will declare it voidable. It is possible for the minor to challenge the contract whilst he is still a minor or after he has attained the age of majority. The courts will probably hold the minor to the contract if it was beneficial to him, if he performed his contractual obligations, if the terms were explained to him and to his parents and were understood by the minor, and if the minor took independent legal advice from a solicitor with experience of music contracts. In addition, if the minor seeks to challenge the contract after he achieved his majority it is likely he will be bound by the contract if he continued to perform his obligations after he had reached his majority, or if he did not challenge or terminate the contract within a reasonable time of reaching his majority.

The court will look at all the contractual terms and the surrounding circumstances to decide whether the contract with the minor, or entered into by the minor and challenged by him after his majority, is voidable.

A record company or promoter will not want to spend a large sum of money developing the minor's career only to find that the contact is then challenged and found to be voidable. It can quite easily cost a record company over £250,000 to bring a record out. No commercial enterprise will be prepared to risk investing such a sum on an artist whom the court may let walk away from a contract. To protect themselves the party contracting with the minor will put as many safeguards in the contract as possible to try and ensure that a court will not find the contract to be voidable. The contractual arrangements should be drafted in such a way that they are beneficial to the minor and give the minor a fair reward for his services. The party contracting with the minor should ensure that the minor's parents or guardians are present when they are dealing with him, that any contract is signed by the minor and his parents or guardians, that the minor obtains independent legal advice from a solicitor experienced with music contracts and that the minor understands the contractual provisions. Also they might seek a guarantor in the contract to guarantee that if the minor successfully challenges the validity of the contract, the guarantor will compensate them for their loss. The guarantor must seek independent legal advice on the proposed terms and effect of the guarantee. The legal advice should be given by a solicitor experienced in music contracts. A guarantor's legal advisor should as stated be independent, that is he should not be the legal advisor to the minor or the party contracting with the minor. The terms should be considered very carefully and, if necessary, the guarantee should be amended to suit what the guarantor is prepared to guarantee, if indeed he is prepared to act as guarantor. The guarantor should ideally only be a guarantor up to the age of the minor's majority. In addition, the guarantor will want to provide a limit on the maximum amount he may be liable for and will want a provision included that any claim against him can only be brought within a year of the minor's majority. Being a guarantor can be a huge financial responsibility. It is not something to enter into lightly, and if there are any doubts the proposed guarantor should not take on the responsibility.

Guarantors

We have seen above that a party to a contract with a minor may seek a guarantor to the contract, and that although the guarantee may originally be drafted with an open-ended liability, it can and indeed should if possible, be cut back so that the guarantor is liable for a specific period of time and for a maximum financial liability. The guarantor may have to provide references so the party contracting with the minor can establish that the guarantor is not a man of straw. At the end of the day if the guarantor does not wish to give a guarantee or cannot get the party contracting with the minor to agree to the terms that he is prepared to guarantee he should not act as guarantor.

It may be understandable that a party contracting with a minor wants a guarantor to the contract with the minor. The party contracting with a minor may intend to spend a substantial sum developing the minor's career. There is the risk, as with all contracts, that the artist does not succeed in the market place and the record company, publisher or concert promoter will lose a large sum of money. With a contract with a minor there is an added risk that the contract might be successfully challenged in court by the minor. That may be one risk too many for a record company, publisher or concert promoter to take, and a guarantor may be required by the party contracting with the minor to reduce the effect of that risk.

There is one occasion where a guarantor will always be required which is where a third party contracts not with the artist but with the artist's limited company. An artist can choose to contract personally or through a limited company which is owned and controlled by him. Where the artist has a limited company he will have an employment contract with his limited company, and his limited company will enter contracts with third parties to provide his services to the third parties. The reason why an artist may set up a limited company and have an employment contract with his own company is usually for tax reasons.

If the artist's limited company is contracting with a third party there is no privity of contract between the artist and the third party. If the limited company goes into liquidation the third party has no contractual right to require the artist to perform under the contract. For this reason the third party should when entering a contract with a limited company which is owned and controlled by the artist require a separate side letter from the artist. The side letter from the artist to the third party should guarantee that the limited company will perform the contract and if the limited company defaults, the artist will personally perform the obligations contained in the limited company/third party contract.

Independent legal advice

The artist will be required by the record company, publisher, manager etc to obtain independent legal advice on the contents of the contract which he is being offered from a solicitor experienced with music contracts. The contract should contain a clause confirming that the artist has taken independent legal advice on the contents of the contract from a solicitor experienced with music contracts. The effect of such a clause in a contract will not stop an artist challenging the terms of the contract in court, nor will it stop, for example, a contract which is actually in restraint of trade from being held by a court to be in restraint of trade. (For Restraint of trade see below). However, where the artist obtains independent legal advice from a solicitor experienced with music contracts and later seeks to challenge the contract, for example, on the basis that when he signed the contract he was a minor or he entered into the contract due to undue influence which was exerted upon him, the record company, publisher, manager etc may be able to use the fact that the artist had received independent legal advice from a solicitor experienced with music contracts along with any other relevant evidence, to persuade the court that the artist was properly advised at the time, was made fully aware of the contractual terms by his solicitor, and so the contract should be upheld.

Restraint of trade

It is very easy to label record companies, publishing companies and managers as the devil incarnate. It must be remembered that they will spend a large amount of their time and money developing unknown artists. There is no guarantee that their investment will succeed. Even if a group becomes a success it is rare that they will do so over night. It is highly unlikely, although it can happen, that money expended by a record company on a group will be recouped by the record company on the strength of one hit single or one hit album. A record company will rarely sign a totally unknown group for a guaranteed five or seven album deal. Newspapers are full of stories of unknown groups signing five album deals for a £500,000 advance. If the truth be told it is often a deal for a single with options for the record company to exercise which, if all the options are exercised will amount to a five album deal. As for the £500,000 advance, usually only a small advance will be paid to the group initially with subsequent advances being paid if the record company exercises their options, which altogether might total £500,000.

Any contract which requires somebody to work exclusively for someone else is restrictive. The music industry has in recent years seen some high profile fall outs between artists and record companies, publishing companies and managers. The Artist Formerly Known as Prince fell out with his record company and believing that he was a slave took to wearing the word "SLAVE" on his face. XTC after falling out with their record company effectively went on strike for six years until they were dropped. Most artists who believe that their relationship, with for example their record company, is beyond repair will adopt a more conventional way to try and extricate themselves from their contract, namely litigation.

Artists who have tried to free themselves from a contract often allege that the contract is in restraint of trade. All contracts providing for the exclusive services of an artist are essentially restraining the artist from working for somebody else. The courts will recognise the sizeable investment which, for example, a record company puts into the development of an artist, and also recognise that the record company will require some time to try to recoup their investment and make a profit. A contract which requires an artist to work exclusively for someone else does not automatically make that contract one which the courts will hold to be in restraint of trade.

The court in *Esso Petroleum Company Ltd* v *Harpers Garage (Stourport) Ltd* [1968] AC 269 looked in detail at the concept of restraint of trade. The approach used in the *Esso* case, and which is the approach the courts will use, is to look at the contract to see if it is capable of attracting the doctrine of restraint of trade. This will mean examining the contract to see if the contract requires the artist to provide his services exclusively to the other party for an agreed period of time. If the contract is capable of attracting the doctrine of restraint of trade then the following questions should be asked:

(a) Does the contractual restriction protect a legitimate interest or does it do more than protect the interest? The person claiming it protects a legitimate interest must show that it does no more than that.

(b) Is the contractual restriction reasonable between the contracting parties?

(c) Is the contractual restriction in the public interest?

In determining whether a contract is in restraint of trade, the court will look at the whole of the contract and at the inter-relationship between the clauses. Some clauses in a contract may on the surface appear to be fair but that may not be the case when the clause is examined with any relevant inter-related clauses. Certainly all the clauses in the contract are of relevance in deciding whether the contract is in restraint of trade, but the main clauses of relevance will probably be:

(a) the clause requiring the artist to provide his services on an exclusive basis,

(b) the term clause including any options to extend the term,

(c) the territory clause,

(d) any clause providing for advances to be paid,

(e) the royalty clause,

(f) the termination clause,

(g) any clause which allows the benefit of the contract to be assigned,

(h) the clause dealing with who owns the copyright in the works,

(i) any clause requiring the party contracting with the artist to exploit the work produced by the artist and dealing with what happens if the work is not exploited.

There have been several legal cases concerning the music industry and restraint of trade. The case of *Schroeder Music Publishing Company Ltd v Macaulay* [1974] 1 WLR 1308 concerned a publishing contract which the court found to be in restraint of trade. *Zang Tumb Tuum Records Ltd and Another v Holly Johnson* [1989] *The Independent*, 2 August 1988 (the Frankie Goes To Hollywood case) concerned recording and publishing contracts which the court found to be in restraint of trade. *Silvertone Records Ltd v Mountfield & Others* and *Zomba Music Publishers Ltd v Mountfield & Others* [1993] EMLR 152 (the Stone Roses case) concerned recording and publishing contracts which were found to be in restraint of trade. The George Michael case, *Panayioutou v Sony Music Entertainment (UK) Ltd* [1994] EMLR 229 concerned a recording contract which the court held was not in restraint of trade.

To see if a contract is in restraint of trade the court will look to see if it was in restraint of trade at the date it was entered into not at the date of the hearing.

If there has been a contract dispute between the parties and it is settled not by litigation but by a negotiated agreement between the parties, the courts will not at a later date re-open the original dispute by letting the artist claim that his contract is in restraint of trade. The courts will not re-open a negotiated settlement on the grounds of public policy. This was made clear in the George Michael case.

If the contract is held to be in restraint of trade the contract is void and unenforceable. Where a contract is void it is void from the date of the court judgment. The effect of this is that the party contracting with the artist will only be able to retain those benefits or rights which have already vested in them prior to the judgment, *e.g.* a publishing company will retain the copyrights in those compositions which were written by the composer and assigned to them prior to the judgment, but the publishing company will not be entitled to an assignment of the compositions which are written by the composer after the judgment.

The courts can if they wish apply the blue pencil test, in other words, they can cut out the restrictive parts of the contract and retain the rest of it. The parties would then be left with a valid contract. They will only do this if the contract makes sense without the restrictive parts. The courts will not use the blue pencil if cutting out the restrictive parts means that the contract has to be amended by them to make sense.

As stated earlier there is no way to guarantee that a contract with an artist will not be held to be in restraint of trade. The only way for record companies, publishing companies and managers to try and avoid the problem is to take the approach that they must be fair and reasonable to the artist in all the contractual clauses. An approach of "do unto others" may be a good approach to take but it is by no means a guarantee that an artist will not bring a successful action for restraint of trade.

Undue influence

Many artists who enter the music business do so at a young age. Hardly any artists, if any at all, come into it with any legal, business or financial experience. Many artists only acquire these skills during the course of their careers, and it is only after they have learned how the industry works that they are able to accurately keep an eye on their finances. Some artists have little interest or ability in controlling what they regard as the boring paperwork side of the business. All they are interested in is recording, touring and having fun. They are happy to trust someone to do the necessary work for them and will sign whatever documents are put in front of them.

The courts are aware that not everybody has business acumen and that one party may rely totally upon another party for advice and will often follow that advice blindly without any question, as for example may happen in a solicitor and client relationship. The law has created the equitable doctrine of undue influence which may provide some form of protection for a person who puts their total trust in somebody. Where undue influence exists a contract which has been entered into by a party due to undue influence is voidable and may be set aside by the courts if it is just and equitable to do so.

Undue influence can either be actual or presumed. The common situation where undue influence is presumed to exist by the court is where there is a fiduciary relationship between the parties, such as between a solicitor and his client or a bank and its customer. A presumption of undue influence will also exist if the courts feel that there is a sufficient nexus between the parties.

Where undue influence is presumed, as may be the case in the relationship between a manager and an artist (if there is a fiduciary relationship between the parties undue influence is automatically presumed to exist, otherwise it has to be established by the artist to the court that the presumption should apply), it will be for the manager to show that the presumption does not apply. He may be able to establish this if he can show that the artist took independent legal advice and that the artist understood the contractual terms. In addition, factors, such as the age and the expertise of the artist, will be taken into account by the court. If the presumption of undue influence applies then the artist will have to establish that the contract he entered into is not at all to his advantage.

There have been several high profile music cases where the courts have looked at the doctrine of undue influence, for example see *O'Sullivan* v *Management Agency and Music Ltd* [1985] 1QB 428, *Armatrading* v *Stone* (1984) unreported, and *Elton John and Others* v *Richard Leon James and Others* [1991] FSR 397. These cases show that the courts will, if they feel it is just and equitable to do so, set aside any agreement which has been entered into where there has been proven undue influence which has not been to the advantage of the weaker party.

It is possible that undue influence may exist between, *e.g.* the artist and his manager, or the artist and his record company, or the artist and his publishing company. Whether there is undue influence depends on the facts of each individual case. What creates the possibility of there being undue influence is a combination of the age and the experience of the artist, whether independent legal advice was taken and understood by the artist, and whether there was a conflict of interest between the parties, for example, the manager advised and persuaded the artist to sign with a record company and a publishing company which were owned and controlled by the manager on terms which were not really favourable to the artist.

EC competition law

The objective of Article 81 of the Treaty of Amsterdam (formerly Article 85 of the Treaty of Rome) is to prohibit agreements between undertakings which restrict or attempt to restrict competition in the EC and affects trade between the member states. This book cannot deal in any detail with the complex subject of competition law. Readers are advised to refer to specialist books on the subject. It is necessary however to touch upon the subject here, albeit only scratching the surface of this specialist area of law, as Article 81 may have an effect, for example, on a recording or publishing agreement. Where any agreement falls within the ambit of Article 81 the agreement is prima facie deemed to be void. There are various ways in which an agreement which falls foul of Article 81 can be valid, examples being where the agreement comes within the Notice of Agreements of Minor Importance, or if Article 81 is exempted under Article 81(3).

The European Court will look at the whole agreement when examining an agreement to see if it restricts competition within the EC. It will essentially ask itself whether the contractual restriction protects a legitimate interest or does it do more than protect that interest. If the agreement does not affect trade between member states, it will be matter for the national competition authorities.

Lawyers for George Michael in the High Court used the arguments that his recording agreement was in restraint of trade or alternatively fell foul of what was then Article 85 but is now Article 81 and was therefore void. (*See* above for Restraint of trade.) The judge in the case, Parker J, did not accept the argument that the agreement fell foul of what is now Article 81. To date no artist has been able to successfully challenge a recording or publishing agreement using the Article

81 argument, nor has there been a decision on the effect of Article 81 on a recording or publishing agreement from the European Court, the House of Lords or the Court of Appeal.

It should be noted that an agreement which is void under Article 81 is void *ab initio* and not from the date of the court judgment. This will mean, for example, that should a composer ever successfully challenge his publishing agreement under Article 81, any copyrights which have purportedly been assigned to the publisher under the agreement will remain vested in the composer. (This should be contrasted with an agreement which is void for being in restraint of trade. Where an agreement is held to be in restraint of trade it is void from the date of the court judgment which means, for example, that a publisher will retain the copyright in those compositions which have already been assigned to him prior to the judgment.)

The Contracts (Rights of Third Parties) Act 1999

The parties to a contract can, by virtue of the Contracts (Rights of Third Parties) Act 1999, grant rights to a third party who is not a party to the contract. The act does not apply to any contract entered into before 11 November 1999. For contracts entered into from 11 November 1999 until 10 May 2000 the act will only apply where the contract makes express provision for the act to apply. For contracts entered into from 11 May 2000 the act will only apply where the contracting parties intend to grant rights to a third party. It should be noted that a third party will only have rights under the contract where the contracting parties intend that he should have rights (or for contracts entered into from 11 November 1999 until 10 May 2000, where the contract makes express provision for the act to apply), and where the third party is expressly identified in the contract eg: by name. The contracting parties can if they want to grant rights to a third party either adopt all or only some of the provisions of the act. The contracting parties should, where they do not want to grant rights to a third party, provide in the contract that the provisions of the act are excluded from the contract and that they do not intend to give rights to any third party under the contract. In addition, where it is intended that a third party is to have rights under the contract, the contracting parties should ideally insert a clause in the contract which allows them to amend the terms of the contract without the need to obtain the third party's consent to the amendment.

Due to the effect that the Contracts (Rights of Third Parties) Act 1999 can have upon a contract it is important for the contracting parties to consider whether or not they intend to grant rights to a third party and to make appropriate provisions in the contract. One occasion where the contracting parties might intend to grant rights to a third party would be where one of the contracting parties is a limited company which is owned and controlled by a third party eg: where the performer's own limited company contracts with a record company to provide the performer's recording services to the record company, a "loan out" agreement. (See Chapter 8 The Recording Agreement, Introduction, for a loan out agreement.)

Cross-collateralisation

The concept of cross-collateralisation for an artist should be accompanied with two words which should be written in letters ten feet high: **be careful**. If the solicitor representing an artist is not aware of the potential problem of cross-collateralisation the artist may find himself seriously out of pocket.

So what is cross-collateralisation? It is best explained by way of a simple example. If we imagine that an artist has entered a three album deal and was paid an advance on signing the contract of £50,000. For the second and third albums the artist was given a guaranteed £50,000 advance for each album upon the commencement of recording the second and third albums. The advances are recoupable but not returnable (in other words recoverable from royalties due to the artist from sales of the recordings made by him for the record company). The artist is on an 11% royalty rate without any deductions. The first album earned £10,000 royalties for the artist, the second and third albums respectively earned £20,000 and £120,000 royalties for the artist. The figures look as follows:

	Advance	*Royalties earned*	*Amount unrecouped*
Album 1	£50,000	£10,000	£40,000
Album 2	£50,000	£20,000	£30,000
Album 3	£50,000	£120,000	–
Total	£150,000	£150,000	

Because of cross-collateralisation the artist will receive no royalties. For Album 1 he had received a £50,000 advance. The £50,000 advance was recoupable from royalties due to the artist from sales of recordings made by him for the record company. For Album 1 he only earned £10,000 in royalties. The £10,000 royalties would not be paid to the artist but would be used to repay the £50,000 advance, so he was £40,000 unrecouped on Album 1. For Album 2 he received another £50,000 recoupable advance. Album 2 only generated £20,000 in royalties so the artist by the end of Album 2 was in total £70,000 unrecouped (£40,000 on Album 1 and £30,000 on Album 2). For Album 3 he received another £50,000 recoupable advance. This album generated £120,000 royalties but this would not be paid to the artist because at the end of Album 2 he was £70,000 unrecouped, and he also owed £50,000 for the advance for Album 3. The £120,000 royalties due to the artist would be taken by the record company to repay the £120,000 which was outstanding.

If the record contract was not cross-collateralised the advance for each album could only have been recouped from sales of that album for which the advance had been paid. That would have meant the record company would have been out of pocket to the tune of £70,000 on the first two albums, whilst the artist would have received £70,000 royalties on Album 3, being the royalties of £120,000 on Album 3 less the advance for Album 3 of £50,000. Every record company will cross-collateralise within a record contract. The record contract is an entire contract not a series of severable contracts, and so any advances paid by the record company to the artist under the terms of the record contract will be recoupable from the royalties which are due to the artist from sales of the recordings made by him for the record company under the contract.

What is not acceptable is cross-collateralisation of a record contract with, for example, a publishing contract. An artist who both composes and performs his own material may be offered a record contract with a record company and a publishing contract with a publishing company at the same time. It will often be the case that the record and publishing companies making the offers are related companies, *e.g.* they are subsidiaries of the same parent company. The situation might arise where the artist finds that he is unrecouped under his record contract because his records have not sold well, yet be owed royalties from his publishing contract because another artist had a hit with one of his compositions. Because this situation could occur, the record company may try and secure a clause which enables them to recoup any unrecouped sums under the record contract from royalties due and payable to the artist under the publishing contract. Such a provision is totally unacceptable for an artist. The artist should ensure that the record company cannot cross-collateralise the record contract with other contracts which he might have, *e.g.* with his publishing or merchandising contracts.

Where the artist is negotiating a record contract with a record company with whom he has not previously contracted, he should ensure that the proposed record contract does not provide that any unrecouped sums under the proposed record contract will be recoupable from any advances or royalties payable under any subsequent record contract which the artist might enter into with that record company. Likewise, where the artist is negotiating a new record contract with his existing record company he should ensure that the proposed new record contract does not provide that any unrecouped sums under the proposed new record contract will be recoupable from any royalties payable under any previous record contract with that record company nor from any advances or royalties payable under any subsequent record contract which the artist might enter into with that record company.

Warranties and indemnities

A warranty is is a statement by one of the contracting parties that certain facts are true. Frequently, the warranted statements are facts which only the person making the statement knows to be true.

Music contracts, like any commercial contract, will contain warranty and indemnity provisions. A breach of warranty enables the injured party to make a claim for damages, although the injured party will have to prove their loss to the court and show the court that they have where possible mitigated their loss. Rescission is not available for a breach of warranty. A warranty clause may be supported in the contract with an indemnity clause. If this is the case where a warranty is breached, the injured party will be able to invoke the indemnity clause.

Examples of some warranties in publishing contracts include that:

(a) the composer is able to enter the contract,
(b) the composer is not a minor,
(c) the composer has not entered into any other contract which conflicts with the contract he is signing,
(d) all songs written by the composer are his own work and are original.

These and other warranties in the publishing contract will often be accompanied by a clause given by the composer indemnifying the publisher against all the costs, liabilities, losses and damage incurred by the publisher arising out of a breach of warranty by the composer. Any warranty clauses must be considered very carefully by both parties and their solicitors. Likewise, the scope of the indemnity clause must be considered very carefully by both parties and their solicitors.

Warranty and indemnity provisions are dealt with in more detail throughout the rest of this book.

Other clauses

As with any commercial contract, music contracts will contain clauses which reflect or modify the common law provisions. These clauses should not be accepted just because they are regarded as standard conditions which are found in every contract. Each clause should be considered carefully to see if it is appropriate for that particular contract. If necessary these clauses should be amended accordingly. The clauses which reflect or modify the common law provisions include:

Notice clause

It may be that the contract requires one party to give notice to the other party in order for a clause under the contract to be implemented, for example options will usually be exercised by one party giving notice to the other of their intention to exercise the benefit of the option. A notice clause may state that the notice should be in writing and sent by recorded delivery or by first class post to the correct address and that it is deemed to have been received at that address on the first working day after it has been posted.

Partnership/joint venture/employment clause

If, for example, there is a management agreement between a manager and an artist there will often be a clause in the management agreement confirming that the contract is not a partnership, joint venture or employment contract. This makes it clear that the intention of the contract is not to create, for example, a partnership as defined by the Partnership Act 1890 which amongst other matters provides that the partners are liable for each other's acts.

Invalidity clause

This clause provides that if any clause in a contract is found to be invalid by the court then the offending clause is deemed to have been severed from the contract whilst the rest of the contract will remain intact. The courts will not rewrite the contract, so if the contract does not stand on its own without the offending clause then the contract will fail. This does not actually increase the power of the court, because even if an invalidity clause is not included in the agreement the courts have a power to sever the offending clause.

Waiver clause

There will usually be a clause stating that any delay in exercising a contractual right does not amount to a waiver of that right.

Law and jurisdiction clause

It is common for there to be a clause confirming that the law of England and Wales will apply to the contract.

The contract will also probably state which is the competent jurisdiction for a dispute to be heard. The contract will often provide that the courts of competent jurisdiction are the courts of England and Wales. A competent jurisdiction clause is different to an exclusive jurisdiction clause. If the competent jurisdiction clause states the courts of England and Wales this does not preclude proceedings being brought in another jurisdiction.

Force majeure clause

A *force majeure* clause should list all the events which are beyond the control of the contracting parties, *e.g.* act of God, civil war, terrorism, strikes, lock outs, which if any of them occur will excuse the party who cannot perform his contractual obligations due to the *force majeure* event. A *force majeure* clause should provide that the party who cannot perform his contractual obligations will not be in breach of contract for non-performance where the non-performance is due to a *force majeure* event. The clause should require the party who cannot perform his contractual obligations due to a *force majeure* event to give notice to the other party of the existence of the *force majeure* event and that it prevents him from performing his contractual obligations. The clause should provide that the contract is suspended whilst the *force majeure* event exists and that the contract will re-commence once the *force majeure* event has ended. As the suspension could last for a substantial length of time there should also be a long stop clause in the contract allowing one party, rather than waiting for the *force majeure* event to end and for the contract to re-commence, to serve a notice on the other party terminating the contract, if the contract is still suspended due to the *force majeure* event after a specified period of time. Where the contract can be terminated due to a *force majeure* event, the contract should contain provisions dealing with what happens where the contract is terminated in such circumstances, *e.g.* any advance paid by a concert promoter to a performer for a concert will, if the concert is terminated due to a *force majeure* event be repaid to the promoter.

Collecting Societies and Music Industry Associations

The Copyright Tribunal

By virtue of the CDPA the Copyright Tribunal has amongst its powers the right to hear certain matters concerning 'licensing schemes' and 'licensing bodies'. The Copyright Tribunal has no power to hear copyright infringement cases.

A 'licensing scheme' is defined in section 116(1)(a) and (b) of the CDPA as a scheme setting out:

> "(a) the classes of case in which the operator of the scheme, or the person on whose behalf he acts, is willing to grant copyright licences, and
> (b) the terms on which licences would be granted in those classes of case."

A "licensing body" is defined in section 116(2) of the CDPA as

> "a society or other organisation which has as its main object, or one of its main objects, the negotiation or granting, either as owner or prospective owner of copyright or as agent for him, of copyright licences, and whose objects include the granting of licences covering works of more than one author."

It should be noted that the Copyright Tribunal only has the power to hear cases under sections 118–123 (the sections which deal with references and applications concerning licensing schemes), and under sections 125–128 (the sections which deal with references and applications concerning licensing by licensing bodies) where the scheme is operated by, or the licence has been granted by:

(a) a licensing body, (it should be noted that the application of sections 125–128 in fact applies to licences which are granted by a licensing body otherwise than in pursuance of a licensing scheme), and

(b) covers works of more than one author, so far as they relate to licences for, or authorise:
   (i) copying the work, (sections 117(a) and 124(a)), or
   (ii) rental or lending of copies of the work to the public, (sections 117(b) and 124(b)), or

(iii) performing, showing or playing the work in public, (sections 117(c) and 124(c)), or

(iv) broadcasting the work or including it in a cable programme service, (sections 117(d) and 124(d)).

Examples of licensing bodies which operate licensing schemes are the Performing Right Society and the Mechanical-Copyright Protection Society (see below). The PRS tariffs are examples of licensing schemes.

The Copyright Tribunal can also by virtue of section 190(1) of the CDPA give consent on behalf of a performer to somebody who wants to make a copy of a recording of a performance where the identity or whereabouts of the person entitled to the reproduction right cannot be ascertained by reasonable inquiry. Where the Copyright Tribunal gives consent under section 190(1) it shall, under section 190(6),

> "in default of agreement between the applicant and the person entitled to the reproduction right, make such order as it thinks fit as to the payment to be made to that person in consideration of consent being given".

The Copyright Tribunal can under sections 93C and 191H hear disputes concerning the equitable remuneration payable where, for example, an author of a literary or musical work or a performer has transferred his rental right in a sound recording or a film to the producer of the sound recording or film. The Copyright Tribunal can also under section 182D hear disputes concerning the equitable remuneration payable to the performer for the exploitation of a sound recording. (*See* Chapter 2 Copyright Law and the Copyright, Designs and Patents Act 1988, Exclusive Rights of the Copyright Owner, Renting or Lending Copies to the Public (for section 93C), Right to Receive Equitable Remuneration where the section 182C rental right in the sound recording has been transferred (for section 191H), and Right for Performers to Receive Equitable Remuneration for Exploitation of a Sound Recording (for section 182D).)

Collecting societies

Collecting societies play a very important role in collecting certain types of income and distributing it to their members. It has been argued, perhaps correctly, that the distribution by some collecting societies is an inaccurate science, as the most popular artists receive the largest slice of the cake but they do not necessarily receive the exact amount they are entitled to. Less popular artists correctly receive a smaller slice of the cake but it is often argued by the most popular artists that the less popular artists receive more than they are actually entitled to.

There is no requirement for an artist or record company to join any collecting society but it is well worth doing so. Taking as an example the Performing Right Society, no publisher or composer is able to keep a check on where, when and how often a particular song is played on the radio, in the clubs, in concert, or on a pub jukebox. The Performing Right Society carries out these functions and many more on behalf of its members by licensing pubs, cafés, hotels and other places where music is played or performed, and by granting blanket licences to radio and television stations to broadcast music.

Performing Right Society

The Performing Right Society (PRS) is closely allied to the Mechanical-Copyright Protection Society Ltd (see below). The PRS and the Mechanical-Copyright Protection Society now work in tandem carrying out their respective functions and are collectively known as the MCPS-PRS The Music Alliance.

The PRS administers the public performance and broadcast of compositions on behalf of their members. The PRS members comprise music publishers, music composers, and lyric writers. There are several ways a music composer or lyric writer whose lyrics have been set to music may be eligible to join the PRS, *e.g.* a composer is eligible to join if he has composed three works each of which must have been either (a) commercially recorded, or (b) commercially published and performed in public at least 12 times within the past two years. (For the other ways a music composer or lyric writer whose lyrics have been set to music may be eligible to join the PRS, see the PRS Members' Handbook and their brochure "What is PRS?".

For a publisher to be eligible to join he must have a catalogue of 15 works out of which at least 10 have been commercially recorded or commercially published. In addition there are other criteria which apply to the publisher each of which must be satisfied before a publisher is eligible to join. The criteria are set out in the PRS *Members' Handbook* and in the brochure "What Is PRS?" and include a requirement that the publisher has acquired rights in at least 10 of the works for a territory within the European Union.

If the membership criteria are satisfied a joining fee of £50 including VAT for authors and £250 including VAT for publishers is payable.

Membership normally lasts for the life of the member although the member may leave if he gives notice under the PRS rules.

As mentioned in Chapter 2, Copyright Law and the Copyright, Designs and Patents Act 1988, the copyright owner has the exclusive right to perform, show or play his work in public (section 16(1)(c)), and the exclusive right to broadcast the work or include it in a cable programme service (section 16(1)(d)). The PRS requires an assignment from its members, of the performing right, namely the right to perform, show or play the work in public, and to broadcast the work or include it in a cable programme service. There are certain rights which the PRS does not control, for example, it does not control the public performance of music specially written for a *son-et-lumière* production and performed in the *son-et-lumière*, nor for the public performance of music specially written for the production of a dramatic work in a theatre when the music is performed in conjunction with the dramatic production. (For examples of other rights the PRS does not control see the PRS *Members' Handbook*, July 1998.) Licenses to use the work under section 16(1)(c) and 16(1)(d) will therefore in nearly all cases be granted by the PRS.

A licence will be required from the PRS where there is a public performance of music. For example, pubs, cafés, restaurants, concert venues, hotels, aircraft, music-on-hold played on telephone switchboards, raves, circuses, ice rinks, music played on the internet require a PRS licence. There is an annual fee payable for the licence. The amount payable is based upon a range of tariffs which take account of matters such as the type of business operated and the size of the premises. The licence is a blanket licence of the PRS repertoire which permits the licensee to play live or recorded music in public.

Radio, television, most UK-based satellite services and some cable operating services will also require a PRS licence. The fees payable are negotiated between the PRS and the various bodies individually *e.g.* the BBC negotiates with the PRS the amount the BBC has to pay for a licence.

The PRS keeps a check on what music is played on radio and on television. This enables them to share out the income it has received amongst its members according to how much each member's work has been used. The PRS receives details of all the music played on certain radio and television stations, *e.g.* BBC network radio, BBC TV, ITV (including GMTV), Channel 4, and S4C. Other radio stations, satellite and cable television services send sample details of the music played to the PRS. The PRS check what music is used by randomly listening to broadcasts and checking them with the details it receives from the broadcasters.

From 1 January 1999 the PRS changed the way it collated the information on music performed live in concert. Previously it kept a list of
"significant venues" which were required to file with the PRS a return
of the songs performed live in concert. In addition, where the royalty
at an event was £500 or more, that event had to file a programme
return of the songs used at the event. The PRS would use these returns
to distribute the income received from those performances. For all
other live performances the PRS distributed the income it received
from the licensed venues not by using a programme return from the
venues but by using a comparison, or as the PRS called it an "analogy",
with the music used on certain radio stations. The PRS has now
stopped using the "significant venue" system and replaced it with a
system detailed in the PRS news 54 supplement. The idea behind the
new system as the PRS has stated in their news 54 supplement is to
make "it possible for any live performance [of a work] to feature in a
distribution" of performance income.

There are certain areas where the PRS has presently waived its right
to collect royalties, for example it does not charge royalties for
performances during divine service or for performances to patients in
hospitals and nursing homes. The PRS has not waived its right to
collect royalties for charity events.

The PRS collects and distributes income from the public performance
of works performed abroad. The PRS is affiliated to performing rights
societies abroad such as SACEM (in France), JASRAC (in Japan), ASCAP,
BMI and SESAC (in America). The PRS collects monies due from this
country to the members of performing rights societies abroad and sends
them to the relevant performing rights society for it to distribute to its
members. In return the affiliated societies collect monies in their country
which are payable to the members of the PRS and will send them to the
PRS for distribution. There is a delay in paying the PRS members monies
due to them from abroad as the money takes time coming into the
foreign collecting society, it takes time processing it and sending it to the
PRS who will then account to the member. If the writer is a big success in
a foreign territory it may be worth him joining the foreign collecting
society as well as the PRS so that he can receive the foreign performance
income directly from the foreign collecting society rather than wait for it
to be sent to the PRS and then wait for it to be sent to him.

Royalties are distributed by the PRS four times a year in April, July,
October and December. The PRS is a non-profit making body and
distributes all its monies to its members after payment of its administration costs and any donations and transfers to reserve funds. The
PRS figures for 1997 show that out of every £1 received 68.5p was

distributed to members of PRS. The administration costs for the year were 13.5p in every pound.

If the songwriter has a publishing contract any performing rights income will be paid by the PRS directly to the parties concerned. The PRS will send a cheque for the publisher's share directly to the publisher and a cheque for the writer's share directly to the writer. The PRS *Members' Handbook* sets out how it will divide up the income for a song between a publisher and a writer where the performing right has been assigned to the PRS. For works which have been written and published by the PRS members, the PRS will pay 50% of the royalties to the publisher and 50% to the writers. This is the normal distribution by the PRS to the publisher and writer unless the PRS has notification from them that the division should be different. Where the division of income is altered by the publisher and writer in writing, the PRS will pay the publisher and writer according to their agreement, although the PRS rules specifically provide that no agreement between the publisher and the writer may provide the publisher with more than 50% of the income and the PRS will not pay more than 50% of the royalties to the publisher. (See also Chapter 7 The Publishing Agreement, Performing and Broadcasting.)

Members can now administer live performances for themselves. The PRS rules allow for a re-assignment to members of the right to perform their work(s) live in public. The PRS (after a Monopolies and Mergers Commission report which included as one of its recommendations that members should be free to administer their live performances them-selves) has established the Live Concert Service. The Live Concert Service will for a fee administer for members the rights in a live performance provided the live performance royalties amount to £1,000 or more and it now accounts to its members far more swiftly than had previously been the case. Therefore, if members have the right to perform their work(s) live in concert re-assigned to them they can choose to do the administration themselves or ask the PRS to arrange for the Live Concert Service to do it for them.

Mechanical-Copyright Protection Society

The Mechanical Copyright Protection Society (MCPS) deals with what is known as the "mechanical right". This is the right to record a composition and to manufacture and distribute copies of the recording of that composition for retail sale to the public for their private use. Where a composer or publisher has appointed the MCPS to deal with the mechanical right, it will be the MCPS which grants the licence, called the "mechanical licence" to the record company to record the composition and to manufacture and distribute copies of the recording of the composition on, for example, record, cassette, CD, mini-disc for retail sale to the public for their private use.

Where a person wants to record a composition for use in a film, video, television programme or commercial, a "synchronisation licence" (more commonly called a "synchro licence") is required. This is a licence to use a composition in timed relation (i.e. synchronised) with visual images. Where, for example, the publisher has appointed the MCPS to administer the composition it will often be the MCPS which will grant the synchro licence. However, the publisher who appointed the MCPS to administer the composition may have withheld the right to grant synchro licences from the MCPS in which case the synchro licence will be granted by the publisher not the MCPS.

It should be noted that some of the large publishing companies are not members of the MCPS and will grant all the relevant licences and collect the royalties themselves.

The MCPS collects royalties known as a "mechanical" or a "mechanical fee" for publishers and composers. If a record company wants to record and release a composition on for example record for retail sale to the public, the royalty rate payable by the record company to the MCPS is 8.5% of the published price to dealers of each record excluding VAT or other taxes (called PPD) which is manufactured for sale. Promotional copies given free of charge, for example, to a radio station for broadcast or to a reviewer for review will not attract a mechanical royalty but there are limits on the number of promotional copies allowed which are royalty free and the packaging must make it clear that it is a promotional copy. Records given free to retailers are not counted as promotional copies and are royalty bearing. It should be noted that the 8.5% is per record not per song. The MCPS collects the royalty and sends it to the relevant publishers after deducting its commission.

Like the PRS, the MCPS grants blanket licences to broadcasters so that the broadcasters can record works administered by the MCPS.

Some major record companies have a central licensing deal with one single collecting society in Europe and pay that collecting society the royalties due rather than deal with the relevant collecting society in each European territory. The advantage for the record companies in doing this is that the royalties payable by them for the use of compositions are either reduced or the record companies receive a rebate from the collecting society with whom they have a central licensing deal.

It should be noted that the mechanical rate is not the same in each European territory. To try and stave off the situation where each European collecting society is trying to obtain its own central licensing deals with major record companies, the western European collecting societies and six major publishing companies entered an agreement known as the Cannes Accord in which it was agreed that by 2001 the mechanical rate for the signatory mechanical collecting societies will reduce to 6%. The Cannes Agreement does allow the collecting societies to pay a rebate to record companies but a percentage limit has been placed on the rebate which is allowed.

Unlike the PRS there are no membership qualifications to join the MCPS and there is no charge for joining the MCPS. Unlike the PRS where it requires an assignment of the performing right, the MCPS does not require an assignment of the right to record a work. The MCPS requires its members to licence it to be the members' sole and exclusive agent. The MCPS Agreement does however allow a member to join other foreign mechanical collecting societies as well as being a member of the MCPS, or to appoint a sub-publisher in another country, but in either case the member must inform the MCPS of this. Where the MCPS have been informed by its member it will not, without the member's consent, collect mechanicals in those countries where the member has joined another collecting society or appointed a sub-publisher. (*See* Chapter 7 The Publishing Agreement for Sub-publishing.)

If a composer has assigned his rights in his work to a publisher there is no need for the composer to join the MCPS if the publisher is a member as the MCPS will collect the relevant mechanicals and account to the publisher.

There are foreign collecting societies which deal with mechanical royalties such as STEMRA (in Holland), JASRAC (in Japan), and the Harry Fox Agency (in the US), and like the PRS, the MCPS has reciprocal arrangements with many foreign collecting societies for the collection of royalties due to its members. The MCPS will also licence mechanical rights abroad either directly or via local foreign societies.

Phonographic Performance Ltd

Phonographic Performance Ltd (PPL) is the body which licenses the public performance and broadcast of sound recordings. It is effectively the equivalent body to the PRS but in relation to sound recordings. PPL requires an assignment of the public performance and broadcast right from the copyright owner of the sound recording, which is usually the record company, and will grant blanket licences to broadcasters to broadcast publicly the record on radio and television, will license pubs, restaurants etc to play the record in their establishments, and will distribute the revenue received according to the use made of their members' sound recordings.

As seen earlier when dealing with the PRS, it is an infringement of copyright to publicly perform a copyright composition without a licence from the copyright owner of the performing right in the composition. It is also an infringement of copyright to publicly perform a sound recording without a licence from the copyright owner of the performing right in the sound recording. However, there is one occasion where the public performance of a sound recording without a licence from the copyright owner of the performing right in the sound recording will not amount to infringement. This exception is the permitted act under section 67 of the CDPA, which allows a sound recording to be played as part of the activities of a club, society or other institution. There will be no infringement if as provided under section 67(2):

> "(a) the organisation is not established or conducted for profit and its main objects are charitable or are concerned with the advancement of religion, education or social welfare, and
> (b) the proceeds of any charge for admission to the place where the recording is to be heard are applied solely for the purposes of the organisation."

As mentioned earlier, (*see* Chapter 2 Copyright Law and the Copyright, Designs and Patents Act 1988), the owner of the copyright in a sound recording, which is usually a record company, is now obliged by virtue of section 182D to pay equitable remuneration to the performers on recordings where they have been broadcast or played in public. PPL pays 50% of the public performance and broadcast income it receives on behalf of the copyright owners of the recordings to the performers. PPL pays this 50% share to one of two performers' collecting societies, namely the Performing Artists' Media Rights Association or the Association of United Recording Artists who will distribute the money which is due to their performer members. Instead of joining the Performing Artists' Media Rights Association or the Association of United Recording Artists a performer can register with PPL who will distribute the money which is due to the performer. It should be noted that PPL will not collect equitable remuneration due from foreign countries (*See* below for the Performing Artists'

Media Rights Association and the Association of United Recording Artists.) The other 50% of the public performance and broadcast income that PPL receives is paid by it to the relevant record companies.

Video Performance Ltd

As well as PPL another collecting society exists for the copyright owners of sound recordings. This is Video Performance Limited (VPL). One of the most effective ways to market a record is to make a video of the song. These videos are sent out to television companies, such as MTV and BBC who use them on programmes like "Top Of The Pops". Frequently, a record becomes a hit not because of the song but because of the video which accompanies it. Commonly, these videos which are made for publicity purposes are at a later date put out on general release for the public. (This helps to some extent to recoup some of the cost of making the video which is frequently astronomical and often far more expensive to make than the record it is promoting.) VPL acts in the same way as PPL and blanket licences the use of videos on, for example, television stations, and video juke boxes in pubs. There are two substantial differences between VPL and PPL. Firstly, there is no assignment from VPL members to VPL of the relevant copyrights. Secondly, as with sound recordings, equitable remuneration is payable where a video has been broadcast or played in public. VPL does not, however, distribute the broadcast and performance income for videos to any performers' collecting society. VPL distributes only to record companies and it is the record companies who account to the performers for their equitable remuneration.

Performing Artists' Media Rights Association Ltd
Association of United Recording Artists

Performing Artists' Media Rights Association Ltd (PAMRA) and the Association Of United Recording Artists (AURA) are collecting societies for performers. AURA is aimed at all performers but primarily at featured artists and studio producers. Similarly, PAMRA is aimed at all performers but primarily at session musicians.

It should be remembered (*see* Phonographic Performance Ltd above) that if a performer does not join PAMRA or AURA he can register with PPL who will collect the equitable remuneration for the broadcast and public performance of sound recordings on which he performed, although, as mentioned earlier, PPL will not collect equitable remuneration due from foreign countries.

PAMRA collects equitable remuneration for its members (currently in excess of 12,500 performers) which is due to them for the broadcast and public performance of sound recordings on which they performed.

Membership of PAMRA is free and upon joining the performer will have appointed PAMRA as his agent in the United Kingdom to, *inter alia*, collect the broadcast and public performance money due to him. The only membership requirement is that the performer has performed on a commercially published recording. Performers can either apply for full membership or if they are members of a foreign collecting society they will apply for associate membership. Full membership means that the performer has appointed PAMRA to collect not only money due in the United Kingdom but also to collect foreign remuneration. Associate membership means that PAMRA has been appointed to collect the remuneration arising in the United Kingdom only, with the foreign society which the performer has joined collecting any foreign remuneration.

PAMRA has entered reciprocal collecting agreements with similar collecting societies in countries, including the Netherlands, Spain, Germany, Croatia and Poland. Other reciprocal agreements are being negotiated at present with France, Japan and Canada.

All the money received by PAMRA is distributed to its members. The only deduction that PAMRA will make from a performer's payment will be an administration fee (not exceeding 15%) to pay for the costs of running the society. PAMRA will pay its members within 60 days of the end of the royalty quarter in which the money was received, *i.e.* for the quarter January to March the payment will be made by PAMRA by May.

AURA represents professional recording artists, performers and studio producers. Like PAMRA, AURA collects equitable remuneration for its members which is due to them for the broadcast and public performance of sound recordings on which they performed. (AURA also act as a lobbying body in the UK and abroad to protect performers' rights.) AURA states in its brochure that its objective is to represent and advise its members in the same way that the BPI represents record companies. The only membership requirement to join is that the prospective member must have either performed on or produced a record which has been commercially released. There is no subscription fee to be a member and there is only one class of membership–Performer Member.

Upon joining the member will have appointed AURA as his exclusive agent to, *inter alia*, collect the broadcast and public performance money due to him. The territory for which AURA is the exclusive agent is the world less any territories where the performer does not want it to represent him. The performer may exclude AURA from acting for him in a particular territory because he might be represented in that territory by the local collecting society and he is happy with the service provided by the local society. If AURA is appointed to only certain territories, the performer will retain his AURA voting rights, although he will lose any extra benefits which AURA might obtain from the foreign collecting society of which he is a member and in which AURA does not represent him.

In order to collect the broadcast and public performance money AURA has set up AURA Services Ltd which is the collecting society. AURA Services Ltd will distribute all the money it collects to its members after it has deducted its costs, expenses and reserves which are currently in the region of 5%. It is AURA's intention to enter reciprocal agreements with foreign collecting societies.

Music industry associations

British Music Rights

British Music Rights (BMR) was established in 1996 and is an organisation whose members are the PRS, the MCPS, the Music Publishers Association and the British Academy of Composers and Songwriters. The aims of BMR as set out in their manifesto "British Music Rights: Understanding the Score" are to show the importance of the British music business in society, to have an input in legislation and technological developments which affects its members, and to act as a "consensus organisation" for its members. Amongst their objectives is for children to have a compulsory music education of one hour per week in school and for the government to provide more money to create more music teaching posts in schools. On the legislation side BMR is actively concerned in ensuring that the internet is properly controlled under copyright law. For example, it is seeking to ensure that payment is made for the use of music on the internet. It is also a lobbying group and has been actively lobbying Brussels on the draft Directive on copyright and related rights in the information society on behalf of its members.

British Phongraphic Industry Ltd

The British Phongraphic Industry Ltd (BPI) is the trade association for record companies. The Directory of BPI Members of 1997 (a directory of the names and addresses of its members with brief details of their areas of business) lists 215 members who as their brochure "Promoting the Business of Music" states "produce the majority of the countrys' recorded music". The subscription for full membership of the BPI is a percentage (about 0.3%) of the company's previous year's turnover.

The BPI carries out many roles for its member companies. For example, it negotiates collective agreements with other industry associations and collecting societies, such as negotiating the mechanical royalty rate payable with the MCPS. It lobbies the UK government and Brussels on matters which are relevant to the music industry and its members. They produce a magazine for their members, *Insight*, which informs them of matters of relevance and importance in the music industry, as well as producing the BPI *Statistical Handbook* which is an annual review of the music business with detailed statistical data.

The BPI promotes the development of music throughout the country, for example, it is actively involved in the annual music industry awards, the BRIT Awards, which are the equivalent of the American GRAMMY Awards; it has established the BRIT Trust which raises money to support the development of music in education, with their main project being the BRIT School for Performing Arts and Technology in Croydon. It is also involved with the annual music Sound City event run by the BPI, the Musicians Union (*see* below for the Musicians Union), BBC Radio 1 and the council of the city holding the event, and along with the British Association of Record Dealers (*see* below for the British Association of Record Dealers) it supports the annual Mercury Music Prize, as well as administering the weekly music charts.

One of the many areas in which the BPI is pro-active is copyright protection via their Anti-Piracy Unit. There is a massive problem throughout the world of sales of pirate, bootleg and counterfeit recordings. Pirate recordings are recordings made by an artist but not commercially released, for example, studio out-takes or different versions of commercially released songs, which have been put on sale without permission from any of the copyright owners. Bootleg recordings are unauthorised recordings from live concerts or from radio or television performances which are sold without permission from any of the copyright owners. Counterfeit recordings are copies of officially released recordings packaged to look exactly like the official release which are sold without permission from any of the copyright owners. The BPI Anti-Piracy Unit is actively involved in trying to stamp out these practices. The Anti-Piracy Unit actively investigates any allegations of which it is aware and will use its expertise to assist the police and trading standards in any criminal investigations and actions. It will also assist and use its expertise in civil copyright and trade mark infringement cases. It also liaises with other industry associations both at home and abroad in an effort to stamp out sales of pirate, bootleg and counterfeit recordings. The pirates, like all criminals, try to keep one step ahead of the game, have now moved into selling via the internet. The Anti-Piracy Unit is aware of the problems the internet poses and has used its expertise in helping to close down web sites which have been selling unauthorised recordings.

Musicians' Union

The Musicians' Union (MU) is the musicians' equivalent to the BPI. As its name suggests it is the trade union representing musicians. The annual subsciption to join the MU depends on the the musician's gross annual earnings from music. For a musician whose gross earnings from music for 1998–99 were over £20,000 the subscription is £192 (or £174 if paid by direct debit).

The MU represents its members' interests in the industry by setting minmum rates of pay for its members and negotiating standard contract terms with the major employers of musicians. For example, it has set the minimum rates of pay for session musicians which have been negotiated with and accepted by the BPI. It has also established set rates for musicians who play live concerts.

The MU represent its members in many other ways. It provides careers advice, information leaflets, a directory of members and a magazine *Musician*, insurance cover for equipment and instruments, public liabilty insurance, free standard form contracts for musicians playing in a live concert, and free advice to members on contracts, including managing, publishing and recording contracts through its Contracts Advisory Service.

Other industry associations

There are several other music industry associations which exist with the aim of developing, promoting and protecting their members in the music industry. Amongst these associations are:

(a) The Music Publishers' Association which is the trade organisation of the music publishing industry.
(b) The International Managers Forum which represents the interests of managers in the music business.
(c) The British Association Of Record Dealers which is the trade association for record retailers and wholesalers.

The Band Register

The Band Register is a body which has been set up to check whether a band name is being used by anybody else. The Band Register is a free service to users and is funded by sponsorship from the Arts Council, Apple computers and the accountants, Baker Tilly.

The name of the band is a very valuable asset. A band can build up a good reputation using a name which it believes is original only to find that the name or a very similar one is also being used by another band. The existence of two bands named the same or similar will usually lead to disputes between the bands over which of them has the right to use the name and can lead to expensive litigation. The cost of changing a band's name may be substantial not only in the cost of advertising the fact that the band still exists albeit under a different name, but also in the fact that it may possibly lose some of its fan base in the course of changing its name. The worst case scenario would be for a band to have released a record which has to be withdrawn from sale due to the fact that another band has the right to use the band name. The amount of money which would be lost if a record has to be withdrawn from sale and re-released under a new band name would be astronomical.

As the band name is important not only in the United Kingdom but throughout the world it is prudent to check with the Band Register that it is safe to use the name before developing a reputation with it. It is true that one word names have a tendency to be in multiple usage and a band should try and choose a name with more than one word in the title. The Band Register will check the name of the band and will advise if there is a name that is the same or similar in existence. This service is certainly one that should be used by a band before it develops any goodwill in its name.

Chapter 5

The Legal Status of Band and Solo Artist

Hired hands

It is not uncommon for a financial investor, such as a businessman, manager, songwriter, production company or record company to want to invest money in setting up and developing from scratch a brand new band in an attempt to capture a share of the extremely lucrative "boy band" or "girl band" market. There is a phenominal amount of money to be made from the teenage and pre-teenage market in record sales and merchandising. One only has to look at the charts to see the proliferation of bands whose music and image is targeted solely at such a young audience. If the right formula is found the sky financially is the limit. For every one of these bands who hit the jackpot, there are dozens of other bands who take off swiftly like a rocket and then fade quickly into obscurity after the first couple of hit records, or who may not even take off at all. (It should be noted that bands are also occasionally set up and developed from scratch by a financial investor to try and capture a share of music markets other than the teenage and pre-teenage market.) Often these put-together bands will be employees of the financial investor and it is the financial investor rather than the band members who will make the decisions about what to record, what image to portray etc.

Most bands are not artificially created by a financial investor but have got together themselves and have developed their own musical identity and image. Such bands are rarely employees of a financial investor and will in the main with the help, support and advice of their manager, publishing company and record company, make their own decisions about what to record, what image to portray etc.

The solo artist

Usually at the start of his career a solo artist will provide his services as a sole trader. It is usually only when he becomes successful that the artist will consider setting up a limited company through which he will provide his services.

As a sole trader the artist will enter all contracts himself in his own name and will pay tax on a self-employed basis. If the artist sets up a limited company he will be a director of the company with perhaps his manager or his accountant or lawyer being the company secretary. He will also be the owner of all the shares in the company. He will enter into a service contract with his company agreeing to provide his company with his services in the music industry. This means that he will be an employee with his employer being his limited company. A third party who wants to use the artist's services will contract not with the artist but with his limited company. The artist will receive a salary from his company as an employee and will receive dividends from the company as a shareholder. A third party, such as a record company, which contracts with the artist's limited company for the artist's services will be concerned that, for example, the artist's limited company might go into liquidation in which case the third party will not be able to require the artist to provide his services because there is no privity of contract between the artist and the third party. To protect itself, a third party should when contracting with the artist's limited company for the artist's services, require a side letter from the artist guaranteeing that he will personally honour the obligations of the contract between the third party and his limited company in the event that his limited company does not do so. The artist should ensure where he is required to enter a side letter that there is a provision in the side letter that he will honour the contractual obligations provided the third party is not itself in breach of the contract.

(There may be tax advantages for the artist in setting up a limited company and being an employee of the company. There are tax, legal and accounting requirements for a limited company which have to be complied with. These are beyond the scope of this book.)

A very successful artist may decide that rather than operate through the medium of one limited company, it would be better to establish a limited company for each field of his musical activities. He may, for example, set up his own publishing company and assign to it the copyright in the compositions, and the company will license third parties to use the copyright works. He may also set up a production company and agree to record for it and it will license the recordings to record companies who will manufacture and distribute the recordings. He may also set up other companies to deal with his touring and merchandising.

The band

A successful band's public image may not reflect what is really going on behind the scenes. A band may appear to the public to be the best of friends, whereas in private they do not get on at all. The public might think that the band runs its business affairs democratically whereas the reality may be totally different. For example, a four piece band could be employees of an entrepreneur and it is the entrepreneur who, as the employer, makes all the career decisions about the band. Alternatively the band could (for want of a better description) be a "real band" rather than a "manufactured band" and the band members make their own career decisions with the help and advice of their manager. A real band may possibly not be a band of equals. For example, their structure may be such that two members make all the decisions or have most of the say whilst the other members have little or no say. Indeed, it may be that two of the band members are in fact employees being employed by the other two.

Partnership or limited company?

A band will run its affairs, either as sole traders (which is rare), or as a partnership or as a limited company. Usually for a band starting out on its career it will manage its affairs through the medium of a partnership. Only when the band becomes more successful might it decide to operate its affairs through a limited company.

No formal documentation is required to set up a partnership as the only requirement needed is for the band members to be carrying on a business in common with the intention of making a profit (by virtue of the Partnership Act 1890 section 1). Most bands will satisfy this requirement and so will be deemed to be a partnership in the eyes of the law and not sole traders. The provisions of the Partnership Act 1890 enable a partnership to be run without a formal partnership agreement as the Act sets out all the terms which will apply where there is no such agreement in existence. Thus the Act provides that all expenses and income will be divided among the members equally and that a unanimous vote (save for the vote of the member to whom the vote relates) is required to expel a member. In addition, if a formal partnership agreement does not deal with a particular matter, the provisions of the Act relating to that matter will apply. It should be noted that the provisions of the Partnership Act are wide ranging and can be hard to rebut — see for example "The Smiths" case, *Joyce v Morrisey and others* [1998] EMLR. A band should always ensure that it has a formal partnership agreement setting out all the terms under which it operates rather than rely on the terms of the Partnership Act. This will ensure that the band's affairs operate exactly how it wants.

A band can also run its affairs through a limited company. Various limited companies could be set up to deal with different aspects of the band's business affairs. As mentioned earlier this would usually be done once a band has become successful although a band may decide to run its business operations through a limited company from the outset. Usually, the company directors and the company secretary will be the band members, and the band members will also be the shareholders in the company. The band members will each enter into a service contract with the limited company and so will be employed by their company. The band members will be paid a salary by their company and will receive dividends as shareholders. Where the band's company enters into a contract with a third party to provide the band's services, the third party will additionally require side letters from each band member guaranteeing that he will personally provide his services which the company has contracted to provide should the company fail to provide them. A third party will require side letters from each band member because his contract is with the company and not with the individual band members. (As mentioned earlier there may be tax advantages for a band to set up a limited company and for the band members to become employees of the company. Also there are tax, legal and accounting requirements which a limited company has to comply with. These are beyond the scope of this book.)

If a band establishes a limited company through which to operate it will need a written shareholders' agreement akin to a partnership agreement setting out what it can do and how it can make decisions. (Amongst the documentation required to establish a private limited company are a Memorandum and Articles of Association. A shareholders' agreement cannot replace the company Memorandum or the Articles of Association, and it may be that to enable some of the matters in a shareholders' agreement to have effect the Articles of Association will need to be altered.)

As mentioned above the band should have a formal partnership agreement rather than rely upon the terms of the Partnership Act 1890, and if a limited company is the preferred method of operation a shareholders' agreement similar to a partnership agreement should be used as well. The question therefore arises what should be in such a document?

The band agreement

Note: the words "band agreement" or "agreement" used below (with the exception of Transferring Shares in the Limited Company which deals with a limited company) can be taken to refer to a partnership agreement and a shareholders' agreement.

There is no such thing as a standard agreement in any area of the music business. Taking a management agreement as an example, if a manager has a roster of artists whom he represents, he will attempt to get artists to sign what he regards as his standard form of agreement, or as near to his standard form agreement as he can get the artist to sign. What is a standard form management agreement for one manager may have little or no bearing to what another manager considers to be his standard form management agreement. However, even though there are no standard form music industry agreements there are certain matters which will be, or should be, covered in every type of agreement. Taking a management agreement again as an example, whether the manager will represent the artist in the United Kingdom, the EU, the world or the world excluding some countries will depend upon the negotiating strengths and weaknesses of the parties and their legal advisers. What can be said is that every management agreement must contain a clause which deals with the territory in which the manager represents the artist. The rest of this chapter will examine a band agreement and will look at the key clauses which should be included, and will make appropriate alternative suggestions for how the clauses may be altered. This approach will be adopted throughout the book when examining other music industry agreements).

Whether or not a partnership or limited company is used the following matters should be dealt with in a band agreement:

Band income

There should be a clause in the agreement which deals with the definition of band income. If successful the band will have several different income streams. Money will come in from record sales, merchandising, touring, equitable remuneration for the broadcast and public performance of sound recordings on which the members of the band performed, and from publishing. There may be other income streams, such as money from band sponsorship, and endorsements of products by the band. It has to be decided if these and any other income which arises will be regarded as band income.

A songwriter who is a member of the band who writes all the band material will not usually want publishing income to be regarded as band income. This is because the songwriter will usually write the material on his own and not with the rest of the band. However, if the other band members occasionally contribute to the songwriting, there should be some provision in the agreement which allows for the publishing income arising from such co-written songs to be band income as well as a provision that they will receive a song-writing credit.

Another area not usually counted as band income is income arising from solo recording projects and from projects such as film acting which arise outside of the band. (Notwithstanding the band agreement, before embarking on any solo album or film project, any record contract or other agreement entered into by the band should be examined to see that the member is not prohibited from carrying out the proposed activity.) (*See* also Working on outside Projects below.)

Division of band income

After the payment of expenses (see below) there will be a division of the band income. The division of income may be an equal split between the band members. This is not always the case. It may be that some members of the band receive a salary only and other members will receive a salary and a division of profits. It may be that the the lead singer is the key person in the band and without him there would be no band; as such he may be given a larger share of the band profits. New members may join an existing succesful band and may well receive only a salary or a salary with a smaller share of profits than other band members which might escalate over a period of time. It is equally possible for the division of income to be made in different percentages for different areas of group income. For example, the band may agree that it will split all the income received for recording equally; merchandising income could be split so that three of the four members receive 20% each for the sales of merchandise with the fourth receiving 40% of the income because his is the face that sells the band merchandise; the equitable remuneration will be in accordance with the amount each band member individually receives from PAMRA, AURA or PPL, and touring monies are split so that two members get 30% each, with the other members receiving 20% each because the two members who receive 20% each have a lesser role on the tour compared to the other two members who receive 30% each.

If the band operates as a limited company it may be that the income will be divided in accordance with the members' shareholding by way of dividend.

There are many ways of dividing band income after expenses. All items and their proposed division should be detailed, and any activities in which the band is not currently engaged should, if possible, be anticipated and there should be a consideration of how to split the income which may arise from such activities.

Band expenses

The agreement will also need to deal with band expenses. The expenses should be shared by the band members in proportion to their share of band income. The expenses which the band will incur include legal fees for negotiating band agreements and for any litigation in which the band is involved either as claimant or defendant, the cost of hiring or buying transportation, the cost of any band travel, accomodation and living expenses for the band whilst on tour, studio hire time, and the hire or purchase of instruments and of a personal address system.

The agreement should make it clear that any money spent for the benefit of the whole of the band is a band expense. There are however some areas which need to be be specifically dealt with in the agreement. Apart from making it clear that any money spent for the benefit of the whole of the band is a band expense and stating the percentage share of the expense for which each member is liable, the agreement should place a limit on how much an individual can spend without consulting the rest of the band. To try and keep some check on this, apart from specifying the amount an individual can spend without consulting the rest of the band, there should be an arrangement with the band's bank, which should also be detailed in the band agreement, that the band's cheques can for example be signed by any one member up to a certain limit, which will be a small sum, say £100 per cheque, and above that figure band cheques should be signed by two or more members of the band. (If the band has a manager, the manager will usually be a signatory to the band account but there should be a limit in the management agreement as to the amount the manager is authorised to spend without consulting the band, and the manager should only be authorised to sign cheques on his own up to a certain value and above that figure one or more band members should be required to counter-sign cheques. *See* Chapter 6 The Management Agreement below.)

Frequently, band money may be used with requisite permission to purchase an item for an individual. The agreement should provide whether the item is owned by the individual or by the band, and where the item is owned by the band whether the individual can buy the item from the band, and if so whether he has to buy it at its replacement value (which is unlikely to be the case), or at its second hand value, or at its value as written down in the band's accounts.

Similarly, there should be a provision dealing with who owns band items purchased with band money if a member leaves the band or the band splits up.

Band name

In many respects the most valuable asset of a band is the band name and the band logo. Some individuals beome known in their own right outside the band context, Keith Flint (The Prodigy), Phil Collins, Peter Gabriel (both ex Genesis), Mick Jagger (The Rolling Stones), and Ronan Keating (Boyzone) being a few examples. However, there are thousands of musicians who are successful only in the context of the band and outside the band are not known in the public eye.

No matter how well known an individual is, a solo album by an artist from a popular band will invariably not sell anywhere near the amount as an album released under his band's name. There are notable exceptions to this statement, for example Paul McCartney, John Lennon and Phil Collins have released solo albums which have sold in numbers which rival their band record sales. There are several reasons why solo albums may not sell as well as a band album. It may be that the solo artist is performing in a style which is different to the band style, he may not be touring or touring on the same scale as his band to promote the album, the record company may not be promoting the record with the same vigour and budget as his band's albums, or the album might be by one of the less popular members of the band. One very important factor which may hold back record sales by a solo artist is the fact that the record is not released under the band name and logo.

An important question that needs to be considered is who exactly owns and can use the band name and the band logo? This must be dealt with in the band agreement. The band name and logo should, if possible, be registered as a trade mark. The agreement may, for example, provide that the founder member owns the name and logo, or it might be the lead singer, or the songwriter in the band, or the majority of the members who perform together, who owns the name and logo. Whatever method is used it is imperative that the agreement deals with this matter. The agreement should provide that where a member leaves the band and he does not own the band name and logo, he cannot use the band name or logo, nor can he use any name or logo which is similar to the band's name or logo. The agreement should not, however, restrict an artist from being able to use his own name.

The ownership and use of the band name and logo is not only important when the band is in the ascendant. There is a very lucrative living to be made by bands on the nostalgia circuit playing their old hits in nightclubs or on reunion tours with other bands from their era. If the ownership and use of the band name and logo is not dealt with on a formal basis there may be more than one band with the same name and logo out on tour playing the same hits which will cause confusion in the public's eyes as to which is the real band. The courts have occasionally become become involved in disputes over the ownership and use of a band's name and logo. It is quite possible that the ownership of the name and logo if it is not dealt with on a formal basis may be held to be an asset owned by the whole band and that each member has the right to use it.

It should be noted that the band will need to give its manager, publishing company, record company, tour agent, promoter, tour sponser and merchandiser the right to use the band's name and logo for specified purposes. (*See* Chapters 6, 7, 8, 9, 10 and 11 below for details).

Working on outside Projects

Frequently, band members want to work on projects outside the band in addition to remaining in the band. For example, an individual member may want to record a solo album or appear in a film or host a television programme. The agreement should deal with whether an individual member can pursue outside projects. This should be acceptable but it should be made clear that outside projects can only be pursued in the individual member's spare time, and that he will devote all the time that is required to fulfill his commitments to the band. It should also be made clear that any outside projects should not compete with the band. The agreement should also deal with the income which arises from an individual working on a project outside the band. The agreement will usually provide that such income belongs to the individual member and will be not be counted as band income. (*See also* Band Income above.)

Hiring and firing

The agreement should deal with how and in what circumstances the band can hire members and how it can fire them. It should specify the vote required to hire or fire a member. Usually the agreement will require a unanimous vote by the band (excluding the vote of the member under discussion) to fire him. The agreement may provide instead that a majority vote will be required. The agreement could possibly be structured so that in certain circumstances a unanimous vote will be required and in all other circumstances a majority vote will suffice to fire a member. Even though a member may be fired by the band he should still be entitled to receive his share of band income for his activities whilst he was in the band, and he should ensure that he has the right to audit the band's accounts to see that he is receiving the right amount of money due to him from his past activities.

Even though the band agreement should contain provisions allowing the band to fire a member, in reality the ability to do so will be subject to the content of any other agreements which the band have entered into. Such other agreements should be checked before firing a band member. It may be that an agreement between the band and a third party will effectively mean that the band cannot fire the member when it wants to because that agreement requires all band members to provide their services to the third party (including the member the band wants to fire). To fire the member of the band would mean that the band are in breach of its agreement with the third party.

As for new members joining, the band agreement should specify the vote required before a new member can join the band. The agreement should also provide the terms and conditions upon which any new member may join the band. The agreement may, for example, provide that a new member will join for a trial period on a salary but with no vote in band affairs whilst on trial. Once he has passed the trial period he will be treated as a full member and will receive possibly a share of band income or a higher salary together with a vote in band affairs. The agreement may also provide that a new member if he passes the trial period will have to buy into the band (possibly in staged payments) and that he will have a share in the band assets. The money from the new member could be used to buy out the interest of any departing member. Any person buying into the band and getting an interest in the band's assets should carry out a full inventory of the assets and the liabilities of the band and should ensure that he has an independent valuation of the assets to ensure that he is not overpaying, although he may have to pay a premium if he is joining an established successful band. A new member will need to establish what rights he has within the band's set up, and what obligations he is taking on. In addition, a new member will require the other band members to give him an indemnity for liabilities which have occurred prior to him joining the band.

Notwithstanding the band agreement, any other agreements which the band has entered into should be checked by the band and the new member to see what conditions there may be on the new member joining. For example, the band's recording and management agreements will have provisions in them concerning new members. Essentially, the recording and management agreements will require any new member to be bound by the terms of these agreements. (*See* Chapter 6 The Management Agreement and Chapter 8 The Recording Agreements for details).

Notice to leave the band

The agreement should not allow a member to leave the band without giving notice. The remaining band members will need time to make any necessary arrangements to enable them to continue without the departing member. For example, if the remaining band members intend to replace the departing member rather than continue without him, they will need time to find a replacement and where the preferred replacement is in another band, they will have to wait for the new member to leave that band to join them. The leaving member's notice period should not be unduly long as this would be too restrictive for him and could inconvenience or jeopardise his career outside the band. However, it should be long enough for the band to be able to make any necessary arrangements to continue without the member and should ensure that he satisfies any immediate or imminent band commitments which exist with third parties.

The agreement may possibly provide that the length of the notice period will depend upon the band's activities at the time the member wants to leave. For example, if the member wants to leave during a tour, the agreement might provide that the notice period will expire at the end of the tour or alternatively at the end of the European or North American leg of the tour, whereas if the member wants to leave at a time when the band is not involved in any major commitments, such as recording or touring, the agreement might provide for a short notice period such as 4 weeks from the date the member gives his notice. The agreement might also be drafted to allow the band to reduce the leaving member's notice period. Such a provision in the agreement may be useful where the band is about to start recording a new album as this will enable it to record without the leaving member and so release the new record with the current line up.

The leaving member's share will need to be bought out by the rest of the band and should be dealt with in the agreement, (*see* Death or Incapacity of a Member below for the provisions which need to be considered on buying out a member's share).

Death or incapacity of a member

The agreement should deal with what happens if a member dies or alternatively becomes incapacitated and can no longer continue to be an active member of the band. The agreement should provide that the member's share will be bought out by the rest of the band. The agreement should deal with how the member's share which is being bought out is to be valued and in particular whether there is to be any payment for his share in the band's goodwill as well as the band's assets.

The band agreement should deal with what will happen to the income it receives if it enters into a merchandising agreement and a member leaves the band. Merchandising is a very lucrative source of income for many bands and for some types of bands it may be their biggest source of income. Certainly, many heavy metal bands may earn more money out of merchandising and touring than they will from record sales. The agreement should ideally provide that any merchandising royalties which the band receives will only be paid to band member for the period he is in the band and that he is not entitled to share in any merchandising royalties relating to the period after he has left the band. (For Merchandising *see* Chapter 11.)

The agreement should specify the period of time over which the deceased/incapacitated member's share is to be bought out and it should provide that interest is payable on the outstanding sum. The interest rate provided for in the agreement should not be a penal rate but should be at a rate commensurate with either the interest rate payable on a particular building society's instant access or a short term notice account, or at a particular bank's base lending rate that is from time to time in force, or perhaps 3 or 4% above that rate. Whichever way the agreement provides for interest to be paid on outstanding sums, it should be at a rate that is fair to both the payer and payee.

The agreement should contain a provision which allows the band's books to be audited by the incapacitated member or by his estate.

If the band is a partnership, the agreement should ideally state that the deceased member's estate or the incapacitated member can only look to the partnership assets and not to the individual partners' personal property for payment when he is bought out. This is because in partnership law a partner does not have limited liability and where he is liable as a partner not only are the partnership assets available to satisfy any liabiltity but also each partner's personal assets outside the partnership can be used to satisfy any partnership liability. A clause in the agreement that only partnership assets can be used to buy out a deceased member's or incapacitated member's share will protect the personal property of each band member from being used to satisfy the liability.

Payment for activities of ex-members

The agreement should detail those activities which the band will continue to pay an ex-member for after he has left the band. An ex-member should continue to be paid for his share of the band income for his past contributions to the band's activities. The band will not, however, want to pay the ex-member for those future band activities in which the ex-member will have no involvement.

It should be noted that most of the agreements which the band enters into with third parties will also contain provisions dealing with how payments due to the band and the ex-member will be dealt with by the third party once a member has left the band, and will also contain clauses dealing with the liability of the band and the ex-member for those expenses which the band and the ex-member has incurred or will incur in the future. For example, the recording agreement will contain provisions about how the record company will pay royalties once a member leaves the band, and will also contain provisions concerning the liability of the band and the ex-member for expenses incurred by them both prior to and after the member has left the band (*See* Chapter 8 Recording Agreements below for further details.)

Indemnities and liabilities of band and ex-members

The agreement should provide that the ex-member will be indem-nified by the band for future liabilities which the band incurs after he has left the band. The indemnity should not however extend to any liability which the band incurs due to the ex-member leaving the band nor should the indemnity extend to those liabilities incurred by the band whilst the ex-member was still a member of the band.

Where the band is a partnership, a band member who is a partner is liable and remains liable to a third party after he has left the partnership for the debts or obligations which were incurred by the partnership whilst he was a partner.

Where the partner, after he has left the partnership, makes a representation to a third party, or a representation is made by someone else with his knowledge to a third party, and the third party relies upon the representation that he is a partner and gives credit to the partnership, the leaving partner may be liable to the third party for the debt. The representation may be either an oral representation, a written representation or a representation by conduct. This is provided for in section 14 of the Partnership Act 1890.

Section 36 of the Partnership Act 1890 requires a partner to give notice of his leaving the partnership. If this is not done the leaving partner will, if a third party does not know that he has left the partnership, be liable to the third party for the acts done by the partnership after he has left. Section 36(1) provides that the partner should give notice that he has left to all those people who dealt with the partnership prior to him leaving. In addition, section 36(2) provides that he should give notice that he has left by placing a notice in the London Gazette. A notice in the London Gazette will act as notice to those people who have not previously dealt with the partnership but who knew who were the partners in the partnership. By giving such notices he will not be liable in respect of debts or obligations incurred after he has left to all those people who dealt with the partnership prior to him leaving and who continue to deal with the partnership, nor will he be liable to those people who knew of the existence of the partnership and who were the partners, and who may deal with the partnership in the future. The leaving partner may, however, still be liable for acts done after he has left if, for example, the third party can show that he did not know the partner had left the partnership and the relevant notice was not given.

It should be noted that where a person ceases to be a partner because of his bankruptcy or due to his death, there is no need to give notice that he has left the partnership and in these situations the leaving partner's estate will not be liable for any acts which are done by the partnership after he has ceased to be a partner.

Where the band is a partnership the agreement should also provide that:

(a) the partnership agreement will remain in force and the partnership will not be dissolved by a member retiring or being expelled from the partnership,

(b) the band stationery will be altered to reflect any change in the partnership lineup,

(c) the bank mandate will be altered where the leaving member is a signatory to the band's bank account.

If a band operates as a limited company, a band member will be personally liable under a contract between the limited company and a third party where he is a guarantor to the contract. The band member will be personally liable where he acts a guarantor not only whilst he is a member of the band but he will also continue to be personally liable after he has left the band unless the guarantee is drafted so that he is automatically released from the guarantee when he leaves the band or unless he can find a suitable alternative person to take his place as guarantor.

As with a partnership agreement, where the band operates as a limited company, there should be a provision in the shareholders' agreement that if a band member leaves that the band stationery will be altered to reflect the change in the directors, and that the band mandate will be altered where the leaving member is a signatory to the limited company's bank account.

General decision making

General band decisions, such as buying musical instruments, should be made by a band vote. The agreement should set out the voting structure to be adopted. The vote could be one vote per member or it could be a weighted vote. The agreement should also deal with what happens where the vote is equal. The agreement may provide that a simple majority vote has to be achieved for the resolution to be passed, or it may be that a particular member in the band or a third party, such as the manager, will have the casting vote. It is somewhat undesireable for a third party who is not a member of the band to have a casting vote in the affairs of the band. It is always preferable that band affairs are decided upon solely by the band. The agreement may set out a second voting system to be adopted if the votes are equal on the first ballot. For example, if the first ballot is based upon one vote per member, the second ballot could be based upon a weighted vote. The agreement may further provide that if the votes are tied on a second ballot the resolution will not pass.

The agreement may provide that a simple majority vote is required for general band matters but for other specified matters a higher percentage vote or a unanimous vote is required. (*See* Hiring and Firing above.)

The agreement may provide for voting by proxy where a member is unable to attend a meeting and vote. A member may authorise the proxy to vote as directed or allow the proxy to use his vote as the proxy feels is appropriate. The agreement may provide that the proxy will be another band member or a third party, such as the absent member's solicitor or accountant or the band's manager.

Signing agreements with third parties

The agreement should clearly state that no member is authorised to sign agreements for the band without the band's express prior authority. This should bring home to the members that they do not have carte blanche to sign agreements for the band. This does not stop members from signing personal agreements, nor does it stop a third party from holding the band to an unauthorised agreement, provided the third party believed that the member who signed the agreement had authority to do so. Obviously with major contracts such as recording and touring contracts, each member will be required by the third party to sign personally. However, for some contracts it may be that the third party will deal with one member believing he is authorised to sign on behalf of the band.

Bank account

The agreement should set out who the signatories to the band's bank account are and the name of the account. As well as detailing the signatories, there should be an arrangement with the band's bank (which should be detailed in the band agreement) that the band's cheques can for example be signed by any one member up to a certain limit (which will be a small sum, say £100 per cheque) and above that figure, band cheques should be signed by two or more band members. In addition, the agreement should place a limit upon how much a member may take out of the band's bank account for personal living expenses.

Meetings with third parties

The agreement should provide that if only some band members are able to attend a business meeting with a third party that they will not express their personal opinion but will give the band's opinion as has been agreed at a previous band meeting. In addition, the agreement should provide that any business decisions which have to be made relating to any such meeting will have to be ratified by the band. The agreement may contain a provision which allows the band to send an authorised representative such as their manager, solicitor or accountant to a business meeting with a third party and that the authorised representative will have the authority to carry out the band's instructions on its behalf.

There are some meetings with third parties which are so important that all the band should be present. However, a member may not be able to attend the meeting, in which case the agreement should allow him to send a representative, such as his solicitor, to attend on his behalf.

Transferring shares in the limited company

The company's Articles of Association will deal with the allotment and transfer of the company's shares. The Articles of Association are open to public inspection. The band will not want the public to know about any restrictions on transferring the company's shares. A shareholders' agreement is a private document not open to public inspection and it may be preferable to deal with restrictions on transferring shares in the shareholders' agreement. Amongst the restrictions to consider are:

(a) Can shares be transferred to people who are not members of the band? (The answer to this will in nearly all cases be no.)

(b) If shares cannot be transferred to people who are not members of the band will an exception be made to allow an individual band member to transfer his shares to his family?

(c) If a new member joins the band in addition to the existing members are the existing members required to transfer some of their shares to the new member? If so, how much of their holding does each member have to transfer?

(d) If an existing shareholder is free to sell some of his shares, does the band have a pre-emption right? If so, if more than one band member wants to buy the shares, will they each be entitled to buy a proportionate part of the shareholding?

(e) If a band member leaves voluntarily or otherwise, is he required to transfer his shareholding to the remaining band members? This will probably be the case as the band does not want the leaving member to have any interest in the band's affairs. However, what if the leaving member's interest has not been bought out but is being bought out over a period of time? Can the leaving member retain his shareholding until he is fully bought out, or will he relinquish a proportionate part of his shareholding each time he receives a part payment?

Disputes

The band may be concerned that where an internal dispute arises which cannot be resolved amicably, the matter might lead to litigation between the members. Litigation, apart from being time consuming and expensive, has one other very important drawback, publicity.

A band may not want the glare of media publicity on its internal affairs. The band agreement may therefore contain a clause to try and avoid the dispute becoming public by providing that if there is a dispute between the band members, the matter will be referred to arbitration. An alternative to an arbitration clause would be for a clause to provide for the dispute to be submitted to a specified form of alternative dispute resolution. It should be noted that an arbitration clause or an alternative dispute resolution clause must be drafted very carefully. For details of how to draft an appropriate arbitration or alternative dispute resolution clause and for the advantages and disadvantages of arbitration and the various types of alternative dispute resolution, the reader should refer to specialist books dealing with these subjects.

Other clauses

Along with the clauses mentioned above, the agreement will contain several other clauses. These may include:

(a) A confidentiality clause. This will require the band members to keep the contents of the agreement confidential. The clause will allow disclosure of the contents of the agreement to the individual band member's lawyer, accountant, bank, financial adviser and manager.

(b) A jurisdiction and choice of law clause. (*See* Chapter 3 Music Industry Contracts.)

(c) An invalidity clause. (*See* Chapter 3 Music Industry Contracts.)

(d) A clause confirming that the agreement reflects the whole of the agreement between the parties and replaces any earlier oral or written agreement.

(e) A non-waiver clause. The effect of a non-waiver clause is to protect the innocent party's rights and remedies for breach of contract against the defaulting party. The non-waiver clause will provide that where the innocent party has not taken action to enforce his rights or his remedies for the defaulting party's breach of contract, such lack of action will not constitute a waiver of the innocent party's rights or remedies.

(f) A *force majeure* clause. (*See* Chapter 3 Music Industry Contracts.)

(g) A notice clause. A notice clause provides how any notice which is required under the agreement should be given, and the date the notice is deemed to have been received. For example, the clause will usually provide that if a letter is sent by first class post by one party to the other and has been correctly addressed, it will be deemed to have been received by the other party two working days after it has been posted. It is possible for the parties to agree to use other methods to send a notice, *e.g.* it might be agreed that a notice can be delivered in person or sent by fax. If a notice is delivered in person, the agreement will usually provide that the notice has been delivered on the day the notice has been left with the other party. If a notice is sent by fax, the agreement will usually provide that delivery of the fax is deemed to have taken place at the time of delivery, provided it has been sent to the agreed address, and provided it has been sent by 4 pm. If the fax is sent after 4 pm the agreement will usually provide that delivery will be deemed to be the next business day.

(h) A clause which provides that the individual band members will sign any documentation which is necessary to carry out the terms of the agreement.

Conclusion

It is very important for a band member to be fully aware of his rights and liabilities within the band. It is very important that these are recorded in a written band agreement, and if the band operates as a partnership it is vital to have a written band agreement to avoid being bound by the terms of the Partnership Act 1890. The implied terms of the Partnership Act 1890 should be closely examined whenever a partnership agreement is being drawn up because if the partnership agreement is silent on a particular point then the implied terms of the Act will apply to that matter which may not be what the band want. For example, the Partnership Act 1890 section 33 provides that if there is no provision in the partnership agreement as to what happens on the retirement, death or bankruptcy of a partner, the partnership is dissolved. This is certainly not what most bands would want and so a partnership agreement should be used to deal with these and all other matters concerning the partnership business.

Many bands will say that they are great friends and they can sort matters out amicably if and when the situation arises and they do not need to waste money on legal fees preparing a formal band agreement. Without any doubt this is the wrong attitude to take. The time to sort matters out is whilst things are amicable and not when things become acrimonious. A band agreement can and should be prepared as soon as the band is formed. The cost of preparing a band agreement which may be only a few hundred pounds is insignificant compared to the litigation costs which may be incurred later on by the band members in disputes over matters which could have been dealt with in the agreement. In addition, any subsequent changes to the terms of the band agreement also should be formally documented.

Chapter 6

The Management Agreement

Introduction

Probably the most important person in an artist's career, with the obvious exception of the artist himself, is his manager. The main responsibilities of a manager are to develop, promote and supervise the artist's career. In addition the manager takes on other responsibilities. He will have to be the artist's father figure, friend and mentor. At the outset of the artist's career the manager may have to be a van driver taking the artist and his equipment to gigs, help carry musical equipment, sound equipment and lights around, as well as help set it all up and take it all down. He may have to deal with the artist's legal and financial problems even though he may not be a lawyer or an accountant. The roles that a manager may have to take on for an artist mean that he has to be prepared to be a jack of all trades. A manager must be a good businessman and understand the workings of the music business; he must be able to develop contacts to help get the artist recording, publishing and other relevant agreements, and he must be able to retain the trust of the artist.

There is no requirement for an artist to have a manager. It is quite feasible for an artist to manage himself. However, it may be difficult for an artist to find the time required to be an effective manager whilst spending time on his musical activities. Some artists are young and inexperienced in business affairs, some artists may not be interested in administration and paperwork and only want to concentrate on their musical activities. Indeed, some artists may have a phenomenal musical talent but no business acumen at all. These are some of the many reasons why an artist may need a manager to represent him.

The management agreement is probably the first and arguably the most important agreement an artist will sign in his career. Johnny Rogan wrote a book about music business mangers called *Starmakers and Svengalis*. In many respects the title of the book sums up what a manager is. Hopefully, a good manager is a starmaker and is a svengali in only the positive meaning of the word. A good manager should be able to open doors for the artist and give him the chance to be a star. A bad manager will not be able to do this and he may be the reason why a very talented artist does not make it in the music business. The choice of whom to appoint as manager is one of the most important decisions that an artist will have to make. He should only appoint someone whom he believes he can trust. However, should the artist only appoint someone with managerial expertise? There is obviously a lot to be said for appointing someone with experience as he will have a lot of contacts in the industry which can be used for the artist, and the artist may be regarded with more credibility by others if he is represented by a known manager. However, there is a possible problem in that if an experienced manager has a roster of successful bands on his books he may not spend all the time which is required to develop a new artist. The problems which exist with appointing an inexperienced manager are that he may be learning the business at the artist's expense, and he probably will not have the necessary contacts to develop the artist's career. However, an inexperienced manager may have time and enthusiasm, which if used effectively may be of more use to an artist than representation by an experienced manager who does not have the time to spend on an artist's career.

The manager and artist relationship is usually one of principal and agent, with the artist as principal and the manager as agent. As the artist is the principal and the manager the agent, where the manager has negotiated an agreement for the artist with a third party (*see* The Rights and Activities Clause below for negotiating and signing agreements) it will be the artist and not the manager who is contracting with the third party, and the manager will not be liable for any breach by the artist under the agreement with the third party. However, it should be noted that if the manager not only negotiates but also purports to enter an agreement between the artist and a third party, the artist will only be bound by the contract with the third party if there was actual or apparent authority for the manager to enter into the agreement. If the third party is not sure that the manager has actual or apparent authority he should make enquiries about the manager's authority to see if the artist will be bound by such an agreement. As will be seen below (*see* The Rights and Activities Clause), the artist will want the management agreement to provide that only he can sign agreements with third parties.

Nowdays it is rare for the manager and artist relationship to be one of employer and employee, although an employer/employee situation may arise if a band or artist is created and financed by the manager (*see* Hired Hands, Chapter 5).

There is no need for there to be a written agreement for a manager to represent the artist. An oral management agreement can exist and may operate successfully until there is a contractual dispute between the parties. It is, however, always best for the agreement terms to be set out in writing. The manager should ensure that the artist receives independent legal advice on the contents of the proposed management agreement from a solicitor with experience of music agreements. This is to help reduce the possibility that the agreement may be successfully challenged by the artist, *e.g.* for undue influence. (For undue influence *see* Chapter 3 Music Industry Contracts above.) Frequently, an artist may not have the finance to pay for independent legal advice. If that is the case the manager should seriously consider paying for, or loaning the artist money to take advice from a solicitor of his choice. The money may be loaned on the basis that it is either a loan which can be paid back to the manager over a period of time, or as an advance which is recoupable against the artist's future professional income. If the manager is concerned about the amount he may have to pay for the artist to receive independent legal advice, he may put a ceiling on the amount of the artist's legal fees that he is prepared to pay or loan. This could be by way of a monetary figure or agreeing to pay the artist's reasonable legal fees.

Oral management agreement

As mentioned above, there is no need for there to be a written agreement in order for a manager to represent the artist. An oral management agreement can exist and may operate successfully until there is a contractual dispute between the parties. Indeed, before a written agreement is prepared, the manager may have been providing his services to the artist for some period of time on the basis of an oral agreement. If there is no written agreement or if a written or an oral agreement does not cover a particular matter(s) the law will imply terms into a management agreement. These implied terms include that:

(a) The manager will personally carry out his obligations to the artist and will do so with due skill and care.
(b) The manager will not allow a conflict of interest to arise between himself and the artist.
(c) The manager will not misuse any confidential information concerning the artist that he acquires. This duty exists not only whilst he is manager but will continue after he ceases to represent the artist.

(d) The manager will keep accounts of all income and expenditure relating to the artist.

(e) The manager is entitled to be indemnified by the artist for any expenses which he incurs on the artists' behalf, but the manager is not entitled to be paid a salary or commission for providing his services to the artist.

An oral management agreement will probably deal with the key terms and, in particular with the matter of the manager's remuneration but will not always cover all the terms of the agreement. However, as mentioned above, if any terms are not dealt with in an oral or a written agreement the law will imply terms into the agreement. It is always best for the parties to agree all the terms they want rather than leave them to be implied by law, and it is certainly a good idea to put an oral agreement into writing as soon as possible.

Key terms

Appointment of the manager

When negotiating the agreement both parties should remember that it is the artist who is appointing the manager and not the other way round. The artist will appoint the manager to be his sole exclusive manager in a defined territory(ies) (*see* below for The territory), and the manager will be required to spend as much time as is necessary to develop the artist's career.

When drafting the clause there should be consideration not only as to what activities the artist is involved in now but also what activities he may want to enter into in the future. For example, the artist may presently only be involved in the music business, but he may have aspirations in the future to go into television presenting or acting. Both the manager and the artist should consider what activities the artist may like to pursue in the future and they should consider whether these activities will be within the scope of the manager's appointment clause.

The appointment clause should make it expressly clear what the manager is appointed to do. The manager would like to see the clause drafted widely so that he is appointed to represent the artist in all his activities in the entertainment business. The artist may well seek to limit the scope of the manager's appointment. For example, the artist may only want to appoint the manager to represent him in the music business. Consideration should also be taken of any other management agreement that the artist has, or has had in the past. If the artist has appointed somebody to manage him in a particular activity, such as acting, and this agreement is still in existence, this activity should be excluded from the appointment clause in the new management agreement. If the artist had a previous management agreement which he believes has expired it should be checked to see that it has expired so that he can validly enter the new management agreement.

The artist may appoint a large management company to be his manager because he wants a particular employee at the management company to handle his affairs. Where this is the case the artist should try to obtain a key man clause in the management agreement providing that if the person he wants to handle his affairs leaves the company or no longer personally handles his affairs then he will be free to terminate the management agreement. A large management company may not, however, be prepared to agree to a key man clause. Their attitude may be that although a capable employee may have left their employment they have other equally capable employees who can handle the artist's affairs properly.

A management company may be the vehicle through which the manager operates his business affairs. Where a manager runs his business affairs via his own management company, an artist who wants to appoint the manager will contract not with the manager but with the manager's company. The artist should in this situation obtain a key man clause in the agreement and a side letter from the manager guaranteeing, inter alia, that if the management company ceases to exist or the manager leaves the company or no longer handles the artist's affairs at the company, that the manager will, if required by the artist, personally represent the artist for the remainder of the term of the management agreement.

The artist may operate his business affairs through his own company in which case it will be his company which will contract with the manager/management company. The manager/management company should ensure when contracting with the artist's company that there is a side letter from the artist guaranteeing that he will personally honour the obligations of the management agreement in the event that his company does not do so. The artist should ensure where he is required to enter a side letter that there is a provision in the side letter that he will honour the contractual obligations provided the manager/management company is not in breach of the contract.

If the manager represents the artist throughout the world, the manager may want the right to appoint agents to help him. The artist may not want the manager to appoint agents to help manage his affairs, but if he is prepared to let the manager do so, he may want the right to be consulted about the proposed agents, or he may want the right to approve the manager's choices. If the manager appoints agents to help him manage the artist's affairs he will want these costs to be paid for by the artist. If it is agreed that these costs will be paid for by the artist they will be dealt with in the agreement in the clause which deals with the manager's commission (*see also* Manager's Remuneration Clause and The territory below).

The appointment clause should not be considered in isolation, but should be considered along with the other clauses in the agreement, and in particular along with the clauses dealing with the term and the territory (*see* The territory and The term below for details).

The territory

The agreement must contain a clause which sets out the territory(ies) in which the manager represents the artist. It used to be fairly common for an artist to have several managers. Each manager would be appointed to be the exclusive manager for the artist in specific countries. Frequently, this would lead to the artist being given conflicting career advice, disputes would arise between each manager over what the artist should be doing at a particular time, and one manager would often blame another manager when something went wrong or when the artist became dissatisfied. It is quite possible and on occasion may be sensible for the artist to have two or three managers each representing him exclusively in specific countries. However, for this to succeed there has to be some sensible channel of comunication between all parties. Nowadays it is becoming more common for the artist to appoint just one manager to represent him throughout the world.

The artist will need to establish whether his manager is capable of representing him efficiently and effectively throughout the world or whether the manager is only capable of representing him properly in certain territories. Some managers may have the contacts and the set-up to represent the artist in the European Union but have no experience or contacts elsewhere in the world. If this is the case the artist should appoint the manager to represent him in the territories in which the manager has expertise, and appoint managers with requisite experience in other territories.

It is possible that the manager may not have a world wide set-up but can still manage the artist throughout the world by delegating some of his responsibilities to others. If the artist is prepared to allow this he should ensure the agreement provides that the manager will ensure that any work which the manager delegates will be properly supervised and carried out. Also, as mentioned above, the artist may want the right to be consulted about any proposed agents to whom the manager wishes to delegate work, or he may require the right to approve the manager's choice of agents. (*See* also Manager's Remuneration Clause below.)

If the artist has previously appointed a manager to represent him in a particular territory(ies) and that agreement is still in existence, the proposed new management agreement must exclude those territory(ies) which are already being managed.

Term

The length of the manager's appointment must be included in the agreement. The Musicians Union recommend that a manager should be appointed for a term of three years, which is made up of a period of one year plus two one-year options.

If the manager has no proven management track record the artist may only want to appoint him for a trial period of say, six months. At the end of the trial period if the artist is satisfied with the manager's performance the manager will continue for a longer period as detailed in the agreement. If at the end of the six month trial period the artist wishes to terminate the agreement he should give 30-days notice to the manager. The agreement should provide how and when the artist can serve the notice, *e.g.* by first class post to the manager at his last known address and that it cannot be sent until the end of the fifth month of the agreement. The clause should ensure that time is not of the essence for serving the notice of termination. If the clause provides that time is of the essence for serving the notice of termination this would mean that if the artist did not serve the notice on time the agreement has not been validly terminated and it automatically continues. Most managers would not be happy to agree to a trial period which can be terminated at the whim of the artist. They may be prepared to agree to a trial period based upon a performance target which if achieved would mean the agreement would continue. (See below for performance targets).

The agreement could be for a fixed term of between three to five years. The artist would most probably like the fixed term to be for three years whilst the manager would like it to be for five years. The artist would prefer a shorter fixed term because this will enable him, should he become successful in this period, to negotiate a new agreement at an early date with his existing manager or with another manager on more favourable terms, or where he has not become successful in this period it will enable him to look for another manager who may be more effective in developing his career. The manager would like a longer fixed term agreement because it takes time to build up an artist's career and earnings potential and he will want a chance to be fully rewarded for as long as possible for all his efforts on behalf of the artist.

The term could be for an initial period of one year with perhaps four separate one-year options exercisable by the manager. The artist would want to provide that the options are only exercisable if the manager achieves stated performance targets. For example, in the first year the manager would be required to use his expertise to obtain agreements which would in total earn a certain amount of money for the artist. If the manager achieves the target figure, he would be allowed to exercise the option to extend the agreement for another year. In the second and subsequent years the manager would be given new higher targets to achieve before he could exercise the next option. If the manager fails to achieve the target set for the year he would not be able to exercise the option and the management agreement would terminate. (Notwithstanding termination of the agreement, the manager and artist will still have ongoing responsibilities to each other. *See* Termination below.) As opposed to, or in addition to setting financial targets for the manager to achieve, the manager might be set a target of obtaining a record or publishing agreement for the artist. If the manager is required to achieve a recording or publishing agreement for the artist, care should be taken in defining what exactly is meant by these terms. For example, does a record agreement mean an agreement for one single only with any record company which would therefore include some fly-by-night operation set up by a friend of the manager, or does it mean an agreement for say up to three albums with a major record company? (What is meant by a major record company would also need to be defined in the management agreement.)

A potential problem the manager needs to consider is what should happen if he is given a financial target to achieve and the artist turns down the work, thereby hindering the manager not only from achieving his target but also depriving him of commission? The manager should ensure the target clause is drafted to include a provision that if the artist turns down any offers of work submitted by the manager, the value of this work is included in the calculation of the target figure. The artist may resist such a provision but he may possibly agree to it being counted towards the target figure if the work is the type of work he has previously done or is seeking to do and the remuneration reflects the amount that would be expected to be paid to an artist of his standing. As for the manager not receiving commission on the work he has offered the artist, the manager would want the commission clause to include a provision that he receives commission on work he secures for the artist but which the artist turns down. The artist may again resist such a clause, but may possibly agree that the manager should be paid commission if the work is the type of work he has previously done or is seeking to do and the remuneration reflects the amount that would be expected to be paid to an artist of his standing (*see below* for Manager's Remuneration Clause).

The agreement should provide a short time limit within which the manager may exercise any option he has to extend the term. Sometimes there may be a provision that if the manager has not informed the artist whether or not he intends to take up the option, that before the agreement can terminate the artist must notify the manager of this whereupon the manager will have a period of time from the artist notifying him to decide whether to exercise the option. Such a provision is unacceptable to the artist as the agreement continues until he takes positive action to terminate it. In any event why should the manager be given a second chance to exercise his option if he has forgotten to do so?

Rights and activities clause

As mentioned above (*see* Appointment of the manager) the agreement should make it specifically clear in which areas the manager represents the artist. A performance criteria may also be inserted into the agreement for the manager to achieve for the artist (*see* The term above).

The artist should ensure the agreement provides that the manager will use his best endeavours in representing and promoting the artist. Any alternative promise offered should be resisted by the artist.

The parties will need to decide whether the manager is authorised to negotiate and sign agreements on behalf of the artist. Certainly the manager would like such authority. The artist should resist giving the manager such wide authority as these agreements relate to his career and the artist will want the final say on them, after he has been advised by his manager and, if necessary, his solicitor and accountant. The artist will probably want the clause to provide for the manager to negotiate agreements but that these can only be signed by the artist. Where the management agreement provides for the manager to nego-tiate agreements on behalf of the artist and that the artist will sign them, the manager will want a clause in the management agreement that the artist will not unreasonably refuse to sign an agreement which the manager has negotiated for the artist.

The only time the artist should possibly consider allowing the manager to actually sign an agreement for him is for a one-off engagement. Even then the artist would want the manager to use his best endeavours to try and consult him first before the manager can sign an agreement for him.

The manager will require the artist to refer any offers of employment to him which relate to the scope of his appointment and which have been made directly to the artist and not to the manager. Such a clause should be accepted by the artist as the manager needs to be able to consider all offers made to the artist to carry out his responsibilities properly.

The manager may seek a clause giving him the right to require the artist to sign any documents which he wants the artist to sign. The artist should resist such a clause as it is his career and the manager should not be allowed to dictate to the artist in this way. Wherever possible the final say always should be with the artist not the manager.

The manager may seek a clause giving him the right to require the artist to attend any promotional interviews which the manager has arranged for him. Again the artist should modify any such clause so that he must be consulted about doing any such interviews, or he should have the final say as to whether he is prepared to do the interview. If the management agreement gives the artist some control over giving interviews, the manager will usually require the clause to be drafted so that the artist will not unreasonably refuse to do promotional interviews. If the artist acts unreasonably, he may be in breach of the management agreement because he may be hindering the manager's ability to carry out his management responsibilities.

The manager will want the right to use the artist's name and likeness, any trade mark belonging to the artist, and the artist's biographical details in order to promote him. This should be acceptable to the artist, provided it is made clear in the agreement that the manager only has the right to use the artist's name and likeness etc to promote the artist in those areas in which the manager is appointed to represent him and not for any other purposes. The artist will want the right to approve any proposed use of his name and likeness etc by the manager in any proposed promotional material. The manager will only want the artist to have qualified approval rights, *i.e.* that the artist will have the right to approve any proposed use of his name and likeness etc in any proposed promotional material with such consent not to be unreasonably withheld.

Artist's warranties and obligations

The warranties and obligations of the artist under the management agreement include that:

(a) he is not a minor,

(b) he is free to enter into the agreement,

(c) he is not suffering from any disability which prevents him from providing his services,

(d) he will carry out any services which he is required to provide under the agreement or any agreement which the manager has obtained for him professionally and to the best of his ability,

(e) the manager is appointed as the artist's sole and exclusive manager in the territory(ies) stated in the agreement,

(f) he has taken independent legal advice from a solicitor with experience of music agreements,

(g) he will keep the contents of the agreement confidential. The clause should allow the artist to disclose the contents of the agreement to his lawyer, accountant, bank and financial adviser,

(h) he will inform the manager of all past professional agreements by which he is bound or may still be bound,

(i) he will not enter into any other management agreement(s) for the territory(ies) in which the manager is appointed,

(j) he will not subsequently vary the terms of any agreement which the manager has negotiated and which he has agreed to,

(k) he will not bring himself, any band members (if he is a member of a band) or the manager into disrepute,

(l) he will keep himself, so far as it it possible to do so, in good health and will pay attention to his personal appearance when in public,

(m) (if the manager wants to take out insurance cover on the artist), the artist will attend a medical examination, if required by the manager's insurance company. He will, where insurance cover has been taken out by the manager, comply with any reasonable requirements of the insurance company to ensure that the insurance policy remains in force.

(n) he will keep the manager informed as to where he can be contacted and as to his availability to perform,

(o) he will not change his image or his professional stage name,

(p) he will undergo any reasonable training that may be necessary so that he can provide his services professionally,

(q) he will not give any interviews without the manager's consent. Such a clause would be unacceptable for an artist and should be deleted from any draft management agreeement as it is his career and he should not be beholden to the manager over giving interviews,

(r) any employment offers he receives which fall within the scope of the manager's activities will be referred by him to the manager,

(s) he will join any relevant collecting societies such as the PRS and either PAMRA or AURA. This clause will be required because the manager wants to ensure that the artist receives the money which is due to him from the relevant collecting societies, and therefore the manager will be able to commission these monies. In addition, the artist will probably be required to join the MU. (*See* Chapter 4 Collecting Societies and Music Industry Associations for the PRS, PAMRA, AURA and the MU),

The Indemnity Clause By The Artist

The management agreement will contain an indemnity clause requiring the artist to indemnify the manager for all the costs, liabilities, losses and damage which have been incurred by the manager due to any breach or non performance by the artist of the management agreement. The artist should try to limit the scope of the indemnity so that he will only be liable to indemnify the manager for specific breaches. In addition, the artist should try to limit liability for the manager's costs to the reasonable costs which have been reasonably incurred by the manager, or to the manager's reasonable legal and other professional costs.

The manager may include a provision allowing him, where he collects the artist's income, to withhold the artist's money in the event of there being any legal action concerning the artist in which the manager is involved. (See below for who is entitled to collect the artist's income). This would enable the manager to offset the money he is withholding against any loss or damage which he incurs, rather than have to pursue the artist for the money due to him under an indemnity clause. The artist should not agree to such a provision. The artist may possibly be prepared to agree to a similar provision which will allow the manager to withhold his money provided:

(i)   the legal action involves a material breach of the artist's obligations, and

(ii) a limit is put on the amount of money which the manager can withhold, and

(iii) any money withheld will be put on deposit to earn interest, and

(iv) that where the threat of legal proceedings does not lead to the issue of court proceedings within a specified time the money which has been withheld will be returned to the artist together with accrued interest.

Manager's obligations

Although the artist will appoint a manager to be his sole exclusive manager in the defined territory(ies), the management agreement will not usually restrict the number of artists whom the manager can represent in the defined territory(ies). The management agreement with an artist will, however, require the manager to use his best endeavours to represent the artist, to spend such time as is necessary to properly represent the artist, and require the manager not to act where a conflict of interest arises between the artist and any other artists whom he manages.

In order for the manager to carry out his responsibilities properly he may need to hire others to carry out certain functions. For example, there will be a need to use a solicitor to examine agreements, and for an accountant to give advice on tax. The management agreement will provide that such costs will be paid for by the artist. The artist may want to put a monetary limit on those costs for which he is responsible. The manager will usually resist this as he will not want to be personally liable to pay the difference between those costs incurred less the amount the artist has contracted to be responsible for. As opposed to putting a monetary limit on the costs the clause might be drafted so that the artist is responsible for any reasonable fees which have been reasonably incurred by the manager.

The artist should ensure the management agreement contains a clause that the manager cannot assign the agreement. The only variation on assignment that the artist may be prepared to accept would be to allow the agreement to be assigned to a management company which is owned and controlled by the manager. An assignment may be acceptable to the artist in this limited case if the agreement is varied to include a key man clause, if the assignee (i.e. the management company) enters a direct covenant with the artist that it will comply with the terms of the management agreement, and if the manager provides the artist with a suitably worded side letter. (See

Appointment of the manager above for the key man clause and for the side letter.)

The manager may seek to limit the times that he is is required to provide his services to the artist. For example, he may seek to provide his services during normal office hours from Monday to Friday. Such times will probably be unsuitable especially as the artist may need to speak to the manager at weekends and in the evenings. The artist should resist any restrictions on the times the manager is available, and he should seek a clause that provides that the manager will be available to provide his services as and when required. A compromise may be that the manager will provide his services to the artist during normal office hours during Mondays to Fridays and at such other times as is reasonably required. The agreement may also provide that the manager will be available to be contacted as and when necessary on a mobile phone and that the number will be given to the artist and others so that the manager can properly carry out his responsibilities to the artist.

The agreement will also specifically oblige the manager to negotiate (and if the agreement permits, sign) agreements relating to the artist. There will also be a specific obligation on him to provide the services for which he has been appointed to represent the artist (*see* Appointment of Manager above).

The agreement should contain a clause which requires the manager to keep the contents of the agreement confidential. The confidentiality clause should allow the manager to disclose the contents of the agreement to his lawyer, accountant, bank and financial adviser.

The agreement will usually provide that the manager's obligations are subject to the performance by the artist of his obligations.

The Indemnity Clause By The Manager

The management agreement should contain an indemnity clause requiring the manager to indemnify the artist for all the costs, liabilities, losses and damage which have been incurred by the artist due to any breach or non performance by the manager of the management agreement. The manager should try to limit the scope of the indemnity so that he will only be liable to indemnify the artist for specific breaches. In addition, the manager should try to limit liability for the artist's costs to the reasonable costs which have been reasonably incurred by the artist, or to the artist's reasonable legal and other professional costs.

Remuneration clause

The artist will only want to pay commission to the manager on income received from agreements which the manager has negotiated. The artist will not want the manager to be entitled to commission on income received from agreements which existed prior to the manager's appointment and which is received during the term of the management agreement. The artist will only want to pay commission to the manager during the term of the management agreement (which will include any options exercised by the manager) and once the management agreement has expired the artist will want the managers' entitlement to commission to cease.

The manager will want his commission to be calculated upon all the gross income (including income from agreements which were not negotiated by him) due to the artist without deduction of any of the artist's expenses. In addition, the manager will want his commission to continue to be payable for as long as possible after the management agreement has expired in respect of any agreements he has negotiated or substantially negotiated for the artist.

The manager and the artist will have to negotiate a half-way house between the artist attempting to limit the commission payable for as short a period as possible and the manager attempting to get the commission payable for as long as possible. The parties will also have to negotiate the rate at which commission will be paid.

The usual commission rate is between 15–25% of the artist's gross income which is derived from the areas in which the manager is appointed to represent the artist before any deduction of the artist's expenses. (The agreement will need to be clear whether the commission is calculated on the income which is actually received by or on behalf of the artist, or the income which is due to the artist.) There are certain deductions, such as the manager's expenses, which will be deducted from the gross figure before the manager's commission is calculated (see below for details). The rule of thumb is that newer artists will pay a higher commission rate and established artists will pay a lower commission rate. Many agreements provide for a fixed commission rate, but there are many other methods which could be adopted to calculate the commission payable to the manager, for example it could be agreed that the manager will receive:

(a) 15% for the first £100,000 income, 20% on the income from £100,000.01 to £200, 000 and 25% on the income from £200,000.01, or

(b) 25% for the first £100,000 income, 20% on the income from £100,000.01 to £200, 000 and 15% on the income from £200,000.01, or

(c) 25% on income from recordings, 20% on income from publishing, 18% on income from live performances, 15% on income from merchandising, or

(d) 20% on all activities in which the manager represents the artist but the total commisssion payable in the first year of the management agreement cannot exceed £150,000, in the second year it cannot exceed £300,000, in the third year it can not exceed £600,000 and so on.

It is possible that the manager may not be paid commission but be paid a salary or a salary with a performance related bonus. Some established international artists may even consider dispensing with a manager and hire staff to run their daily affairs with their business affairs being run by their solicitor or accountant who will be paid for the time they spend at their hourly charging out rate. Some managers may, instead of being on commission, be paid as if they were a member of the band and be paid an equal share of the band's net profits. If the manager is to receive an equal share of the band's net profits instead of commission, care should be taken to define in the management agreement what exactly is meant by "net".

The management agreement should be checked to ensure that if the artist provides his services through a limited company the commission payable to the manager is only calculated on the income due to or received by the artist's company. The artist will be paid a salary from his company and the manager should not commission this as well because this would amount to the manager receiving double commission, namely from the artist's company and from the artist's salary.

The artist should also ensure the agreement provides that as the manager will be entitled to commission any advances which are payable under agreements between the artist and a third party, *e.g.* a recording agreement, the manager is not entitled to receive commission on any royalties which would have been paid to the artist but which are used by the third party to recoup the advance. If the manager were allowed to commission the advance and any royalties which were used to recoup the advance this would amount to the manager receiving double commission. The advance is effectively a loan to the artist by the third party which will be recouped by the third party from future royalties, and the artist will not actually receive any royalties until such time as the advance as been fully recouped.

The artist will want the agreement to provide that the manager receives commission on the money which is actually "received", whereas the manager will seek the commission to be paid upon what is "due" even if has not yet been paid. The manager will argue that he has brought in the work for the artist, that it is not his fault if a third party has not yet paid the artist for his services and that he should be paid his commission and not be penalised for the failure of the third party to pay. The artist will argue that it may be true that the manager obtained the work for him, but he should not have to pay the manager commission for work he has provided and not yet been paid for, as this would mean not only has he presently provided his services for free with the possibilty of never being paid if the third party goes into liquidation or bankruptcy, but until such time as he is actually paid it is causing him a financial loss to provide the services, as he is paying commission on money which he has not yet, and may not ever receive. As to whether the manger is paid on income "received" or "due" will depend on the negotiating strengths of the parties.

The agreement should provide that it is the manager's own responsibility to pay for those costs which are directly attributable to the running of his own business. The manager will therefore be expected to pay for his own office expenses which will include rent, business rates, heating, lighting, stationery, and staff. This is different to the costs which the manager incurs specifically for the benefit of the artist. Those costs which are incurred by the manager specifically for the benefit of the artist should be recoverable from the artist's income. The artist will want a clause in the agreement which requires the manager to provide receipts for any expenses which he wants to reclaim and in addition the artist will want to limit the amount which the manager can reclaim. Rather than putting a monetary figure on the amount which the manager can reclaim, it is common practice for the agreement to provide that the manager will only be repaid for his reasonable expenses which have been reasonably incurred by the manager specifically for the benefit of the artist. Another limitation which the artist might seek to put into the agreement concerning the manager's expenses would be to require the manager to obtain prior authority from him before incurring expenses above a certain figure. The artist will also want a clause in the agreement which provides that the manager can only reclaim his expenses out of the income from which he represents the artist and not from any income which the artist receives. Also if the manager can appoint agents to help manage the artist, the agreement should deal with whether the agent's costs are an expense recoverable from the artist's income.

It should be noted that if commission is calculated on the artist's gross income, the manager's expenses should be deducted from the gross figure before commission is calculated.

At the outset of his career the artist will probably have little or no money to live on. He may need to buy musical equipment and clothing in order to perform and may need to go into the recording studio to record a demo tape to be able to send to record and publishing companies to try and raise interest in him. Apart from borrowing money from family or friends or trying to get a bank loan, the only other possible source of finance will be the manager. The manager may be prepared to lend the artist money to help him launch his career. The manager will want the agreement to provide that any loan he makes to the artist is an advance which is recoupable from the artist's income. In addition, the agreement will also provide that any musical instruments, clothing or any other items which he buys with the loan will remain the property of the manager until such time as the advance has been fully recouped. The manager may also try and add a clause providing that any loan made by him to the artist will be treated as a debt repayable by the artist, to the extent that it has not been recouped from the artist under the management agreement. The artist could try to resist such a clause being inserted in the agreement on the basis that it is not his fault if any loan is not recouped, rather it is the manager's fault because he has not promoted him successfully and if he had done so more income would have come in from which the manager would have been repaid.

Sometimes the manager will find suitable offers of work for the artist which the artist for no apparent reason decides to turn down. The manager will therefore lose the chance to earn commission. The manager will not want to work for nothing and will want a clause in the agreement which provides that he will be entitled to be paid commission on work which he finds for the artist which the artist turns down. The artist will resist such a clause in the management agreement on the basis that it is his career and if he does not feel that a particular offer is suitable he has the right to turn it down. The manager will argue that the work is of the type the artist is seeking and that he should be paid commission if the artist has a flight of fancy and rejects suitable offers of work. If the artist is prepared to agree that the manager should be paid commission for work which he turns down, he should ensure the management agreement is drafted in such a way that it provides that the work the manager has obtained is similar to the work, in terms of pay and conditions, which he has done in the past and which would be expected to be carried out by an artist of his standing, or if it is of a type which he has not previously been involved in, it is in an area in which he has expressed an interest in becoming involved, and which reflects his professsional standing in the field of entertainment in which he is known.

On rare occasions an artist might be given a gift, such as a Ferrari or a Bentley, by a grateful concert promoter at the end of a tour, or by a record company to reflect their pleasure at their record sales, or by a record company to reflect some landmark in the artist's career, *e.g.* 20 years in the music business. The manager will want to commission payments in kind and personal gifts which have been made to the artist. The artist will probably resist the manager having the right to commission personal gifts. The manager will argue that he should be paid commission upon any personal gifts the artist might receive from grateful third parties on the basis that the manager obtained the agreement which led to the relationship between the artist and the third party and therefore if it had not been for the manager the artist would not have received the gift. The manager might also argue that the gift is an equivalent to a further advance or a higher royalty, albeit in the complete discretion of the donor, and is therefore commissionable.

Sometimes an artist will not be paid for his services in money but will instead be paid in commodities such as oil. This may happen where, for example, an artist perfoms in a country where the country's currency is volatile. The manager should be entitled to commission payments in kind because the payment in kind is an alternative method to paying the artist for his services. The agreement should, however, provide a method for calculating at what stage a payment in kind is commissioned, *e.g.* is it commissioned on the value when the artist takes delivery of the payment in kind or when he sells the payment in kind? The agreement should also provide what deductions can be made from the payment in kind before the manager can commission it, *e.g.* the artist should be allowed to deduct from the agreed value of the payment in kind the costs he incurs in selling the payment in kind.

As mentioned above the manager's commission is usually between 15–25% of the artist's gross income which is derived from the areas in which the manager is appointed to represent the artist before any deduction of the artist's expenses. (The agreement will need to be clear whether the commission is calculated on the income which is received by or on behalf of the artist or on the income which is due to the artist.) There are certain deductions which should be made from the artist's gross income before the manager's commission is calculated. The deductions include:

(a) VAT.

(b) Tour support if it is given by the record company to the artist. Tour support is money which may be given to the artist to enable him to perform live in concert. Touring is notoriously expensive and for new or less established artists a tour will run at a loss. Artists may want to go out on tour to promote their latest album but often they cannot afford to do so. The record company will usually want its artist to tour to promote the album and to encourage him to do so it may offer him tour support. This is money given to the artist to offset a loss incurred on the tour. (*See also* Chapter 8 Recording Agreements.) The manager should not be able to commission tour support as it is not money which is due to the artist, but is money paid to the artist to offset a loss.

(c) Where a tour makes a profit, receipted tour costs, *e.g.* travel and hotel expenses of the artist and his road crew, his road crew's wages, and any money which the artist has to pay an established artist/band to perform as the opening act on tour.

(d) Tour agent's costs. (These are usually in the region of 10–15% of the gross tour receipts). (*See* Chapter 9 Touring, Tour Agent Agreement, Tour Agent's Remuneration.)

(e) Any hire fee paid by a promoter to the artist for the use of the artist's own sound and lighting equipment on tour. (*See* Chapter 9 Touring, Tour Agreement, Promoter's Obligations.)

(f) Any monies paid by the artist's record company to an independent record producer or engineer. If the artist is also the producer and/or engineer of his album he will be paid an additional sum(s) to perform these functions by the record company, in which case these monies belong to the artist and would be commissionable. However, if the artist is not the record producer and/or he is not the engineer, these monies do not belong to the artist and so should not be commissionable by the manager.

(g) Any recording costs or video recording costs paid for by the artist or recoupable by the record company from the artist.
It should be noted that recording costs and video recording costs will be paid for in one of two ways. Either the record company will give the artist an additional recoupable advance specifically to enable the artists to pay the recording costs (this advance should not be subject to manager's commission as it is not the artist's personal money but it is money the artist is given specifically to pay for recording). Alternatively,

the record company will pay the recording and video recording costs itself. Either way these costs will usually in the end be paid for by the artist as they will be recoupable from the artist's royalties. (See Chapter 8 Recording Agreements — deductions from the gross royalty.)

(h) Litigation costs relating to the areas in which the manager represents the artist which have been incurred pursuing monies which are due to the artist from, *e.g.* a publisher, record company, promoter. Only those litigation costs which have not been recovered from the other party to the litigation should be deducted.

Collection of income

Another area which must specifically be dealt with in the management agreement is who is entitled to collect the artist's income. There are several ways of dealing with this, for example:

(a) The manager will collect the income. Obviously, this is what the manager wants. However, the artist will try and resist this as it is his money, save for the manager's 15–25% commission. The artist will be concerned that the manager might possibly either run off with his money or go into liquidation or bankruptcy. If the manager insists on collecting the income and the artist is prepared to agree to this, the manager should be required to account to the artist monthly or at least quarterly, and in the event that the manager receives large sums, such as recording or publishing advances or royalties, he should be required to account to the artist within seven days of their receipt.

There should be a provision that any money received by the manager will be paid into a bank acccount before any commission is deducted. The bank account should not be the manager's bank account. It should be a separate trust bank account either in the name of the artist or in the names of the artist and the manager. Any interest earned on the money should belong to the artist although the manager will want to be able to commission the interest earned. The artist and the manager should both be required to sign any cheques issued on the account, although there may be provision allowing the manager to be the sole signatory for small cheques of, say, £100. The artist will be paid his money from the trust bank account either by way of a cheque or by a direct transfer from the trust bank account to his personal bank account. Where the payment is by way of a direct bank transfer the agreement should set out the name of the artist's bank, the account name, number and sort code to enable the payment to be made directly into the account.

(b) The manager will collect the income with the exception of any recording or publishing income which will be collected by the artist (which the manager would probably not accept) or the artist's accountant (which the manager would be more likely to accept) who will then account to the manager with his commission. This removes from the manager the right to collect what is likely to be the artist's largest sources of income. The manager will still collect some of the artist's income, such as the income from touring, merchandising (if he represents the artist for merchandising) and personal appearances. If the artist is likely to earn substantial sums from touring or merchandising then he should consider removing the right of the manager to collect this income as well.

(c) The manager will collect the income for the first year or two years of the agreement (if it is anticipated that the artist will not earn substantial sums during that period) and thereafter the artist or the artist's accountant will collect the income and will account to the manager with his commission. An extra safety valve could be inserted to provide that if during the time the manager collects the income the artist signs a recording or publishing agreement or any other agreement which will bring in sizeable income, any monies from these agreements will not be collected by the manager but by the artist or the artist's accountant who will account to the manager with his commission.

(d) The manager will collect the income during the agreement term (in which case the matters discussed at (a) above will still be relevant), and after the agreement has ended the artist will collect the income and account to the manager with his commission.

(e) The artist will collect the income and will account to the manager with his commission. The manager will certainly resist any such suggestion as he will be concerned that the artist might run off with his commission or that the artist might become bankrupt before he has been paid his commission, or where he has contracted with the artist's company rather than the artist in person that the artist's company might go into liquidation before he has been paid his commission.

(f) The artist's accountant will collect the income and will account to the manager with his commission. This may be acceptable to the manager if he cannot persuade the artist to let him collect the money.

Where the manager collects the artist's income there should be a provision in the agreement requiring the manager to maintain proper accounts relating to the artist's income which will be kept at the manager's registered office or main place of business. In addition, the manager will be required to send the artist a detailed statement of account when paying the artist the money which is due to him. The manager may insert a clause giving the artist, for example, one year from receipt of the accounts to object to their accuracy. The artist should not accept any clause which allows the manager to reduce the six-year contractual limitation period to object to the accounts. The agreement should also contain an audit clause which will allow the artist or his professionally qualified accountant to inspect, audit and take copies of the manager's books and records to determine the accuracy of the accounts. The clause will usually require the artist to give notice of his intention to carry out the audit, and will limit the inspection to one inspection a year at the artist's expense. In addition, the clause will usually provide that the audit will take place at the manager's registered office or main place of business and will take place during the manager's normal business hours. There may be an additional restriction that the accountant carrying out the audit for the artist is not presently engaged on another audit of the manager on behalf of another artist.

The agreement should provide that where the artist has been underpaid by a specified sum, *e.g.* he has been underpaid by at least £5,000, or has been underpaid by a specified percentage, *e.g.* 10%, whichever is greater, that the cost of the audit will be paid for by the manager. The agreement should provide that where the artist has been underpaid, the manager will account to the artist for the under-payment. The artist should ensure that the clause is drafted so that the manager accounts for any underpayment immediately and that the manager pays interest on any underpaid sum at 3 or 4 % above a stated bank's base rate from time to time in force.

The audit clause should contain a provision that the information disclosed to the artist and/or his accountant is confidential information and will not be disclosed to anyone other than the artist's professional advisers. The manager will usually require a copy of the artist's final audit report to be sent to him.

Where the artist or his accountant collects the income, the manager will want a detailed statement of account sent to him with his commission and will require audited accounts to be sent to him once a year. The matters discussed in the above paragraphs concerning where the accounts are to be kept, the right to audit, the mechanics and cost of the audit, underpayment, that the information is confidential, and requiring a copy of the final audit report to be sent to the audited party are also relevant in this situation. Likewise any attempt by the artist to cut back the six-year contractual limitation period for the manager to object to the accounts should not be accepted by the manager.

The artist's solicitor should try to obtain a provision in the agreement that, notwithstanding who collects the artist's income, the manager's right to receive commission is conditional upon the artist not terminating the agreement because of the manager being in material breach of contract. The manager will strongly resist any such provision being included in the agreement.

The manager may insert a clause in the agreement which allows him, where he collects the artist's income, to retain such amount of the artist's money as he deems necessary as a reserve for future expenses which he anticipates he will incur for the artist in the future. Where the artist's money is collected by the artist or his accountant, the manager may want a clause giving him the right to be sent such amount of the artist's money as he deems necessary for him to hold for such a reserve. The artist will not want any such provision in the agreement. At most the artist might be persuaded to agree to a clause which will either allow a "reasonable" reserve, or a specified sum to be retained.

Occasionally, the artist may find that a party with whom he has contracted is delaying or refusing to pay him for his services. The artist should ensure that the management agreement does not allow the manager to commence legal proceedings in his name. Because of the time, expense and possible publicity involved for the artist in litigating, the decision to litigate should rest solely with him after consultation with the manager.

Manager's remuneration after agreement has ended

As mentioned earlier, the artist will only want to pay commission to the manager during the term of the management agreement (which will include any options exercised by the manager) and once the management agreement has expired he will want the manager's entitlement to commission to cease. In contrast, the manager will want his commission to continue to be payable for as long as possible after the management agreement has expired in respect of any agreements that he has negotiated or substantially negotiated for the artist. The manager will have to put a lot of effort into obtaining suitable agreements for the artist and he should be financially rewarded for his work. Imagine the situation where, with six months left to run on the management agreement, the manager obtains long term world wide recording and publishing agreements for the artist. The manager will be entitled to commission on any advances paid to the artist during the term of the management agreement, but if his right to receive commission were to automatically cease at the expiration of the management agreement, he will lose the chance to commission any further advances and royalties the artist may receive from the agreements which he had secured for the artist. The artist will want to cut off the manager's right to receive commission at the end of the management agreement because any new manager he appoints will want to commission all the income he earns from the activities in which the new manager represents him. If the artist is not careful, he could find himself paying two sets of commission on the same income, namely to his previous manager if the previous manager is entitled to receive commission beyond the term of the management agreement, and to the new manager under the new management agreement.

The artist will obviously not want to pay two sets of commission on his income. To guard against this problem a clause should be included in any management agreement which will ensure that the artist will not pay commission twice on the same income, or if he does it will only be for a short period of time. The clause which should be inserted to deal with this situation should ideally provide that the commission payable after the end of the term to the manager will be tapered so that it will reduce from a 100% entitlement to a zero entitlement over a period of time. There are many ways this clause could be drafted, *e.g.* the manager could be paid commission after the term as follows:

For a period of 10 years after the term he will receive

(i)   for the first five years after the term, full rate commission on records which have been recorded and released during the term, and thereafter for the next five years half rate commission,

(ii)   for the first five years after the term, full rate commission on compositions which have been written, recorded and released during the term, and thereafter for the next five years half rate commission,

(iii) for the first five years after the term, half rate commission on records which have been recorded during the term but released after the term, and thereafter for the next five years quarter rate commission,

(iv) for the first five years after the term, half rate commission on compositions which have been written during the term but recorded and released after the term, and thereafter for the next five years quarter rate commission,

(v) for all other income he will receive,

(aa) full commission rate for the first two years after the term, thereafter,

(bb) 80% of the full commission rate for the next two years, thereafter,

(cc) 60% of the full commission rate for the next two years, thereafter,

(dd) 40% of the full commission rate for the next two years, thereafter,

(ee) 20% of the full commission rate for the next two years,

(vi) at the end of the 10-year period he will no longer be entitled to commission any of the artist's income.

A tapering clause will enable the manager to continue to commission the artist's income from those areas in which he represented the artist for a period of time after the management agreement has ended, albeit the commission rate will reduce over a period of time, and will enable the artist to move on and earn money without having to pay the manager commission in perpetuity.

If the artist appoints a new manager and agrees to pay him commission on income arising from agreements entered into prior to the new manager's appointment, he may be able to persuade the new manager to accept a lower but gradually increasing commission rate on this income. The objective for the artist is to try and ensure that the total commission which he pays to his previous manager and to his new manager does not amount to more than the total full rate commission which he would pay to one manager.

Clauses relating to band

The above clauses apply whether the manager represents a solo artist or a band. If the management agreement is with a band there are additional clauses which need to be included. These include:

(a) A clause providing that the members of the band remain jointly and severally liable to the manager. (A departing member (see below for the clause in the management agreement dealing with a departing member) will require an indemnity from the remaining members concerning future liabilities incurred by them. This should be provided for in the internal band agreement. (*See* Chapter 5 The Legal Status of Band and Solo Artist for details.))

(b) A clause providing that the manager represents the band as a whole as well as each individual member of the band. (See below for the departing member clause).

(c) A clause which the manager may require which provides that nobody can leave the band without his previous consent which can only be given in writing. Such a clause is unacceptable to the band members and they should not agree to this. At most they may agree to consult with or notify the manager of their desire or intention to leave. The provisions concerning departing members should also be dealt with in the internal band agreement and in the recording agreement (*See* Chapter 5 The Legal Status of Band and Solo Artist for the Band Agreement. *See also* Chapter 8 Recording Agreements.)

(d) A clause providing that the band will allow the manager the right to use the band's name and likeness, any trade mark belonging to the band, and the band's biographical details in order to promote them. The band should ensure the agreement makes it clear that the manager can only use their name and likeness, any trade mark belonging to them and their biographical details to promote them in those areas in which the manager is appointed to represent them and not for any other purposes. The band will also want to approve any proposed use by the manager of their name and likeness, any trade mark belonging to them and their biographical details in any promotional material. The manager may only be prepared to consult the band about the proposed use of the band's name and likeness etc on any proposed promotional material. Where the manager is prepared to let the band have approval rights the manager will usually only agree to the band having qualified approval rights i.e. that the band will have the right to approve any proposed use of their name and likeness etc in any proposed promotional material with such approval not to be unreasonably withheld.

(e) A clause which the manager may require which provides that he and not the band owns the band name. The band should not accept any such clause unless they are a band which has been put together by the manager, *i.e.* they are employed by the manager. (See Chapter 5 The Legal Status of Band and Solo Artist, Hired Hands.)

(f) If the manager collects the band income and distributes it to the band members there should be a clause dealing with how he divides up the income amongst the band members. This should reflect the division of income set out in the internal band agreement. (*See* Chapter 5 The Legal Status of Band and Solo Artist.)

(g) A clause which the manager may require allowing him to terminate the agreement should a member(s) leave and/or new members join with the effect that the constitution of the band's membership is substantially different to that which he agreed to manage.

(h) A clause which the manager may require allowing him to approve whether any new or additional members can join the band. This is unacceptable to the band members and should be resisted by them unless they are a band which has been put together by the manager, *i.e.* they are employed by the manager. (*See* Chapter 5 The Legal Status of Band and Solo Artist, Hired Hands.) It should be the band's and not the manager's decision as to who can join them and the mechanics of how they decide should be detailed in the internal band agreeement (*See* Chapter 5 The Legal Status of Band and Solo Artist, The Band Agreement.)

Departing and new band members

A discussion of the additional matters which should be dealt with in the management agreement covering new band members and departing band members is set out below:

(a) Where a band member leaves the band, under the terms of the management agreement which he had signed, he will be required to remain with the manager whether he performs as a solo artist or as a member of another band. He will when leaving the band want an indemnity from the remaining band members concerning future liabilities incurred by them. This should be provided for in the internal band agreement. (*See* Chapter 5 The Legal Status of Band and Solo Artist.)

(b) The manager may want a clause which provides that a departing member will not use the band name. This clause is inappropriate in a management agreement unless they are a band which has been put together by the manager, *i.e.* they are employed by the manager. The use of the band name should be dealt with in the internal band agreement (*See* Chapter 5 The Legal Status of Band and Solo Artist).

(c) Where a new member intends to join the band, the band's management agreement will usually require the new member to appoint the band's manager to represent him and will usually require the new member to become a party to the band's existing management agreement. This will cause a problem for an established musician who already has a manager. Indeed, the established musician's management agreement will usually contain a similar clause requiring the band to appoint the established musician's manager to represent them and to become a party to the established musician's existing management agreement. This situation will need to be sorted out before the established musician and the band work together. If the situation can not be sorted out amicably and the established musican (whom we will call party 1) and the band (whom we will call party 2) are determined to work together, then unless party 1 or party 2 can find a legitimate ground to terminate his own management agreement, the only way for the parties to work together is for party 1 and/or party 2 to fire his manager and so breach his management agreement. If we assume that party 1 fires his manager and so is in breach of contract, his manager will be in a position to sue him for the breach of contract. Party 1's manager can seek, for example, damages or an order for specific performance of the management agreement against party 1. In addition, party 1's manager may possibly have an action against party 2 and party 2's manager for inducing party 1 to breach his management agreement. In reality, the courts will not grant an order for specific performance of the management agreement against party 1, as specific performance is an equitable remedy and the courts will award damages instead as they are not able, nor do the courts believe it to be desireable, to force people to work together where a business relationship has broken down. It should be noted that a management agreement will contain a warranty from the artist that he is free to enter the management agreement. If party 1 is in breach of his existing management agreement and wants to sign with another manager, he will not be able to give this warranty in the new management agreement. If he did give such a warranty he would be in breach of the new management agreement which would enable the new manager to sue him for damages. Party 1 should ensure that this warranty in the new agreement is re-drafted to reflect the situation.

(d) The manager may possibly provide money to the band, *e.g.* to enable them to live or to buy equipment or stage clothes. If the manager provides money to the band, the management agreement will at the very least provide that the money is recoupable from the band's income from the areas in which the manager represents the band. There may be a problem as to what happens if the money has not been recouped and a member decides to leave the band. The management agreement should make provision for such an eventuality. A band member would ideally like the management agreement to provide that where he leaves the band his income will no longer be used to help pay back any amount still outstanding to the manager. It is unlikely that the manager would agree to such a provision as he might not be able to recoup his money from the income of the remaining members, especially where the remaining members lose their popularity without the departing member. In addition, it would be unfair on the remaining band members who, where the departing member's income is not used to help pay back any amount still outstanding to the manager, would find that they remain responsible for the outstanding amount. In the unlikely event that the manager agrees to such a clause being included in the management agreement, a prudent solicitor negotiating the management agreement for the band should seek an additional clause providing that where a member leaves the band, where his income is released from being used to recoup any amount outstanding to the manager, the remaining band members' responsibility to recoup any amount outstanding to the manager would be reduced proportionately. The manager would obviously like to use both the departing member's band income and the income he earns in the future after he has left the band from the activities in which the manager represents him, to help recoup any outstanding money which was provided by the manager to the band for the band's use. The band's solicitor should resist any clause in the management agreement which allows a departing member's income which he earns in the future after he has left the band from the activities in which the manager represents him from being used to recoup any outstanding money lent by the manager to the band for the band's use. At most, only the departing member's band income should be used for such recoupment. In addition, the band's solicitor should resist any clause which allows a band member's income from non-band activities from being used to recoup any money lent by the manager to the band for the band's use.

Termination

The agreement should contain provisions as to when the management agreement will automatically terminate. The agreement should also contain provisions as to when an aggrieved party has the right to elect to terminate the management agreement. The agreement may provide that where a terminating event occurs which entitles an aggrieved party to elect to terminate the agreement, before he can elect to terminate the agreement, he must serve a notice on the other party giving notice of the terminating event and requiring it to be remedied within a period of 30 days. Only if the terminating event has not been remedied within that time can he then terminate the agreement. The circumstances where termination will or may occur include:

(a) Where one party has been in material breach of contract, the other party has the right to terminate the agreement.

(b) Where one party becomes either bankrupt or enters into a voluntary arrangement or any company through which he operates goes into compulsory or voluntary liquidation (save for the purposes of reconstructing or amalgamating a solvent company), or becomes insolvent or has a receiver, manager, or administrative receiver or provisional liquidator or administrator appointed, the agreement will automatically terminate.

(c) Where one party has been convicted of a criminal offence the other party has the right to terminate the agreement. This provision should be drafted so that it does not allow termination if the conviction is for a minor offence such as speeding. The criminal conviction which will give rise to a right to terminate should only be for a serious criminal conviction. The definition of "serious conviction" must be included in the agreement so that both parties are in no doubt as to what will or will not give rise to a right to terminate.

(d) The artist has the right to terminate where the manager has failed to meet any performance targets placed upon him.

(e) A right for the manager to terminate where he is managing a band and the membership of the band is substantially different to that which he had originally contracted to manage.

(f) At the end of the contractual term the agreement will automatically terminate whereupon the artist will be free to sign with another manager.

The termination clause will usually contain a provision that, notwithstanding termination, both parties must continue to comply with the clauses of the management agreement to the extent that they are not affected by termination. For example, if the agreement is terminated by the artist due to a material breach of contract by the manager, although the artist can terminate the agreement, both parties will still be bound by any clause in the agreement providing for confidentiality.

Suspension

The agreement will usually contain a clause allowing the manager to suspend rather than terminate the agreement whilst there is a breach of contract existing which has arisen through no fault of the manager. If there is a suspension clause there should be a provision in the agreement that before suspension can occur the manager must give the artist notice that the agreement will be suspended if the artist has not rectified the breach within a period of time, *e.g.* 28 days. The agreement should also list the circumstances where the manager can invoke a suspension clause.

Where the agreement is suspended the term is frozen from the date of suspension. The term re-commences once the breach has been rectified. A suspension clause may provide that the artist is not required to provide his services until the breach has been rectified. In addition, a suspension clause may also provide that the manager does not have to make any payment of monies due to the artist until the breach has been rectified. The artist's solicitor should not agree to a provision in the suspension clause which provides that the manager can withhold the artist's money during a period of suspension.

The circumstances where suspension may occur include:

(a) Where the artist refuses to provide his services under the agreement.

(b) Where a *force majeure* event occurs. It should be noted that where suspension occurs due to a *force majeure* event that the agreement should not require the manager to give the artist notice that the agreement will be suspended if the artist has not rectified the situation within a period of time. This is because the *force majeure* event is not due to the artist's fault nor is rectifiable by the artist. (*See* Chapter 3 Music Industry Contracts, Other Clauses, for *force majeure*, for the provision of a notice of *force majeure*, and for the provision of a long stop clause where the agreement is suspended for *force majeure*.)

The agreement may provide that notwithstanding the manager's right to suspend the agreement, he may instead elect to terminate the agreement immediately. Alternatively, the agreement may provide that, notwithstanding the manager's right to suspend the agreement, for certain specified events, *e.g.* if the artist refuses to provide his services, the manager may elect to terminate the agreement immediately, whereas for other events, *e.g.* force majeure, termination can only occur 14, 21 or 28 days after the agreement has been suspended and the event which gave rise to suspension has not been rectified.

The suspension and termination clauses should be drafted to make it clear that any legal right or remedy which existed prior to suspension and/or termination is not affected by suspension and/or termination. (Also see below for a non-waiver clause.)

Other clauses

Along with the clauses mentioned above, the agreement will contain several other clauses. These include:

(a) A clause which will allow the manager to promote himself to others that he is the artist's manager.

(b) A jurisdiction and choice of law clause. (*See* Chapter 3 Music Industry Contracts.)

(c) An invalidity clause. (*See* Chapter 3 Music Industry Contracts and Chapter 5 The Legal Status of Band and Solo Artist.)

(d) A clause emphasising (if this is what has been agreed between the parties) that the manager is not allowed to sign agreements on behalf of the artist.

(e) A clause confirming that the manager has no rights to any of the artist's copyrights, moral rights or performer's rights, nor the right to use the artist's name, likeness, any trade mark belonging to the artist or the artist's biographical details, except where expressly authorised in the agreement.

(f) A clause confirming that the management agreement does not constitute a partnership, joint venture or employment relationship between the manager and the artist.

(g) A clause making it clear that the manager has the right to represent other artists.

(h) A clause confirming that the agreement reflects the whole of the agreement between the parties and replaces any earlier oral or written agreement.

(i) A non-waiver clause. (*See* Chapter 5 The Legal Status of Band and Solo Artist.)

(j) A *force majeure* clause. (*See* Chapter 3 Music Industry Contracts.)

(k) A notice clause. (See Chapter 5 The Legal Status of Band and Solo Artist.)

(l) A clause dealing with the Contracts (Rights of Third Parties) Act 1999. (See Chapter 3 Music Industry Contracts.)

Chapter 7

The Publishing Agreement

Introduction

A publisher helps to promote, exploit and administer a composer's works and collect in the monies due from their expoitation (with the assistance of the PRS and possibly the MCPS). (*See* Chapter 4 Collecting Societies and Music Industry Associations for the PRS and the MCPS.) A publisher may also be able to use his contacts in the music business to help an artist who is not only a composer but also a performer obtain a recording agreement. Frequently, the composer will produce demo recordings of his compositions for the publisher to use to attract interest in the compositions and these demos can be used to attract the interest of record companies in the artist as a performer.

Historically a music publisher's main source of income was from sales of sheet music. Although this is still an important source of income, it is essentially a secondary source of income for musical compositions. The primary sources of income for musical compositions are performing rights, synchronisation licences (known as synchro licences) which are licences permitting a song to be used in timed relation to television or film footage, and mechanical licences which are licences permitting a song to be recorded and released for sale to the public.

It is possible for an established composer to make a substantial living without the need for a publisher. A composer may be courted by publishers who, knowing that the composer is not prepared to assign all the copyright in his works in exchange for publishing services, (which as will be seen is standard in most term publishing deals), will try and lure the composer into deals which will ensure that the composer will either retain all the copyright in his works, or will entail the composer retaining some of the copyright in his works with the remaining part of the copyright being assigned to the publisher. (*See* Administration Agreements and Co-publishing Agreements below.)

The majority of composers need a publisher's services and are not able to survive alone. Perhaps in the short term one of the main reasons why a composer would need a publisher is that the publisher will usually pay an advance, which is non-returnable but is recoupable from future royalties, *i.e.* the composer is not required to return the advance or any part of it if the publisher does not recoup the advance out of the income earned from exploiting the compositions. The advance can be used by the composer to live. In addition, a composer may need a publisher because publishing is a very specialised business and a good publisher has the contacts and ability to promote and exploit the works to their full potential, so maximising their financial worth. A publisher will deal with all the paperwork involved in publishing the works, and he will keep track of and collect in all the income due from expoiting the works.

It is very possible that an artist who is both a composer and a performer may not be offered a publishing and a recording agreement at the same time. Sometimes artists may be offered both at the same time, but on many occassions a publishing agreement is offered first which will lead to a subsequent offer of a recording agreement, and on other occassions a recording agreement is offered first which will lead to a subsequent later offer of a publishing agreement. Some music industry lawyers say if a recording and publishing agreement are not offered at the same time that from their experience a publishing agreement will usually be offered first; others will say that from their experience a recording agreement will be offered before a publishing agreement. The truth really lies in between, in that it varies from case to case. Often an artist who composes and performs his own material will be offered a publishing agreement and a recording agreement at the same time. If a publishing agreement has been signed and there appears to be no current interest in signing the composer to a recording agreement, the existence of a publishing agreement may lead to a fairly swift offer of a recording agreement because a good publisher may be able to use his contacts to help the composer find a record deal. If there is currently only a recording agreement on the table a publishing agreement may swiftly follow if the artist is recording his own material as there will be publishing income coming in from the artist recording his own material and this will attract a publisher as he can see a potential income stream which he can commission if he signs the artist to a publishing agreement. A publisher will also find it easier to promote material which has been or is being recorded.

As mentioned above, an artist who composes and performs his own material will often be offered a publishing agreement with a publishing company and a recording agreement with a record company at the same time. It will often be the case that the publishing and record companies making the offers are related companies, *e.g.* they are subsidiaries of the same parent company. If this is the case the solicitor negotiating the publishing and recording agreements for the artist must examine both agreements to ensure there are no clauses in the agreements which have been included to favour the non-contracting company. For example, the artist's solicitor should ensure the agreements are not drafted in such a way as to allow cross-collateralisation between the two agreements. Cross-collateralisation within an agreement may be acceptable, but cross-collateralisation between two different agreements is unacceptable. The effect of cross-collateralisation between a publishing agreement and a recording agreement will allow any monies due to the artist under his publishing agreement to be used to pay any unrecouped sums under his recording agreement, and vice-versa. (*See* Chapter 3 Music Industry Contracts above for cross-collateralisation.)

The artist's solicitor when considering and negotiating the proposed terms of a publishing agreement should also examine the terms of any recording agreement which the artist may already have or which is being offered at the same time as the publishing agreement. There will be clauses in the recording agreement that need to be taken into account when considering and negotiating the proposed terms of a publishing agreement. For example, the recording agreement will contain a controlled composition clause which has an effect on the artist's compositions and so will need to be considered when negotiating the proposed terms of a publishing agreement. (See below for the controlled composition clause.) (For the same reasons when the artist's solicitor is considering and negotiating the proposed terms of a recording agreement he should also examine the terms of any publishing agreement which the artist may have or which is being offered at the same time as the recording agreement.) Where the artist's solicitor is considering the proposed terms of a publishing agreement and there is no recording agreement in existence or on offer (or where the artist's solicitor is considering the proposed terms of a recording agreement and there is no publishing agreement in existence or on offer), he obviously has nothing to compare the proposed agreement against. In this situation, the artist's solicitor would have to consider and negotiate the agreement on offer on the basis of what clauses he would commonly expect to find in the other agreement.

This chapter assumes the artist is both a composer and a performer, that the artist has interest from both a publishing and a recording company, and that the publishing company is looking to sign the composer to a term publishing agreement (in other words the composer agrees to compose and assign his works to the publisher for a period of time).

Before examining in detail the clauses in a term publishing agreement there follows a brief examination of administration, co-publishing and sub-publishing agreements.

Administration agreements

An administration agreement is an agreement whereby one party, the composer, retains 100% of the copyright in his works but uses a publisher to promote the works, to grant licences under the terms of the administration agreement and to collect in and distribute the income from the exploitation of the works throughout the world.

An administration agreement may be used where the composer is established, his works are in demand, and he wants to retain all the copyright but he does not have the time or the ability to exploit the value of his works to their maximum potential, nor does he have the ability to perform all the necessary administrative chores which go with exploiting his works. The publisher who is acting here as an administrator will receive an administration fee in the region of 15–25% of all the income earned during the agreement.

Co-publishing agreements

A co-publishing agreement is an agreement where two or more people have a share in the copyright of the works. For example, an established songwriter may be prepared to assign for a period of time some of the copyright in his works in exchange for a non-returnable but recoupable advance and for a share in the publisher's income.

If the composer owns 100% of the copyright in his works he may be prepared to assign for a period of time say for example, 40% of the copyright to a publisher in exchange for a 50:50 split in the publisher's income from these works. If the works in the first year of a co-publishing agreement earn £200,000, the split between the composer and the publisher will be as follows:

> **Composer (60% of copyright).**
> £120,000 due to composer, *i.e.* 60% of £200,000.
> **Publisher (40% of copyright).**
> £80,000 due to publisher, *i.e.* 40% of £200,000, **BUT** the £80,000 is shared 50:50 between the composer and the publisher. So the publisher is entitled to £40,000 and the composer is entitled to £40,000.

FINAL ACCOUNT FOR YEAR 1.

Composer due £160,000 (£120,000 plus £40,000).
Publisher due £40,000 (£80,000 minus £40,000 due to the composer under the 50:50 split of the publisher's share).

Note 1. Often a publisher would pay a non-returnable but recoupable advance to the composer under the agreement. If this were the case here the £40,000 due to the composer from the publisher would be used to recoup the advance.

Note 2. The co-publishing agreement may provide that the publisher may deduct certain items, *e.g.* an administration fee of 15% from the £80,000 before the 50: 50 division occurs.

Apart from the division of copyright ownership and the division of the publisher's share of income between the publisher and the composer, a co-publishing agreement will deal with many other contractual matters. One particular area relates to the administrative arrangements involved in publishing. For example, will the publisher have the exclusive right to administer the works, or will the publisher have the exclusive right to administer the works but with restrictions which stop him from granting certain types of licence without obtaining the composer's consent?

Another example of where co-publishing may occur is where two composers who are each bound under publishing agreements to different publishers decide that they want to collaborate to write songs together (see below for collaborations). The composers' respective publishing agreements will contain provisions dealing with collaborating with other composers (see below for details), but if the collaboration is to go ahead their publishers will need to sort out how the copyright, income division and administrative arrangements will work. The administrative arrangements can work in several ways, for example, they may agree that:

(a) one publisher has the exclusive right to administer the works, or

(b) one publisher has the exclusive rights to administer the works but with restrictions which stop the publisher granting certain types of licence without the other publisher's consent, or

(c) both publishers will administer their own share of the works, which will mean that if anybody wishes to use the work they will need to obtain a licence from each publisher for the share they administer, or

(d) both parties can administer the whole of the work and grant non-exclusive licences but neither publisher can grant exclusive licences.

The division of income between the respective publishers will usually be in the same ratio as the copyright has been divided. However, there may be cases where the copyright division may not accord with the income division, for example, an established songwriter may collaborate with a relatively unknown songwriter and the copyright may be split 50: 50 but the income may be split more favourably in favour of the established songwriter because it is his name which will increase the usage of the song.

Sub-publishing agreements

A publisher based in England may not be capable of exploiting a composer's works in certain territories and will need to appoint publishers in these territories to enable the works to be exploited worldwide. A publisher who is not capable of exploiting a composer's works in certain territories will enter into agreements with foreign publishers based in these territories, known as sub-publishing agreements, whereby the sub-publisher will be granted the right by the publisher, in the form of a licence, to exploit the works in a particular territory and collect the income from exploiting the works in that territory. A composer who wants to sign with a publishing company which is part of a worldwide group of publishing companies may find that the publisher wants to appoint companies within the group to sub-publish his works. There should be no problem with this, provided the composer is prepared to allow the publisher to appoint sub-publishers and provided the sub-publishing agreements are negotiated at arm's length and so do not contain terms which are more favourable to the sub-publisher than would be found in a sub-publishing agreement between a publisher and an unconnected sub-publisher. (A publisher based in England should obviously not be permitted to appoint a sub-publisher for England. If the composer wants to sign to a publisher who wants to do this he should question the publisher's ability to be a publisher and should seriously consider looking for an alternative publisher.)

A sub-publisher will be appointed by the publisher for a specified period of time which is usually between three and five years. The term of the sub-publishing agreement including any rights extension period should not exceed the term plus the rights extension period of the publishing agreement. (*See* Common clauses in Term publishing agreement below for the rights extension period.) The sub-publishing agreement should detail what rights the sub-publisher is being granted and the territory(ies) for which he is appointed.

A sub-publisher will, for the term of the sub-publishing agreement and for the territory defined in the sub-publishing agreement, fulfill the role of the publisher for the compositions which are the subject of the sub-publishing agreement. The sub-publisher will promote, exploit, administer and collect in the monies relating to the compositions covered by the sub-publishing agreement (with the assistance of the foreign equivalent of the PRS and possibly the foreign equivalent of the MCPS). (*See* Chapter 4 Collecting Societies and Music Industry Associations above for the PRS and the MCPS.) The sub-publisher may possibly pay the publisher a non-returnable but recoupable advance for the right to administer the compositions covered by the sub-publishing agreement. In return the sub-publisher will earn commission on the money received from the exploitation of the works in the territory.

Generally, the sub-publisher's commission will be in the region of 10–25% of the money earned in the territory. However, the actual percentage commission payable depends upon the type of exploitation involved as different types of exploitation will be commissioned at different rates, *e.g.* for sheet music if the sub-publisher licenses a third party to print the sheet music the sub-publisher will receive between 15–25% of the licensed income, whereas for performing income the sub-publisher may receive up to 50% of the publisher's share of the performing income. The reason why the sub-publisher may receive up to 50% of the publisher's share of the performing income is that the composer's share of the performance income is paid directly to the composer by the PRS (once it has been collected by the foreign collecting society and remitted back to the PRS for distribution to the composer), and therefore the only performance income from which the sub-publisher can seek commission is the 50% publisher's share. As the publisher under PRS rules will only be paid a maximum of 50% of the performance income the sub-publisher will need to receive 50% of the publisher's share to enable the sub-publisher to earn the equivalent of 25% of the total performance income earned in the territory.

A sub-publisher will usually seek and generally obtain a higher commission rate for cover recordings made of any of the compositions which are the subject of the sub-publishing agreement. A cover recording should be defined in the sub-publishing agreement so that it is clear exactly what the sub-publisher can charge a higher commission rate upon. A cover recording should be defined in the sub-publishing agreement and will often be defined as a recording of a composition which has been recorded locally in the territory, in the local language, by a local artist, and released in the territory. The sub-publisher may expect a commission rate in the region of 40–50% of the income earned and received in the territory for a cover recording. Tight drafting of the meaning of a cover recording should ensure that there is no dispute between the publisher and the sub-publisher as to whether a particular recording is a cover version and whether the sub-publisher is entitled to a higher rate of commission on that version. Another particular problem with a cover version is that although it is easy to distinguish between sales of the original and sales of the cover version of the composition (because they will show up with different catalogue numbers on the record company records) and so it is easy to calculate how much the sub-publisher is entitled to at the higher and lower rate, if the sub-publisher has negotiated a higher rate for the performance of cover recordings, it is usually not possible to calculate the public performance money attributable to the original composition and the cover version. This is because the collecting societies register the composition under the song title and do not distinguish between the original and the cover version. If the sub-publisher has negotiated a higher commission rate for the performance income for a cover version of the composition there should be a formula in the agreement which provides how this will be calculated, *e.g.* the division of performance income between the original composition and the cover version might be based upon the percentage that sales of the cover version bears to the total number of record sales for the composition in the territory. The logic behind this method, albeit not scientifically foolproof, is that airplay and public performance is directly related to record sales.

The sub-publishing agreement should provide that if an adaptation, alteration, arrangement or translation of a composition has been made, the sub-publisher will ensure that any new copyright created will be assigned to the publisher with the sub-publisher retaining the right to exploit any such adaptation, alteration, arrangement or translation of the composition in the territory under the terms of the sub-publishing agreement. In addition, the moral rights position of the author of any adaptation, alteration, arrangement or translation of the composition should be dealt with in the sub-publishing agreement.

The sub-publishing agreement should provide that if a cover version has been obtained, the sub-publisher will provide the publisher with a copy of the lyrics and will also provide an English language translation. The publisher should have a right to approve the lyrics of a cover version before it is recorded.

The collecting societies will, as their name suggests, collect in the money for each composition and distribute it to those entitled. However, they can only distribute to those members who have registered their interest in the composition. If the collecting society collects in money and does not know to whom it should be sent, the money will be retained. The money retained by a collecting society is commonly known as "black box" money. To ensure a publisher gets paid for the compositions he controls, he should ensure that he always registers his interest in each composition with the mechanical collecting society.

In some countries, *e.g.* France and Holland, after a period of time any undistributed income will be paid out to local registered publishers. The sub-publishing agreement may possibly deal with how any black box income which may be distributed by a mechanical collecting society should be dealt with between the publisher and sub-publisher. The publisher may be able to persuade the sub-publisher in the sub-publishing agreement to account for a percentage of any black box income that the sub-publisher receives. The sub-publisher will frequently resist any attempt by the publisher to share in the black box income. If the publisher's catalogue is an important catalogue which is worth a lot of money to the sub-publisher, the publisher may be able to get some of the black box income which the sub-publisher may receive. Whether the publisher can get some of the black box income depends upon the negotiating strengths of the parties. If the publisher shares in the black box income there will need to be a mechanism to calculate how much the publisher is entitled to receive. The mechanism could, for example, be based upon the proportion that the income the sub-publisher earns from publishing the publisher's catalogue bears to the total income the sub-publisher earns from all publishing.

The publisher should ensure the sub-publishing agreement provides that all the income due to the publisher from the sub-publisher is calculated "at source". This means that the money due to the publisher from the sub-publisher will be calculated on the earnings of the composition in the country where it was earned. So if the money was earned in Italy the percentage due to the publisher will be calculated on the income that arose in Italy. This will prevent double or more than double deductions of commission before it reaches the publisher. For example, if there is a sub-publishing agreement between an English publisher and a Dutch sub-publisher covering the EU, if the agreement provides that the publisher receives 80% of the income earned "at source" if £100 is earned in Italy the publisher will receive £80 and the sub-publisher will retain £20. If there was no "at source" provision the £100 could be subject to double commission as the money collected by the Italian office of the Dutch sub-publisher will be commissioned by the Italian office which will take £20 and then remit £80 to the Dutch sub-publisher in Holland which will take its commission of £16 (20% of £80) and then send £64 to the English publisher. The English publisher by having an "at source" provision will in this example have received £80 rather than £64 if there was no "at source" provision. Without an "at source" provision if the money was sent from the Dutch sub-publisher's offices in Italy to its offices in Germany, then on to its offices in Belgium, then on to its offices in Austria and finally on to Holland, each office could take its cut, thereby reducing the amount due to the English publisher.

A publisher should include a provision in the sub-publishing agreement that the sub-publisher is not allowed to appoint a sub-sub-publisher. Such a provision will avoid possible problems for the publisher tracing which sub-publisher has received what money. It will also avoid possible disputes between the sub-publishers and the publisher that each sub-publisher is entitled to commission the same sources of income which would if correct reduce the amount of money due to the publisher. In addition, the publisher should include a provision which prohibits the sub-publisher from assigning the sub-publishing agreement.

The publishing agreement should contain a clause which provides that where the composer terminates the publishing agreement any royalties which are payable by the sub-publisher to the publisher will be paid directly by the sub-publisher to the composer. Where the publishing agreement contains such provisions, any sub-publishing agreement should contain similar provisions.

The matters discussed above are the some of the more important provisions which specifically relate to sub-publishing agreements. A sub-publishing agreement will obviously contain many more contractual provisions, *e.g.* accounting, auditing clauses (many of which will be similar to those contained in a composer: publisher term publishing agreement which is dealt with below).

Term publishing agreements

A composer who is not a recognised composer will usually be offered one of two types of publishing agreement: either a single song agreement or a term agreement. A single song agreement, as the name suggests, is a publishing agreement for a specific song. A term agreement is one whereby the composer agrees to write exclusively for the publisher for a period of time and the copyright in these compostions will belong to the publisher for the term and the rights extension period stated in the publishing agreement. (See below for The term and the Rights extension period). As the composer will agree to write exclusively for the publisher, care should be taken over the terms of the agreement to ensure the agreement is not liable to be held to be in restraint of trade. (*See* Chapter 3 Music Industry Contracts for Restraint of trade.)

A publishing agreement will usually be between a composer and a publisher, although there may be occasions when a term publishing agreement will be between a composer's company and the publisher. If the publisher contracts with a composer's company, the publisher should ensure the composer's company has the copyright in the compositions vested in it so that it can therefore validly assign the copyright to the publisher. The publisher should also ensure that there is a side letter from the composer guaranteeing that he will personally honour the obligations of the publishing agreement if his company does not do so provided the publisher/publishing company is not in breach of the publishing agreement.

The copyright in the compositions under a term publishing agreement will either be licensed or more commonly assigned to the publisher for a period of time. As there will be a licence or assignment of copyright to the publisher, it will be the publisher who personally contracts with third parties to use the compositions.

Songwriting teams

As seen earlier (*see* Chapter 2 Copyright Law and the Copyright, Designs and Patents Act 1988), if a composer has written a composition there will usually be two copyrights in the work, namely copyright in the words as a literary copyright, and copyright in the music as a musical copyright. These are two separate and distinct copyrights. If the composers are a songwriting team, *e.g.* Elton John and Bernie Taupin, and one writes the words the other writes the music, the publishing agreement will usually state that each work is a separate copyright work. The publishing agreement will need to deal with how the composer's share of the income from each separarate copyright work will be divided between them. Usually the composer's share of the income from the words and the music will be divided equally between the composers even though one of them solely writes the words and the other solely writes the music. However, a 50:50 split of the composer's share of the income from the words and music may not be appropriate. For example, an established successful lyricist may decide to form a songwriting partnership with a new composer with little track record and they enter into a publishing agreement with an established publisher. In this situation a 50: 50 split of the income from the words and the music may not be appropriate. The lyricist may, for example, want 100% of the composer's share of the income from the lyrics and 50% of the composer's share of the income from the music to reflect his belief that the publishing agreement was offered due to his reputation and that any demand for the use of the compositions is primarily due to his reputation. The percentage split of the composer's share of the income from the words and the music needs to be agreed between the songwriting team with the agreed split being inserted into the publishing agreement. If the publisher is not informed of the agreed split the publishing agreement will usually provide that the composer's share of the income from the words and the music will be divided equally between the composers.

If the composer(s) have signed a publishing agreement and they are also performers in a band, the band agreement should also provide how the income earned by the composer under the publishing agreement is dealt with between the band members. (*See* Chapter 5 The Legal Status of Band and Solo Artist.)

As mentioned above, the reason a publishing agreement will separate composers' income into income from the words and income from the music is because a songwriting team may have an unequal division of income between the words and the music which will need to be reflected in the publishing agreement. It is also possible that the words and music as separate and distinct copyright works may be used one without the other, *e.g.* the music may be set to a different set of words. If the publishing agreement separates the composers' income into income from the words and income from the music it will be clear from the publishing agreement how much each party is entitled to receive from the use of that particular copyright work.

Usually a songwriting team will sign one agreement with the publisher rather than two separate publishing agreements. Where a songwriting team is signed to a publisher the songwriters should ensure that the publisher keeps separate accounts for each composer and that the publisher is not able to cross-collateralise between the composers. There are several situations where this could cause a problem for one of the composers. For example, let us assume that there are three composers in a songwriting team and they received an advance from the publisher under their publishing agreement which is shared equally between them. The composers share the composers' share of the income from the words and the tunes which they write together equally. The advance is unrecouped. In this senario the song-writing team all have the same account balance, *i.e.* they are all unre-couped for the same sum. Now imagine that one of the songwriting team decides he no longer wants to compose with the team and so leaves to write on his own. The solo composer now writes a compo-sition that becomes a worldwide hit. The hit composition puts the solo composer into a position where he is now recouped and he will now receive royalty cheques from the publisher. However, if the agreement allows the publisher to cross-collateralise between the composers the solo composer's account which is recouped will be used to recoup the accounts of the other two members of the old songwriting team. The successful composer will be paying out of his own money to recoup the accounts of the other composers. This would not have occurred if there was a provision in the publishing agreement that there can be no cross-collateralising between the individual composer's accounts.

A songwriting team will also want to ensure if possible that the publishing agreement does not provide for joint and several liability where one of the songwriting team is in breach of contract.

The publisher may insert a provision in a songwriting team publishing agreement which allows him, when exercising an option, to choose which member(s) of the songwriting team he wishes to keep under contract. Such a provision allows the publisher to keep the star composer(s) in the songwriting team and to drop the less talented member(s). Any such provision should be resisted by the songwriting team.

If a band composes together a publisher may sign all the members of the band to a publishing agreement. In addition to the publishing agreement which contains the contractual provisions as they exist between the publisher and the band, the band agreement should also deal with the relevant provisions of the publishing agreement as they affect the internal working arrangement of the individual band members. (*See* Chapter 5 The Legal Status of Band and Solo Artist.) Some clauses will be duplicated in both the publishing and band agree-ments, for example, both should contain the same provisions detailing how publishing income is divided between the individual band members, how the order of the writing credits will appear on the record and other published versions of the composition, *i.e.* written by Alan Ashurst, Charles Chaucer, Brian Banks and Dave Dawes, and detail what happens if a member leaves the band or a new member joins.

Collaborations and co-writing

There are occasions when a composer who has a publishing agreement wants to compose with somebody who is not a party to the publishing agreement. The composer should check his publishing agreement to see whether he is allowed to do so and if so on what terms.

Sometimes a publishing agreement requires the composer to obtain the consent of his publisher before he composes with someone else. Some agreements require the composer to tell the proposed collaborator that he already has a publishing agreement and that the proposed collaborator must grant the composer's publisher the same copyright and publishing rights that the composer has given to his publisher. The proposed collaborator will in return share pro-rata with the composer the royalty rate which the composer receives under his publishing agreement.

Some publishing agreements require the composer to get the proposed collaborator to enter into a publishing agreement with the composer's publisher. This requirement may be for a single song agreement or possibly for a single song agreement which with options could become a term publishing agreement.

The above clauses may not be acceptable to a proposed collaborator who although he may want to work with the composer may not want to have any contractual arrangement with that particular publisher. In addition, any clause which requires the composer to get a proposed collaborator over whom he has no control, *e.g.* such as requiring the composer to get the collaborator to enter into a publishing agreement with the composer's publisher, should be resisted by the composer. It is more than likely that the proposed collaborator has his own publishing agreement which contains clauses restricting his ability to collaborate with the composer. If both the composer and the proposed collaborator have their own publishing agreements, before any collaboration can take place their respective publishers will have to sort out the terms of any proposed collaboration. In particular, they will need to sort how the copyright and income is divided between the parties and how the publishing of the composition(s) will be handled by the publishers.

It should be noted that some publishing agreements provide that at least 50% of the copyright in the composition has to be delivered to the publisher for it to count towards the minimum commitment. A composer would prefer this provision to be amended so that any percentage of the copyright which he delivers to the publisher will count towards the minimum commitment. (*See* Minimum commitment below.)

The controlled composition clause

Before looking at the common clauses in the term publishing agreement, it is necessary to look at the controlled composition clause in the recording agreement for records which are released in the US and Canada. It should be noted that some record companies will want such a clause to apply to records which are released in all the territories covered by the recording agreement. (*See* Chapter 8 Recording Agreements, Mechanical Licences for how to try to deal with a recording agreement controlled composition clause). As mentioned earlier, (*see* Introduction above), the artist's solicitor when considering and negotiating the proposed terms of a publishing agreement should also examine the contents of any recording agreement which the artist may already have or which he is being offered at the same time as the publishing agreement. This is because there will be clauses in the recording agreement that need to be taken into account when considering and negotiating the proposed terms of a publishing agreement. (Likewise, when the artist's solicitor is considering and negotiating the proposed terms of a recording agreement he should also examine the contents of any publishing agreement which the artist may have or which is being offered at the same time as the recording agreement.) The controlled composition clause in a recording agreement is possibly the best example of why the artist's solicitor should, when considering and negotiating the proposed terms of a publishing agreement, also examine the contents of any recording agreement which the artist may already have or which he is being offered at the same time as the publishing agreement.

A recording agreement will often define a controlled composition as a composition which has been written by, or is owned by, or is controlled by the recording artist. Therefore, if the artist is a composer and a recording artist and he has written a composition which he wants to record, this composition will be regarded as a controlled composition under his recording agreement.

A mechanical licence will need to be obtained from the copyright owners of the words and music of a song to enable the artist to record the song for his album, for copies of the recording to be made, e.g. on cassette, CD and for copies of the recording to be distributed to the shops for sale to the public. If the artist is a composer and a recording artist and he wants to record one of his own songs, the mechanical licence will be obtained either from himself as the composer or where he has a publisher, from the publisher. As will be seen below, it is the record company's responsibility to pay the mechanical licence fees.

In the United States and Canada the cost of a mechanical licence to record a composition is determined by the length of each composition. In the United States from 1 January 2000, the cost of a mechanical licence for a composition lasting five minutes or less is 7.55 cents for each recording. This is known as the statutory rate. If a composition lasts over five minutes the rate is 1.45 cents for each minute or fraction of a minute that the composition lasts.

Outside the United States and Canada the cost of a mechanical licence is calculated in completely different way. The method of calculation in this country is based upon a percentage of the published dealer price ("PDP") which is the price the record company sells the record to dealers. The current rate is 8.5% of the PDP excluding VAT. The 8.5% royalty covers all the compositions on the record, therefore, the same amount is payable by the record company whether there are six, eight, 14 or 17 compositions on the record. To calculate what percentage of the 8.5% of the PDP the composer/publisher of an individual composition is entitled to receive, the total playing time of the whole record is divided by the total playing time of the composition. For example, if there are 10 compositions of five minutes each, the total playing time of the record is 50 minutes and each composition is entitled to 10% of the 8.5% of the PDP. If there are 10 compositions, five of which are 2 minutes 30 seconds long and five of which are 7 minutes 30 seconds long the total playing time of the record is 50 minutes. A composition lasting 2 minutes 30 seconds will be entitled to 5% (and a composition lasting 7 minutes 30 seconds will be entitled to 15%) of the 8.5% of the PDP.

Record companies, like all businesses, do not like paying out money before they have received money. Record companies have to incur substantial expenses before they actually sell any of their artists' recordings. As well as the normal costs involved in recording, manufacturing, and promoting the recordings, the record company will usually pay the artist a non returnable but recoupable advance against future record sales. As record companies will be paying for the mechanical licences to use the compositions on the recordings, they may commonly find that they are paying mechanical licence fees to use the compositions to a composer who is also their recording artist to whom they have given an advance under the recording agreement which is unrecouped. Unless the record company is able to cross-collateralise the recording and publishing agreement (which as mentioned above the artist's lawyer should ensure does not happen), the record company will find itself paying sizeable sums to an artist in his capacity as a composer which they would want, but cannot use to recoup the recording advance given to the artist in his capacity as a recording artist. (Where the composer has a publishing agreement the mechanical licence fee will be paid to the publisher which the composer will partially benefit from in the form of royalty payments from the publisher. Therefore, the record company will still be paying money which will reach the artist in his capacity as a composer which they would want, but can not use to recoup the recording advance given to the artist in his capacity as a recording artist.)

As seen above, in this country the mechanical rate is based upon a set figure (8.5% of PDP) irrespective of the number of compositions on the record, whereas in the United States and Canada the mechanical rate is per composition and is based upon the length of each composition. Therefore, in the United States and Canada the length and number of compositions included on a recording determine the amount of mechanicals the record company has to pay. The record company will include a controlled composition clause in the recording agreement to limit the amount of mechanicals it will have to pay to a composer who is also its recording artist (or where he has a publishing agreement, to his publisher) where it releases his compositions in the US and Canada. As mentioned above, some record companies will want such a clause to apply to records which are released in all the territories covered by the recording agreement. (*See* Chapter 8 Recording Agreements, Mechanical Licences for how to try to deal with a recording agreement controlled composition clause). Also, some record companies will try to limit the mechanicals payable on all the compositions the artist wants to record and not just on controlled compositions. (*See* Chapter 8 Recording Agreements, Mechanical Licences for how to try to deal with a recording agreement which contains a clause limiting the mechanicals payable on all the compositions which the artist wants to record.)

As already mentioned a controlled composition clause will enable the record company to limit the amount they have to pay for a mechanical licence in the United States and Canada for the use of a controlled composition. They will usually say that they will only have to pay 75% of the "minimum" statutory rate for the use of each controlled composition. This means the rate is based on a composition lasting five minutes or less, even if the composition lasts for more than five minutes. In addition, the rate is fixed to a particular date (*e.g.* the date the composition was recorded or the date of delivery of the master recordings to the record company) thereby avoiding any record company liability to pay 75% of a higher rate should the minimum statutory rate increase.

Notwithstanding the record company reducing the amount of mechanicals to (say) 75% of the minimum statutory rate, the record company could still face substantial mechanical licence fees where the artist records a large number of compositions for his record. This is because, as has been mentioned earlier, in the United States and Canada, the mechanical fee is per composition not per record. Alert to this problem record companies will include a clause in the recording agreement limiting the total amount of compositions for which they will pay a mechanical fee per album. For example, the record company may say that there is a limit of 11 or 12 times 75% of the minimum statutory rate for a CD, and 10 times 75% of the minimum statutory rate for a cassette. This means that the record company will only pay for 10 compositions on a cassette at 75% of the minimum statutory rate, *i.e.* they will only pay mechanicals to a maximum of 56.625 cents per cassette.

A clause in the recording agreement which

(a) limits the amount payable per controlled composition and
(b) puts a ceiling on the number of compositions for which a mechanical licence fee is payable

enables the record company to limit the total amount of mechanical licence fees for which it has agreed with the artist it will be responsible.

Where the controlled composition clause applies to all the territories covered by the recording agreement, the recording agreement will, as well as dealing with the mechanical licence fee payable for the US and Canada, also need to deal with the mechanical licence fee payable for all the territories save for the US and Canada. The fee may be for example 75% of the industry rate (i.e. 75% of the 8.5% of PDP).

The effect of a controlled composition clause is that:

(a) If the artist is a composer and a recording artist, where he records his own compositions he will have to do so at a lower mechanical rate. If he has a publishing agreement or intends to sign one, it is imperative that his solicitor ensures that a clause is inserted into the publishing agreement providing that the publisher will license his compositions to the record company at the rate provided for in the recording agreement. If this clause is not included in the publishing agreement the publisher can refuse to grant the artist's record company a mechanical licence at the lower rate which was agreed between the artist and the record company in the recording agreement. In reality what would happen in this situation is that the publisher will grant a mechanical licence at the normal rate e.g. for the United States the publisher will grant a mechanical licence at the statutory rate and the difference between the statutory rate and the lower mechanical rate provided for in the controlled composition clause in the recording agreement will be paid for by the artist out of his own pocket.

(b) If the performer wants to exceed the total limits in the controlled composition clause, *i.e.* (a) the per composition limit and (b) the total amount payable per CD or cassette, any excess will be paid for by the artist out of his own pocket.

It should be noted that a controlled composition clause may be drafted to provide that all compositions which the artist intends to record and not just compositions written by, owned by or controlled by the artist will be licensed at a lower rate. This provision should be resisted by the artist's solicitor. An artist will not usually be able to get another composer or his publisher to accept a royalty rate which is less than the normal rate. If the artist's recording agreement does contain such a provision and the artist wants to record another composer's composition, all the artist can do is either tell the composer or his publisher that he will not record the composition unless the composition is licensed at a lower rate or the artist will have to pay the difference between the normal and lower rates himself out of his own pocket.

The record company may possibly agree to some variation in the proposed controlled composition clause in the recording agreement. (This will be dealt with in Chapter 8 Recording Agreements, Mechanical Licences.)

Common clauses in term publishing agreement

The term

The term of a publishing agreement, which is the period for which the composer will compose and will deliver the minimum commitment to the publisher, will usually be for a set period with a series of options. (*See below* for Minimum Commitment. For what is meant by compose and deliver see Composer's Warranties and Obligations below). For example, the term may be for a one-year period with three or four one-year options. (Some publishing agreements provide that if the publisher has not notified the composer whether he intends to exercise the option, the composer must send the publisher a notice asking him whether he intends to exercise the option and in addition the publisher will have a period of time from the composer's notice to decide whether to exercise the option. Any such provision should be resisted by the composer's solicitor. After all the publisher should be on the ball and he should know when the option is exercisable. It should not be the composer's responsibility to notify the publisher of his right to exercise an option.) If the publishing agreement is being entered into at the same time as a recording agreement and the publishing and recording companies are related companies, the term of the publishing agreement may be the same length as the term of the recording agreement.

Minimum commitment

The composer will have to satisfy a minimum commitment during the term and during each option period. The minimum commitment may be that the composer has to compose and deliver a certain number of compositions during the term and during each option period. For example, the agreement may require the composer to compose and deliver 20 compositions during the term and 20 further compositions during each option period. (For what is meant by compose and deliver, see Composer's warranties and obligations below.) Where a number of compositions is required to satisfy the minimum commitment, the solicitor acting for the composer should establish whether the composer is capable of composing the number of compositions required to satisfy the minimum commitment. If not, the composer's solicitor should attempt to negotiate a more realistic minimum commitment. The composer's solicitor should ensure that the minimum commitment clause allows the composer where he has co-written a composition to count his percentage share of the copyright in the co-written composition which he delivers to the publisher towards the minimum commitment. (*See also* (c) below for further comments about the minimum percentage which the publisher may require for a co-written composition to count towards the minimum commitment.)

Sometimes the minimum commitment is not based upon a writing criteria but upon the recording and release of the compositions on a record. Such a clause is only appropriate if the composer is also a recording artist with a recording agreement. However, even if he is both a composer and a recording artist with a recording agreement, great care should still be taken with such a minimum commitment clause. A minimum commitment clause for the term may, for example, require an album to be recorded by the composer which contains 100% of the composer's compositions and which has been released by a major record company in the United Kingdom and in the United States. Several problems arise with such a clause. There needs to be a definition of what constitutes an album, what is a major record company and what constitutes release. For example, a release may be defined as a commercial release of the album (as defined) by a major record company (as defined) on the major record company's top line label. These terms need to be drafted in such a way that they are not too onerous on the composer so that he can satisfy the minimum commitment. Three problems arise with the example minimum commitment clause.

(a) The requirement to have the album released in the United Kingdom and the United States is onerous in that it is difficult enough to guarantee that a record will be released in one territory let alone two territories, and in any event unless the artist has a clause in his recording agreement guaranteeing the record company will release the record, any requirement in a minimum commitment clause that his record will be released by a record company is beyond his control.

(b) There is a requirement that the album contains 100% of the composer's compositions. This means that if the composer records a composition written by somebody else, then he has not satisfied the minimum commitment. The figure of 100% should therefore be reduced, say, to 75% to allow the composer to record compositions written by somebody else. This should also enable the artist to satisfy the minimum commitment clause.

(c) The requirement that the album contains 100% of the composers' compositions would mean that if the composer co-writes a composition and records it for the album, that he has not satisfied the minimum commitment. The figure of 100% should be reduced, say, to 75% to allow the composer to co-write and record his co-written compositions and so enable him to satisfy the minimum commitment clause. In addition there should be a provision in the minimum commitment clause which allows the composer where he has co-written and recorded a composition, to count his percentage share of the copyright in the co-written and recorded composition which he delivers to the publisher toward the minimum commitment.

Therefore if the composer has co-written and recorded two compositions and in one of them he has 70% of the copyright and in the other he has 30% of the copyright, the composer is effectively delivering a total of one composition (i.e. 70%+30%=100% = one composition) to be counted toward the minimum commitment. The publisher may want the minimum commitment clause drafted to provide that a co-written composition which is recorded by the composer will only count towards the minimum commitment if he receives at least 50% of the copyright in the composition from the composer. This is because the publisher ideally wants 100% of the copyright in each composition. The publisher will not want odds and ends of 5 or 10% of the copyright in each composition used to count towards the minimum commitment as such small amounts of copyright require as much if not more effort to promote and will bring in less commission. The composer would prefer any such clause which provides that a composition will only count toward the minimum commitment if the publisher receives at least 50% of the copyright to be amended so that any percentage of the copyright which he has in a composition which he has co-written and recorded will count towards the minimum commitment. (*See also* Collaborations above for details of other provisions which may affect the ability of the composer to collaborate.)

As can be seen, a minimum commitment clause must be examined carefully to see if the composer is capable of complying with it for the term and each option. If the composer does not satisfy the minimum commitment this will have two consequences for the composer.

1. The minimum commitment clause along with any clause dealing with any advance payable to the composer will provide either that any subsequent advance(s) payable will be suspended until the minimum commitment has been satisfied, or any subsequent advance(s) will be reduced in proportion to the amount of compositions delivered as against the minimum commitment required. If, for example, the minimum commitment for the first year was 20 compositions, if the composer only writes 15 compositions any subsequent advance will be 75% of the advance he would have received had he satisfied the agreed minimum commitment.

2. If the minimum commitment has not been satisfied, the agreement will provide that the term (or the option) will be extended until the minimum commitment has been satisfied.

This will also mean that the date(s) for the exercise of any subsequent option(s) under the agreement will be put back in time.

One problem that will exist for a publisher under any clause that allows for the term or any option to be extended until the minimum commitment has been satisfied is that the composer could claim the agreement is in retraint of trade. This argument is, as has been seen earlier, one that artists have used in the past and with some considerable success. In an attempt to protect the publisher from an allegation that the agreement is in restraint of trade there should be a long stop provision in the agreement providing that if the minimum commitment has not been satisfied the term (or the option term) will continue until it has been satisfied but in any event the term (or the option term) will not last for more than two years. This will provide a maximum length that the term or any option term can last and may enable the publisher to rebut an allegation by the composer that the publishing agreement is in restraint of trade.

Rights extension period

As mentioned above, the agreement term is the period for which the composer will compose and will deliver the minimum commitment to the publisher, *e.g.* for a term of three years the composer will compose and deliver to the publisher a total of 20 compositions a year. (For what is meant by compose and deliver *see* Composer's Warranties and Obligations below.) The publishing agreement may provide that the copyright in the compositions will be assigned to the publisher for the full copyright term and for any renewals and extensions of copyright. A composer should not give the publisher copyright in the compositions for the full copyright term and for any renewals and extensions of copyright. The composer should allow the publisher a reasonable time to exploit the compositions to enable the publisher to recoup his expenditure and to make money from his efforts exploiting the compositions.

Most publishing agreements rather than provide for the copyright in the compositions to be assigned to the publisher for the full copyright term and for any renewals and extensions of copyright will provide the publisher instead with a shorter period which is known as the rights extension period, also known as the rights period. The rights extension period which will usually be for a period of 15 to 20 years, is the period of time over and above the agreement term which the publisher has to exploit the compositions which were delivered to him by the composer during the term. The publisher will therefore have the right to exploit the compositions for the agreement term and the rights extension period. At the end of the rights extension period the publisher will no longer have the right to exploit the compositions. The publisher may provide that the rights extension period is, say, 15 years but will be 20 years for those compositions for which the publisher has obtained a cover recording or a synchronisation use. (The term cover recording will need to be defined so that it is clear what entitles the publisher to a longer rights extension period. A cover recording will often be defined as any recording other than (i) a recording of the composition which has been produced by the composer or (ii) a recording of the composition by the composer as a solo performer or with others, or (iii) a recording by a third party which is made due to the direct effort of the composer to get the third party to record the composition.)

It should be noted that at the end of the rights extension period there will be some income which is still to be received by the publisher, *e.g.* from record companies, which is attributable to the exploitation of the compositions by the publisher during the rights extension period and upon which the publisher is entitled to commission. The agreement should deal with who will collect this income. The publisher will usually want the agreement to provide that at the end of the rights extension period he can collect in the income which is attributable to the exploitation of the compositions during the rights extension period for a period of one year. Such a clause does not allow the publisher to continue to exploit the compositions after the rights extension period but merely allows him to collect in the income which is outstanding at the end of the rights extension period.

Once the agreement term (including any options which the publisher may take up) has ended, the composer is free to sign a publishing agreement with another publisher. The compositions under the previous agreement cannot usually be licensed or assigned by the composer in a subsequent publishing agreement because they remain with the previous publisher for the term of the rights extension period. The composer can only licence or assign these compositions in any subsequent publishing agreement if the rights have re-vested in him. (*See* Re-assignment of Compositions below.) (It should be noted that where the publisher re-assigns the compositions to the composer, the re-assignment may have to be subject to, and with the benefit of, any agreements which the publisher has entered into with third parties relating to the compositions. Where this is the case if the composer licenses or assigns these compositions in a subsequent publishing agreement, the licence or assignment by the composer to the new publisher should be subject to, and with the benefit of, those agreements which still relate to the compositions.)

Where the composer enters a subsequent publishing agreement with a new publisher and licenses or assigns his previous compositions to the new publisher, the new publisher will want a clause in the publishing agreement which allows him to collect the income from the previous compositions during the term of the agreement and during the rights extension period. Where the previous publishing agreement gives the previous publisher the right to collect, for a period of time after the rights extension period any income which is due and outstanding from exploiting the compositions during the rights extension period, the new publishing agreement should exclude the new publisher's right to collect this money for the period that the previous publisher has this right.

Territory

The publisher will want the right to publish the compositions worldwide. Generally, a composer will grant the publisher rights for the world. Some very successful composers may be able to limit the territories for which the publisher is appointed and so will appoint different publishers for different territories. (If the territory is not worldwide it will usually be limited to named countries, although it is possible to limit the territories to defined regions, *e.g.* North America and Canada, or by reference to language, *e.g.* granting publishing rights for countries whose primary language is Spanish.)

Not all publishers have the ability to exploit compositions throughout the world. Each territory has its own peculiarities and generally it is best for a publisher to be based in the territory where a composition is going to be exploited so that the publisher can use his local knowledge and contacts to exploit the composition to its maximum potential. A composer may attempt to use this argument to try to limit the publisher's territory. Most publishers will not accept this argument as they will say that even if they are not based in each territory they have their own contacts in each territory who can and will exploit the compositions properly. This will be done by the publisher entering sub-publishing agreements for the exploitation of the compositions. (See above and below for sub-publishing agreements.)

Grant of rights to the publisher

The composer will either assign or exclusively license the copyright in the compositions which are the subject of the publishing agreement to the publisher. The composer would prefer to grant a licence (which is a contractual right) whereas the publisher would prefer an assignment (which is a property right) of the copyright in the compositions.

Whether a licence or an assignment is granted the composer should ensure the agreement provides that any rights granted by the licence or assignment are conditional upon the publisher performing his contractual obligations. (*See below* for Publisher's Obligations).

If the compositions are assigned, the rights clause will contain a title guarantee from the composer to the publisher. The composer should be able to give "full title guarantee" which means that the rights in the compositions are free from all charges and encumbrances and are free from all other third party rights other than any charges, encumbrances or rights which the composer does not and could not reasonably be expected to know of. Full title guarantee is the best title guarantee available and the publisher will expect the composer when assigning the compositions under the agreement to give this guarantee. If the compositions are licensed no title guarantee will be given. A licence which is a contractual right does not have a title guarantee, whereas an assignment which is a property right would usually have a title guarantee.

As mentioned above, the composer will either assign or exclusively license the copyright in the compositions which are the subject of the publishing agreement to the publisher. There needs to be very careful consideration of exactly what works are included in the publishing agreement. The publisher will often seek rights to all the composer's past works as well as those which will be created in the future. The composer must consider very carefully not only whether he is prepared to give the publisher rights over his past compositions but also whether he is able to give the publisher those rights. It may be that the composer had a previous publishing agreement and the compositions which his new publisher wants will probably still be controlled by his previous publisher by virtue of the rights extension clause. If the composer is not able to give the new publisher rights over any of his past compositions he should specifically exclude these from the agreement. From a drafting perspective rather than have a clause which provides that the composer grants the publisher rights in all his past compositions except for certain named compositions, it would be better specifically to name all those compositions which the publisher will receive and all those compositions which are excluded from the agreement.

The rights which the composer will usually grant the publisher in the compositions may include the right to:

(a) use the title of composition,
(b) use the characters featured in the composition,
(c) print sheet music,
(d) grant mechanical licences,
(e) grant synchronisation licences,
(f) translate the lyrics into another language,
(g) alter, adapt, add to, delete parts from, the lyrics and the music,
(h) translate the lyrics.

The rights which the composer may grant the publisher may be restricted by the composer, *e.g.* the composer will allow the publisher to grant synchronisation licences but he may stop the publisher from granting a synchronisation licence for certain types of use, for example, he may not want his compositions associated with tobacco products and so the publisher will be stopped from granting synchronisation licences for such uses, or he will allow the publisher the right to translate the lyrics but he will want the right to approve the translated lyrics. (Other examples where the publisher's rights may be restricted by the composer are examined below).

As was seen earlier, (Chapter 4 — Collecting Societies and Music Industry Associations), the Performing Rights Society, the PRS, requires an assignment from its members of the performing right in the compositions. As the publisher will require the composer to join the PRS, the publishing agreement should expressly exclude an assignment of the performing right in the compositions to the publisher.

In addition to the rights in the compositions, the publisher will want the right to use the composer's name and likeness, any trade mark belonging to the composer, and the composer's biographical details in order to promote the compositions. This should be acceptable to the composer, provided it is made clear in the agreement that the publisher only has the right to use the composer's name and likeness etc to promote the compositions and not for any other purposes. The composer will want the right to approve any proposed use of his name and likeness etc by the publisher in any proposed promotional material. The publisher will often only be prepared to consult the composer about the proposed use and content of any proposed promotional material which bears the composer's name and likeness etc. Where a publisher is prepared to let the composer have approval rights, the publisher will at most usually only agree to the composer having qualified approval rights, *i.e.* that the composer's approval will not be unreasonably withheld.

The publisher will want the composer to waive all his moral rights which he has under the CDPA. Although the composer may be prepared to waive the section 84 false attribution right and the section 85 right to privacy of certain photographs and films, he will not want to waive the section 77 right to be identified as the author of a work (the paternity right), nor the section 80 right to object to the derogatory treatment of his work (the integrity right). Indeed the author will want to protect the section 77 paternity right by asserting his right in accordance with the provisions of section 78. The composer may be prepared to accept a contractual right to be attributed as the author of the compositions in exchange for him agreeing not to assert his statutory paternity right. However, the composer should ensure that the contractual right to be attributed as the author of the compositions is not qualified in any way before he agrees to waive his statutory paternity right. The composer should be very wary about waiving his statutory integrity right under section 80 of the CDPA. The publisher will require a waiver of the integrity right from the composer as without it the publisher will be seriously hampered in his ability to exploit the compositions to their maximum potential. The composer will be equally concerned to ensure that his compositions are not used in a way in which he does not approve. A compromise solution which would enable the composer to waive his integrity right would be if the publishing agreement contains an absolute prohibition on his compositions being used for certain activities, *e.g.* if the composer has a strong dislike for alcohol he could bar his compositions being used in connection with advertising alcoholic products, and there could be a provision that the composer can approve the use (which the publisher will require not to be unreasonably withheld) of his compositions for other listed activities which the composer may have some concerns about associating with his compositions.

As for the other moral rights namely, the section 84 false attribution right and the section 85 right to privacy of certain photographs and films, these will in practice be of little concern to a composer and the composer will usually be prepared to waive these rights. However, if the composer is concerned that the publisher might be inclined to attribute a sub-standard composition written by someone other than him to him then he should not waive the section 84 right. (The publisher/composer relationship is based considerably on trust, and if the composer is concerned that the publisher might be inclined to attribute a sub-standard composition written by someone other than him to him then perhaps the composer should question whether he should in fact be entering a publishing agreement with the publisher.)

Composer's warranties and obligations

The obligations under the publishing agreement will require the composer to compose solely and exclusively for the publisher during the term of the agreement. The exclusive nature of the agreement means that the publisher should try to ensure the agreement is not one which is likely to be in restraint of trade (*see* Chapter 3 Music Industry Contracts above for Restraint of trade).

The word "compose" will need to be defined and will include all the musical compositions and lyrics which have been written by, and composed by the composer, either alone or in collaboration with others. The definition will often include any musical arrangements, adaptations and orchestrations by the composer, either alone or in collaboration with others. (*See* above for Collaborations.)

There will be obligations upon the composer to satisfy the minimum commitment (see above for the Minimum commitment) and for the delivery to the publisher of the compositions which form the subject matter of the agreement. The word "delivery" will need to defined in the agreement so the composer knows exactly what he has to send to the publisher when he has written a composition. "Delivery" may mean that the composer is required to send the publisher a musically notated copy of the written composition with a written copy of the lyrics. The term "musical notation" may be drafted to require the composer to send not only the musical notation of the melody line but also the musical notation for all instruments intended to be used on the composition and the vocal arrangements. "Delivery" may be drafted in such a way that all the composer needs to send the publisher is a recorded demo of the composition. Many publishing agreements require "delivery" not only of a demo recording of the composition but also the musical notation of the melody line, the full instrumentation and vocal arrangement together with a written copy of the lyrics. If the composer is not able to write a musical notation, the agreement should be checked and if necessary amended by his solicitor to ensure that "delivery" will be satisfied by receipt of a recorded demo of the composition. The composer will also be required to supply the publisher with details of the appropriate writing credit(s) for the compositions.

The composer will be required to execute any necessary confirmatory documentation which the publisher requires to enable him to exploit the compositions. For example, a confirmatory copyright assignment of the composition will be required by the publisher so that the publisher can register the composition with the PRS and the MCPS.

Other obligations which will be placed upon the composer will include a requirement:

(a) To compose during the term to the best of his ability.

(b) To join the PRS.

(c) To keep the contents of the agreement confidential. The clause will allow disclosure of the contents of the agreement to the composer's lawyer, accountant, bank, financial adviser and manager.

(d) To keep the publisher informed as to where he can be contacted.

(e) (That if the publisher wants to take out insurance cover on the composer), the composer will attend a medical examination, if required by the publisher's insurance company. He will, where insurance cover has been taken out by the publisher, comply with any reasonable requirements of the insurance company to ensure that the insurance policy remains in force.

(f) To compose and represent himself only under his professional name.

(g) (Where the minimum commitment clause is based upon the recording and release of the composer's compositions), to record and release the compositions with a major record company. (*See* Minimum commitment above for recording and releasing compositions with a major record company.)

The publisher may want the right to require the composer to compose with other people selected by the publisher. The composer should not agree to this. There is nothing wrong with the publisher suggesting that the composer collaborates with somebody else but there should be no obligation upon the composer to work with someone chosen by the publisher.

The publisher may need the help of the composer to exploit the compositions to their maximum potential. The publisher may therefore want a clause in the agreement requiring the composer to help him promote the compositions. As the composer will have other professional commitments which will need to be honoured he should ensure that the clause is drafted so that he will only be required to help promote the compositions subject to his availability. In addition, the composer will want the publisher to give him, for example, 14 days' advance notice of when he is required to help promote the compositions, and may also want to limit the amount of promotional work that he is required to do to a maximum number of days a year. The composer should require the publisher to pay those travel, hotel and other expenses which he incurs whilst helping the publisher to promote the compositions.

The warranties which the composer will have to give the publisher include that:

(a) He is the owner of the compositions.

(b) He is a qualifying person under the CDPA. (*See* Chapter 2 Copyright Law and the Copyright, Designs and Patents Act 1988, Author requirement (s154) for the qualifying person under the CDPA.)

(c) The compositions are original.

(d) None of the compositions have been previously exploited and there are no restrictions on the use of the compositions. Any compositions which have been previously exploited (*e.g.* under a previous publishing agreement) or which are subject to restrictions on their use (e.g. because they have been written in collaboration with another person and the composer does not own all the copyright in them) should be excluded from the warranty.

(e) The compositions are not obscene, defamatory, blasphemous, nor infringe any copyright or third party rights.

(f) There is no litigation or threat of litigation concerning any previous compositions which are being licensed/assigned to the publisher under the publishing agreement.

(g) He is not a minor.

(h) He is free to enter into the agreement.

(i) He is not suffering from any disability which prevents him from providing his services.

(j) He has taken independent legal advice from a solicitor with experience of music agreements.

(k) He will keep the contents of the agreement confidential. The clause should allow the composer to disclose the contents of the agreement to his lawyer, accountant, bank, financial adviser and his manager.

The indemnity clause by the composer

The publishing agreement will contain an indemnity clause requiring the composer to indemnify the publisher for all the costs, liabilities, losses and damage which have been incurred by the publisher due to any breach or non performance by the composer of the publishing agreement. The composer should try to limit the scope of the indemnity so that he will only be liable to indemnify the publisher for specific breaches of the agreement. In addition, the composer should try to limit liability for the publisher's cost to the reasonable costs which have been reasonably incurred by the publisher, or to the publisher's reasonable legal and other professional costs.

The publisher may include a provision allowing him to withhold the composer's royalties in the event of there being any legal action concerning the composer in which the publisher is involved. This would enable the publisher to offset the money he is withholding against any loss or damage which he incurs, rather than have to pursue the composer for the money due to him under an indemnity clause. The composer should not agree to such a provision. The composer may possibly be prepared to agree to a similar provision which will allow the publisher to withhold his royalties provided:

(i) the legal action involves a material breach of the composer's obligations, and

(ii) a limit is put on the amount of money which the record company can withhold, and

(iii) any money withheld will be put on deposit to earn interest, and

(iv) that where the threat of legal proceedings does not lead to the issue of court proceeding within a specified time the money which has been withheld will be returned to the composer together with accrued interest.

Publisher's obligations

The obligations which will be placed upon the publisher will include a requirement:

(a) To pay the composer a non-returnable but recoupable advance(s).

(b) To collect the income due from the exploitation of the compositions.

(c) Twice a year, within for example 30 days of the end of each accounting period, to send a royalty statement to the composer.

(d) To send along with the royalty statement any royalty money which is due to the composer.

(e) To keep accounts of all income which he has received relating to the exploitation of the compositions. (*See* Accounting and auditing below.)

(f) To publish, promote and exploit the compositions. The composer will want an obligation on the publisher to use his best endeavours to publish, promote and exploit the compositions. The publisher may only be prepared to use his reasonable endeavours. Whether a best endeavours or reasonable endeavours clause will be given will depend upon the negotiating strengths of each party and their solicitors.

(g) To inform the composer when a composition has been used.

(h) To ensure that the relevant copyright notices are inserted when the composition(s) are used.

(i) To register the works with the PRS and the MCPS.

(j) (where the composer has a recording agreement with a controlled composition clause) to grant a mechanical licence to the composer's record company for him to record his compositions at the rate provided for in his recording agreement (*See* The controlled composition clause above).

(k) To take legal action to protect the compositions if the copyright in them has been infringed, and to consult with and keep the composer informed as to the progress in any such action. The publisher will want the composer to indemnify him for any legal costs he incurs in pursuing any such action.

(l) To defend any legal action which alleges copyright infringement by the composer, and to consult with and keep the composer informed as to the progress in any such action. The publisher will want the composer to indemnify him for any legal costs he incurs in defending any such action.

(m) To keep the contents of the agreement confidential. The confidentiality clause should allow the publisher to disclose the contents of the agreement to his lawyer, accountant, bank and financial adviser.

The indemnity clause by the publisher

The publishing agreement should contain an indemnity clause requiring the publisher to indemnify the composer for all the costs, liabilities, losses and damage which have been incurred by the composer due to any breach or non performance by the publisher of the publishing agreement. The publisher should try to limit the scope of the indemnity so that he will only be liable to indemnify the composer for specific breaches of the agreement. In addition, the publisher should try to limit liability for the composer's costs to the reasonable costs which have been reasonably incurred by the composer, or to the composer's reasonable legal and other professional costs.

Sub-publishing

The sub-publishing agreement between a publisher and sub-publisher was considered above. The publishing agreement between the composer and the publisher will usually contain provisions which allows the publisher to appoint a sub-publisher where necessary.

The composer will be concerned to ensure that his compositions will be exploited to their best potential and that the income to which he is entitled will not be reduced by the appointment of any sub-publisher.

The composer would ideally want the publishing agreement to provide that his royalties from exploiting his compositions in a foreign territory will be calculated "at source". This means that the money due to the composer would be calculated on the earnings of the composition in the country where it was earned. A publisher will frequently not agree to such a clause. Only the most successful composers may be able, (if they are very fortunate), to get such a clause in their publishing agreement. A publisher will not accept an "at source" clause because this would mean the composer's royalty would be calculated before the sub-publisher has deducted his commission and therefore the sub-publisher's commission will come out of the publisher's share. The only deductions which would be made if an "at source" basis of calculation were used would be the commission deducted by foreign collecting societies and any VAT or sales tax payable in the territory. The publisher will want to calculate the composer's royalties on a "receipts" basis, which means the composer's royalties will be calculated on the money which the publisher has received after the deduction of the foreign collecting societies' commission, any VAT or sales tax payable in the territory, and the deduction of the sub-publisher's commission and other agreed expenses as set out in the sub-publishing agreement.

For example, if the publishing agreement contains a clause providing for the composer's royalties to be calculated "at source" and the composer receives a 60% royalty, and a sub-publishing agreement exists providing the sub-publisher with a 25% commission, if (after deducting the commission of the collecting society and VAT in the territory) the sub-publisher has generated income of £100,000 from the compositions in the territory covered in the sub-publishing agreement, the composer will be entitled to £60,000 of that money, the sub-publisher will be entitled to £25,000, and the publisher will be entitled to £15,000. If the publishing agreement did not contain an "at source" provision for calculating the composer's royalty, but instead contained a provision that the composer's royalty would be calculated on a "receipts" basis, under a "receipts" basis the sub-publisher would be entitled to £25,000, the composer would be entitled to £45,000 (60% of £75,000, being the £100,000 less the £25,000 commission due to the sub-publisher), and the publisher would be entitled to £30,000 (40% of £75,000).

If the composer is unable to get his income calculated "at source", he should still attempt to limit the amounts which can be deducted due to the existence of any sub-publishing agreements which cover his compositions. For example, the composer could:

(a) seek a clause in the publishing agreement requiring the publisher to ensure that the income payable by the sub-publisher to the publisher under a sub-publishing agreement is calculated "at source". This will avoid the possibility of double deduction of commission and therefore the publisher's income under the sub-publishing agreement, (out of which the composer's commission is calculated) is maximised. (*See* Sub-publishing agreements above for how double commission may arise), or

(b) seek a clause in the publishing agreement placing a ceiling on the amount of commission that is payable to a sub-publisher.

The composer should not let the publisher appoint more than one sub-publisher in each territory. Some publishers will not agree to such a limitation. If the composer is prepared to concede this point he should only do so on the basis that there is a maximum amount of income that can be retained by the sub-publishers in each territory. This will ensure that the composer's income is not diminished by the existence of more than one sub-publisher operating in a territory. In any event the publisher should not be allowed to appoint a sub-publisher for the territory in which the publisher is based and operates. If the publisher requires a clause allowing him to appoint a sub-publisher where he is based and operates, the composer should consider whether the publisher is actually capable of being an effective publisher and whether he can carry out his required responsibilities.

Sometimes a publisher will enter a sub-publishing agreement for the whole of the publisher's catalogue. Frequently, the sub-publisher will pay the publisher a non-returnable but recoupable advance on account of royalties. The publisher will not account to the composer for the advance as the sub-publishing agreement covers all the publisher's catalogue, not just the composer's compositions. If the composer has international standing he may possibly be able to persuade the publisher to agree to a clause in the publishing agreement that will enable him to share in any sub-publishing advance paid for the whole of the publisher's catalogue. The basis of the composer's argument for sharing in the advance is that the sub-publisher's main interest in entering into the sub-publishing agreement is because of the composer's compositions. If the publisher accepts the argument, and he certainly will resist it if at all possible, a mechanism will need to be agreed in the publishing agreement which provides how the sub-publishing advance is to be shared between the composer and the publisher, *e.g.* the composer will be entitled to the percentage of the advance that equals the percentage that his compositions earned for the publisher in the year prior to the sub-publishing agreement as compared to the total earnings by the publisher for all the publisher's compositions in the year prior to the sub-publishing agreement.

Although the composer will not usually be able to share in any sub-publishing advance paid for the whole of the publisher's catalogue, the composer should be able to negotiate a clause in the publishing agreement which provides that where the publisher enters a sub-publishing agreement for the composer's compositions and receives a non-returnable but recoupable advance, the advance will be shared 50:50.

The composer's solicitor should ensure the publishing agreement contains a requirement that any sub-publishing agreement:

(a) Term and rights extension period will not last longer than the term and rights extension period in the publishing agreement.
(b) Cannot be assigned or sub-licensed by the sub-publisher.
(c) Will not allow the sub-publisher to appoint a sub-sub publisher.

(d) Will contain a clause which requires the sub-publisher to pay any royalties directly to the composer and not to the publisher where the composer has terminated the publishing agreement. (*See* Termination below.)

(e) Will require the sub-publisher (where the composer has a recording agreement which contains a controlled composition clause which covers the sub-publisher's territory), to grant a mechanical licence to the composer's record company for him to record his compositions at the rate provided for in his recording agreement. (*See* The controlled composition clause above.)

(f) Will not, where the sub-publisher and the publisher are related companies, contain terms favourable to the sub-publisher which would not normally be granted by a publisher to an unrelated sub-publisher.

(g) Will require any new copyright created in any cover version or in any adaptation, alteration, arrangement or translation of the compositions to be assigned by the sub-publisher to the publisher. The composer will want this provision because in due course he will require the publisher to assign these copyrights to him.

The advance

As mentioned above, in the short term one of the main reasons why a composer would need a publisher is because the publisher will usually pay an advance which is recoupable from future royalties. The advance can be used by the composer to live. A publishing agreement will usually contain option clauses. If an option is exercised the composer will usually be paid a further advance. The composer should ensure the advance payable increases for each option. In addition, the composer should ensure that even if his account is not recouped, each advance is payable in full and cannot be used to recoup any outstanding sum. For example, if the composer has a publishing agreement and he was originally paid an advance of £30,000 and the publisher decides to exercise the first option which requires a further advance to be paid of £40,000, if the composer was £15,000 unrecouped at the time of the option being exercised, he should still receive the £40,000 further advance and not £25,000 (*i.e.* £40,000 less £15,000 to pay back the unrecouped sum).

Obviously, the composer would like any advance to be paid in full at the earliest opportunity, whilst the publisher would like to pay the advance in stages over a period of time subject to the composer performing his contractual commitments.

The agreement may provide for the advance to be paid in stages, for example, £10,000 on signing the agreement (or on an option being exercised), and £10,000 when the composer has delivered the minimum commitment to the publisher. The minimum commitment will frequently be defined by the composer composing and delivering a minimum number of compositions. Where this is the case the composer should ensure the agreement allows him to deliver part of a composition and that it will be counted towards the minimum commitment requirement (*see* Minimum commitment and collaborations above). Alternatively, where the minimum commitment is defined by the recording and release of the compositions on a record, the stages when the advance is paid could be that a certain amount will be payable when the composer has recorded his compositions and a certain amount will be payable upon the commercial release of the record.

If the advance is linked to recording and releasing the composer's compositions, the composer may be able to negotiate a further advance which is dependent upon record sales. For example, he may be able to negotiate a further advance should his record achieve sales in excess of 100,000 copies and a further advance if the record sells in excess of 250,000 copies, or the advance could be linked to sales in certain territories, for example, a further advance is payable upon sales in excess of 50,000 copies in the United Kingdom, and a further advance is payable for sales in excess of 50,000 copies in other specified territories. It is possible that there might be a further advance based upon the chart positions of the compositions in a recognised music industry chart as compiled by CIN or Billboard.

The advance could be based upon the amount of income the composer has generated during the previous contractual period but subject to a floor and a ceiling figure. A floor is the minimum advance payable and a ceiling the maximum advance payable. The calculation of the advance will therefore be made in the knowledge that there is a minimum and a maximum advance payable, irrespective of the figure reached under the proposed method of calculation.

The advance could be structured as a rollover advance, so that once it has been recouped a further advance will be paid, and once that has been recouped another advance will be paid and so on. It is possible to have a rollover advance based upon a percentage of the composer's income during the previous contractual period but subject to a floor and a ceiling figure.

The agreement will provide that any advance payable is conditional on the composer fulfilling the minimum commitment required under the publishing agreement. If the minimum commitment has not been satisfied when an option period arises, the agreement will provide that any further advance payable will be reduced proportionately.

Ways to exploit compositions and royalty rates payable

The advance paid to the composer is recoupable from the royalties due to him from the publisher. The amount of royalties payable will depend upon the particular use and the amount of use which is made of the compositions. As mentioned earlier (*see* Sub-publishing above), the composer would ideally want the calculation of royalties due to him to be on an "at source" basis. The publisher will resist this and will want the calculation of royalties due to the composer to be on a "receipts" basis. (*See* Sub-publishing above for "at source" and "receipts".)

As has been seen throughout this book the use of a copyright work requires permission in the form of a licence or assignment from the copyright owner. The composer's compositions can be exploited in many ways to generate income. The main uses of a composition are:

Mechanical

A mechanical licence, more commonly called a "mechanical", is required from the copyright owner of the composition to record the composition and to manufacture and distribute copies of the recording of the composition for retail sale to the public for their private use on, for example, record, cassette, CD, Mini-Disc. The mechanical licence will either be issued by the publisher or he may have appointed the MCPS to deal with the issue of mechanical licences on his behalf. (*See* Chapter 4 Collecting Societies and Music Industry Associations for the MCPS). The cost of a mechanical licence is 8.5% of the PDP. (*See* The controlled composition clause above for how a mechanical licence is calculated.) The composer will expect the publishing agreement to provide that he will be paid between 50–75% of this amount.

Synchronisation

A synchronisation licence, more commonly called a "synchro" licence is required from the copyright owner of the composition to use the composition in timed relation (*i.e.* synchronised) with visual images such as a film, video, television programme or commercial. (A transcription licence is required from the copyright owner of the composition to use the composition on radio commercials.) The cost of a synchro licence will depend upon the popularity of the composer and the composition as well as the use to which, and the medium in which, the composition is put. For example, if the composition will be used for a couple of seconds in the background of a television drama the use fee will be less than if a large portion of the composition is used for a major motion picture. The composer will expect the publishing agreement to provide that he will be paid between 50–75% of this amount.

If the composer is also a recording artist and has a recording agreement or is seeking a recording agreement, he should consider inserting a clause into the publishing agreement requiring the publisher to grant a synchro licence without charge to the composer's record company to enable them to make a video to accompany the composition. This clause should, if possible, be inserted into a publishing agreement as some recording agreements require a free synchro licence if the record company is going to make a video to accompany the composition, and the recording artist/composer will not want his publisher refusing his record company a free synchro licence. The publisher will not usually be prepared to grant a free synchro licence to the composer's record company to make a video to accompany the composition where the video is being made for sale to the public. However, the publisher may be prepared to grant a free synchro licence to the composer's record company to make a promotional video to accompany the composition.

Performing and broadcasting

The performing and broadcasting of musical compositions, such as by by a band live in concert, or by cafés, pubs, clubs, hotels, restaurants etc playing a radio or CD player or jukebox on their premises, or by radio stations, requires the consent of the copyright owner of each of the compositions being performed. The copyright owner obviously cannot monitor all the performances of his compositions and so will assign the performing right to the PRS who will license and collect in the relevant fees due for the performances of the compositions.

As was seen earlier, where the composer has a publishing agreement the PRS will directly account to the composer with his share of the PRS money and will directly account to the publisher with his share of the PRS money, but the PRS will not send the publisher more than

50% of the total monies due. (*See* Chapter 4 Collecting Societies and Music Industry Associations for the PRS and how the PRS operates.) The publishing agreement will often entitle the composer to more than 50% of the money which has been collected by the PRS after the deduction of the PRS's costs of collection but will require the composer to notify the PRS that he is only to receive 50% of the money. The reason why the agreement may be drafted like this is that if the agreement provides for, say, a 60:40 composer/publisher split and the PRS is told it is a 50: 50 split, the composer will receive 50% directly from the PRS and the extra 10% (making the agreed 60% as per the publishing agreement) from the publisher. However, the 10% will only be paid by the publisher to the composer once the composer's account is recouped. Alternatively, the publishing agreement may entitle the composer to 50% plus a specified percentage of the publisher's share of the PRS monies. The specified percentage will only be paid by the publisher to the composer once the composer's account is recouped.

The composer will expect the publishing agreement to provide that he will be paid between 50–66% of the total performing and broadcasting rights monies which have been collected by the PRS after the deduction of the PRS's costs of colllection.

Sheet music

The right to copy, print, distribute and sell printed copies of the lyrics and a musical notation of the composition will require the consent of the copyright owner of the composition. The composer will expect the publishing agreement to provide for him to be paid between 10-15% of the retail sale price. This is the figure which the Musicians Union recommends a composer should receive.

Commonly the name and a photograph of the recording artist (who may also be the composer) of the composition(s) may be on the front cover of the sheet music. An additional sum may be payable for this. The composer should obtain a provision in the publishing agreement that where he is also a recording artist that the publisher cannot commission any additional sum paid to use the recording artist's/composer's name and likeness on the sheet music. The composer will argue that this money is for using his name and likeness and not for the use of the composition. The publisher will want to commission this additional sum. Whether this additional money will be commissioned by the publisher will depend upon the negotiating strengths of the parties.

Other uses of compositions

The composer should ensure the publishing agreement provides that where the composition is used in ways which have not been specifically dealt with in the agreement, he will be paid commission for these uses. The composer should expect to be paid the same percentage rate which he gets for mechanicals. Other ways in which the composition could be used include using extracts from the lyrics in novels and printing the lyrics in magazines.

It is common for a record to contain a printed version of the lyrics in the accompanying CD booklet. The publisher is entitled to charge a fee for this use, however, in practice the publisher will not usually do so.

Deductions from royalties

Having seen the main ways a composition can be exploited and the royalty rate payable to the composer for each type of exploitation, it is necessary to examine how the royalty is actually calculated. The agreement will usually provide that the composer's royalty rate will be calculated on the gross money received by the publisher for exploiting the compositions after certain deductions. (The composer would prefer the royalty to be calculated not only on money received but also on money due to the publisher for exploiting the compositions after certain deductions.) The deductions which are made may include:

(a) VAT on monies the publisher has received.
(b) The collecting societies' costs.
(c) Usually, the sub-publisher's commission. (*See* Sub-publishing above for the sub-publisher's commission.)
(d) The costs the publisher incurs preparing a demonstration recording (a demo) of the composition(s). A demo is a recording (usually not of a quality suitable for commercial release) which can be used by the publisher to promote and encourage recording artists to record the composition. (A demo can also be used by a composer to encourage interest from a record company to sign him as a recording artist.) Not all publishers charge the composer for the costs incurred in recording demos. It is a matter of negotiation between the parties whether all, part or none of the costs of demo recordings will be deducted from the composer's royalties.

Some publishers may try and charge the composer an administration fee for handling the compositions or try and charge the composer for the publisher's normal business expenses, such as office rental, telephones, staff wages. The composer should not agree to pay these charges. There is no absolutely no need for the publisher to charge an administration fee as he gets commission from exploiting the composer's compositions, and the costs of running the publisher's business are not the composer's responsibility.

The royalty provision and any deductions must be carefully examined to ensure the composer does not suffer any double deductions, *e.g.* that the sub-publisher's commission if it is deducted is only deducted once not twice in the calculation of the amount due to the composer.

Accounting and auditing

The publishing agreement should contain an accounting provision clause requiring the publisher to maintain proper accounts relating to the composer's compositions which will be kept at the publisher's registered office or main place of business. The agreement will usually provide that the publisher will prepare a royalty statement of account twice a year. The accounting period will usually be 30 June and 31 December. The agreement will usually provide that the accounts will be sent to the composer within 90 days of the end of each accounting period with a cheque for any royalties which are payable. It is possible, although not at all easy, to get the publisher to agree to account four times a year. The composer will not want to wait 90 days from the end of the accounting period to receive any money due to him. The composer should try and reduce the 90-day period to either 60, 45 or 30 days. There should be little problem in getting the publisher to agree to account within 60 days of the end of the accounting period, but the composer may well find the publisher will resist an attempt to move the time period to account any closer to the actual accounting period.

The publisher may insert a clause giving the composer, for example, one year from receipt of the accounts to object to their accuracy. The composer should not accept any attempt by the publisher to reduce the six-year contractual limitation period to object to the accounts.

The publishing agreement should contain an audit clause which will allow the composer or his professionally qualified accountant to inspect, audit and take copies of the publisher's books and records to determine the accuracy of the accounts. The clause will usually require the composer to give notice of his intention to carry out the audit, and will limit the inspection to one inspection a year at the composer's expense. In addition, the clause will usually provide that the audit will take place at the publisher's registered office or main place of business and will take place during the publisher's normal business hours. There may be an additional restriction that the accountant carrying out the audit for the composer is not presently engaged on another audit of the publisher on behalf of another composer.

The agreement should provide that where the composer has been underpaid by a specified sum, *e.g.* he has been underpaid by at least £5000, or he has been underpaid by a specified percentage, *e.g.* 10%, whichever is greater, that the cost of the audit will be paid for by the publisher. Where the composer has been underpaid the agreement should provide for the publisher to account to the composer for the underpayment. The composer should ensure the clause is drafted so that the publisher accounts for any underpayment immediately and that the publisher pays interest on any underpaid sum at 3 or 4% above a stated bank's base rate from time to time in force.

The audit clause should contain a provision confirming that the information disclosed to the composer and/or his accountant is confidential information and will not be disclosed to anybody except the composer's professional advisers. The publisher will usually require a copy of the composer's final audit report to be sent to him.

The composer will need to specify in the agreement the address to which the publisher should send the accounts and any royalty cheque. Usually the address to which they will be sent is the composer's home address. The composer may want the accounts to be sent to his accountant with the royalty cheque paid by the publisher directly into his bank account, in which case the publisher will need to be given the name of the composer's bank, the account name and number and the sort code to enable payment to be made directly into the account. The composer should also insert a provision to allow him to give notice to the publisher requiring the accounts and any royalty cheque to be sent to a different address and/or bank account.

The composer's management agreement should be examined to check whether the composer's publishing advance(s) and royalties have to be sent to his manager, in which case the publishing agreement should provide for these to be sent to the manager, or notice should be given by the composer to the publisher to send them to the manager. Where the monies are to be sent to the composer's manager, the publishing agreement should provide that the manager's receipt for the monies will satisfy the publisher's duty to pay the advance or royalties to the composer.

Where the composer is part of a songwriting team (*see* above for Songwriting teams), the publishing agreement should deal with how the royalties are to be divided between the songwriters. Usually the publishing agreement will require the publisher to divide the royalties equally between the songwriters unless he has been given written notice signed by all the songwriters to divide the royalties for a particular composition(s) in a different proportion.

Termination

The agreement should contain provisions as to when the publishing agreement will automatically terminate. The agreement should also contain provisions as to when an aggrieved party has the right to elect to terminate the publishing agreement. The agreement may provide that where a terminating event occurs which entitles an aggrieved party to elect to terminate the agreement, before he can elect to terminate the agreement, he must serve a notice on the other party giving notice of the terminating event and requiring it to be remedied within a period of 30 days. Only if the terminating event has not been remedied within that time can he then terminate the agreement. The circumstances where termination will or may occur include that:

(a) Where one party has been in material breach of contract, the other party has the right to terminate the agreement.

(b) Where one party becomes either bankrupt or enters into a voluntary arrangement or any company through which he operates goes into compulsory or voluntary liquidation (save for the purposes of reconstructing or amalgamating a solvent company), or becomes insolvent or has a receiver, manager, or administrative receiver or provisional liquidator or administrator appointed, the agreement will automatically terminate.

(c) Where one party has been convicted of a criminal offence the other party has the right to terminate the agreement. This provision should be drafted so that it does not allow termination if the conviction is for a minor offence, such as speeding. The criminal conviction which will give rise to a right to terminate should only be for a serious criminal conviction. The definition of "serious conviction" must be included in the agreement so that both parties are in no doubt as to what will or will not give rise to a right to terminate.

(d) The composer has the right to terminate where the publisher has failed to meet any performance targets placed upon him.

(e) At the end of the contractual term the agreement will automatically terminate whereupon the composer will be free to sign with another publisher for those compositions which he will compose in the future. It should be remembered that the original publisher retains the right to publish the compositions which have been licensed or assigned to him for the rights extension period (*see* above for Rights extension period).

The termination clause will usually contain a provision that, notwithstanding termination both parties must continue to comply with the clauses of the publishing agreement to the extent that they are not affected by termination. For example, if the agreement is terminated by the composer due to a material breach of contract by the publisher, although the composer can terminate the agreement, both parties will still be bound by any clause in the agreement providing for confidentiality.

Where the composer terminates the publishing agreement, for example, due to a material breach of contract by the publisher, the compositions which have previously been assigned to the publisher will still belong to the publisher despite the composer terminating the agreement. The composer will therefore require a clause in the publishing agreement which provides that where he terminates the publishing agreement, the compositions which have previously been assigned to the publisher will be re-assigned to him. The publisher may have granted mechanical, synchronisation or other licences in relation to some if not all of the compositions, in which case any re-assignment clause should provide for the compositions to be re-assigned to the composer subject to, and with the benefit of, any licences which the publisher has granted. (*See also* Re-assignment of Compositions below.)

(An assignment of the compositions should be contrasted with a licence of the compositions by the composer to the publisher. A licence is a contractual right which does not pass ownership of the copyright to the publisher, whereas an assignment is a property right which will pass ownership of the copyright to the publisher. The licence will be conditional upon the publisher performing his contractual obligations and will also provide that if the publisher becomes either bankrupt or enters into a voluntary arrangement or any company through which he operates goes into compulsory or voluntary liquidation (save for the purposes of reconstructing or amalgamating a solvent company), or becomes insolvent or has a receiver, manager, or administrative receiver or provisional liquidator or administrator appointed, then the licence will automatically terminate. Where a licence terminates automatically by reason of bankruptcy etc, or is terminated by the composer, for example, due to a material breach of contract by the publisher, or where both the contractual term and the rights extension period have expired, the ownership of the copyright will remain where it was on the grant of the licence, in other words, with the composer. It should be noted that the licence will be drafted so that the publisher can grant mechanical, synchronisation or other licences in relation to the compositions. The licence agreement between the composer and publisher will provide that where the publisher has granted mechanical, synchronisation or other licences in relation to any of the compositions, the termination of the licence will be subject to, and with the benefit of, any such licences which the publisher has granted.)

The composer's solicitor should ensure that there is a clause in the publishing agreement which provides that where the composer terminates the publishing agreement that the composer will have the right to collect any royalties directly from the sub-publisher(s). (Any sub-publishing agreement should contain provisions which reflect how royalty payments will be made where the composer terminates the publishing agreement.) *See also* Sub-publishing above.

The publisher may want a clause inserted into the agreement which provides that where he terminates the agreement, the composer will only be entitled to be paid royalties up to the date of termination. The composer's solicitor should not accept any such provision in the agreement.

Suspension

The agreement will usually contain a clause allowing the publisher to suspend rather than terminate the agreement whilst there is a breach of contract existing which has arisen through no fault of the publisher. The circumstances where suspension may occur include:

(a) where the composer refuses to provide his services to the publisher,

(b) where the composer is unable to provide his services to the publisher due to illness, disability or injury,

(c) where a *force majeure* event occurs. It should be noted that where suspension occurs due to a *force majeure* event that the agreement should not require the publisher to give the composer notice that the agreement will be suspended if the composer has not rectified the situation within a period of time. This is because the *force majeure* event is not due to the composer's fault not is it rectifiable by the composer. (*See* Chapter 3 Music Industry Contracts, Other Clauses, for *force majeure*, for the provision of a notice of *force majeure*, and for the provision of a long stop clause where the agreement is suspended for *force majeure*).

The publisher might insert a provision into the suspension clause which provides that he will not have to pay the composer any money due to him whilst the agreement is suspended. The composer's solicitor should not accept any such provision in the agreement.

(For a more detailed discussion on suspension of the agreement *see* Chapter 6 The Management Agreement, Suspension.)

Re-assignment of compositions

The publishing agreement should contain provisions for the re-assignment by the publisher of the copyright in all the compositions (or in the case of (d) below for the re-assignment of the copyright in specific compositions) to the composer in certain situations. The clause should provide that the publisher will execute any document which the composer requires to effect a re-assignment of the copyright. (It should be noted that if the right for a re-assignment arises due to one of the situations referred in (b) below, the publisher cannot execute a valid re-assignment on the happening of any of these events. This is why (b) below contains a provision for a deemed automatic re-assignment of the compositions to the composer.) The agreement should provide that where the publisher has granted mechanical, synchronisation or other licences for any of the compositions, the re-assignment of these compositions will be subject to and with the benefit of any licences which the publisher has entered into with third parties. The re-assignment of the copyright in the compositions to the composer should occur where:

(a) There has been a material breach of contract by the publisher and the composer has terminated the agreement.
(b) The publisher becomes either bankrupt or enters into a voluntary arrangement or any company through which he operates goes into compulsory or voluntary liquidation (save for the purposes of reconstructing or amalgamating a solvent

company) or becomes insolvent, or has a receiver, manager, or administrative receiver or provisional liquidator or adminis-trator apponited. The agreement should provide that if any of these situations occurs there is deemed to be an automatic re-assignment of the copyright in the compositions to the composer. (It should be noted that if the parties are aware at the time of entering the agreement that there is a serious chance of the publisher, for example, becoming insolvent, then a clause which provides for the re-assignment of the copyright to the composer in such a situation could be regarded as a pref-erence and so could be set aside.) It is suggested following *Orwin* v *Attorney-General* [1998] FSR 415 that the effect of such a clause is to provide an equitable re-assignment of the copyright to the composer. (In *Orwin* a company passed a special resolution that in the event of the company being wound up etc, all copyrights would vest in the director. The company was struck off the company register subsequent to the special resolution. Mummery LJ in the Court of Appeal said *obiter* that it was possible for the special resolution to act as an equitable assignment of the copyright to the director.)

(c) The rights extension period under the agreement has expired. (*See* above for Rights extension period.)

(d) a composition has been assigned to the publisher and the publisher has not exploited it within a specified period of time. The agreement will need to define exactly what is meant by "exploitation". For example, exploitation may be defined to mean that the composition has to be recorded and commer-cially released within a specified period of time. The time period will usually be from the end of the agreement term, so, for example, if the composition was assigned to the publisher during the term and is not recorded and commercially released within two years after the end of the contractual term (which will probably be defined so as to include any options which have been exercised), the composition will be re-assigned to the composer. Where the time period to exploit the compositions is calculated from the end of the publishing agreement there is a problem for the publisher where he receives compositions from the composer near the end of the agreement term. If, for example, the agreement was for a fixed five-year term and compositions were delivered to the publisher in the first few months of the agreement, the publisher could do nothing with them for about five years plus an extra one or two years before the composer could require them to be re-assigned for lack of exploitation. If another batch of compositions were delivered to the publisher in the last few months of the agreement the publisher would only have about one or two years to exploit the compositions before the composer could require them to be re-assigned for lack of exploitation. Where the time period to exploit the compositions runs from the end of the agreement term, the publisher should be given as much chance to exploit the later delivered compositions as he has to exploit those delivered earlier in the term before the composer can require them to be re-assigned for lack of exploitation. This can be achieved by creating a two-fold time period to exploit the compositions, *e.g.* the publisher must exploit the compositions within one year after the end of the agreement term but in any event he has a minimum of three years from the composer delivering the compositions to exploit them.

The composer should ensure the publishing agreement provides that where a composition has been adapted, altered, arranged or translated, that any copyright which exists in any adaptation, alteration, arrangement or translation of the composition will be assigned to the composer along with the re-assignment of the copyright in the composition.

Other clauses

Along with the other clauses mentioned above, the agreement will contain several other clauses. These may include:

(a) A clause allowing the publisher to promote himself to others as the composer's publisher.

(b) A jurisdiction and choice of law clause. (*See* Chapter 3 Music Industry Contracts.)

(c) An invalidity clause. (*See* Chapter 3 Music Industry Contracts and Chapter 5 The Legal Status of Band and Solo Artist.)

(d) A clause confirming that the publishing agreement does not constitute a partnership, joint venture or employment relationship between the publisher and the composer.

(e) A clause confirming that the publishing agreement reflects the whole of the agreement between the parties and replaces any earlier oral or written agreement.

(f) A non-waiver clause. (*See* Chapter 5 The Legal Status of Band and Solo Artist.)

(g) A *force majeure* clause. (*See* Chapter 3 Music Industry Contracts.)

(h) A notice clause. (*See* Chapter 5 The Legal Status of Band and Solo Artist.)

(i) A clause which provides that the composer and publisher will sign any documentation which is necesssary to carry out the terms of the agreement. For example, the composer will when required sign any confirmatory assignment or licence relating to the compositions, and the publisher will when the agreement terminates re-assign the compositions to the composer. Where the composer terminates the agreement early, for example, due to a material breach of contract by the publisher, the publisher may become awkward and refuse to sign any document re-assigning the compositions to the composer. To avoid the possibility of this problem occurring, the composer might require the publisher to grant a power of attorney to the composer so that he can execute any re-assignment of the compositions on behalf of the publisher.

(j) A clause which prohibits either party from assigning the agreement. Where assignment is permitted in certain circumstances and/or is permitted subject to certain conditions the clause should detail the relevant circumstances and conditions which apply.

(k) A clause dealing with the Contracts (Rights of Third Parties) Act 1999. (See Chapter 3 Music Industry Contracts.)

Chapter 8

The Recording Agreement

Introduction

For many performers the likelihood of them being offered a recording agreement with an established record company is extremely remote. A performer will usually need to have a fair degree of talent as a performer, good commercial material to perform, a certain amount of good looks and charisma and a lot of luck, especially as he has to persuade the record company that he is what it is looking for at that particular time. Timing is also a crucial factor in that the performer's image and material has to be in line with the current public trend or better still anticipate the next public trend.

Some performers attract the attention of more than one record company and a bidding war may ensue to get them to sign a recording agreement. Usually, however, a performer will only have one record company interested in signing him. The performer, if he has only has one record company currently interested in signing him, will often be prepared to sign any document put in front of him rather than turn it down in the hope that a more suitable deal might possibly be offered to him in the future by another record company. The performer will understandably be concerned that this will be his only chance to get a record deal and that a bird in the hand is worth two in the bush. In addition, the performer may be swayed by the advance on offer and be prepared to take the money now and not concern himself about whether the royalty package offered is acceptable.

The terms offered to a performer will depend upon whether there is any competition to sign the performer and whether the interested record company is a major (*i.e.* BMG, EMI, Sony, Universal, Warners) or an independent record company. (A major record company is a company which has all the facilities to put the record into the shops, *i.e.* they can manufacture, distribute and sell the record to the retailer, whereas an independent record company has to use other companies to get the record into the shops.)

There are essentially three types of recording agreement:

1. A direct signing agreement, where the performer personally signs a recording agreement with the record company.

2. A loan out agreement. Under this arrangement the performer sets up his own limited company "LC" and enters into an agreement with "LC" to record exclusively for them. "LC" then enters into a recording agreement with the record company to supply or "loan out" the performer's recording services to the record company. To protect the record company the performer will have to give the record company a side letter guaranteeing that he will personally provide his services should "LC" cease to exit or fail to provide the performer's services.

3. A production agreement. Under this agreement the performer enters an agreement with a company which is not owned by the performer "TP" to record exclusively for them. "TP" then enters into an agreement with the record company to license the performer's recordings to the record company. To protect the record company the performer will be required to give the record company a side letter guaranteeing that he will personally provide his services to the record company should "TP" cease to exit or fail to provide the performer's recordings.

Although some recording agreements are extremely long, running to many dozens of pages and contain complex provisions, the basics of a recording agreement are simple to understand. Essentially, the performer, in exchange for royalties and an advance which is non returnable but recoupable against royalties, agrees to record exclusively for the record company and allows the record company to record, manufacture, distribute and sell his recordings. In addition, the record company provides the money to make the recordings which will be recoupable against the performer's royalties and will usually agree to release the recordings for sale to the public.

The record company will want to own the copyright in the sound recordings for the full copyright term. As was seen in Chapter 2 Copyright Law and the Copyright, Designs and Patents Act 1988, section 11(1) of the CDPA provides the general rule that the author of a copyright work is the first owner of the work, and section 9(2)(aa) provides that the author of a sound recording is the producer. The producer is defined in section 178 as the person who makes the necessary arrangements for the creation of the sound recording. The record company will require a clause in the recording agreement providing that where the copyright in the sound recordings vests in the performer, he will assign the ownership of the copyright in the sound recordings to the record company. This clause will be in the agreement in case the performer produces his own recordings. Similarly, where a third party produces the performer's recordings the producer's agreement will contain a clause which provides that the producer will assign the ownership of the copyright in the sound recording to the record company. (See also Chapter 2 Copyright Law and the Copyright, Designs and Patents Act 1988, The owner of the work, The producer of a sound recording *above*.)

As will be seen later recording costs are paid for by the record company but are recoupable from the performer's royalties. Assuming the performer is successful and he has recouped his advance, recording costs and any other recoupable sums, he will have paid for the sound recordings which are owned by the record company. It is only fair that the record company which is making a substantial economic investment in the performer should be able not only to earn back its investment but also earn a return on its investment. There is certainly an argument that a performer who is fully recouped and so has paid for the sound recordings should in fact own the sound recordings after the record company has had a reasonable period of time to earn a return on its investment. As sound recordings are a valuable asset, the performer's solicitor should try and negotiate a clause in the recording agreement which provides for the copyright in the sound recordings to be assigned or re-assigned to the performer and for the physical property of the master tapes to be handed over to the performer, say, 10 or 15 years after the end of the contractual term. Although the performer's solicitor should seek such a clause in the recording agreement, most record companies will have the same response to such a request – no, no, and no again. In the unlikely event that the record company agrees to assign or re-assign the copyright in the sound recordings to the performer, it will usually only be prepared to do so if the performer is recouped or is prepared to repay the record company any unrecouped sums, and provided the performer pays its reasonable legal fees for the assignment or re-assignment and a nominal sum of, say, £250 per master track. Where the record company has agreed to assign or re-assign the copyright in the sound recordings to the performer, the recording agreement should provide that the assignment or re-assignment is subject to and with the benefit of any licences which the record company has granted to third parties to use the sound recordings. (*See also* Termination below.)

A record company should be aware of the problems involved when entering into a recording agreement with a minor, and of the possibilty of the agreement being challenged for being in restraint of trade or undue influence. The record company will require the performer to obtain independent legal advice upon the contents of the recording agreement from a solicitor with experience of music agreements. (*See* Chapter 3 Music Industry Contracts for Minors, Independent legal advice, Restraint of trade and Undue influence.)

Perhaps the most complex area in any recording agreement is the royalty clause. There are three reasons why the royalty clause is so complex.

1. There are many different formats in which the performer's recordings can be sold to the public and many different ways in which the performer's recordings can be used, each of which will generate different royalty rates, *e.g.* LP, cassette, CD, mini-disc, DVD, CD-ROM, licensing the recording for a television advertisement or for a film soundtrack, downloading the recording via the internet, using the recording on a compilation of recordings such as the NOW series.
2. There are different price ranges in which the same recording may at some time be sold to the public, *e.g.* usually a CD will initially be brought out on the record company's top line label at full price, after a period of time it may be released at mid-price, and at a later date it may be released at budget price.
3. There are various deductions such as for packaging which need to be taken into account before the royalty payable can be calculated.

The performer may be swayed to sign with a particular record company because of what appears to be the high royalty rate being offered. This high royalty rate will in reality be much lower after taking into consideration the deductions, the different price ranges in which the recordings may be sold, the different formats in which the performer's recordings can be sold to the public and the different ways in which the performer's recordings can be used. For this reason, the performer's solicitor and his manager should look closely at the royalty rate on offer and calculate what it is really worth, based on hypothetical sales figures, and advise the performer accordingly. It is very possible that a 16% royalty rate offered by record company A may in fact be worth less than a 12% royalty rate offered by record company B.

This rest of this chapter will look at the key clauses in the recording agreement. The chapter assumes that the performer is signing directly to a record company for a long term recording agreement rather than for a single song and that there is at present no other record company interested in the performer. Only once the agreement has been examined and negotiated by a solicitor should the performer (in conjunction with his manager and after considering their solicitor's advice) decide whether to accept it, although the reality of the situation is that if this is the only offer on the table the performer will sign anything so that he can be a recording artist.

The Recording agreement

The parties

The parties to the recording agreement will be the record company and the performer. Where the performers are a band the individual band members will each sign the agreement. As will be seen later on, (*see* Leaving members below), the record company will require the services of each individual performer to record for them exclusively whilst they are members of the band, and where an individual performer ceases to be in the band the record company will reserve the right to require the individual performer to record exclusively for them whether they join another band, set up another band or wish to perform as a solo artist.

Under the recording agreement the performer is allowing the record company to record (*see* Grant of rights by performer for what is a recording), and exploit his performances, usually throughout world, for the full period of the performer's rights. (*See* Chapter 2 Copyright Law and the Copyright, Designs and Patents Act 1988 for Duration of performer's rights.) The record company will require the right to exploit all the performer's performances and to exploit them in all formats (*see* Grant of rights by the performer below for details). In consideration of these rights the performer who signs a recording agreement will receive a non returnable advance which is recoupable against royalties, royalties for sales and other uses made of his performances, the right to receive equitable remuneration where the performances are played in public or included in a broadcast or cable programme service, and the right to receive equitable remuneration where the performer has transferred his rental right in the sound recording to the producer of the sound recording. (*See* Chapter 2 Copyright Law and the Copyright, Designs and Patents Act 1988 for details of the performer's right to receive equitable remuneration.)

Where a performer who has a recording agreement with a record company uses session musicians on his recordings, the session musicians will give their consent to the record company to record and exploit their performances under the standard Musicians' Union agreement.

Territory

The record company will usually require the performer to give them worldwide rights. It may be that the performer is contracted to another record company for a particular territory, in which case the performer will want to exclude that territory from the agreement.

It is quite possible for the performer to have recording agreements with several record companies covering different territories throughout the world, *e.g.* one for the United Kingdom, one for North America and Canada, and one for the rest of the world. Obviously, when the performer enters into a recording agreement he should only contract for deliverable territories. If the record company is prepared to accept less than the world the agreement will specifically state those territories which are excluded from the ambit of the agreement, and the record company may try and obtain a warranty from the performer that he will use his best or reasonable endeavours to require the excluded territory not to release his recordings in the excluded territory before the record company has done so in one or more of its territories. The reason why the record company may try and obtain such a warranty from the performer is it may be concerned that initial sales of the recordings in its territories may be affected by the importation of copies of the recordings from the excluded territory before the recordings can be released by the record company in its territories.

Minimum commitment

The term, which will be an initial term plus options exercisable by the record company, will be drafted so that it inter-relates with the number of recordings the record company requires from the performer. The number of recordings the record company requires is called the minimum commitment. For example, in the initial term the minimum commitment required from the performer may be for him to make enough recordings for two singles, and in addition at the request of the record company enough recordings for a long playing record. (See below for the definition of a single and a long playing record.)

During the initial term the performer's solicitor should attempt to get the record company to require an album's worth of recordings from the performer rather than only one, two, or three singles with an option for the record company to require an album. The performer will want a guarantee that he will be able to record and release at least one album, rather than let the record company decide upon the success or failure of a couple of singles as to whether it wants to continue its relationship with him and require an album from him. If the record company refuses to agree to a minimum commitment of an album and will only commit to a couple of singles, the performer's solicitor should try and get the record company to agree to spend a minimum guaranteed sum promoting the singles and he should try to get the record company to guarantee (rather than have an option) that it will require an album if a single achieves a certain number of sales or a top 30 chart place within a specified period of time after it has been released in a designated territory.

A single may, for example, be defined as three recordings of different compositions, none of which are instrumentals or which have been previously recorded by the performer. The definition will usually provide that each of the compositions will be of a certain minimum and maximum length and will in addition provide an overall maximum length for the single. A long playing record may, for example, be defined as not less than ten recordings of different compositions, none of which are instrumentals or which have previously been recorded by the performer, each lasting (say) not less than 3 minutes nor more than 6 minutes 30 seconds and together lasting not less than 35 minutes. The reason why the definition will usually provide that a single will be of a maximum length and a long playing record of a minimum length is to satisfy the eligibility requirements for entry into the singles and albums sales charts.

The performer's solicitor should consider the proposed definition of a single and long playing record carefully with the performer. Where necessary these definitions should be amended to suit the type of compositions which the performer intends to record. For example the definition of a long playing record will need to be different for a performer like Mike Oldfield who records rock symphonies consisting of two tracks (as in *Tubular Bells*) as well as more conventional 10 track rock albums or for a punk band which records compositions which each last for less than 3 minutes.

The agreement will often contain a clause that if more than a certain amount of compositions are contained on a long playing record, it will be defined as a double album. This will affect the royalty rate payable to the performer. (*See* Royalty rates for different formats and different types of exploitation below for details.) The performer's solicitor should try to remove any such clause, or if he cannot get the clause removed, he should attempt to raise the number of compositions which can be contained on a long playing record before it will be defined as a double album. As well as a clause dealing with what constitutes a double album, the recording agreement will also contain a clause that the record company's consent is needed for the performer to release a double album. Where the record company will not agree to remove a clause in the recording agreement relating to what constitutes a double album, the performer's solicitor should try to remove any clause in the agreement which requires the record company's consent for the performer to release a double album. It is however unlikely that a record company will agree to this where it originally proposed such a clause in the agreement. This is due to the fact that double albums generally sell in lesser numbers that single albums and because double albums are usually priced at less than twice the price of a single album. It is also for these reasons that the record company will usually include a clause in the agreement that if a double album is released it will only count as a single album for the purposes of the performer's minimum commitment.

The minimum commitment will often state that neither a live recording of the performer in concert nor the release of a greatest hits or best of record will count toward the minimum commitment. In addition, the record company will often not want to release a live album as they do not usually sell in the same quantities as studio recorded material. The performer will want a live/greatest hits/best of album to count towards the minimum commitment, but the record company will not usually agree to this as the compositions have previously been recorded by the performer and released by the record company. It is becoming common for live albums to contain material which the performer has not released before, and for greatest hits/best of albums to contain two or three newly recorded tracks to entice fans who have all the other material on the album to purchase the compilation. The performer's solicitor may be able to persuade the record company that any compositions which have been included on a live/greatest hits/best of album which have not been previously released should count towards the minimum commitment.

The agreement will require the recordings made by the performer to be master recordings. The term master recording will be defined in the agreement. Put very basically, a master recording is the original tape recording or any other method which is used to record music professionally, *e.g.* computer disk. The lead vocals, backing vocals, and each instrument will be recorded onto separate tracks on the tape. Once the performances have been recorded onto the tape it is then edited, mixed (the levels between each of the instruments and the vocals on the tracks are balanced), and equalised (eq'd) (simply balancing the treble, bass and mid-range). From the edited, mixed and equalised tape another tape is made which will be used in the manufacture process of CDs, cassettes, mini discs, LPs.

Term

The record company should be aware that the length of the term needs to be long enough to enable it to make a financial return on its investment in the performer whilst ensuring that it is not so long that it might be held by the courts to be in restraint of trade. It should be remembered that the courts will look at all the terms of the agreement, including how long the whole of the agreement will last if all the options are exercised, together with any extensions of time provided for in the agreement for late delivery of the minimum commitment by the performer in deciding whether an agreement is in restraint of trade. As a guideline, restraint of trade cases seem to suggest that the maximum acceptable length of term including options is seven years.

The length of the term can be drafted in several ways. For example:

(a) the term **will last for a period of one year** during which time the performer will satisfy the minimum recording requirement, or

(b) the term **will last until 180 days after the delivery** of the minimum recording commitment **but in any event** the term will last **not less than** one year **nor last for more than** 18 months in total, or

(c) the term **will last until 180 days after the release** in the United Kingdom of the minimum recording commitment **but in any event** the term will last **not less than** one year **nor last for more than** 18 months in total, or

It should be noted that in (b) the term is defined by reference to delivery, whereas in (c) the term is defined by reference to release. The release of the record by the record company may be easily six to nine months after the delivery of the record by the performer to the record company.

Options

Some recording agreements provide that where the record company has not exercised an option, the agreement will continue until the performer has given it notice that it has not exercised the option and the record company will then have an extra period of time, *e.g.* four weeks from the performer's notice, to decide whether or not to take up the option. If the record company does not take up the option within the time period given under the performer's notice, the performer will only then be free to enter into a recording agreement with another record company. The performer's solicitor should delete any clause requiring the performer to give notice and extra time to the record company to decide whether to exercise an option. It is the record company's and not the performer's responsibility to keep an eye on when an option clause in its favour becomes exercisable.

It is quite common for the performer to fall behind in the recording sessions and so be unable to deliver the minimum commitment on time. The record company will often require a right allowing it to elect to terminate the agreement if the performer does not deliver the minimum commitment on time. In addition, where the performer has not delivered the minimum commitment on time the agreement will provide that the term will automatically be extended. The performer should only agree to the automatic extension of the term where the delay is his fault. Due to the possibility of the agreement being in restraint of trade, the record company should insert a long stop date beyond which the automatic extension cannot run, *e.g.* if the performer does not deliver the minimum commitment during the intial period, the initial period will automatically continue until the minimum commitment has been delivered, although the initial period shall not exceed a period of two years. In addition, where there has been late delivery of the minimum commitment the agreement will usually provide for an extension of time for the record company to exercise any option it might have. It is only fair that where the performer has not delivered the minimum commitment the record company should have an extension of time to decide whether to exercise an option to retain the performer. To do so it needs to evaluate the recordings which it cannot do until it has received them from the performer. The extension provided for in the agreement to exercise the option may easily be in the region of 180 days following delivery of the minimum commitment. The performer's solicitor should ensure where the agreement provides for an extension of time to exercise an option that this only operates where the delay in delivering the minimum commitment is the performer's fault. In addition, the performer's solicitor should try and cut back the time period allowed to the record company to decide whether to exercise the option. The record company should not require too long an extension to decide whether to exercise the option due to the possibility of the agreement being in restraint of trade.

The agreement should be drafted to make it clear that where an option is not taken up, all subsequent options will automatically lapse and the agreement is automatically terminated, enabling the performer to look for another deal with another record company.

Stories often abound in newspapers and magazines that a performer has signed a record deal for eight albums for a £1,000,000 advance. In reality, the performer has most likely signed a recording agreement for one or two albums for a £50,000 advance with the record company having a series of options. Where the record company exercises each option it will pay the performer a further advance. If all the options are exercised the record deal will be for a total of eight albums for £1,000,000. As the record company will have a series of options over the performer's recording services, at each option date it can decide either to exercise the option where the performer is still popular or decide not to take up the option where the performer's popularity has declined. This will enable the record company to drop the performer once he loses his popularity and will save the record company the substantial costs involved in recording and releasing his albums.

The performer should ensure that any option clause is drafted so that he will receive an increased advance on the exercise of each option by the record company. For example, if the recording agreement was for an initial one year term with an advance of £50,000 with four options of one year each, the performer might seek a further advance of £100,000 on the exerise of the first option, £150,000 on the exercise of the second option, £200,000 on the exercise of the third option and £250,000 on the exercise of the fourth option. There are other ways that the performer can provide for an increased advance on the exercise of the option (*see* Advances and Royalties below). In addition, when each option is exercised the performer should ensure the recording budget, his royalty rate, and any royalty escalations also increase (*see* Advances and Royalties below).

The record company will usually insert a clause into the agreement providing that the performer cannot start recording his second or subsequent albums until he has delivered his previous recording, and that the performer cannot deliver the new recording until nine months after he has delivered his previous recording. This enables the record company to ensure that it only receives one record at a time to promote and that these recordings are the performer's current style of performance and from the record company's point of view hopefully still in touch with current fashion, whereas his older recordings which if it was obliged to accept under the agreement might be out of fashion. In addition, this will prevent the performer signing a long term agreement with the record company and presenting it with the whole of his contractual commitment in one go, whereupon he will be free to leave and sign with another record company.

Sometimes a performer might record an album, deliver it to the record company and then disappear for several years only to come back saying that he is ready to record his new album. A record company may be prepared to allow the performer to record after such a long time span where it believes he will still be popular with the public. To protect against the possibility of a performer who has gone out of fashion suddenly wanting to record after a long time gap since his last album, the record company will insert a clause into the agreement providing that if the performer has not delivered his next album within 18 months of delivering his previous album the record company can terminate the recording agreement.

Grant of rights by performer

The agreement should provide that the grant of rights by the performer is conditional upon the record company complying with its contractual obligations.

The performer will usually grant the record company the exclusive right to his services as an audio and audio-visual recording artist in the defined territory for the defined term. (*See* above for Territory and Term.) Apart from being given the right to record the performer's performances, the record company will also need the right to manufacture, distribute and sell copies of the recordings of the performer's performances on LP, cassette, CD, mini disc and on any other formats which are now known or which may come into existence in the future. As was seen earlier in Chapter 2 Copyright Law and the Copyright, Designs and Patents Act 1988, Rights in performances, the performer has rights in his performances under sections 182(1)(a), (b), (c), 182A(1), 182B(1), 182C(1), 183(a) and (b) and 184(1)(a) and (b). The recording agreement will contain a provision which gives the performer's consent for the record company to do those acts which are detailed in these sections. This will enable the record company to exploit the performer's performances. The consent will be given to enable the record company to exploit the recordings for the full period of the performer's rights and/or any renewals and extensions of the performer's rights.

There may be a problem with the performer agreeing to provide his services to the record company as an audio-visual recording artist. This is because an audio-visual recording will include films, television and video and so will catch the performer's work not only as a recording artist but also as a film actor or television presenter. The record company will usually not object to the performer working as a film actor or television presenter, although it has a right to these services under the agreement, provided it does not interfere with his work for the record company as a musical recording artist. However, even though the record company would usually give their consent for the performer to work as a film actor or television presenter, if the performer is presently engaged in such activities or it is envisaged that he may want to do so in the future, the clause should be amended to exclude these activities being granted to the record company.

The recording agreement will give the record company the right to lease, license and sell the recordings. Therefore, it is the record company and not the performer which has the right to allow others to use the recordings in, for example, an advertisement, a television programme or a film. A performer may not want the recordings to be used to advertise certain products, *e.g.* he may not want his recordings to be used to promote the sales of meat where he is a vegetarian, or to be associated with particular television or film scenes, *e.g.* he may not want his music being used in a sex scene. The performer should, where he has strong preferences against the recordings being used in certain situations, either seek a total bar on such use or require the record company to seek his approval before they can be used. A record company will usually be sensitive to a performer's feelings on such matters and will often agree to prohibitions on the use of the recordings in certain situations.

The exclusive nature of the record company's rights to the performer's services means that the performer cannot make recordings for other companies whilst he is under contract to the record company.

Sometimes a performer is invited to contribute to a recording made by another performer who is contracted to another record company. A performer may want to make a "guest" appearance on this record but is prohibited from doing so because he is exclusively contracted to his record company, and will need the record company's consent to "guest" on the record. The performer's solicitor should ensure the recording agreement allows the performer to make "guest" appearances on other performer's records. The record company will often agree to this but on terms such as:

(a) The record company will be credited on the cover or inner sleeve of the record for letting the performer make a "guest" appearance, *i.e.* "John Smith appears courtesy of ABC12 Record Company Ltd".

(b) The performer will only "guest" not be a "featured artist" on the record and will only be credited on the record sleeve, record packaging, and adverts for the record as a "guest".

(c) The size of any "guest" credit on the record sleeve, record packaging, and adverts for the record will be the same size as the "guest" credit for any other performers who "guest" on the record.

(d) No photographs of the performer can be included on the record sleeve or record packaging nor on any advertisements for the record.

(e) Where the performer is a member of a band and is "guesting" as an individual he will only be credited under his own name and there will be no reference to the name of the band.

(f) Any "guest" appearance will not interfere with any commitment he has under his recording agreement.

The exclusive nature of the record company's rights to the performer's services means that if the performer wants to record some of his songs for radio or television, e.g. for a Radio 1 session, then he will need his record company's permission to do this. The record company will usually allow the performer to record his songs for radio or television as it is good free publicity. However the record company will usually only allow these recordings to be used by the radio or television station for broadcast purposes only. The performer would like to be able to record his songs for broadcast on radio or television without having to seek the prior consent of his record company. If the record company will not agree to amend the agreement to allow for this, the performer's solicitor should try and obtain as an alternative that the record company's consent to allow the performer to make recordings for broadcast on radio or television will not be unreasonably withheld.

The rights clause will also provide that where the sound recording copyright vests in the performer that he will assign it to the record company. This clause will be in the agreement in case the performer produces his own recordings. (*See* above for a discussion of the sound recording copyright.)

The record company will require the right to adapt, add to, alter, delete material from, and re-arrange material on the sound recordings which contains the performer's performances. The performer may not be prepared to grant the record company all of these rights, and where the performer has concerns these should be carefully negotiated with the record company. The record company may be prepared where the performer has some legitimate concerns to agree to some restriction upon these rights, *e.g.* it may agree not to delete any lyrics from the sound recording where it might mean that the deletion would equate to a derogatory treatment of the author's literary work under the CDPA. Notwithstanding any rights which may be granted by the performer to the record company to adapt etc the sound recordings which contains the performer's performances, the record company will need to be aware that any adaptation etc of the sound recordings may amount to a derogatory treatment of the author's literary or musical work. Where this might amount to a derogatory treatment, the record company should get consent from the author(s) of the work to make the adaptation etc.

The performer will be required to grant the record company the right to use his name and likeness, his biographical details and any trade mark belonging to him, and where he is in a band the right to use the band's name and likeness, the band's biographical details and any trade mark belonging to the band in order to promote and exploit the recordings. Unless the performer/band is giving the record company merchandising rights (for which see below), the performer/band should ensure that the record company only has the right to use the performer's/band's name and likeness etc to promote and exploit the recordings and not for any other purposes. The performer/band will want the record company to submit any proposed promotional material which bears his/their name and likeness etc to him/them for his/their approval. The majority of record companies will often only be prepared to consult the performer/band about the proposed use and content of any proposed promotional material which bears the performer's/band's name and likeness etc. Where a record company is prepared to let the performer/band have approval rights the record company will at most usually only agree to the performer/band having qualified approval rights, *i.e.* that the performer's/band's approval will not be unreasonably withheld.

Some record companies will try to obtain the performer's merchandising rights so that they can license them to merchandising companies, collect the royalty income from the merchandising companies, take a percentage of the royalty income for themselves and account to the performer with the balance. In addition, the record company will be able to earn interest on the performer's share of the merchandising royalties until it has to account to the performer. The recording agreement may also contain a provision that the record company can use the performer's share of the merchandising royalties to recoup any sums which are unrecouped under the recording agreement. If the performer were to allow the record company to have his merchandising rights he should not agree to any provision allowing the record company to use his merchandising royalties to recoup any sums which are unrecouped under the recording agreement. Because of the potential value of merchandising a performer should strongly resist giving the record company his merchandising rights. The performer should ideally contract directly with a merchandising company of his own choice. If the performer does give the record company his merchandising rights they should only be given on terms which would usually be given to a merchandising company which is unrelated to the record company.

Some record companies with a related merchandising company might try to get the performer to sign a merchandising agreement with their related merchandising company. If the performer agrees to give his merchandising to a merchandising company which is related to the record company he should only do so on terms which would usually be given to a merchandising company which is unrelated to the record company. In particular, there must be no provision allowing for cross-collateralising the merchandising and recording agreements. (*See* Chapter 3 Music Industry Contracts for Cross-collateralisation and Chapter 11 Merchandising.)

In the music industry trade newspaper, *Music Week* (1 May 1999) it was reported that one major record company had offered a band a recording agreement which contained a clause giving the record company ownership and control of the band's website. As the article pointed out a performer's website has two very useful purposes. Firstly, it can be used to promote a performer, and secondly, it can be used to sell the performer's recordings and his merchandise. As such it is a potentially lucrative source of income. The performer's solicitor should be aware that record companies may now want ownership and control of a performer's website and want a percentage of the income derived from the performer's website. The performer should resist giving such rights over his website to a record company. It should be noted that the record company can take action against the performer if he uses his website to release (either for purchase of for free downloading) demo recordings, unreleased recordings, or recordings which have already been released by the record company, where these recordings were made by the performer under an exclusive recording agreement with the record company.

Performer's warranties and obligations

The warranties and obligations of the performer under the recording agreement include that:

1. He is a qualifying person under the CDPA. (*See* Chapter 2 Copyright Law and the Copyright Designs and Patents Act 1988, Author requirement (s154(4) for the qualifying person under the CDPA.)
2. He is not a minor.
3. He is free to enter into the agreement.
4. He is not suffering from any disability which prevents him from providing his services.
5. He will carry out the services which he is required to provide under the agreement professionally and to the best of his ability.
6. He has taken independent legal advice from a solicitor with experience of music agreements.
7. The material which he records will not be obscene, defamatory, blasphemous or infringe any copyright or third party's rights.
8. The compositions comprised in any recordings made specifically for the record company under the agreement have not been previously recorded by the performer.
9. Where he is required to assign any rights to the record company, he is free to assign them to the record company.
10. He is free to use his professional name, and in addition where the performers are a band, that they are free to use the band name.
11. He will perform under his professional name, and in addition where the performers are in a band, they will perform under the band name, and will not use any other name to perform under. (Perhaps as Prince who at one stage adopted an hieroglyphic as his professional name, which nobody knew how to translate, spell or pronounce in English, the clause should be extended to provide that the performer will not use any other professional name, nor adopt any symbol or hieroglyphic as a professional name.)
12. He will keep the contents of the agreement confidential. The clause will allow disclosure of the contents of the agreement to his lawyer, accountant, bank, financial adviser and his manager.
13. He will waive his moral rights. As mentioned in Chapter 2 Copyright Law and the Copyright, Designs and Patents Act 1988, moral rights belong to the author of a literary or

musical work. Performers do not have moral rights, however a performer who is also the author of a literary or musical work would as the author have moral rights in the literary or musical work.

Although as a performer it does not matter if he waives moral rights (as he has none as a performer), his solicitor should check the clause does not also provide that he waives his moral rights as the author of any literary or musical work he has written. Any such reference in the clause should be deleted by the performer's solicitor.

14. He will not record with any other performer without first obtaining the record company's permission. (*See* Grant of rights by the performer above for "guest" appearances and how these can be dealt with in the agreement.)

15. He will deliver the minimum commitment required within the time provided for in the agreement. (See above for Minimum commitment.)

16. He will not use any samples on his recordings unless his record company has been informed beforehand and their use has been cleared. (*See* Chapter 2 Copyright Law and the Copyright, Designs and Patents Act 1998, Exclusive rights of copyright owner, Copying *for* sampling.)

17. Where the performer writes his own compositions, he will only record his own original compositions. The clause will also provide that the compositions must be new material and must not have been previously recorded. It may be that the performer will want to record some compositions written by other composers. This clause prohibits this. The performer's solicitor should amend the clause to allow the performer to record other people's compositions, although if the record company is signing the performer because he is a singer-song-writer rather than as a vocal interpreter of other people's compositions, it may put a limit upon the number of other people's compositions which he may record.

18. He cannot start recording his second or subsequent albums until he has delivered his previous recording to the record company, and he cannot deliver the new recording until say nine months after he has delivered his previous recording. (*See* Minimum commitment, Term, Options, above for details of why this clause is required by the record company.)

19. The recordings will be "technically and commercially acceptable". The performer will want to resist any reference to

the recordings being "commercially" acceptable. The record company will not usually be prepared to remove a reference to the recordings being "commercially" acceptable for a non-established performer. An established performer who may be negotiating a new recording agreement may be able to persuade the record company to remove a requirement that the recordings will be "commercially" acceptable on the basis of his proven commercial reputation.

20. He will record the material which has been selected by the record company. The record company will also require the performer to record at the recording studios which it has chosen and will require him to work with its chosen producer. The record company will not, due to its substantial financial investment, allow a non-established performer to make such choices on his own. At most a record company may agree to select the choice of material, the recording studios and the producer together with a non-established performer, although the record company will want the final say on such decisions. Established performers negotiating a new recording agreement will usually be able to negotiate more favourable terms relating to the material to be recorded, and the recording studios and producer to be used, although the record company will usually want to be consulted about such matters or will want qualified approval rights i.e. the right to approve the performer's decisions with such approval not to be unreasonably withheld.

The agreement will also provide that he will make himself available, will attend, co-operate and participate, as and when required at the recording sessions and any video recording sessions (including rehearsals for the recording sessions and any video recordings sessions and at the mixing and editing stages of the recording and video recording process).

The agreement should also deal with who will select and prepare the artwork for the record covers. Where the performer is not established the agreement will provide that the record company will do this, although the performer may be able to get consultation rights. The record company may agree to an established performer having the right to select and prepare the artwork for the record, although the record company will usually want consultation rights. Some established performers may be able to get the right to select and prepare the artwork without any need to consult the record company, although the record company will want the performer to warrant that the artwork is neither obscene, blasphemous, defamatory, nor infringes any copyright or any other third party rights. If possible the performer should attempt to get the record company to agree that a guaranteed minimum budget will be available for the artwork for each release, and that it will raise the guaranteed minimum budget for each subsequent release.

21. He will re-record those recordings which the record company has deemed under the terms of the agreement to be unacceptable, *e.g.* where they are not technically acceptable.

22. He will not re-record any material which he has recorded for the record company for anybody else for a period of five years after the term. This clause is an attempt to protect and maximise the economic value of the recordings as it enables the record company to exploit the recordings for five years after the term without any competition from similar recordings which might be made by the performer for another record company for which he might subsequently sign. After the five year period has expired the performer can re-record the material for another record company. The performer will want to cut back the length of the re-recording restriction to three years. In addition, the performer may be able to obtain a provision that he can re-record any recordings made by him which have not been released by the record company within one year after the end of the term.

23. He will, as and when required by the record company, participate in the making of promotional videos to accompany his recordings. The cost of making a video is frequently more expensive than the cost of making a record. Record companies are frequently loathed to commit themselves to finance the making of promotional videos, even though the finance is recoupable from the performer. The record company will often insert a requirement into the agreement that the performer will make a video to promote his recordings, as and when required. The performer will want the record company to commit itself to make a certain number of promotional videos, *e.g.* the performer might want a video made to accompany each single released. (*See* Record company's obligations (e) below *and see* Royalties below for how the cost of making videos is dealt with in the agreement.)

The agreement should provide who has control where a video is made over *e.g.* the video storyline, its producer and director. As the record company is initially paying the substantial video recording costs in nearly all cases it will want to have total control over the making of the video, although the performer may be able to negotiate either the right of approval, with such approval not to be unreasonably withheld, or the right to be consulted by the record company about the making of the video. (*See* Record company's obligations (e) below *and see* Royalties below for how the cost of making any videos and royalties payable on sales of videos will be dealt with in the agreement.)

24. He will not change his musical style or his professional image. The record company will want this clause to prevent what could be perceived as an inappropriate change of musical direction by the performer, *e.g.* they would have serious misgivings if the performer was a long haired, heavy metal performer whose professional image was that of a typical heavy metal performer suddenly deciding that he wanted to perform in the style of and adopt the image of a jazz singer. The performer will not want the record company completely controlling his musical style or his professional image and will resist a very restrictive clause. It may be possible to agree a less restrictive clause which will allow the record company some control over the performer's musical style and image, thereby allaying its concerns that the performer will not suddenly attempt to re-create himself in a completely new and unrelated field of music, whilst allowing the performer to have some latitude to change his musical style and image as his career develops and as public tastes change. A clause that might be acceptable to both the record company and the performer could be one which provides a list of musical styles in which the performer can perform that are deemed to be acceptable, with an acceptance that the professional image may change to reflect the musical style being performed. In addition, the clause could provide a list of musical styles which are not acceptable to the record company.

25. He will endeavour to stay in good health. The record company may require a best endeavours or a reasonable endeavours clause from the performer.

26. (If the record company wants to take out insurance cover on the performer), the performer will attend a medical

examination, if required by the record company's insurance company. He will, where insurance cover has been taken out by the record company, comply with any reasonable requirements of the insurance company to ensure that the insurance policy remains in force.

27. He is a member of, or will join the Musicians' Union.

28. He will not do anything which will bring himself or the record company into disrepute. This is commonly known as a morals clause. Some performers might be offended by the provision of a morals clause in the recording agreement and will want it removed. It should be noted that even if the record company will not agree to remove a morals clause from the agreement that it will only take action against a performer for a breach of the clause where his behaviour is extremely bad.

29. He will inform the record company of his current address and telephone number and will keep it informed as to where he can be contacted.

30. He will keep the record company informed of his proposed professional plans, *e.g.* where and when he will be touring. This will enable the record company to tie in record releases, national and local special promotions, local radio and television personal appearances and advertising campaigns to increase record sales. The record company may additionally require the performer to arrange a concert tour around the release of a single or album, and it may even want to approve or consult with the performer over the proposed dates, venues and tour budgets. This is not only to enable the record company to promote the records in the locality around the time of the concerts, but because it may be giving tour support to the performer (*see* Royalties below for tour support).

31. He will attend photo shoots. The performer will want the clause to provide that he will be available, subject to other prior personal or professional commitments, that he will be given a period of notice, *e.g.* seven days' notice, before the record company needs him, and that it will pay for his travel and other expenses incurred in complying with the clause. If the record company agrees to pay the performer's expenses the clause will provide that the expenses should be reasonable expenses which have been reasonably incurred and the company will require receipts to be provided.

32. He will make himself available for personal appearances and interviews which the record company reasonably requires to

promote the recordings. The performer will want the clause to provide that he will be available subject to other prior personal or professional commitments, that he will be given a period of notice, *e.g.* seven days' notice, before the record company needs him, and that it will pay for his travel and other expenses incurred in complying with the clause. If the record company agrees to pay the performer's expenses the clause will provide that the expenses should be reasonable expenses which have been reasonably incurred and the company will require receipts to be provided.

33. (Where royalties are to be paid by the record company directly into the performer's bank account), he will supply the record company with the name of his bank, the account name and number and the sort code to enable the payment to be made directly into the account.

The indemnity clause by the performer

The recording agreement will contain an indemnity clause requiring the performer to indemnify the record company for all the costs, liabilities, losses and damage which have been incurred by the record company due to any breach or non performance by him of the recording agreement. The performer should try to limit the scope of the indemnity so that he will only be liable to indemnify the record company for specific breaches. In addition, the performer should try to limit liability for the record company's costs to the reasonable costs which have been reasonably incurred by the record company, or to the record company's reasonable legal and other professional costs.

The record company may include a provision allowing them to withhold the performer's royalties in the event of there being any legal action concerning the performer in which they are involved. This would enable the record company to offset the money they are withholding against any loss or damage which they incur, rather than have to pursue the performer for the money due to them under an indemnity clause. The performer should not agree to such a provision. The performer may possibly be prepared to agree to a similar provision which will allow the record company to withhold his royalties provided:

(i)   the legal action involves a material breach of the performer's obligations, and

(ii) a limit is put on the amount of money which the record comany can withhold, and

(iii) any money withheld will be put on deposit to earn interest, and

(iv) that where the threat of legal proceedings does not lead to the issue of court proceedings within a specified time the money which has been withheld will be returned to the performer together with accrued interest.

Record company's obligations

The obligations which the record company will be expected to give include that:

(a) It will release the recordings and make them commercially available to the public. The clause should provide that it will release those recordings which are acceptable within a specified period of time, *e.g.* within a period of six months after they have been delivered to the record company. (*See* Performer's warranties and obligations (19) above for what is an acceptable recording.) It should be remembered that an agreement which does not contain an obligation to release may make the agreement liable to be in restraint of trade. The clause should provide that the recordings will initially be released to the public on the record company's top line label at full price. The record company will usually guarantee a release in the United Kingdom but will frequently not guarantee to release the record in other territories. The performer may be able to negotiate that the record company will guarantee release in some other territories as well as the United Kingdom, or may be able to get a guaranteed release in some other territories if, for example, the record achieves a top 10 placing or sales of 50,000 within three months of being put on sale in the United Kingdom.

Where, for example, the performer has not delivered the minimum commitment, or the recordings are not technically acceptable, the record company can rely upon the fact that the performer is in breach of his contractual obligations and it can legitimately refuse to comply with its obligation to release the recordings. The record company may, however, decide not to release the recordings for invalid reasons, for example, the people in the record company who believed in the performer have left (as is quite common in such a fast-moving industry) to be replaced by other people who do not have the same interest or belief in the performer. To allow for the possibility that the record company may, without any valid contractual reason, decide not to release the record, the performer should require a clause in the agreement which enables him to serve a notice on the record company requiring it to release the record within a specified time period, and that if the record company does not release the record in the time period provided for in the notice, then the performer can either:

(i) serve another notice on the record company terminating the agreement (which will include any future options) whereupon the record company will hand over the master tapes of the unreleased recordings to the performer and will assign/re-assign the copyright in them to the performer, or

(ii) serve another notice on the record company, whereupon the record company will hand over the master tapes of the unreleased recordings to the performer and will assign/re-assign the copyright in them to the performer. The difference to (i) above is that in this scenario the recording agreement is not terminated.

Although (i) and (ii) above provide for the performer to obtain the unreleased recordings, the record company will not give them up lightly. If (and it is a big if) it is prepared to let the performer obtain the unreleased recordings, it will usually want the performer to repay the record company for the recording costs which have been incurred, and for its reasonable legal fees incurred in assigning the copyright in the sound recording and a nominal sum of, say, £250 per master track. Most record companies will not readily agree to a clause which enables the performer to obtain any unreleased recordings. A record company might instead agree to a clause which provides that where the record has not been released in a particular territory(ies), if another record company is interested in releasing these recordings on terms which are similar to those contained in the performer's recording agreement, it will grant a licence to that record company to release them but only in the territory(ies) where the record has not been released. The record company will also want the licensed record company to pay it all the royalties. The royalty money received will be divided between the performer and the record company in the proportions set out in the recording agreement as if it and not the licensed record company had released the record, and it will in due course pay the performer his share, provided of course he is recouped, otherwise this money will be used to reduce his account deficit with the record company. Finally, in addition to the record company taking a share of the royalty income from sales of the licensed recordings, the record company will take an additional override royalty of between 2–5%, which the record company deducts from the royalty money it receives from the licensed record company before it is divided up between itself and the performer. Essentially, this is a fee for the record company agreeing to, and implementing, the clause in the agreement relating to licensing the unreleased recordings to another record company.

(b) (In some agreements the record company may agree that) having released the recordings on its top line label at full price it will not bring the record out on any mid-price label or budget price label for an agreed minimum period of time, *e.g.* it will not bring out the record on any mid-price label until a period of two years after the initial release of the record on their top line label, and it will not bring out the record on any budget price label until a period of four years after the initial release of the record on its top line label.

(c) It will provide the recording facilities for the performer and will pay for the costs of the recording. The clause will provide that the recording costs will be paid for by the record company as an additional advance. This means that although the record company initially pays the recording costs they are recoupable from the performer's royalties, and if the performer is successful he and not the record company will in the end pay for the recording costs. Recording costs are recoupable from royalties due to the performer from all of the recordings made during the term of the agreement. This means that if an album has flopped the unrecouped recording costs can be recovered out of the royalties due to the performer from hit albums recorded during the agreement.

The definition of recording costs must be examined very closely to ensure that only those items relating to recording costs are recoupable from the performer, (*see* Royalties below for what are recording costs).

It may be possible for the performer to obtain a guarantee that the record company will make a minimum amount available to record each album, and that the guaranteed minimum amount will increase for each album, or that it will be increased if the record company exercises an option.

(d) The released recordings will contain a credit naming the performer as the performer of the recordings. This is to prevent any possibility that the record company might release the recordings without crediting the performer as the performer of the recordings.

(e) It will, at its own expense, promote the performer and his recordings. The performer would ideally want the record company to agree to use its best endeavours to promote the performer and his recordings. The record company will usually only agree to a reasonable endeavours clause.

It should be noted that if the record company uses a specialist promotions company in addition to its own in-house promotions department to promote a recording that the record company will usually deduct half of the external company's costs from the gross royalty. The performer's solicitor should ensure that a ceiling is placed upon the amount of cost that can be deducted for specialist promotions per single and album, e.g. that half the cost of specialist promotions incurred by the record company can be deducted from the gross royalty up to a maximum of £x per single and £y per album. (*See also* Deductions from the gross royalty (h) below *and* Items not to be deducted form gross royalty (d) below.)

Also, the agreement will usually provide that any costs incurred by the record company promoting the performer in a way that it would not usually do, such as running a national radio and/or television campaign, will be shared between the record company and the performer. Where this happens the record company would pay the costs incurred but half of these costs would be recoupable from the gross royalty. (*See also* Royalties, Deductions from the gross royalty (i) below, Items not to be deducted from gross royalty (d) below and Royalty rates for different formats and different types of exploitation (s) below.) Where there is such a provision in the agreement, if the performer cannot get the record company to remove it, then he should try and:

(i)   reduce his percentage contribution, and
(ii) get the right for him to approve the content of the campaign, or at the least he should try and get consultation rights, and
(iii) get the right for him to approve the campaign budget.

In addition, the performer's solicitor should check whether the royalty rate is affected by such advertising. It may be that the royalty rate is reduced by the record company for records sold in the territory(ies) where a special promotional campaign takes place during the time of that campaign. (*See* Royalty rates for different formats and different types of exploitation (s) below.) The performer would not want to be responsible for half of the special promotional campaign costs and also have the royalty rate on the records sold during the time of a special promotional campaign reduced. If the performer is responsible for half of the special promotional campaign costs he should not have his royalty reduced on the records sold during the time of the special promotional campaign. If the record company wants to do a special promotional campaign at its own expense then it might be acceptable for the royalty rate to be reduced for records sold in the territory(ies) where a special promotional campaign takes place during the time of that campaign.

Promotional videos are commonly used by the record company to promote the record and the performer. They are notoriously expensive to produce. A single video may easily cost more to make than recording a whole album. A promotional video is made to help increase record sales. Promotional videos may be commercially exploited by being put on sale to the public, but the money made from video sales will not usually, if ever, recoup the video recording costs. The performer will usually have to negotiate a clause in the agreement requiring the record company to make promotional videos. Because of the costs involved, the record company would ideally prefer promotional videos to be made as and when it wants rather than have to make them on the occasions specified in the recording agreement, *e.g.* whenever the performer releases a single. (*See also* Performer's warranties and obligations (23) above.) Where a video is made the record company will pay for the video recording costs but will want them to be recoupable from the performer. The record company will try to make all the video recording costs recoupable from the performer's record royalties and from his video royalties (which are likely to be very small in comparison to his record royalties). This will mean that a successful selling performer may well find 100% of the video recording costs are offset against his record royalties, which would therefore substantially reduce the record royalties payable to him. The performer's solicitor should, if he cannot get the record company to agree to recoup video recording costs only from the performer's video royalties (which the record company will rarely if ever agree to), amend the clause to provide that 50% of the video recording costs can be added to the performer's record recording costs and so can be recouped from his record royalties and the other 50% of the video recording costs can only be recouped from the performer's video royalties.

(f) Where it is under an obligation to make a certain number of videos the performer may possibly also get the record company to agree to spend a minimum amount to record each video. (*See also* Performer's warranties and obligations (23) above.) The performer's solicitor might also be able to obtain a clause in the agreement that the record company will not only spend a minimum amount to record each video but it will also increase the minimum amount it has guaranteed throughout the term of the agreement, *e.g.* the minimum guarantee spend will be higher for videos made to accompany the second album than for videos made to accompany the first album.

(g) It will pay for tour support. Most record companies will agree to some sort of tour support provision in the agreement. Tour support is money which is given by the record company to pay for the losses incurred by the performer whilst on tour. Many performers such as The Rolling Stones earn considerable sums out of a concert tour. However, most performers starting out on their career cannot afford to tour. Some established performers actually charge the support band, who may be known performers themselves, to tour with them as it helps to defray their touring costs and increase their touring profits. Some venues, far from paying performers, will require the performers to pay them for playing in their venue. Most performers need to tour to promote their records. A record company will often agree to provide tour support because touring is promotion, and promotion helps sell records. If the performer cannot tour because he cannot afford to, this will seriously affect record sales, if not even kill the performer's career before it has had a chance to get off the ground. If the record company agrees to provide tour support there will be conditions placed upon such support. It will probably want to approve the proposed concert dates, venues, and most matters concerning the concert including, most importantly, the proposed tour costs. To enable the record company to establish whether the tour has made a loss and so require it to pay tour support, the agreement will detail exactly what are the allowable expenses which can be deducted from tour income, *e.g.* receipted travel expenses, hotel accommodation, and equipment hire up to a certain amount will be regarded as allowable expenses, whilst, for example, commission on tour income payable by the performer to his manager will not be an allowable expense. The record company will not agree to an open-ended liability to pay for any tour losses and will put a limit on the amount it will provide. The record company may, where it is prepared to pay tour support, want the tour support to be recoupable from the performer's royalties. The performer should resist tour support being recoupable from his royalties and should ensure that it is treated as a record company expense on the basis that it is standard promotion for the record.

(h) It will pay the advances specified in the agreement, and will both during and after the agreement term collect in the income from exploiting the recordings and will pay the performer his royalties at the rates set out in the royalty clause. (*See* Royalties below for details.) It will either pay the royalties into the performer's bank account, or if so directed will send the royalties to his manager, in which case the clause will provide that the manager's receipt will satisfy the record company's duty to pay the royalties to the performer.

(i) It will keep accounts detailing the number of the performer's recordings sold, the income received from other uses of the recordings, *e.g.* from licensing a recording for use in a television advertisement, and the amount of royalties which are due to the performer. (*See* Accounting and auditing below.)

(j) It will keep the contents of the agreement confidential. The clause should allow the record company to disclose the contents of the agreement to its lawyer, accountant, bank and financial adviser.

The indemnity clause by the record company

The recording agreement should contain an indemnity clause by the record company requiring the record company to indemnify the performer for all the costs, liabilities, losses and damage which have been incurred by the performer due to any breach or non performance by the record company of the recording agreement. The record company should try to limit the scope of the indemnity so that he will only be liable to indemnify the performer for specific breaches. In addition, the record company should try to limit liability for the performer's costs to the reasonable costs which have been reasonably incurred by the performer, or to the performer's reasonable legal and other professional costs.

Advances

A performer will want to ensure he can get as large an advance from the record company as possible. Indeed, many performers are more concerned about the size of the advance than the royalty rates which they will be paid for sales and other uses of their recordings. The size of the advance will depend upon the status of the performer, upon how many record companies are chasing the performer for his signature, and upon the type of music the performer plays, *e.g.* a jazz musician may not necessarily expect to get as large an advance as a rock musician because jazz music does not sell in the same numbers as rock music. Indeed, some performers may not even be offered an advance at all. As an extremely rough guide, a new performer may get an advance from a token figure up to £100,000. It must be stressed that the upper limit is extremely rare for a new performer. The advance figure will usually be toward the bottom end of the spectrum. For an established performer the size of the advance will depend to a considerable extent upon his past sales and how much the record company believes his sales record will continue in the future. An established performer may be able to command a sizeable advance with the top end being in the region of £250,000. For super-stars, frequently the sky is the limit and they can to a large extent not only name their price but also the terms of the agreement.

The advance is non-returnable but recoupable against royalties, *i.e.* the performer will not be required to return the advance or any part of it if the record company does not recoup the advance out of the income earned from exploiting the recordings. Where a performer is being chased by more than one record company, or is an established performer or superstar, in addition to an advance, he may be able to get a signing on fee which will not be recoupable, or may be able to negotiate that part of the advance is paid as a non-recoupable signing on fee.

In only a few cases will the whole of the advance be paid to the performer on signing the agreement. The record company will usually pay the advance in stages throughout the term of the agreement. The agreement will usually provide that a percentage of the advance will be paid upon signing the agreement, a percentage when the performer starts recording, a percentage on delivery of the recordings and a percentage on the release of the recordings.

The performer's solicitor should try to negotiate a clause in the agreement which will provide for a further advance to be paid if a specified event(s) occur. For example, a further advance could be paid if the record achieves either a particular number of sales or a particular chart placing within a specified period of time after its release in the UK. As an alternative, if the actual recording costs are less than then minimum amount which has been guaranteed by the record company — the difference between the two could be paid as a further advance.

The performer's solicitor should ensure that when the record company exercises an option that a further advance is paid and that the further advance is higher than any previous advance. Rather than have a fixed figure in the agreement, there may be a provision allowing for a formula to be used to calculate the advance payable when an option is exercised. For example, the agreement may provide that if an option is exercised a further advance will be payable (which will be payable in specified stages) and that the advance will be 50% of the royalties earned on sales in the UK on the record company's top line label during the first nine months of release of the album which was released prior to the exercise of the option. (Greatest Hits or Best of albums should be excluded here and the album released previously should be used to calculate the advance.) In any event the advance being paid might be specified as being not less than £75,000 and not more than £175,000.

The performer's solicitor may be able to obtain a provision that a further advance will be payable if the record company releases a greatest hits or best of album. Where the record company agrees to pay such an advance, it will usually provide that any money which is unrecouped when the further advance is payable will be deducted from that advance. In this case the performer's solicitor should try to obtain a floor figure for the further advance, e.g. where the further advance is £60,000 less any unrecouped amount but with a floor of £20,000, if the performer has £50,000 unrecouped, he will receive a further advance of £20,000 and not £10,000.

Some companies will pay the performer an additional sum of money as a further advance to cover recording costs, in which case it is the performer's responsibility to write the cheques to pay the recording costs. Other record companies prefer not to give the performer a further advance to cover recording costs and instead write the cheques to pay the recording costs themselves. Whichever method is used, the recording costs will be treated as money spent by the record company which is recoupable from the performer's royalties.

Where the agreement provides that advances are payable in stages and that the record company will pay the performer an additional sum as a further advance to cover the recording costs, the performer's solicitor should check the agreement to ensure that the performer will be paid the recording costs advance in time for him to pay these costs as and when they fall due.

The performer's solicitor should try to ensure that when the record company exercises an option, the advance payable for exercising the option is payable in full (albeit in stages) and cannot be used by the record company to recoup any unrecouped balance on the performer's account.

Royalties

Usually royalties are paid on a percentage of the sale proceeds of the recordings. It is important that the performer's solicitor checks exactly what is meant in the agreement by "sale proceeds". Sale proceeds will usually be either:

(a) the wholesale price of the recordings (commonly called dealer price or published dealer price "PDP") excluding VAT, or

(b) a fictional retail price. The fictional retail price is created by taking the wholesale price excluding VAT and multiplying it by a percentage (which is 129% for CDs and 131% for cassettes).

In addition, most record companies will provide that royalties are paid on the sale proceeds which they have received, thus ensuring that they do not pay royalties where they have not been paid themselves.

(*See also* Chapter 7 The Publishing Agreement, The controlled composition clause, where a percentage of PDP is used to calculate the cost of a mechanical licence.)

Although royalties are usually paid on a percentage of either PDP or the fictional retail price, before the actual amount of royalties due to the performer can be calculated, the cost of the record packaging has to be deducted. For CDs the packaging deduction is 25% and for cassettes 20%. The reason why packaging is deducted is because the record company maintain it is paying the performer for sales of the recordings and not for sales of the recordings and the packaging in which the recording is contained. The packaging deduction are industry standard figures used and do not reflect the actual cost of packaging, which in reality is less than 25% for CDs and 20% for cassettes. (The recording agreement will specify how the recordings will be packaged, *e.g.* it will set out the number of pages the CD booklet can have. If the performer wants special packaging like Pink Floyd's Pulse CD which has a cardboard cover with a flashing red light set in the spine of the cover into which the CD case fits, or wants a different coloured CD plastic case, or merely extra pages in the CD booklet, the record company will if it agrees to the request charge a higher packaging deduction and/or seek to reduce the royalty rate for the record. (*See also* Royalty rates for different formats and different types of exploitation below.) The figure which is reached after the packaging costs have been deducted is called the royalty base.

The royalty rate the record company is prepared to pay the performer depends upon the same criteria used in deciding the advance they are prepared to pay the perfomer. The royalty rate recommended by the Musicians' Union for a new performer is between 10–14% of the fictional retail price. The equivalent rate if the record company pays royalties based on PDP is 13–18%. (The reason the royalty rate is usually higher where PDP is used is because PDP is about 30% lower than the fictional retail price. Therefore, a royalty based upon the dealer price should be 30% higher to equate to a royalty based upon the fictional retail price). (*See also* Royalty rates for different formats and different types of exploitation below.)

The royalty base should be multiplied by the royalty rate to give the royalty rate per record. The royalty rate per record should then be multiplied by the number of records sold which will give the gross royalty due to the performer. (See below for a worked example.)

(It should be noted that some independent record companies instead of paying royalties on a percentage of the sale proceeds will instead pay the performer a royalty based upon the "net profit" before VAT from the exploitation of the recordings. The performer can expect to negotiate a royalty in the region of 40–60% of the net profit. The performer's solicitor must check what items the record company proposes to deduct from the gross income and that these items are acceptable deductions. Essentially, the acceptable deductible items from gross income are the actual costs which are payable by the record company to others, *e.g.* recording costs. The record company's own operating expenses, *e.g.* rent, staffing, heating, lighting are not acceptable deductions.)

Deductions from the gross royalty

The performer does not get paid the gross royalty. There are certain deductions which will be made from the gross royalty. The deductions are for:

(a) Free copies. Between 5–10% of the gross royalties will be deducted for free copies which have been distributed by the record company to the record shops to encourage them to stock more copies of the performer's recordings. Some record companies may not put a limit on the amount of free copies which they can distribute or insert an unacceptably high figure. The performer's solicitor should ensure that a limit of between 5–10% for free copies is inserted into the agreement.

(b) Promotional copies. The record companies will send copies of the record to radio and television stations and club disc jockeys to encourage them to play the record.

Promotional records (called promos) are packaged in either the same packaging as that used for copies which are on retail sale and can be differentiated from retail copies by the fact that the CD case, and/or the actual CD packaging, and/or the CD itself is stamped as a promotional copy, or it may be packaged in less elaborate packaging than the copies which are on retail sale, *e.g.* the CD might just be packaged in a simple white cardboard sleeve with no artwork with details of the tracks printed on the cover.

Certainly, promos records are a vital way to promote the performer and his record; they help increase awareness of the record and will usually increase record sales. As promos are given away free and not sold the record company will not pay the performer a royalty for them. Although promos are a necessary and useful marketing tool, the performer's solicitor should be concerned about the number of promos which might be given away. The performer's solicitor should therefore insert a limit in the agreement on the number of promos which can be given away and which do not bear a royalty.

(c) Breakages. A few record companies may try to deduct between 5 and 10% for breakages. The performer's solicitor should resist a deduction for breakages. In reality CDs, casssettes etc do not break easily. The reason why record companies originally made a deduction for breakages is because in the days of 78 rpm records, records were liable to break very easily because they were made of shellac. Nowadays some record companies seek a deduction for breakages because it reduces the actual royalty payable. If the record company wants a deduction for breakages and refuses to delete it, the performer's solicitor should try and negotiate an increase in the royalty rate by an amount which cancels out the deduction for breakages.

(d) Some record companies may try to deduct between 5 and 10% for returns. The record company only pays royalties on record sales and not on records which it has manufactured and distributed to the record shops for them to sell. The record company may manufacture and distribute 80,000 copies of the record in different formats to the shops but that does not mean that 80,000 copies will sell. Certainly, some will be returned by the shops as they cannot sell them, and in the worst scenario if the record is an absolute turkey 80,000 records may come back to roost with the record company. Some record companies may insert a provision in the recording agreement allowing them to deduct between 5 and 10% for records which have been returned as unsold. Although this might seem on the surface to be an acceptable deduction, the performer's solicitor should delete any such clause where the agreement also contains a clause which allows the record company to keep a reserve out of the royalties to allow for returns. (*See* below for Reserves against returns.) Any clause allowing the record company to deduct between 5 and 10% for returns where there is a separate right for the record company to hold back a reserve against returns is unnecessary and is just a way of reducing the royalty due to the performer.

(e) The advance paid to the performer (including, any additional advance given by the record company to the performer for him to pay for the recording costs).

(f) The recording costs, where the record company actually pays for them instead of advancing extra money to the performer for him to pay them.

Whether the performer or the record company actually writes the cheque for the recording costs, at the end of the day they are recoupable from the performer's royalties. The agreement should define exactly what is meant by recording costs. It will include the cost of the record producer, the studio engineers, the cost of session musicians who are used, the hire of the equipment including the hire of any instruments, the cost of the recording tape and the cost of the studio hire. (*see also* below for the Producer.)

The definition of recording costs may include items such as the cost of remixing the recordings and of cutting. These are items which the performer will not want to be responsible for. The performer will only want to be liable for those costs which are incurred in making acceptable recordings. The performer does not want to be liable for any of the costs, such as the cutting costs which have to be incurred in converting and manufacturing the recordings into LPs, CDs, cassettes, etc. These costs should be the responsibility of the record company.

The performer will need to pay the costs of mixing the recordings but he will not want to be responsible for any remixing costs because the recording once mixed, provided it is an acceptable recording, is the finished product from the performer's point of view. Remixing is the taking of an acceptable finished recording and putting a different musicial slant on it. Remixing is very popular especially for dance music and in many cases a remix helps to sell records. The remixed version of a recording may be the reason why the record is a hit. (There are many thousands of examples of records which have been remixed, *e.g.* see Toni Braxton's soul ballad, "Un-Break My Heart", Everything But The Girl's pop song "Missing", and Terrorvision's rock/metal tune "Tequilla" each of which were re-mixed into a dance version.) An acceptable recording can be and often is re-mixed into many different versions and the performer will not want to be liable for these costs as they will substantially reduce his royalty.

(g) Video recording costs. As mentioned above, (*see* Record company obligations (e) above), the record company will try to make all the video recording costs recoupable from the performer's record royalties and from his video royalties (which are likely to be very small in comparison to his record royalties). This will mean that a successful selling performer may well find 100% of the video recording costs are offset against his record royalties, which would therefore substantially reduce the record royaties payable to him. The performer's solicitor should, if he cannot get the record company to agree to recoup video recording costs only from the performer's video royalties (which the record company will rarely if ever agree to), amend the clause to provide that 50% of the video recording costs can be added to the performer's record recording costs and so can be recouped from his record royalties and the other 50% of the video recording costs can only be recouped from the performer's video royalties.

(h) Promotion costs charged by a specialist promotions company which may be used in addition to the record company's own in house promotions department, *e.g.* a plugging company which will use their contacts with radio producers and programmers to help the record company get the record directly to these people in the hope that they will listen to it and put it on the radio station playlist. Although the record company has its own staff who promote the record, many of the people who have the best contacts do not work as record company employees but work independently of them. Specialist promotions companies can make the difference between a record being a success or a failure and are often used by record companies. Where a specialist promotions company is used, half the cost is usually deducted from the gross royalty. The performer's solicitor should ensure that a ceiling is placed upon the amount of costs that can be deducted for specialist promotion per single and album, e.g. that half the cost of specialist promotion incurred by the record company can be deducted from the gross royalty up to a maximum of £x per single and £y per album.

The costs charged by a specialist promotions company should be distinguished from record company in house promotions costs which should not be deducted from the gross royalty. (*See* Record company's obligations (e) above and Items not to be deducted from gross royalty (d) below.)

(i) Where the record company promotes the performer's record in a way that it would not normally do, *e.g.* by running a national radio and/or television campaign, the record company will usually deduct half of these costs from the gross royalty. As mentioned above, (see Record company's obligations (e) above, the performer's solicitor should check whether the royalty rate is affected by such advertising. It may be that the royalty rate is reduced by the record company for records sold in the territory(ies) where a special promotional campaign takes place in a specified time period. The performer would not want to be responsible for half the costs of a special promotional campaign and also have the royalty rate on the records sold during the time of the campaign reduced. If the performer is responsible for half of the campaign costs he should not have his royalty reduced on the records sold during the time of the special promotional campaign. If the record company wants to do a special promotional campaign at his own expense then it might be acceptable for the royalty rate to be reduced for records sold in the territory(ies) where the campaign takes place. (*See* also Record company's obligations (e) above, Items not to be deducted from gross royalty (d) below and Royalty rates for different formats and different types of exploitation (s) below.)

Items not to be deducted from gross royalty

There are are certain items which should not be deducted by the record company from the gross royalty. These are:

(a) the cost of designing the artwork for the sleeve,
(b) the cost incurred in manufacturing LPs, CDs, cassettes etc,
(c) the cost of distributing the records,
(d) the cost of promoting and advertising the recording.
As mentioned above, (*see* Deductions from the gross royalty (h) above), half of any promotion costs charged by a specialist promotions company is usually deducted from the gross royalty, but in house promotions costs should not be deducted from the gross royalty as they are a business operating expense which should be borne by the record company.

Also as mentioned above, (*see* Record company's obligations (e) above) the agreement will usually provide for the sharing of any costs incurred by the record company in promoting the performer in an exceptional manner, such as radio and/or television campaigns. Thus the record company would pay the costs incurred but half the costs would be recoupable from the gross royalty. (*See also* Deductions from the gross royalty (i) above and Record company's obligations (e) above, and Royalty rates for different formats and different types of exploitation (s) below). This type of promotion should be distinguished from the record company's normal promotion which should not be deducted from the gross royalty.

(e) any tour support. (*See* Record Company's Obligations (g) above for tour support.)

(f) mechanical licence fees and mechanical royalties.

Record companies should pay the performer royalties for sales of all the recordings. However, some record companies do not pay the performer royalties based on 100% of sales, but pay only on 85 or 90% of sales. The reasoning behind this is that the record company is allowing itself a margin for breakages. If the record company proposes a royalty based upon 85 or 90% of sales this should be resisted by the performer's solicitor, who should either insist on royalties being paid on 100% of sales, or ensure that the royalty rate is uplifted to take account of the fact that royalties are paid on 85 or 90% of sales.

The agreement should be checked to ensure that it does not contain a deduction for breakages (*see* Deductions from the Gross Royalty (c) above for breakages), a deduction for returns (*see* Deductions from the Gross Royalty (d) above for returns), and a provision for royalties to be paid on 85 or 90% of sales. There should be no need for the record company to make any deduction for breakages, any deduction for returns, nor for royalties to be paid on less than 100% of sales as the agreement will usually contain a provision which enables the record company to withhold royalties due to the performer as a reserve against returns. (*See* below for Reserves against returns.) Any attempt by the record company to make deductions for breakages and returns and to pay only on 85 or 90% of sales where there is a provision allowing the record company to withhold royalties due to the performer as a reserve against returns is an unacceptable way of reducing the royalties due to the performer.

Reserves against returns

As mentioned above, the record company will want to withhold royalties due to the performer as a reserve against returns due to the fact that it pays royalties on records which have been sold and not on records which have been distributed. Although the records may appear to the performer to have sold, the record company has only shipped them to the shops in the hope that they may sell. The record company will therefore want to withhold royalties due to the performer as a reserve against returns until it is clear whether the records have sold. (See below for how the performer's solicitor should deal with such a provision in the agreement). The reserve will be based upon the gross royalties due to the performer. It is only fair that the record company should be allowed to withhold some of the performer's royalties as a reserve against returns in case the record does not sell and is returned to the record company. The performer's solicitor should ensure that the agreement does not allow the record company carte blanche to decide the amount of the performer's royalties which it can withhold as a reserve against actions. The performer's solicitor should ensure that the agreement only allows the record company to withhold a fixed percentage of the performer's royalties as a reserve against returns. This fixed percentage will depend on the status of the performer. An acceptable reserve for a performer with no track record would be in the region of 20–25% whereas for an established performer the reserve may be in the region of 5–10%. If the record company agrees that it can only withhold a fixed percentage of the performer's royalties as a reserve against returns, it may require the percentage which it can withhold to be different for each format in which is releases the record. For example, it may want a 20% reserve for CDs, 20% for cassettes, 20% for LPs, 35% for Mini Discs and 50% for singles. The reason why the record company may want a different percentage for each format in which it releases the record rather than a standard across the board percentage is because it knows it is likely to have far more returns of singles and of new formats such as Mini Disc than for CDs, cassettes and LPs. In addition, where the record company agrees that it can only withhold a fixed percentage of the performer's royalties as a reserve against returns, it will usually want the right to increase the fixed percentage which it can withhold if, for example, it allows the performer who may be a pop singer, to release a jazz style album or a Christmas-themed album.

The performer's solicitor should ensure the agreement provides that the balance of any reserve which has been withheld by the record company (namely the amount left after deducting from the reserve the royalties which are no longer payable because records have been returned) will be liquidated – i.e. paid to the performer — at the latest two years after the record has been initially distributed. The performer's solicitor should try to ensure that the balance of any reserve will be liquidated rateably during the two years over four accounting periods (i.e. 30 June and 31 December each year) rather than wait for the two years before the balance of any reserve is liquidated. (*See* Accounting and auditing below for royalty accounting.) In addition, the performer's solicitor should try to ensure that any reserve which is withheld by the record company will be held in a bank account to earn interest which is payable to the performer.

The producer

The choice of producer can often make the difference between a record being a success or a failure. In many respects the producer is the person who takes the performer's compositions and ideas and by using his own creative and technical ability will transform them into a commercially acceptable product. Some producers may be regarded as unofficial members of the band, *e.g.* Sir George Martin and The Beatles. Others, who are equally as important, take a performer or a band and add their unique production style to the performer's musical style, *e.g.* Quincy Jones, William Orbit, Jam and Lewis, Babyface, and Brian Eno to name but a few. A successful producer will recreate or even help write the compositions which the performer will record.

A producer may want a fee to produce the performer as well as royalties and a non-returnable but recoupable advance. In addition, the producer will, if he helps the performer to write compositions for the record, usually want a co-writing credit and a share in the publishing royalties. A successful producer's record royalty will be up to 5% of the fictional retail price. Usually the producer's record royalty will be in the region of 3% of the fictional retail price.

The producer's production fee, advance and record royalties are strictly speaking the performer's responsibility and have to be paid for by the performer out of any monies he receives from the record company and where these monies are insufficient to pay the producer, the performer will have to pay the producer out of any other source of income which he may have.

As will be seen below, the producer will frequently be entitled to receive his royalties at an earlier stage than the performer. The performer's solicitor should try to obtain a provision in the recording agreement that the record company will actually pay the producer's royalties and will treat these payments as additional advances which are recoupable from the performer's royalties. The performer's solicitor should also try to obtain an additional provision in the recording agreement that where the record company pays the producer's royalties, that part of the producer's royalties will not be recoupable from the performer. If the record company agrees to the first provision, it might agree to the additional provision, where it wants the performer to work with a particular producer and the producer wants more than a 3% royalty. In such a case the record company might agree that the excess royalty over 3% is not recoupable from the performer.

If the record company will not agree to pay the producer's royalty the performer will have to pay the producer himself, in which case the performer should set money aside from any advance he receives from the record company so that he can pay the producer's royalties. Even where the record company will not agree to pay the producer's royalties, the performer's solicitor should still try to obtain a provision in the recording agreement similar to the additional provision discussed at the end of the previous paragraph.

Care should be taken to ensure that the producer does not receive a higher royalty than the performer. In addition, care should be taken to ensure that the calculation of the producer's royalty in the production agreement contains the same deductions as in the performer's agreement e.g. for packaging, free copies and promos, and the same royalty rates for different formats and different types of exploitation. (*See below* for Royalty rates for different formats and different types of exploitation.) A detailed discussion of a production agreement is beyond the scope of this book.

As mentioned above, the producer will frequently be entitled to receive his royalties at an earlier stage than the performer. This is because the performer will only receive royalties from the record company once he is in a recouped position, in other words, after the record company has recouped, inter alia, any advance, recording costs, half of any video recording costs which have been added to his recording account, half the costs charged by specialist promotions companies, and half the costs incurred by the record company promoting the record in a way it would not normally do. In comparison, all the producer will usually have to recoup is the advance which was paid to him. It should be noted that the production agreement will usually provide that the producer will be entitled to royalties on every copy of the recording sold, but that he will not actually be paid any royalties until such time as the recording costs have been recouped.

(The production agreement may provide that the recording costs will be recouped at the combined performer and producer royalty rate prescribed in the recording agreement i.e. if the recordings are only ever released on CD and the performer gets a royalty of £1 per CD which includes a 30p royalty for the producer, the recording costs will be recouped at a royalty rate of £1. Alternatively, the production agreement may provide that the recording costs will be recouped at the performer's royalty rate which in this case is 70p, i.e. £1 less the 30p producer royalty.)

A prudent producer will obviously be concerned that the performer will not be able to pay him any monies which are due to him. Therefore the producer should ensure that the production agreement provides that the record company will be responsible for paying any monies which are due to him.

Royalty calculation example

Having seen in detail how the royalty is calculated it would be useful to see a worked example showing how the pieces fit together. If we assume the following:

(a) The performer has negotiated his first recording agreement with a royalty rate for CDs of 12% of the fictional retail price.

(b) The performer receives an advance from the record company of £10,000.

(c) For the purposes of this example the fictional retail price of a CD is £10. (This figure has been reached by taking the wholesale price excluding VAT and multiplying it by 129%).

(d) For the purposes of this example the first album will be only ever be released on CD on the record company's top line label at full price in the United Kingdom.

(e) There is a packaging deduction of 25%.

(f) The producer of the album receives a 2% royalty rate. (The calculation of the producer's royalty which is set out in the production agreement contains the same deductions (*e.g.* for packaging, free copies and promos) as are in the performer's recording agreement.) The record company has agreed to pay all the producer's royalties and also agreed that the producer's royalties will not be recoupable from the performer. (*See* The producer above for how the producer's royalties are usually dealt with. This unusual provision has been included in order to make the calculation easier to follow.)

(g) Recording costs are £100,000.

(h) Video recording costs come to £100,000 but only half of this sum (£50,000) is recoupable from record royalties. The other half is recoupable out of video royalties.

(i) An independent promotions company is used to promote the album and it has charged £40,000, of which only half (£20,000) is recoupable from record royalties.

(j) Free copies and promos total 10% of sales (which was the limit agreed upon by the performer and the record company in the recording agreement).

(k) There is no deduction for breakages in the agreement.

(l) There is no deduction for returns in the agreement.

(m) Sales of the CD total 350,000 copies.

(o) The record company will retain 20% as a reserve against returns. (The record company withholds the reserve based upon the gross royalty total.) The agreement provides that any unused reserve will be liquidated two years after the record has been initially distributed. There is no provision in the agreement for any unused reserve to be liquidated over four accounting periods during the two year period.

(Fictional retail) CD price	£10.00
Minus	–
Packaging (25%)	£ 2.50
Royalty base	£ 7.50

Royalty base	£ 7.50
Multiplied by	×
Performer's royalty rate	12%
Royalty per CD	£ 0. 90p

Royalty per CD	£0. 90p
Multiplied by	x
CD sales	350,000
Gross royalty total	£315,000

Gross royalty total	£315,000
Minus	–
Free goods and promos (10%)	(£31,500)
Recording costs	(£100,000)
Video recording costs	(£50,000)
(50% of £100,000)	
Independent promotion	(£20,000)
(50% of £40,000)	
Advance received from	(£10,000)
the record company	
Total royalty due to the	£103,500
performer from the record	
company	

Although the performer appears to be entitled to a royalty of £103,500 on album sales of 350,000 copies the record company will not pay the whole £103,500 to the performer as there is a 20% reserve against returns against the gross royalty, namely £63,000, *i.e.* 20% of £315,000. The performer is only entitled at this stage to a royalty of £40,500. The £63,000 which has been withheld by the record company will be liquidated two years after the record has been initially distributed.

Royalty rates for different formats and different types of exploitation

As mentioned earlier (*see* Royalties above) the royalty rate recommended by the Musicians' Union for a new performer is 10–14% of the fictional retail price. The equivalent rate if the record company pays royalties based on PDP is 13–18%. This is the recommended royalty rate for a recording which is sold on the record company's top line label at full price in the United Kingdom, (which will be called in the examples below "full rate"). The royalty rate will depend upon the format in which the recording is released, *e.g.* the full rate royalty for a CD might be, say, 14% of PDP, whereas the full rate royalty for a cassette might be, say, 16% of PDP. In addition, if the recording is:

(a) Released on the record company's mid-price label, the royalty rate will be in the region of 66.6% of the full rate.
(b) Released on the record company's budget label, the royalty rate will be in the region of 50–66.6% of the full rate.
(c) Sold to the armed forces, the royalty rate will be in the region of 50% of the full rate.

(d) Sold to libraries or other educational establishments, the royalty rate will be in the region of 50% of the full rate.

(e) Released as a 12" single, the record company may try to get the performer to accept that a certain number will be royalty free. The performer's solicitor should try and ensure that all copies will bear a royalty or limit the numbers which are royalty free. The royalty rate will be in the region of 75% of the full rate.

(f) Released as a single, the royalty rate will be in the region of 75% of the full rate.

(g) Released as a picture disc, there will be no royalty payable on the sales of these copies. There was a fashion in the late 1970s and early 1980s for singles and indeed some albums to be released as picture discs with a picture contained within the record, *e.g.* The Cars My Best Friend's Girl single was released with a picture of a car on the record itself. Picture discs are still occasionally released and may help push the record into the charts encouraging the public to buy the standard release format. The performer will be concerned that if all sales of the record are on picture disc, he will not earn any royalties. The record company will resist any attempt by the performer's solicitor to get the full single or album royalty rate for a picture disc, but will usually agree to limit the number of records which will be released on picture disc, *e.g.* to 5,000 or 10,000 copies.

(h) Released in territories outside the United Kingdom, the record company will reduce the royalty rate for these territories. The record company may divide the world excluding the United Kingdom into major territories and the rest of the world. For the major territories, which will need to be defined, the record company will pay a royalty rate in the region of 60–85% of the full rate. For the rest of the world the royalty rate will be in the region of 50–60% of the full rate. The performer's solicitor should try to get full rate irrespective of where the record is released. However, it is highly unlikely that the record company will agree to this and the performer's solicitor should instead try and raise the percentage figure offered, and ensure that all the major territories where records are sold are included within the definition of major territories. In addition, the performer's solicitor should ensure that any territory where the performer is popular is included within the major territory definition.

(i) Given away as free copies or as promotional copies to radio stations etc, there will be no royalty payable (because the record company has given them away and not sold them). The performer's solicitor should put a limit on the number of promo copies the record company can give away which are not royalty bearing (*see also* Deductions from the gross royalty (a) and (b) above for free copies and promos).

(j) Sold on new technology, *e.g.* Mini Disc, DVD, the royalty rate will be in the region of 50–90% of the full rate. In addition, the record company will usually require a higher packaging deduction than that charged for CDs and cassettes. The record company's attitude is that new formats such as Mini Disc cost more to manufacture than established formats, the packaging is more expensive for new formats compared to established formats such as cassette, and sales for new formats are negligible compared to estabished formats.

The performer will not want the royalty reduced for sales of the recordings on new technology. Some performers still receive a reduced royalty rate on CD sales because their recording agreement at the time treated CD as new technology. Many formats which have been launched by the industry have not taken off with the music-buying public, *e.g.* DAT (Digital Audio Tape) and DCC (Digital Compact Cassette), and a reduced royalty rate for record sales on these formats would not have substantially affected the perfomer. However, care should be taken when considering whether to accept a reduced royalty rate for sales on new technology because what is a new format today could become an important way to sell recordings in the future; see, for example, sales of recordings via the internet on MPEG3 files which at present are small but are predicted to grow substantially in the near future.

The performer's solicitor should try to obtain the full rate for sales of recordings on new technology, but the record company will not usually agree to this. The performer's solicitor may as an alternative try to limit the time period for which a reduced rate will be paid for sales on new technology, *e.g.* the performer will be paid a reduced rate for sales on a new format for three years after the recording is first released on that format and thereafter he will be paid the full rate, or alternatively the performer will be paid a reduced royalty rate for sales on a new format until the record company pays other performers full rate for that format whereupon the performer will also be paid the full rate.

(k) Sold via record clubs, the royalty rate will be in the region of 50% of the full rate. In some cases the record company as opposed to paying a royalty based upon the full rate will instead pay a royalty in the region of 50% of the net money received by the record company from licensing the record to the record club. The word 'net' will need to be defined to ensure that only valid deductions from gross are made. The performer may be able to secure a higher royalty rate where the record club and the record company are related companies *e.g.* they are subsidiaries of the same parent company.

Record clubs entice members to join by making special membership joining offers and by offering loyalty schemes. For example, the record club may offer five records from a selected list for £1 each to get people to join, and to retain members it may offer a special deal e.g. after 10 purchases the member can have one record free. The recording agreement will usually provide that the performer will not be paid a royalty where the record is sold by the record club at a nominal price to entice people to join or where it is given away by the record club to members. The performer's solicitor should resist a clause which provides that the performer will not be paid a royalty in these situations. At the very least the performer's solicitor should try to ensure that a limit is placed upon the number of the performer's records which are royalty free.

Many performers will not want their latest record to be sold through a record club for a period of time after its initial release. This is because of the lower royalty rate paid for record club sales. In addition, some performers feel that if the record is available to record club members for £1, or as a free record if the member buys 10 other records, it might give the impression that the record is a flop and that the record company is desperate to shift it at any cost. The performer may therefore seek a clause in the agreement that a record will not be sold through a record club until one year after its' initial release. Many record companies will not usually agree to such a provision because record club sales depend considerably on new or recent releases being available for club members to purchase and record companies need to make such releases available to record clubs to sell along with their back catalogue.

(l) Released on a best of or greatest hits record of the performer, the royalty rate will usually be the full rate. Some record companies may only offer 50% of the full rate and try to justify the rate on the basis that it is re-using existing recordings and not new recordings, and that the recordings were paid full rate when they were originally released. The performer's solicitor should resist any such reduction, especially as a greatest hits album may be the performer's best selling record and he should seek full rate on the basis that the release of a greatest hits album may adversely affect future sales of the performer's previous albums. If all the most popular material is collected on one album, it is possible that those people who have not got the performer's previous albums may not buy them in the future because they have collected all the tracks they want on one album, rather than having to buy several of the performer's previous albums to collect these tracks. The record company may try and counter this argument by saying that the purchase of a greatest hits album will encourage the purchase of the performer's previous albums because people may want to discover the performer's less well known recordings.

The tracks on the greatest hits album will come from various stages of the performer's career and be taken from albums which may have attracted different royalty rates. The royalty rate for the greatest hits album will be pro rata to the albums from which they were taken. For example, if the greatest hits album contained 12 tracks with four tracks from the first album which attracted a 12 % royalty, two tracks from the second album which also attracted a 12% royalty, three tracks from the third album which attracted a 13% royalty, and three tracks from the fourth album which attracted a 15% royalty, the royalty rate for the greatest hits album would be 13%. The recording agreement needs to deal with what royalty rate is payable on tracks used for a greatest hits album where the albums from which the recordings were taken had escalating royalty rates. For example, if the first two albums had a royalty rate of 12% and the rate escalated to 13% for sales over 100,000 copies, and further escalated to 14% for sales over 200,000 copies, if the first album sold 120,000 copies and the second album sold 235,000 copies will the royalty rate for the tracks taken off these albums for the greatest hits album be at the basic 12% rate or at the higher rates of 13% for the tracks taken from the first album and 14% for the tracks taken from the second album? The recording agreement should deal with this point. In addition, the performer's solicitor should, if possible, get an escalated royalty rate on sales of the greatest hits album. (For escalations *see* Escalating royalty rate below.)

(m) Released by the record company on a compilation record alongside recordings by the record company's other performers, the royalty rate is pro rata to the number of tracks on the album, *e.g.* if there are 40 tracks on the album and one of these is by the performer, the royalty rate is 1/40th of the performer's full royalty rate. Some performers do not want their recording used in compilations with other performers' recordings, in which case their solicitor should insert a clause in the recording agreement which prohibits such use.

(n) Released by a record company under licence from the performer's record company on a compilation record with other performers' recordings, the royalty will usually be in the region of 50% of the net money which the performer's record company receives from the licensee for the use of the performer's recording. The word 'net' will need to be defined to ensure that only valid deductions from gross are made.

As mentioned in (m) above, some performers do not want their recording used in compilations with other performers' recordings, in which case their solicitor should insert a clause in the recording agreement which prohibits such use.

(o) Released by the record company on a sampler record, *e.g.* XYZ Record Company's "New Artists Sampler For 2000 Volume 1" which is sold to the public at a cheap price of £1.99, there will be no royalty payable. The record company will not pay a royalty as the use of the recording is to get the public interested in their performers and is a way of promoting them to get the public to go out and buy records by each performer on the sampler.

Performers should consider whether they are happy for their recordings to be used in such a way and if not they will want a clause in the recording agreement which prohibits the use of the recordings on such sampler releases.

(p) Sold to jukebox companies for use in jukeboxes, there will be no royalty payable.

(q) Sold as a deletion or sold as a cut-out or sold for scrap, there will be no royalty payable.

The record company will delete an album from its catalogue when it believes the album has been fully exploited at full price, mid-price and budget price and has no more sales potential. It will notify record shops of its intention to delete the album from its catalogue from a particular date and the record shops can return any copies they have during this period to get a credit. After this date the record company will not accept returns of the album and it is deleted from its catalogue. Where an album has been deleted and the record company has residual stock of the album, the record company may sell the residual stock for whatever price it can get, and will cut the album sleeve with a hole puncher, hence the term cut-out, to show that it is not a full priced album.

The record company will sell an album at scrap to be melted down and used for some other purpose when there are copies left over which cannot be sold as cut-outs.

The performer's solicitor should try to obtain a clause in the recording agreement which prohibits the record company from cutting-out an album for, say, 2 years after it has been initially released. In addition, the performer's solicitor should, where the recording agreement allows the record company to cut-out an album, obtain a clause in the agreement which will enable the performer, should he so wish, to buy all the cut-outs from the recording company at the best price which the record company has been offered for them.

(r) Licensed by the record company for use in a television advertisement or for inclusion in a film or television programme, the performer will be paid a royalty in the region of 50% of the net money received by the record company. The word "net" will need to be defined to ensure that only valid deductions from gross are made.

(s) Promoted by the record company in an exceptional way, e.g. running a national radio and/or television campaign. The record company will usually deduct half the costs of such promotion from the gross royalty and may also reduce the royalty during the time of the special promotional campaign for records sold in the territory(ies) where the special promotional campaign takes place to 50–66.6% of the full rate.

As mentioned above, (*see* Deductions from the gross royalty (i), Items not to be deducted from gross royalty (d), and

Record company's obligations (e)), the performer will not want to be responsible for half of the special promotional campaign costs and also have the royalty rate on the records sold during the time of the special promotional campaign reduced. If the performer is responsible for half of the special promotional campaign costs he should not have his royalty reduced on the records sold during the time of the special promotional campaign. If the record company wants to do a special promotional campaign at its own expense then it might be acceptable for the royalty rate to be reduced for records sold in the territory(ies) where a special promotional campaign takes place during the time of that campaign.

(t) Released as a double or triple album, the royalty rate is a percentage of the full rate calculated as the percentage that the selling price of the double or triple album bears to two or three times the selling price of a single album. For example, if a single album sells for £13.99 (£14 for round figures) and the performer releases a double album and it sells for £15.99 (£16 for round figures), the royalty rate on the double album is 8/14ths of the full rate, *i.e.* £16 (for the double album) over £28 (twice the price of a single album). The reason why the royalty rate is reduced for a multiple album is that they usually do not sell in such quantities as a single album and the selling price of a double or triple album is less than the two or three times the selling price of a single album so the record company's profit margin on the album will be less. (*See also* Minimum commitment above.)

(u) Used as a premium, the royalty will be in the region of 50% of the net amount of money received by the record company from the company wanting to use the recording. The word "net" will need to be defined to ensure that only valid deductions from gross are made.

A premium is a record which is used to promote another product, *e.g.* send in five ring pulls from a fizzy drink can and for the cost of a stamped addressed envelope, the drinks company will send out a cassette containing three tracks by the performer.

Many performers do not want their recordings used in such a way. As premiums are only a small source of income for the record company, it will usually agree to a clause in the recording agreement prohibiting such use of the performer's recordings.

(v) Packaged at the performer's request in a way that is not how the record would normally be packaged, the record company will, if they agree to the performer's packaging request, charge a higher packaging deduction and/or may also seek to reduce the royalty rate for the record. (For normal packaging deductions *see* Royalties above.) Although the recording agreement will detail the normal packaging deductions it will not set out the special packaging deductions or the royalty rate for specially packaged records as the record company is not able to calculate the cost of the special packaging at the time of the agreement as it will not know the type of packaging the performer requires, and the performer will not know what he wants until a much later date, which is usually about the time he records the single or album which he wants specially packaged. The deductions for special packaging and the royalty rate for specially packaged records will therefore have to be negotiated between the parties at a later date. The performer's solicitor should try to avoid there being any extra packaging deduction in addition to a reduction in the royalty rate for a specially packaged record.

Some recording agreements allow the performer to have some extras over and above the normal packaging specification, so he can, for example, have a couple of extra pages inserted in the CD booklet accompanying his album which will enable him to include extra photos of him and allow him more space to thank everybody for their help in making the record (and it does seem that everybody gets thanked although lawyers often get forgotten!).

(w) Discounted in price by the record company to shop chains or others who buy records in bulk quantities, the record company will either want to alter the definition of sale proceeds to take into account the discount offered by the record company, thereby reducing the royalty payable (see above for the definition of sale proceeds), or will want to reduce the royalty that is paid by the same percentage as the discount given by the record company. The performer's solicitor should resist any clause which reduces the performer's royalty where the record company has given a discount on record sales to bulk buyers of the record.

Escalating royalty rate

The performer's solicitor should try to ensure that the royalty rate will escalate for a record when it achieves certain sales targets. If the record company agrees to this, it will usually provide that the escalating royalty rate will only apply to records which are sold on the company's top line label at full price within, for example, 2 years of the record's release. In addition, the record company will often provide that the escalating royalty rate will only apply to records that are sold in the United Kingdom. The record company might agree to an escalating royalty rate for worldwide sales, in which case the sales targets will be much higher than the targets which would apply for an escalating royalty rate for United Kingdom sales.

An escalating royalty rate might provide, for example, that the royalty rate in the United Kingdom for an album sold on the record company's top line label at full price is 13%, escalating to:

(i)   14% if the album sells in excess of 50,000 copies in the United Kingdom (a silver record),

(ii) 15% if the album sells in excess of 100,000 copies in the United Kingdom (a gold record),

(iii) 16% if the album sells in excess of 300,000 copies in the United Kingdom (a platinum record),

within 2 years of the album's release. An escalating royalty will usually only apply to the particular record which has achieved the sales target. Subsequent records will usually start off at the base royalty rate and only escalate once they achieve the relevant sales targets. If the targets are worldwide, the escalating royalty rates might be triggered by sales targets of (say) 500,000, 1,000,000 and 2,000,000.

Usually an escalating royalty rate will only apply to those records sold from the target figure onwards, e.g. using the royalty rate figures from above, if the first album sold 350,000 copies on the record company's top line label at full price within two years of release, sales of the first 50,000 copies will attract a 13% royalty, sales of copies 50,001 to 100,000 will attract a 14% royalty, sales of copies 100,001 to 300,000 will attract a 15% royalty and sales of over 300,001, will attract a 16% royalty.

An escalating royalty rate can be applied to singles as well as albums. The target figures to achieve for singles may be, for example: 500,000, 750,000 and 1,000,000.

As well as obtaining an escalating royalty rate where a record achieves certain sales targets, the performer's solicitor should ensure that whenever the record company exercises an option, that the royalty rate and the escalating royalty rate for albums and singles recorded during the option period is automatically increased from the previous royalty rate payable.

Mechanical licences

(Before reading this section it is suggested that The controlled composition clause dealt with in Chapter 7 The Publishing Agreement should be re-read.)

Apart from advances and royalties the record company will be liable to pay for the right to use the compositions on the record and accompanying video. The record company will therefore be liable for:

(a) Mechanical licence fees payable to the composer/publisher to enable the compositions to be recorded, and to enable copies to be manufactured, distributed and sold to the public on CD, cassette etc. (See (b) below for the mechanical licence fee for videos.)

As was mentioned earlier, (*see* Chapter 7, The Publishing Agreement, The controlled competition clause), the record company will want a controlled competition clause in the recording agreement for the United States and Canada. As was also mentioned earlier, some record companies will want such a clause to apply to all the territories covered by the recording agreement. Any clause which gives a favourable mechanical rate to the record company reduces the mechanical royalty which is payable by the record company to the composer/publisher.

The performer's solicitor should examine the proposed controlled composition clause very carefully to see how he can improve its terms for the performer. The improvements that might be sought include:

(i) A provision, where the record company is seeking a favourable mechanical rate for all the territories covered by the recording agreement, that the favourable rate will only apply to the United States and Canada. It should be noted that the record company will not usually agree to restrict its favourable mechanical rate to the United States and Canada where it is seeking that rate for all territories covered by the recording agreement.

(ii) An increase in the mechanical rate payable based on sales of the record, e.g. the rate payable will be 75% of the mechanical rate for the first 500,000 copies sold, 80% for sales between 500,001 and 1,000,000 and 85% for sales from 1,000,001 copies onwards.

(iii) An increase in the mechanical rate on later albums, e.g. the rate payable will be 75% of the mechanical rate for the first two albums, 80% for the next two albums and 85% for subsequent albums.

If the record company agrees a higher mechanical rate on later albums, the recording agreement should specify whether the release of a greatest hits/best of album will attract a mechanical royalty of 75% or whether the royalty rate is determined by when the record is released, *i.e.* if it is the fourth album released it will attract an 80% mechanical rate. There are other ways for the mechanical rate to be calculated for a greatest hits/best of album, *e.g.* it might be based upon the total mechanical rate payable for the tracks at the rate paid on the albums from which the tracks were taken before any escalation for sales, divided by the number of tracks on the greatest hits/best of album. If, for example, the mechanical rate for the first two albums was 75%, 80% for the next two albums, and 85% on subsequent albums, if the greatest hits/best of album comprises 12 tracks with three tracks taken from the first two albums, four tracks taken from the next two albums and five tracks taken from subsequent albums, the record company will pay a 80.83% mechanical rate (*i.e.* $(3 \times 75) + (4 \times 80) + (5 \times 85) \div 12 = 80.83$).

(iv) An increase in the maximum number of compositions per record for which the record company will pay a mechanical royalty. (*See* Chapter 7 The Publishing Agreement, The controlled compositions clause for details.)

It should be noted that some recording agreements will provide that all compositions which the performer intends to record (and not just compositions written by, owned by or controlled by the performer) will be licenced at a favourable mechanical rate. This provision should be resisted by the performer's solicitor because in most cases the composer/publisher of a composition not written by, owned by or controlled by the performer will not be prepared to licence the composition at a favourable rate. Where there is a favourable mechanical rate for all compositions, the record company will seek to deduct the difference between the licence fee payable and the favourable rate provided for in the agreement from the performer's royalties. It should be noted that even if the performer's solicitor manages to get the record company to accept that the favourable mechanical rate will not apply to compositions which are not written by, owned by or controlled by the performer, there will still be provisions in the agreement which will have an effect on the total amount of mechanicals for which the record company has agreed that it will be responsible. For example, the agreement will contain a provision that the mechanical rate for the US and Canada will be the minimum statutory rate. At the end of the day, if the total amount of mechanicals payable exceeds the total amount for which the record company has agreed to be responsible, the record company will take the excess it pays from the performer's royalties.

(b) synchronisation and mechanical licence fees payable to the composer/publisher to enable the recorded compositions to be used on video. The record company will often want a clause in the recording agreement which provides that no licence fees will be payable where recorded compositions are used on a promo video. This is because the video has been made purely to promote sales of the recorded compositions. The record company should, however, be required to pay licence fees where the videos of the recorded compositions are sold to the public. The performer's solicitor should ensure that any favourable synchronisation and mechanical licence fees to use the compositions on video only applies to controlled compositions which will need to be defined in the agreement and not to all compositions (for the reason why, see (a) above).

Equitable remuneration

As was mentioned earlier, the performer is entitled to receive equitable remuneration under section 191G of the CDPA where he has transferred his section 182C rental right in the sound recording. (*See* Chapter 2 Copyright Law and the Copyright, Designs and Patents Act 1988, Right for performers to receive equitable remuneration, where the section 182C rental right in the sound recording has been Transferred, for section 191G, and Rights in performances, Performer's rights, for section 182C.)

Also, as was mentioned earlier, the performer is entitled to receive equitable remuneration under section 182D of the CDPA where the sound recording is broadcast or played in public. The PPL will collect the income on behalf of the record company for the broadcasting or public performance of the sound recording and will now pay 50% to PAMRA or AURA who will distribute it to their members (or where performers have registered with the PPL, the PPL will account to the performers for their share of the income), and the other 50% will be sent by the PPL to the record company. (*See* Chapter 2 Copyright Law and the Copyright, Designs and Patents Act 1988, Right for performers to receive equitable remuneration, For the exploitation of a sound recording, for section 182D. *See* Chapter 4 Collecting Societies and Music Industry Associations for PPL, PAMRA and AURA.)

Clauses specifically relating to bands

All the matters discussed so far in this chapter are relevant whether the performer is a solo artist or a member of a band. Where a recording agreement is offered to a band additional matters need to be dealt with in the agreement.

Advances and royalty payments

The recording agreement should reflect what has been agreed in any internal band agreement concerning the division of advances and royalties between the band members. The recording agreement should also contain a provision which enables the band to notify the record company of any change in the division of advances and royalties between the band members. (*See* Chapter 5 The Legal Status of Band and Solo Artist for The band agreement.) Where the band members want any advances and royalties paid by the record company into their bank accounts, the record company will need the name of each band member's bank, the account names and numbers and the sort codes to enable payment to made directly into the relevant bank account. Where the band want any advances and royalties paid to their manager then the record company will need to be supplied with the manager's details. Where the record company is requested to pay monies to the band's manager, the record company will insert a provision into the recording agreement that the manager's receipt for the monies will satisfy its duty to pay any advance or royalties to the band.

Leaving members

When a record company signs a band it will always insert provisions into the recording agreement detailing what happens when a member decides to leave the band. The record company must try to ensure that any leaving member clause is drafted in such a way that it would be unlikely to be found by the courts to be in restraint of trade. (See Chapter 3 Music Industry Contracts for Restraint of trade).

The recording agreement will be signed by each member of the band and will provide that the band members are jointly and severally liable for breaches of the agreement. The band's solicitor should ensure there is a clause in the recording agreement which provides that where a member leaves the band, the remaining band members will not be liable for any future breaches of the agreement by the leaving member once he has left the band, and that the leaving member will not be liable for any future breaches of the agreement by the remaining members once he has left the band. (*See also* Chapter 5 The Legal Status of Band and Solo Artist, Indemnities and liabilities of band and ex-members for the indemnity by the band to an ex-member and the ex-member's liability to third parties after he has left the band.

It is arguable that the band's most valuable asset is the band name. One international rock star acknowleged the value of his band's name by saying that his band was so successful that if they put out a record of silence under the band name, it would still sell a million copies. He did, however, go on to say that the band could only do this once as the band's goodwill would be eroded immediately. Certainly, a successful band will guarantee increased record sales by the use of the band name and logo on the record. The record company will require the band members to record and perform under the band name. In addition, the record company will want the right to use each individual band member's name and likeness, any trade mark belonging to each individual band member, and each individual band member's biographical details, as well as the band's name and likeness, any trade mark belonging to the band, and the band's biographical details to promote their recordings during and after the term of the recording agreement. (*See also* Grant of rights by performer and Performer's warranties and obligations (11) above.) The recording agreement will provide that where a member leaves the band, the remaining members or those members designated by the record company will continue to record under the band name. This clause is usually acceptable but consideration should be had to the situation where the band is named after one of the members, and that member leaves the band. Where the band is named after one of the members the recording agreement should ideally provide that if the member after whom the band is named leaves the band, only the leaving member has the right to use the band name.

The leaving member cannot just walk out of the band as and when he wants. He may, for example, have to give notice under the band agreement. He may also not be able to leave when he wishes because of his contractual touring commitments. In addition, he has contractual commitments under the recording agreement which require him either to record for the record company as a member of the band, or where he leaves the band the record company will have the right to retain his services to record for them as a solo performer or in any band which he sets up or joins.

The record company will require a leaving member to give them written notice of his intention to leave the band. The record company will then have a period of time to decide their options *viz-à-viz* the leaving and remaining members. The agreement will allow the record company to, for example, either:

(a) terminate the recording agreement for the leaving member and the remaining band members, or

(b) terminate the recording agreement for the leaving member only. The remaining band members would still be bound by the recording agreement to record for the record company, or

(c) terminate the recording agreement for the remaining band members only. The leaving member would still be bound by the recording agreement to record for the record company either as a solo artist or in any other band of which he is a member, or

(d) require the remaining band members to continue to record for them as a band under the recording agreement and require the leaving member to continue to record for them under the recording agreement either as a solo artist or in any other band of which he is a member.

The band's solicitor should ensure that a time limit is placed upon the record company to decide whether or not it wants to retain the services of the leaving member and/or the remaining band members. Although the record company is fully aware of the band's ability and marketability, it may be concerned about the ability and marketability of the leaving member without the rest of the band and the rest of the band without the leaving member. It is possible that the band's chemistry only existed when all the members played together. The record company will often include a provision in the recording agreement which enables it to require a demo recording from the leaving member and/or the remaining band members to help it decide whether to retain either one.

Where there is such a provision in the recording agreement, the band's solicitor should ensure that the record company has a time limit from its receipt of the leaving member's notice to require a demo recording from the leaving member and/or the rest of the band members – and that the record company has a further time limit from receipt of the demo recording to decide whether to retain either party or both.

Where the record company decides to retain the recording services of the leaving member, the recording agreement which he signs with the band will provide the contractual terms relating to him recording as a solo artist or in another band. The contractual terms will be substantially the same as those which applied prior to him leaving the band, although the maximum length of the agreement will be for the unexpired residue of the band's recording agreement, and the record company may try to reduce the advances and royalty rate payable to the leaving member for his recordings as a solo artist or in another band. The record company will attempt to justify any reduced advances and royalties on the basis that the advances and royalties paid to the band are shared between all the band members and therefore they should be reduced when he leaves the band and makes recordings as a solo artist or in another band to reflect the share he was entitled to as a band member. Where the agreement contains lower advance and royalty provisions for a leaving member's recordings as a solo artist or in another band, the band's solicitor should try and get the advance and royalty levels raised on the basis that, if the record company wants the leaving member to continue recording for it, it must believe his records will be commercially successful in the future and he should be properly rewarded for proving his ability as a performer in the past.

The recording agreement should provide that once a member has left the band, the record company will set up two separate accounting ledgers, one relating to the leaving member, the other relating to the remaining members. The band's solicitor should check the recording agreement provides that as at the date a member leaves the band a pro rata share of any band deficit will be transferred to his leaving member's ledger. (Likewise as at the date a member leaves the band a pro rata share of any band credit should be transferred to the leaving member's ledger.) The agreement should also provide that the leaving member is not responsible for any part of the remaining members' expenses incurred after the date he has left the band and that the remaining members are not responsible for any part of the leaving member's expenses incurred after the date he has left the band. The leaving member will continue to receive royalties on the band recordings on which he performed and his pro rata share of these royalties will be credited to his leaving member's ledger, with the band's pro rata share of the royalties credited to the band's ledger. The leaving member will obviously not receive any royalties on recordings made by the band after he left the band, nor will the band receive any royalties on recordings made by the leaving member where they did not appear on the leaving member's record. What must be avoided in the recording agreement is any clause which allows the record company to use the leaving member's royalties to pay off any deficit on the band's ledger or allowing the band's royalties to be used to pay off any deficit on the leaving member's ledger.

Solo recordings by band member

The recording agreement may contain provisions allowing band members to make solo records. If the record company allows a member of the band to make a solo record, the recording agreement will usually make it expressly clear that the band's recording obligations take priority and a solo record will not be released within a specified period of time after any band recording has been released by the record company. This is to ensure that sales of a band record are not reduced by the release of a solo record. In addition, the recording agreement may also provide that the recording of a solo record can only take place if the band is not touring. The record company puts the band's career above a band member's proposed solo career because, with few exceptions, a solo record by a band member will not sell in anywhere near the numbers as a record by the band.

The band's recording agreement should contain all the contractual provisions relating to a band member's proposed solo recordings, including, for example, provisions dealing with the royalty rate and any advance which is payable and that the record company will set up a separate ledger relating to the band member who is making solo records. The band's solicitor should ensure that only a pro rate share of any band deficit can be debited to the band member's solo record ledger and that only a pro rate share of any band royalties can be used to recoup any deficit on the band member's solo record ledger.

The band's solicitor could try to obtain a clause in the agreement which provides that where the record company is prepared to let the band member make a solo record that the band member can negotiate a solo recording agreement with another record company and if the other record company offers better terms to record as a solo performer, the band's record company will have, say, a four week term to match the terms. Ideally the band's solicitor should provide that time is of the essence for the record company to decide if it wants to match the terms. If the record company is prepared to match the terms, the band member will then be required to make solo recordings for it. If it decides not to match the terms – or, if time is of the essence, is out of time – the band member can sign a solo recording agreement with the other record company.

If the record company is prepared to agree to such a provision, it may require a provision in the agreement that where the band member signs a solo recording agreement with another record company, the band member's solo royalties will be paid to them and that it will take an override royalty of 2–3%. This will enable the record company to use the royalties to recoup the solo band member's pro rata share of any band deficit. It also enables the record company to earn interest on these royalties because it will not account to the solo band member with them until the next accounting period and it can take a 2–3% share of the royalties for itself on the basis of it being its fee for releasing the band member from the contractual requirement to record exclusively for it. The band's solicitor should strongly resist any such clause in the recording agreement because the royalties will take much longer to reach the band member and it is not reasonable for the record company to recoup the solo band member's pro rata share of any band deficit if it was not prepared to take the risk of financing a solo record. It is also arguable that the record company should not receive an override royalty for releasing the band member from the exclusivity clause where the exclusivity it actually wants is for the member to record with the band not as a solo performer.

Some recording agreements contain a clause which allows the band member to negotiate a solo recording agreement with another record company where the record company he is contract to does not want him to record a solo album for them. Where there is such a clause there will also usually be provisions in the agreement similar to those discussed in the previous paragraph e.g. relating to matching rights, a requirement for the band member's solo royalties to be paid to the record company and for the record company to take an override royalty.

New band members

The recording agreement will often not allow the band unilaterally to add a new member. The recording agreement will often provide that the record company must approve any proposed new band member. In addition, the proposed new member and the band members will be required by the record company to sign a confirmatory document acknowledging that as from the date of the confirmatory document the new member has joined the band, that he will be bound by the terms of the recording agreement with the band, and that all members of the band are jointly and severally liable for breaches of the recording agreement, with the new member only being liable for future breaches of the recording agreement.

Accounting and auditing

The recording agreement should contain an accounting provision clause requiring the record company to keep accounts detailing the number of the performer's recordings sold, the income received from other uses of the recordings, *e.g.* from licensing a recording for use in a television advertisement, and the amount of royalties which are due to the performer. The record company will be required to keep the accounts at its registered office or its main place of business.

The recording agreement will usually provide that the record company will send the performer a statement of account twice a year, e.g. 90 days after 30 June and 31 December, showing full details of all the monies which have been received by the record company for record sales and for other uses of the performer's recordings, together with a cheque for the royalties due. The agreement will usually provide that royalties will only be paid on record sales and on other uses of the performer's recordings for which the record company has been paid and that no royalty will be paid for records which have been sold and then returned to the record company. The performer will not want to wait 90 days from the end of the accounting period to receive any money due to him. It may be possible to reduce the 90-day period to 60 days but the record company will resist an attempt to move the time period to account any closer to the actual accounting period.

The record company may insert a clause giving the performer, for example, one year from receipt of the accounts to object to their accuracy. The performer should not accept any attempt by the record company to reduce the six year contractual limitation period to object to the accounts.

The recording agreement should always contain an audit clause which allows the performer or his professionally qualified accountant to inspect, audit and take copies of the record company's books and records to determine the accuracy of the accounts. The conditions applied to the right to audit will be tightly controlled by the record company. For example, the record company will want to limit the documents to which the auditor has access. The record company will usually only want to allow the auditor access to their sales ledgers. To enable the auditor to have a more complete picture which will help him pick up more easily any irregularities, he will want to have access to other record company documentation, *e.g.* he will want to have access to manufacturing and distribution ledgers, and copies of any licences granted by the record company to use the recordings. This will help the auditor to verify the number of records made, the numbers sold, the numbers returned, the type of sales of these recordings and the amount distributed as free copies. (*See* Royalty rates for different formats and different types of exploitation above for how different types of sale of the same record will bear different royalty rates and Deductions from the gross royalty above for free goods.)

The audit clause will usually require the performer to give notice of his intention to carry out the audit, and will limit the inspection to one inspection a year at the performer's expense. In addition, the clause will usually provide that the audit will take place at the record company's registered office or main place of business and will take place during the record company's normal business hours. There may be an additional restriction that the accountant carrying out the audit for the performer is not presently engaged in another audit of the record company on behalf of another performer.

The agreement should provide that where the performer has been underpaid by a specified sum, *e.g.* he has been underpaid by at least £5,000, or has been underpaid by a specified percentage, *e.g.* 10%, whichever is greater, that the cost of the audit will be paid for by the record company. Where the performer has been underpaid, the agreement should provide for the record company to account to the performer for the underpayment. The performer should ensure the clause is drafted so that the record company accounts for any under-payment immediately and that the record company pays interest on any underpaid sum at 3 or 4% above a stated bank's base rate from time to time in force.

The audit clause should contain a provision that the information disclosed to the performer and/or his accountant is confidential infor-mation and will not be disclosed to anyone except the performer's professional advisers. The record company will usually require a copy of the performer's final audit report.

The performer will need to specify in the agreement the address to which the record company should send the accounts and any royalty cheque. Usually the address to which they will be sent is the performer's home address. The performer may want the accounts to be sent to his accountant with the royalty cheque paid by the record company directly into his bank account, in which case the record company will need to be given the name of the performer's bank, the account name and number and the sort code to enable payment to be made directly into the account. The performer should also insert a provision to allow him to give notice to the record company requiring the accounts and any royalty cheque to be sent to a different address and/or bank account.

The performer's management agreement should be examined to check whether the performer's recording advance(s) and royalties have to be sent to his manager, in which case the recording agreement should provide for these to be sent to the manager, or notice should be given by the performer to the record company to send them to the manager. Where the monies are to be sent to the performer's manager, the recording agreement should provide that the manager's receipt for the monies will satisfy the record company's duty to pay the advance or royalties to the performer.

Termination

The agreement should contain provisions as to when the recording agreement will automatically terminate. The agreement should also contain provisions as to when an aggrieved party has the right to elect to terminate the recording agreement. The agreement may provide that where a terminating event occurs which entitles an aggrieved party to elect to terminate the agreement, before he can elect to terminate the agreement, he must serve a notice on the other party giving notice of the terminating event and requiring it to be remedied within a period of 30 days. Only if the terminating event has not been remedied within that time can he then terminate the agreement. The circumstances where termination will or may occur include:

(a) Where one party has been in material breach of contract the other party has the right to terminate the agreement. The effect of the performer terminating the recording agreement is that he will then be free to sign with another record company. The record company with whom he terminated the agreement will still retain the copyright in the sound recordings which the performer made for them for the full period of copyright, *i.e.* 50 years. The record company will not agree to a clause which provides for the copyright in the sound recordings to be assigned or re-assigned to the performer where he terminates the agreement. (See also (c) below dealing with whether the copyright in the sound recordings will be assigned to the performer where the agreement expires by effluxion of time.)

(b) Where one party becomes either bankrupt or enters into a voluntary arrangement or any company through which he operates goes into compulsory or voluntary liquidation (save for the purposes of reconstructing or amalgamating a solvent company), or becomes insolvent or has a receiver, manager, or administrative receiver or provisional liquidator or administrator appointed, the agreement will automatically terminate.

(c) at the end of the contractual term the agreement automatically terminates and the performer will be free to sign to another record company. As in (a) above the record company will retain the copyright in the sound recordings which the performer made for it for the full period of copyright, *i.e.* 50 years. As mentioned at the beginning of this chapter, see Introduction above, because sound recordings are a valuable asset, the performer's solicitor should try and negotiate a clause in the recording agreement which provides for the copyright in the sound recordings to be assigned or re-assigned to the performer and for the physical property of the master tapes to be handed over to the performer, say, 10 or 15 years after the end of the contractual term. Although the performer's solicitor should seek such a clause in the recording agreement, most record companies will have the same response to such a request: no, no, and no again. In the unlikely event that the record company agrees to assign or re-assign the copyright in the sound recordings to the performer, it will usually only be prepared to do so if the performer is recouped or is prepared to repay the record company any unrecouped sums, and provided the performer pays its reasonable legal fees for the assignment or re-assignment and a nominal sum of, say, £250 per master track. Where the record company has agreed to assign or re-assign the copyright in the sound recordings to the performer, the recording agreement should provide that the assignment or re-assignment is subject to and with the benefit of any licences which the record company has granted to third parties to use the sound recordings.

The termination clause will usually contain a provision that, notwithstanding termination, both parties must continue to comply with the provisions of the recording agreement to the extent that they have not been affected by termination. For example, if the agreement is terminated by the performer due to a material breach of contract by the record company, although the performer can terminate the agreement, both parties will be bound by any clause in the agreement providing for confidentiality.

The record company may want a clause inserted into the agreement which provides that where it terminates the agreement, the performer will only be entitled to be paid royalties up to the date of termination. The performer's solicitor should not accept any such provision in the agreement.

Suspension

The agreement will usually contain a clause allowing the record company to suspend rather than terminate the agreement whilst there is a breach of contract existing which has arisen through no fault of the record company.

The circumstances where suspension may occur include:

(a) where the performer refuses to provide his services to the record company,

(b) where the performer is unable to perform because of illness or disability,

(c) where a *force majeure* event occurs. It should be noted that where suspension occurs due to a *force majeure* event that the agreement should not require the record company to give the performer notice that the agreement will be suspended if the performer has not rectified the situation within a period of time. This is because the *force majeure* event is not due to the performer's fault not is it rectifiable by the performer. (*See* Chapter 3 Music Industry Contracts, Other clauses, for *force majeure*, for the provision of a notice of *force majeure*, and for the provision of a long stop clause where the agreement is suspended for *force majeure*.)

The record company might insert a provision into the suspension clause which provides that it will not have to pay the performer any money due to him whilst the agreement is suspended. The performer's solicitor should not accept any such provision in the agreement.

(For a more detailed discussion on suspension of the agreement see Chapter 6 The Management Agreement, Suspension.)

Other clauses

Along with the clauses mentioned above, the agreement will contain several other clauses. These may include:

(a) A jurisdiction and choice of law clause. (See Chapter 3 Music Industry Contracts.)

(b) An invalidity clause. (See Chapter 3 Music Industry Contracts and Chapter 5 The Legal Status of Band and Solo Artist.)

(c) A clause confirming that the recording agreement does not constitute a partnership, joint venture or employment relationship between the record company and the performer.

(d) A clause confirming that the recording agreement reflects the whole of the agreement between the parties and replaces any earlier oral or written agreement.

(e) A non-waiver clause. (See Chapter 5 The Legal Status of Band and Solo Artist.)

(f) A *force majeure* clause. (*See* Chapter 3 Music Industry Contracts.)

(g) A notice clause. (See Chapter 5 The Legal Status of Band and Solo Artist.)

(h) A clause which provides that the performer and the record company will sign any documentation which is necesssary to carry out the terms of the agreement.

(i) A clause which prohibits either party from assigning the agreement. Where assignment is permitted in certain circumstances and/or is permitted subject to certain conditions the clause should detail the relevant circumstances and conditions which apply.

(j) A clause dealing with the Contracts (Rights of Third Parties) Act 1999. (See Chapter 3 Music Industry Contracts.)

Chapter 9

Touring

Introduction

Many performers will be offered a recording or publishing agreement only after they have built up a live following over a period of time. The record and publishing company usually like to see that a performer has a following before signing him as the following can be used as a starting base to build up the performer's career in the recording and publishing industry. There are performers who are signed on the basis of a handful of live appearances but such signings are few compared to the number who are signed only after they have served their apprenticeship on the touring circuit. There are other ways apart from live performing which may lead to the offer of a record and/or publishing deal, *e.g.* being a celebrity with an established following in a different area of the entertainment business, being a club DJ, having the looks and style being sought after by a manager trying to build up a boy/girl band, or getting asked to do an influential radio session, such as "The John Peel Sessions". However, the most common way to get the eyes and ears of the people in the industry who have the power to sign a performer is to build up a reputation and following live in concert.

With some notable exceptions, such as with dance music, most types of music depend on live concerts, tours, and personal appearances on television and radio to promote the performer and increase record sales. Many bands such as The Grateful Dead, U2 and The Rolling Stones have made a lot of money out of touring, and tour merchandising, but many bands will in fact lose a lot of money from touring. Indeed, many bands who want to tour extensively around the country or abroad cannot afford to do so. This is why record companies will often pay performers tour support which enables them to go out on tour and promote their records live in concert. (For tour support *see* Chapter 8 Recording Agreements, Record company's obligations (g).)

Some performers, for example, many heavy metal bands, make more money from touring, tour sponsorship and tour merchandising than they do from publishing and record sales. For most performers with recording and publishing agreements the reason why they tour is to help increase their income from record sales and from publishing. Live performing can also be used as an opportunity for a performer to try out new unrecorded material on his audience. Breaking even on a tour, or at best making a small profit, is the most many performers can hope to achieve at the start of their career.

Concert tickets can be expensive and the public may believe that the performer earns a lot of money from each show. Certainly, as mentioned above, some performers will undoubtedly walk away from a concert with a lot of money, but the price of a ticket does not all go into the performer's pocket. A concert ticket to see a major international rock band may cost £25, £30 or £35 plus, but the band is lucky to clear 25 to 30% of the ticket price for themselves after they have paid the cost of food, accommodation and transport for themselves and their touring staff, the wages of their own touring staff, their manager's and tour agent's commission, and income tax on their concert performance fee. The ticket price also incorporates the money which is payable to the PRS for the public performance of the compositions in the concert, VAT payable to Customs and Excise on the ticket price, and the costs the promoter incurs staging the concert, namely advertising the concert, hiring the venue, hiring venue staff for the concert including security staff, paying for police to be present in and around the venue, hiring sound and lighting equipment, and hiring any support band(s). Finally, a percentage of the ticket price includes an amount for the promoter's profit for staging the concert.

Touring may be fun for many performers but it is time consuming, can be very tiring and expensive and takes a performer away from his home base. For some performers touring can be very lucrative and tour sponsorship and the sale of tour merchandise can help increase tour profitability. (*See* Chapter 10 for Tour Sponsorship and Chapter 11 for Merchandising.) For many performers touring is a means of helping to sell records whilst the tour itself may struggle to break even. It should not be forgotten that many bands who may get along in the studio and live separate lives outside the studio are forced to live together on tour, which can and often does lead to fall outs and, at worst, a break up of the band. Whilst on tour promoting a record, a performer may be expected to write material for his next album. Touring generally does not help improve the creative writing process. A performer's first album comprises the best material he has assembled over the months and years whilst waiting for a record deal. The second album may have to be written quickly on the road almost from scratch as all the best material from the past will have been used up on the debut record. The "difficult" second and third albums may often establish how talented a perfomer really is. The performer's manager must ensure that the performer is not out on the road all the time. There should be time away from touring so that the performer is able to re-charge his batteries. In addition, the manager should ensure if at all possible that there is time set aside away from touring to enable the performer to concentrate his efforts solely on writing and recording new material. A balance has to be established between promoting the present material on tour and having time to write quality new material. If the performer does not have adequate time to compose new material, this will have an adverse effect on his career, and may in the worst case bring about a premature end to his career.

The tour agent agreement

(Note. The tour agent agreement is an agreement between a tour agent and the performer for the tour agent to use his contacts to obtain offers from concert promoters and others for live personal appearances by the performer. The tour agreement is an agreement between the concert promoter and the performer containing the terms and conditions for the live personal appearance in concert by the performer.)

The tour agent will use his contacts to get the performer live concerts and other live personal appearances. At the start of the performer's career the tour agent will have to work hard to persuade promoters to book the performer for concerts. Once the performer becomes well known promoters will be chasing the tour agent to book the performer for concerts. The tour agent will liase closely with the performer's manager and may possibly liase with his record company ensuring the performer tours at the most sensible times, *e.g.* any tour should coincide with an album release rather than with nothing new to promote. The tour agent with the performer's manager will put together a suitable tour itinerary with days set aside for the performer to rest. The tour itinerary should go from place to place in a logical sequence on the map. The only time when a tour should not follow a logical sequence on the map is if there is a prestigious concert which can only be held at a particular time and place which will benefit the performer to perform at.

The tour agent will, with the manager and promoter sort out all the relevant ticket arrangements, *e.g.* ticket pricing and how and when tickets are released on sale to the public.

The tour agent should refer all offers he receives to the performer's manager who will consult with the performer and decide whether to accept the offer. The tour agent agreement should make it expressly clear that although the tour agent may negotiate the terms of any proposed personal appearance agreement, he has no authority to enter any binding contract for the performer to provide his services.

The tour agent agreement usually provides that the tour agent will collect the concert fee and any advance for the concert from the promoter. If the tour agent has been given such authority he will collect in these monies from the promoter and distribute them to the performer in accordance with the terms of the tour agreement between the performer and the promoter. (*See* The tour agreement below for details.)

Parties

The parties to a tour agent agreement will often be the tour agent himself and the performer.

The performer may, however, appoint a large tour agent company to be his tour agent because he wants a particular employee at the company to handle his affairs. Where this is the case, the performer should try to obtain a key man clause in the agreement providing that if the person he wants to handle his affairs leaves the company or no longer personally handles his affairs then he will be free to terminate the agreement. A large tour agent company may not, however, be prepared to agree to a key man clause. Its attitude may be that although a capable employee may have left its employment, it has other equally capable employees who can handle the performer's affairs properly.

A tour agent company may be the vehicle through which the tour agent operates his business affairs. Where a tour agent runs his business affairs through his own tour agent company, a performer who wants to appoint the tour agent will contract not with the tour agent but with the tour agent's company. The performer should in this situation obtain a key man clause in the agreement and a side letter from the tour agent guaranteeing, inter alia, that if the company ceases to exist or the tour agent leaves the company or no longer handles the performer's affairs at the company, that the tour agent will, if required by the performer, personally represent the performer for the remainder of the term of the tour agent agreement.

The performer may operate his business affairs through his own company in which case it will be his company which will contract with the tour agent/tour agent company. The tour agent/tour agent company should ensure when contracting with the performer's company that there is a side letter from the performer guaranteeing that he will personally honour the obligations of the tour agent agreement if his company does not do so provided the tour agent/tour agent company is not in breach of the tour agent agreement.

Publicity

The agreement should allow the tour agent to represent himself as the performer's sole and exclusive tour agent. The performer should grant the tour agent the right to use his name and likeness, his biographical details and any trade mark belonging to him, and where he is in a band the right to use the band's name and likeness, the band's biographical details and any trade mark belonging to the band, solely for the purpose of getting him/the band live appearance bookings. The performer/band will want the right to approve any proposed use of his/their name and likeness etc by the tour agent in any proposed promotional material. The tour agent will only want the performer/band to have at most qualified approval rights, *i.e.* the performer/band will have the right to approve any proposed use of his/their name and likeness etc in any proposed promotional material with such approval not to be unreasonably withheld.

Scope of tour agent's representation

The agreement must establish whether the tour agent represents the performer for all his personal appearances relating to the entertainment industry or whether the appointment is limited to personal appearances relating to the performer's career in the music industry.

The agreement will provide that the tour agent is the performer's sole and exclusive tour agent in the field in which he has been appointed. The performer will be required to notify the tour agent of any offers for personal appearances which he receives directly or indirectly (*e.g.* communicated to him by his manager) during the term of the agreement and which covers the scope of the tour agent's representation. There will also be a provision that if the performer makes a personal appearance during the term of the agreement which is within the scope of the tour agent's area of representation and which has not been introduced to him by the tour agent, the tour agent will be entitled to commission on the personal appearance fee. The performer should specifically exclude the right to commission any personal appearance which has been negotiated by a previous tour agent and which has been fulfilled during the term of the new tour agent's agreement. If the agreement does not contain this provision, the performer would be liable to pay two tour agent's commission for the personal appearance arranged by his previous tour agent, *i.e.* to his previous and his new tour agents.

Term and territory

The tour agent will usually want a minimum fixed term of three years. Usually at the start of the performer's career the tour agent will spend a considerable amount of time trying to get promoters interested in booking the performer, and the performer will usually not be paid much money from concert appearances. The tour agent's commission will usually be small and will be hard earned. As the performer becomes established, the offers start to come in and the concert fees start to increase. At this stage the tour agent will be able to earn more commission.

A performer may be worried that the tour agent may not obtain sufficient personal appearances for him during the term. The performer may prefer to give the tour agent a target to achieve, for example, the term will be for a fixed term of one year during which time the tour agent would be required to use his expertise to obtain personal appearances which would in total earn a certain amount of money for the performer. If the target is achieved the term will continue for another two years and at the end of the two year period the term will continue until one party gives the other six months' written notice to terminate the agreement. If the tour agent is given a target to achieve before the agreement can continue, the tour agent should ensure the agreement provides that if he obtains personal appearances for the performer which the performer unreasonably rejects, the value of these rejected engagements will count towards the income target figure. If the tour agent does not have any such protection the performer can ensure the agreement will not continue by rejecting all personal appearance offers. In addition, where a target figure has to be achieved before the agreement can continue, the tour agent will want the agreement to provide that income from personal appearances performed after the fixed term which were obtained by him during the fixed term will count towards the target figure.

The tour agent will usually want to represent the performer throughout the world. If the tour agent only has the expertise to represent the performer in certain territories the performer may want to limit the tour agent to representing him in those territories. Some tour agents may have good contacts with other tour agents in those territories where they are not able to represent the performer. The performer should, along with his manager consider whether the tour agent should be allowed to appoint sub-tour agents in those territories where he is not capable of representing the performer, or whether it is better for the performer to contract directly with tour agents in those territories. If it is agreed that the tour agent will appoint sub-tour agents for those territories where he is not capable of representing the performer, the agreement should provide that the tour agent and not the performer will be responsible for the sub-tour agent's commission.

Tour agent's obligations

The tour agent will be required to use his best endeavours to obtain suitable live personal appearances for the performer. He will be required to submit to the performer or his manager details of all offers for the performer's personal appearances which are made to him.

The agreement should specify whether the tour agent is allowed to negotiate the detailed terms of any proposed agreement between the performer and a promoter. Where the tour agent has authority to negotiate the detailed terms, he will not usually be allowed to sign the proposed agreement on behalf of the performer. Usually the tour agent will be required to submit the proposed final form of the agreement to the manager for approval and signature by the performer. The tour agent agreement should provide that where the tour agent submits any proposed agreement for approval or for approval and signature by the performer, the performer's approval or approval and signature will not be unreasonably withheld.

The performer should not be required to repay nor contribute towards the normal business costs the tour agent incurs in representing him. The tour agent, like a manager, is responsible for his own business running costs, *e.g.* office rent, staff, heating, lighting. The tour agent should, however, be repaid his travel and hotel accomodation expenses if they were incurred by him solely on behalf of the performer, *e.g.* he had to travel to meet and negotiate the terms of a proposed agreement with a promoter. The expenses must, however, be reasonably incurred and the amount claimed for each item must be reasonable. In addition, the tour agent should provide receipts for any expenses being claimed.

The tour agent will often be responsible for collecting the money from the promoter for the performer's personal appearances. Where the tour agent is responsible for collecting the money, the tour agent agreement will usually require the tour agent to put the money into a separate trust bank account in the name of the performer or in the names of the performer and the tour agent. The agreement should ideally provide that the signatures of both the tour agent and the performer are required for any cheques which are issued on the account. The agreement should also deal with when the tour agent will account to the performer with his personal appearance monies. The agreement should provide that the provisions in the tour agreement between the performer and the promoter concering the release of the personal appearance monies by the tour agent will apply, and that the tour agent will account to the performer with the personal appearance monies which he has received from the promoter within seven days of the period provided for in the tour agreement. (See also The tour agreement, Performer's warranties and obligations and Promoter's obligations below.) In addition, the tour agent should be required to send to the performer (or if required by the performer, he will send to the performer's manager or accountant) a detailed statement of account of the performer's personal appearance monies which he has received. This should be sent at the same time as the tour agent accounts to the performer with his personal appearance monies. The performer will be paid his personal appearance money either by way of a cheque or by a direct transfer from the trust bank account to his personal bank account. Where the payment is by way of a direct bank transfer, the agreement should set out the name of the performer's bank, the account name and number and the sort code to enable the payment to be made directly into the account. The performer's management agreement may require the performer's personal appearance money to be sent to his manager. Where this is the case the tour agent agreement should contain a provision requiring the performer's personal appearance money to be sent to the performer's manager. In addition, there should be a provision in the agreement that the manager's receipt for the monies will satisfy the tour agent's duty to pay the personal appearance monies to the performer.

The promoter may be prepared to pay a deposit in advance of the concert fee/share of gate receipts. (*See* The tour agreement, Performer's warranties and obligations and Promoter's obligations below for the payment of a deposit by the promoter.)

Although the promoter could:

(i)   send any deposit to the tour agent with instructions to hold it and only release it to the performer or his manager after the concert has been performed, and

> (ii) account directly to the performer or his manager with the balance of the money due after the concert,

he would prefer to account to one person throughout. Indeed, the promoter will certainly not want to pay any deposit monies to the performer or the performer's manager as he will be worried that if the performance does not take place, the performer may have spent the deposit monies and so not be able to repay him. As the promoter will probably have an established business relationship with the tour agent and no doubt believes the tour agent is more trustworthy than the performer, he would prefer to account throughout to the tour agent and not to the performer or his manager.

Where the tour agent collects the money due for the performer's personal appearances, the tour agent agreement should state the capacity in which the tour agent holds any deposit he receives. To reflect what the promoter will want, the tour agent agreement should provide that any deposit paid to the tour agent will be held by the tour agent as stakeholder. This means that the tour agent cannot release the deposit until the concert(s) has been performed. It is most unlikely that the tour agent will hold any deposit as agent for the performer as this would allow the performer to use the deposit before he has performed the concert and the promoter could have problems recovering it if the performer has spent the money and not given the concert. Similarly it would be even more unlikely that any deposit would be held by the tour agent as agent for the promoter, as the promoter could pay any advance before the concert and then at any time before the performance tell the tour agent to return it to him. The tour agent agreement will also need to provide for what happens to any interest earned on any deposit monies. The agreement should provide that the performer is entitled to any interest earned on the money although the tour agent may be able to negotiate that he can commission the interest.

Sometimes a promoter may give a tour agent a gift/inducement to get him to get the performer to perform a concert. Any such gift must be accounted for by the tour agent to the performer as the tour agent owes a fiduciary duty to the performer. Even though the tour agent is duty bound to account to the performer for such gifts, the agreement should make it expressly clear that this is the case. The agreement should also provide that the tour agent is entitled to commission on the value of such gifts.

The agreement should contain an accounting provision clause requiring the tour agent to maintain proper accounts relating to the performer's personal appearance money which will be kept at the tour agent's registered office or main place of business. The tour agent may insert a clause giving the performer, for example, one year from receipt of the accounts to object to their accuracy. The performer should not accept any clause which allows the tour agent to reduce the six-year contractual limitation period to object to the accounts. There should also be an audit clause in the agreement which will allow the performer or his professionally qualified accountant to inspect, audit and take copies of the tour agent's books and records to determine the accuracy of the accounts. The clause will usually require the performer to give notice of his intention to carry out the audit, and will limit the inspection to one inspection a year at the performer's expense. In addition, the clause will usually provide that the audit will take place at the tour agent's registered office or main place of business and will take place during the tour agent's normal business hours. There may be an additional restriction that the accountant carrying out the audit for the performer is not presently engaged on another audit of the tour agent on behalf of another performer.

The agreement should provide that where the performer has been underpaid by a specified sum, *e.g.* he has been underpaid by at least £5,000, or has been underpaid by a specified percentage, 10%, whichever is greater, the cost of the audit will be paid for by the tour agent. The agreement should provide that where the performer has been underpaid, the tour agent will account to the performer for the underpayment. The performer should ensure that the clause is drafted so that the tour agent accounts for any underpayment immediately and that the tour agent pays interest on any underpaid sum at 3 or 4 % above a stated bank's base rate from time to time in force.

The audit clause should contain a provision that the information disclosed to the performer and/or his accountant is confidential information and will not be disclosed to anyone other than the performer's professional advisers. The tour agent will usually require a copy of the performer's final audit report.

Tour agent's remuneration

It is rare for the tour agent to be paid an advance against commission by the performer. If an advance is paid to the tour agent by the performer it will usually be non-returnable but recoupable against the commission due to the tour agent. Any such advance may be paid in full upon signing the agreement or spread over a period of time.

The tour agent will usually just be paid commission. The commission rate is usually in the region of 10–15% of the performer's gross earnings from personal appearances, although the tour agent may be prepared to accept a commission of less than 10% where the performer earns substantial sums from his personal appearances.

Gross earnings will need to be defined in the agreement and may be defined as the income earned by the performer, (or the income earned by the performer and received by the tour agent, the performer, his manager or anyone acting on behalf of the performer), from his personal appearances which have been obtained by the tour agent, the performer, his manager or anyone acting on behalf of the performer during the term, and which are performed during or after the term, less any VAT payable by the promoter on any personal appearance fee, less any reasonable legal costs incurred in collecting the money for the personal appearance. The definition of gross earnings will need to make it clear that the tour agent is only entitled to commission the personal appearances for which he is appointed to represent the performer, and that he is not entitled to commission any tour support which the performer receives from his record company, nor any money paid to record the perfomer's performance.

The definition of gross money should deal with whether the tour agent is entitled to be paid commission on engagements performed during the term but which were negotiated prior to the agreement, and whether the tour agent is entitled to be paid commission on personal appearances negotiated during the term but performed after the term. From the performer's standpoint the tour agent should not be paid commission on engagements performed during the term but which were negotiated prior to the agreement. The performer should, however, be prepared to pay commission for engagements which were negotiated by the tour agent during the term and which were performed wholly or in part after the term. The agreement must specifically deal with whether the tour agent is entitled to commission where a promoter, who originally engaged the performer through the tour agent, wants to re-engage the performer after the end of the agreement term, and whether the tour agent is entitled to commission where the promoter, after the expiry of the tour agent agreement, wants to add extra tour dates to the tour which was originally negotiated by the tour agent.

Termination, suspension and other clauses

For details about the termination, suspension and other clauses which should be included in a tour agent agreement *see* Chapter 3 Music Industry Contracts, Chapter 5 The Legal Status of Band and Solo Artist, Chapter 6 The Management Agreement, Chapter 7 The Publishing Agreement and Chapter 8 Recording Agreements.

The additional clauses which should be included in a tour agent agreement include:

(a) A termination clause.

(b) A suspension clause.

(c) A confidentiality clause.

(d) A clause which provides that the performer has been advised to obtain and has obtained independent legal advice on the contents of the agreement from a solicitor with experience of music agreements.

(e) A jurisdiction and choice of law clause. (*See* Chapter 3 Music Industry Contracts.)

(f) An invalidity clause. (*See* Chapter 3 Music Industry Contracts and Chapter 5 The Legal Status of Band and Solo Artist).

(g) A clause emphasising that the tour agent has no rights to any of the performer's or his band's copyrights, moral rights or performers' rights, nor the right to use the performer's or his band's name, likeness, biographical details or any trade mark belonging to him or his band except where expressly authorised in the agreement.

(h) A clause providing that the tour agent agreement does not constitute a partnership, joint venture or employment relationship between the tour agent and the performer.

(i) A clause making it clear that the tour agent has the right to represent other performers.

(j) A clause confirming that the agreement reflects the whole of the agreement between the parties and replaces any earlier oral or written agreement.

(k) A non-waiver clause. (*See* Chapter 5 The Legal Status of Band and Solo Artist.)

(l) A *force majeure* clause. (*See* Chapter 3 Music Industry Contracts.)

(m) A notice clause. (*See* Chapter 5 The Legal Status of Band and Solo Artist.)

(n) A clause which provides that the tour agent and the performer will sign any documentation which is necesssary to carry out the terms of the agreement. (*See* Chapter 7 The Publishing Agreement.)

(o) A clause confirming that the performer is free to enter into the agreement.

(p) An indemnity clause. (*See* Chapter 3 Music Industry Contracts and Chapter 6 The Management Agreement.)

(q) A clause dealing with the Contracts (Rights of Third Parties) Act 1999. (See Chapter 3 Music Industry Contracts.)

The performer should ensure the tour agent agreement contains a clause that the tour agent cannot assign the agreement. The only variation on assignment that the performer may be prepared to accept would be to allow the agreement to be assigned to a company which is owned and controlled by the tour agent. An assignment may be acceptable to the performer in this limited case if the agreement is varied to include a key man clause, if the assignee (i.e. the company) enters a direct covenant with the performer that it will comply with the terms of the tour agent agreement, and if the tour agent provides the performer with a suitably worded side letter. (See Chapter 6 The Management Agreement, Appointment of the manager above for the key man clause and for the side letter.)

The tour agreement

It is not easy for a performer at the start of his career to find venues which will let him play live in concert. Even if the performer can find venues to play, the chances are he will be paid next to nothing to perform.

Many performers at the start of their career will have to play for free or, if lucky, they may be given a few drinks on the house. Some venues will even charge the performer to play. These venues will either charge the performer a fee to play or will sell him a certain number of tickets for the evening he is playing which the performer can try and sell on to the public in an attempt to recover some of the money he spent purchasing them.

Some venues will not pay the performer to play but will instead share the gate receipts. Some venues may even pay the performer a nominal sum of money up front as a non-returnable but recoupable advance for his share of the gate receipts. There is no hard and fast rule as to what percentage of gate receipts the performer may receive. It all depends upon the generosity or otherwise of the venue owner and the performer's negotiating ability. It is possible that a venue owner may be prepared to pay the performer all the net gate receipts, *i.e.* after the venue owner has recovered his expenses. The reason why a venue owner may be prepared to pay the performer all the net gate receipts may be because he is running a restaurant or bar rather than a proper concert venue and he is using the performer to bring in diners and drinkers, and the ticket price after the venue owner has recovered his expenses equates to the fee he would have been prepared to pay the performer to play.

The idea that a performer may have to pay to play may continue when the performer has become established. There is a tendency for some top international performers who are on tour to charge support acts a fee to open for them. The fee may be purely a cash fee to play or may be dressed up as a fee to use their sound and lighting equipment. The opening act for a top international performer may be only too pleased to pay because the audience will associate them with the star and it will be excellent publicity to play in front of such a large audience. The opening act may, however, not be able to afford to pay a fee to open because after, inter alia, the tour agent's commission, their own touring expenses and the fee to open the concert have been deducted from the fee they are being paid by the promoter to play they would be making a substantial financial loss. Their record company may feel that the opportunity to open a large concert for a top international superstar is worth paying for due to the publicity it will attract and so the record company might be prepared to pay tour support to enable them to open the concert. (For tour support *see* Chapter 8 Recording Agreements, Record company's obligations (g).)

The costs of a performer going on tour may be substantial. Until the performer has achieved some level of success he will find that life on the road is not a five-star experience. Even if the performer is successful and living a five-star lifestyle on tour he will soon find out that it is not the record company, nor the publishing company, nor usually the promoter who picks up his hotel and other bills on tour. The person who picks up these bills is the performer. The performer should remember that the more he spends on himself on tour the less money he will bring home at the end of the day.

To start with touring is more a case of living in the tour van with the rest of the band and tour crew, eating in motorway cafes and take away restaurants, with occasional stays in a bed and breakfast. From the concert fee the band will have to pay the tour agent's commission, the manager's commission, wages for the tour crew, the cost of hiring and running the tour van, the hire purchase of musical equipment and possibly, the sound and lighting equipment they use, the costs of repairs to equipment, various insurance premiums, and their individual living expenses whilst on the road. Even where the performer cuts his lifestyle back, touring will still be a costly and at times not a very glamorous way of life. As mentioned earlier, some performers can make a lot of money from touring and indeed heavy metal bands may make more money from touring than from record sales, but for most performers touring is the main way to help promote and sell records, rather than a way for them to make a living.

It should be noted that a tour agreement may comprise two separate documents which together will form the tour agreement. The first document is the promoter's standard terms and conditions. The second document is a schedule or rider to the standard terms and conditions which will detail the performer's specific personal requirements for the tour, *e.g.* the food he wants provided at each venue and the technical requirements such as sound and lighting equipment which the performer needs for the tour. The rest of this chapter assumes that all the contractual provisions are contained in one document. This chapter also assumes that the performer is being paid to perform in concert by the promoter and that the promoter does not own the concert venue.

Parties

The promoter, who is responsible for booking the venues and promoting the concerts, will usually be a limited company rather than an individual. The performer will either contract personally or via a limited company which is owned and controlled by him. The principles discussed above concerning either or both of the parties to a tour agent agreement being a company apply equally to a tour agreement. (*See* The tour agent agreement, Parties above.)

Publicity

The performer should grant the promoter the right to use his name and likeness, his biographical details and any trade mark belonging to him, and where he is in a band the right to use the band's name and likeness, the band's biographical details and any trade mark belonging to the band solely for the purpose of advertising and promoting the concerts.

The performer/band will want the right to approve any proposed use of his/their name and likeness etc by the promoter in any proposed advertising and promotional material. The promoter may only be prepared to consult with the performer/band about the proposed use of the performer/band's name and likeness etc on any proposed advertising and promotional material. Where the promoter is prepared to let the performer/band have approval rights, the promoter will usually only agree to the performer/band having qualified approval rights, *i.e.* the performer/band will have the right to approve any proposed use of his/their name and likeness etc in any proposed advertising and promotional material with such approval not to be unreasonably withheld.

The performer may be required to attend a photo shoot at a specified time to be photographed for the tour advertising material. As mentioned above, the performer will want the right to approve any advertising and promotional material which the promoter wants to use. The agreement should set out where the performer's name and logo will appear on any advertising material together with the size of the performer's name credit. Where the performer is the headline act the agreement should provide similar provisions concerning the support act(s). The performer will want to ensure the advertising makes him appear to be the headline act and that the name of the support act(s) does not detract from the fact he is the headliner. The tour agreement should also provide that all concert advertising will include a reference to the performer's tour sponsor. The performer should ensure that the provisions in the tour agreement concerning a reference to the tour sponsor in the concert advertising mirrors what he has agreed with the tour sponsor in the tour sponsorship agreement, *e.g.* as to the size of the reference to the sponsor. (*See also* Chapter 10 Tour Sponsorship, The tour sponsorship agreement, The sponsor's rights).

Performer's warranties and obligations

The primary obligation of the performer in a tour agreement is that he will perform in concert at the venue(s), date(s) and time(s) specified in the agreement and that he will perform to the best of his ability.

Where the performer is entering into a tour agreement rather than a one off concert agreement, he will usually be required to warrant that he will not perform a concert(s) for anyone else during the tour. This is to give the promoter a period of exclusivity to promote the performer on tour. Some promoters may try to extend the period of exclusivity by requiring the performer not to perform any concert(s) for anyone else for a period of time before and after the tour. The performer should resist a clause extending any exclusivity before and after the tour. The promoter may also try and prohibit the performer from appearing on television or radio without his permission during the tour. The promoter might seek this restriction to enhance the exclusivity of the concert(s). The performer should strongly resist any such restriction. The performer should at most only agree that he will not make a live concert appearance for television or radio during the tour without the permission of the promoter and that any such restriction will not apply to any live concert appearance which he made for television or radio prior to the date of the tour agreement and which is broadcast during the tour, nor to him making any appearance on television or radio to perform a maximum of, say, two compositions to promote a single or album.

The performer will want to choose the compositions he will perform in concert and he should not accept a clause in the agreement which requires the promoter's prior approval of the compositions he intends to perform. Some performers become tired of playing their most popular songs night after night and may prefer to drop them and play their more obscure and less popular back catalogue songs along with the songs from their latest record. The promoter may be concerned that a performer may want to drop his best known songs from his set. To protect against this some promoters allow the performer to choose the compositions which he will perform but may require him to include some or all of his best known songs in each concert performance. Perhaps the only time when a promoter may choose the material is where the performer is unknown and is being hired as the cabaret for a hotel dinner dance. Even in this situation the promoter is more like to choose the musical style, *e.g.* middle of the road music, pop music, rather than actually choose the compositions which will be performed. The one limitation which a promoter will put on any performer's choice of compositions is that he must not include a composition in the performance which is defamatory, obscene, blasphemous, infringes any third party's right, or which may possibly affect the public's sensitivities at the time. The performer will also be required to give his performance in his usual style, *e.g.* if he is a pop singer he will perform in a pop music style and not re-interpret his music in any other musical style.

The agreement might contain a clause providing that the performer will conduct himself at all times during the concert(s) in a proper manner and will not do anything which will bring himself, the promoter or the venue(s) into disrepute. Whether the promoter requires a conduct clause in the agreement depends upon the type of performer being booked. A promoter may require a conduct clause if, for example, he is booking a boy band as he will be concerned that they do not do or saying anything on stage which prejudices their squeaky clean image. A conduct clause may not be appropriate for a band that sells itself on its bad behaviour, although the promoter may require a modified version of the conduct clause for such performers which allows them to portray their usual image on stage but prohibits any behaviour which may be regarded as worse than their usual stage behaviour.

The performer will be required to warrant that the tour agent agreement contains a provision that any deposit paid by the promoter to the tour agent for a concert performance(s) will be held by the tour agent as stakeholder.

The performer will be required to ensure his musical equipment and any sound and lighting equipment which he intends to use will be installed in the venue in time for the concert, and that he will perform a sound check before the concert. The promoter will have to ensure the performer and his tour crew will be given access to the venue in proper time to install the equipment and to carry out a sound check. (*See* Promoter's obligations below.) The performer will also be required to warrant that all the equipment he intends to use in concert is in good working order and will be safe to use.

The agreement should provide that where the performer does not have his own sound and lighting equipment, he will give the promoter details of the sound and lighting equipment he needs, say, 14 days in advance of the concert so the promoter can arrange for it to be hired in time.

The agreement will provide that the performer will be responsible for his own actions, for the actions of his tour crew at the concert venue, as well as being responsible for any damage which he and/or they cause at the concert venue. The performer will be required to indemnify the promoter for any breach of this obligation. In addition, the performer will be required to warrant that he has appropriate insurance covering any loss which might arise from any breach of this obligation.

Occasionally, a performer has to cancel a concert or a series of concerts due to illness. The promoter will require the performer to inform him as soon as he is aware of any illness or disability which will stop him performing in concert. The promoter will want the right for his doctor and/or his insurer's doctor to examine the performer. The insurer's doctor will want to examine the performer to ensure that any claim being made on the cancellation insurance cover taken out by the promoter is valid.

Security is the responsibility of the promoter (*see* Promoter's obligations below). To enable the promoter to provide proper security at each venue he will need to know the names of the performer's tour crew and all other personnel associated with him who will be at the concerts. Some personnel associated with the performer need access to only certain parts of the venue, *e.g.* hairdressers need back stage access, whilst the lighting crew need access back stage and on stage. The performer must provide the promoter with a list of people he needs at the venue together with details of the areas in the venue these people are permitted to enter. The promoter may want the performer to send him photos of these people so that laminate security passes can be made. Security is an extremely important responsibility for the promoter and can only be done effectively if the performer provides the promoter with proper details of who is allowed where. In addition, the agreement should require the performer to give the promoter a list for the evening of each concert of those guests who can come back stage after that evening's show and party with the performer, *e.g.* friends, family, record company executives, local radio and television presenters and journalists. The performer will also be required to supply the promoter with details of the cars, lorries and vans which need to be parked at the venue(s) so that the promoter can arrange the necessary car park passes (*see also* Promoter's obligations below for parking vehicles at the venue(s)).

The performer will have to warrant that he is able to enter into the tour agreement and that there are no other agreements in existence which will prevent him from performing at the venues on the dates and times agreed.

Where he is signing a band for a tour the promoter will be worried that one or more of the performers may leave the band prior to or during the tour. The agreement will contain a clause providing that all those performers who are band members when the agreement is signed will satisfy the tour commitments. Such a clause will not in reality stop a band member walking out prior to or during the tour. No court will grant the promoter an order for specific performance requiring the band to perform together. Because of this the agreement will also contain a clause providing that where one or more members leave the band prior to or during a tour the promoter can terminate the agreement. The band may want to modify this clause to provide that the promoter can only terminate the agreement where, for example, a named key member such as the lead singer or the lead guitarist after whom the band is named leaves.

Where the performer uses back up musicians in his performance the tour agreement should provide that it is the performer's responsibility to pay the back up musicians and that they will not be paid less than Musicians' Union rates.

Promoter's obligations

It is the promoter's responsibility to find suitable venues for the concerts and to book them for the dates required. The promoter will be required to ensure that the venues comply with all relevant laws and regulations, *e.g.* any licences which are required to hold the concert have been obtained, that the venues comply with all health and safety requirements, that the venues are registered with the PRS, and that a concert set list will be sent to the PRS after the concert together with the money payable for performing the compositions in concert.

The promoter must make himself fully acquainted with the venue's rules and regulations and with any other regulations which apply to the venue, such as any local authority regulations dealing with the maximum audience capacity allowed at the venue. The promoter should inform the performer of any regulations which may affect his performance, *e.g.* the maximum sound level which is permitted at the venue and when the concert including any encores must end.

The promoter must ensure the venue is available before and after the concert to enable the perfomer to unload, set up, dismantle and reload his stage and musical equipment. The promoter should ensure that someone is at the venue at all times to supervise the whole process. The promoter should also make sure the venue will be available for the perfomer to carry out soundchecks and, where the performer requires, rehearsals for the concert.

The promoter should ensure there are proper dressing room and back stage facilities for the performer and his band and that there are adequate parking facilities at the venue for the performer's cars and for the lorries and vans carrying the tour equipment. Any car park passes needed for access to the venue's car park should be obtained by the promoter from the venue owner.

It should be the promoter's responsibility to hire any equipment such as electrical generators and the sound and lighting equipment which the performer needs to perform at the venue. The performer will obviously have to inform the promoter of his requirements, say, 14 days in advance of the concert so the promoter can arrange for the necessary equipment to be hired in time. (*See* Performer's warranties and obligations above.) Often the performer will use his own sound and lighting equipment. Where this happens the agreement should provide that the promoter will hire the performer's sound and lighting equipment from him. As it is the promoter's responsibility to pay for the hire of such equipment it is only fair that where the performer uses his own equipment, the promoter should pay him a hire fee for its use.

The agreement should require the promoter to ensure that no audio or audio visual recording of the concert will be made and that no photographs will be taken at the concert without the consent of the performer. The promoter will be required to include a statement on the concert tickets informing the audience that they are not allowed to record the concert or take photographs at the concert. The agreement should also provide that where the performer wants to record his performance that he will notify the promoter in advance with details of the people who need access to the venue to make the recording and with details of the equipment which needs to be brought into the venue to enable the recording to be made. The agreement should require the promoter to apply for the venue owner's consent for the performer to record the performance. Any fee required by the venue owner for giving his consent is payable by the performer. The agreement should provide that where the venue owner has given his consent for the recording to be made at the venue that the promoter will ensure that access to the venue is available for the people making the recording and for their equipment.

Although the promoter will be responsible for promoting and advertising the concert the agreement should provide that he will not be allowed to book radio, television or newspaper interviews which requires the performer to be in attendance. Any promotion which needs the attendance of the performer should only be booked by the promoter if the performer has consented to appear.

The promoter will either have to consult with the performer about the proposed advertising and promotional material, or will have to supply it to the performer for approval. (*See also* Publicity above.) The promoter must ensure the size and positioning of the performer's name credit, that of any support act(s), and that of the performer's tour sponsor conforms to the specifications required by the performer. Where the performer is the headline act the performer will usually want the right to approve the support act and the length of their appearance at the concert.

The performer will want to ensure that only his tour sponsors will be able to directly associate themselves with the tour. Indirect association with the tour can occur in the form of ambush marketing. Ambush marketing is an extremely effective and a comparatively cheap way of a company indirectly and legitimately associating itself with an event without being an official sponsor of the event. For example, if a marathon race is officially sponsored by a company the company can advertise that they are the sponsors of the event. A competing company who have not paid for the right to be an official sponsor might choose to try and buy up the advertising hoardings around the marathon route. Consumer research has shown that a high percentage of the public believes that the ambush marketer is in fact an official sponsor of the event. The performer cannot prevent ambush marketing but he can limit anybody whom he has not approved from directly associating himself with the tour by inserting a clause into the tour agreement which bars the promoter from entering into an agreement with a third party which would allow the third party to directly associate himself with the tour. This would, for example, stop the promoter from entering into an agreement with a company allowing it to have its name on the tour advertising material, and would also prevent the promoter entering into an agreement with a company to sell it concert tickets which it can give away in an advertising campaign. The performer should also require the promoter to warrant that the venue hire agreement between the promoter and the venue owner will contain a similar restriction upon the venue owner.

The promoter will be required to recruit and pay for security staff for the concert(s). (It should be noted that some venues will insist that the promoter uses its security staff in which case the promoter will pay the venue for the use of its staff.) The promoter should be required to supply the security staff and the performer's personnel with walkie talkies to enable efficient communications to be maintained throughout the whole venue. Where security staff have to be pre-approved by the venue owner or by the local or any other authority, the promoter should be required to obtain the necessary approval(s).

The performer should supply the promoter with a list of people whom he needs at the venue together with details of the areas these people are permitted to enter. The promoter should be responsible for devising a suitable security pass scheme and for arranging the manufacture and distribution of the necessary security passes.

It is the promoter's responsibility to arrange the necessary insurance cover for the tour — such as cancellation and public liability insurance. The tour agreement should specify the insurance cover which is required and which is the promoter's responsibility to arrange. Some risks will be covered by the venue's insurance, in which case it may be possible for the promoter to rely on that insurance provided it adequately covers risks, is sufficient in amount and provided that the venue's insurers are prepared to note the interests of the promoter, performer and (if required) the performer's sponsor on the policy. The tour agreement should require the promoter to provide the performer with evidence that all the necessary insurance has been arranged and that such insurance is on risk. The performer will also want a provision in the tour agreement that his interest will be noted on the insurance policy(ies) and evidence will be provided that it has been noted. (The performer should arrange his own insurance to cover theft, loss or damage to his equipment and for any damage he or his tour crew might cause at the venue.) Where the performer has a sponsorship agreement or wants to obtain sponsorship, he should ensure that the tour agreement reflects the need for the sponsor to have evidence of insurance cover for the tour and for the sponsor's interest to be noted on such insurance policies. (*See also* Chapter 10 Tour Sponsorship, the Performer's warranties and obligations below for tour insurance relating to the sponsor.)

The promoter may be prepared to pay a deposit, *i.e.* an advance on account of the concert fee/share of the net gate receipts. (See below for what are net gate receipt.) If a deposit is to be paid by the promoter, the agreement should specify when the promoter will pay the deposit and the balance of the monies, *e.g.* the deposit will be paid 28 days before the concert and the balance will be paid immediately after the concert. The agreement should also detail to whom the promoter is to pay the deposit and to whom he is to pay the balance of the monies. The promoter will want to pay the deposit and the balance of the monies to the tour agent. The promoter will want the tour agent to hold the deposit as stakeholder until the performer has given the concert whereupon the tour agent can release the deposit to the performer. Where the deposit is to be paid for a tour, the agreement should provide whether the tour agent is to release the deposit only after the whole tour has been completed or whether, as the performer would prefer, the tour agent can release the deposit to the performer in stages, *e.g.* if the deposit covers a series of 20 concerts the agreement could provide for the tour agent to release a proportionate part of the deposit after the performer has played each concert. The agreement should also deal with when the tour agent can release the balance of the monies to the performer. For a one off concert, the agreement should provide that the tour agent can release the balance monies to the performer as soon as they are received by the tour agent from the promoter. Where the agreement is for a tour, the performer will want the tour agent to be able to release the balance monies for each concert as soon as they are received by the tour agent from the promoter rather than having to wait until the end of the tour before the tour agent is able to release them to him. (See also The tour agent agreement, Tour agent's obligations above.)

The promoter might agree to pay the performer a share of the net gate receipts and guarantee the performer will be paid a minimum amount irrespective of the actual gate, *e.g.* if the performer receives 85% of the net gate receipts and the promoter guarantees the minimum the performer will be paid is £30,000 for the concert, the performer will receive £30,000 even if the performer's 85% of the net gate receits would have amounted to less than £30,000.

As mentioned throughout this book, the word "net" will need to be defined so that the promoter and performer are aware of what can be deducted from the gross gate receipts. Gross gate receipts are monies received from ticket sales, any fees the promoter charges for setting up stalls to sell merchandise at the venue, and any other money the promoter receives from the concert, less VAT on the ticket sale price, and the costs charged by ticket agencies for selling tickets. The net gate receipts are gross gate receipts less the promoter's expenses. The promoter's expenses which can be deducted should be itemised in the agreement as should the maximum amount which can be deducted per item, *e.g.* a maximum of £50,000 can be deducted for advertising during the tour, and a maximum of £70,000 can be deducted for hiring venues during the tour. The promoter should be required to keep receipts for the expenses he is seeking to deduct from the gross gate receipts. (Rather than set a limit which can be deducted per item for the tour, the limit could instead be a limit per item per concert, *e.g.* for smaller venues the maximum amount which can be deducted by the promoter for advertising will be set at a lower limit than that permitted for larger venues. This should ensure that the promoter 's expenditure for the concerts is spent according to the size and importance of each venue.)

The items which the promoter will seek to deduct as expenses include the cost of:

(a) hiring the venue,
(b) hiring sound and lighting equipment,
(c) advertising the concert(s),
(d) printing the concert tickets,
(e) relevant insurance cover,
(f) hiring staff including security staff for the venues,
(g) PRS monies payable for each performance.

Where the performer is on tour rather than performing a single concert, he will need money for his living expenses. Life on the road even at the cheapest level frequently costs more than living a similar lifestyle at home. The tour agreement may provide that the promoter will pay the performer a certain amount of money daily or each week to help towards the performer's living expenses whilst on tour. Any such money advanced by the promoter is recoupable from the tour fees payable to the performer. The tour agent will be concerned that the cheque from the promoter for the tour fee may not cover his commission, due to the deduction by the promoter of any living expense advances. The tour agent could seek the balance of any commission due from the performer, but it is possible that the performer may not have sufficient money to pay the tour agent. To prevent this problem the tour agreement should provide a maximum amount which the promoter can advance to the performer for his living expenses. Whenever he advances living expenses to the performer the promoter should obtain a signed receipt for the money. The promoter will need a receipt to send to the tour agent to show the deductions made from the tour fees are correct. Whether the performer is responsible for paying his own travel and accommodation expenses will need to be negotiated between the parties. The promoter will generally not be prepared to pay the performer's travel and accommodation expenses. If the promoter agrees to pay the performer's travel and accommodation he may do so on the basis that these costs are treated as an expense which can be deducted from the gross gate receipts. The performer would not want any travel and accommodation which is paid for by the promoter to be a deductible expense but would want them to be paid in addition to his share of the net gate receipts. Whether they will be a deductible expense or treated as an additional payment to the performer will depend upon the negotiating strengths and weaknesses of the parties.

Where the performer is paid a share of the audience gate receipts, it is vital that the tour agreement contains provisions enabling the ticketing arrangements to be checked. If there are not proper checks on the ticketing arrangements an unscrupulous promoter can easily fail to account for the correct monies due to the performer. To ensure that the performer is paid the correct money where he is entitled to a share of the gate receipts, the agreement should include:

(a) Details, or where they are not available at the date of the agreement, the promoter must supply the performer within a set period of time after the parties have entered the agreement with details of:
    (i) the seating plan for each concert venue. A copy of the seating plan for each concert venue should be given to

the tour agent and the performer's manager, or where the performer has one, his tour manager. The seating plan which is to be provided should relate to the seating which will be in place for the concert, *e.g.* taking into account the stage layout, the placing of the sound and lighting equipment and the mixing desk used by the performer for the concert. This may be different to the standard seating plan used by the venue.

(ii) the maximum audience attendance permitted for each concert venue.

(iii) the ticket prices for each concert venue.

(iv) the gross amount of money which would be generated from ticket sales from a sell out concert at each concert venue.

(b) Details for each concert venue of the number of tickets printed in each price range and of the number of tickets printed in total. The agreement will require the promoter only to print and distribute for sale the number of tickets which the performer and the promoter have agreed for each venue. The agreement should also provide that the tickets for each venue will be consecutively numbered, and that the tickets will only be sold at face value.

(c) A limit on the number of free tickets allocated to the promoter and the venue for each concert. The agreement should prohibit the promoter and the venue from selling these tickets. Although the tickets will be for the best seats in the house, the performer will want to ensure that the promoter and the venue cannot have free tickets for the front 10 or 15 rows in the venue. This is to ensure that real fans can buy these tickets and so help generate a proper atmosphere for the performer and the rest of the audience at the concert. (In addition, provision should be made for the performer, his manager, his tour sponsor, his publisher and his record company to have a certain number of free tickets. These tickets should be for the best seats in the house. For the reason given above the performer will probably not want his manager etc to have tickets for the front 10 or 15 rows in the venue. The performer will probably want tickets for specific areas such as the venue's box seats or those areas used for corporate hospitality.)

(d) A provision that the promoter will make available to the tour agent and the performer's manager, or where the performer has one, his tour manager, at a specified time(s) before each concert, details of how many tickets have been sold in advance of each concert and of the number of tickets sold in each price range.

(e) A provision that will allow the performer to have representatives on the doors to count the number of people attending each concert.

(f) A provision that the promoter will allow the tour agent and the performer's manager or tour manager or other designated representative of the performer to attend the ticket box office at each venue to inspect and take copies of the ticket sales records to enable the performer to carry out an audit of the ticket sales.

(g) A provision that the promoter will give the tour agent and the performer's manager or tour manager details of the ticket box office takings immediately after the concert.

(h) A provision that the promoter will, for a specified period of time, retain all the ticket stubs and unsold tickets from each concert, and will allow the performer's representatives to examine them. These can be used as a cross-checking reference in an audit of the ticket sales.

If the performer is being paid a share of the audience gate receipts there should be a provision in the tour agreement requiring the promoter to maintain proper accounts, and for the accounts to be kept at the promoter's registered office or main place of business. In addition, the promoter should be required to provide a detailed statement of account with the performer's share of the gate receipts. As mentioned above, the tour agreement should contain a provision as to whom the promoter is to pay any deposit and to whom the balance of the monies should be paid e.g. to the performer, or his manager, or as will be most likely, to the tour agent. (See also The tour agent agreement, Tour agent's obligations above.) The agreement should provide that where the promoter pays the performer's monies to a third party that the third party's receipt for the monies will satisfy the promoter's duty to pay the performer. The promoter will usually pay the performer's personal appearance money by cheque or by a bank transfer. (It should be noted that some promoters are required to account immediately after the concert in cash.) Where the payment is by a bank transfer the agreement should set out the name of the bank, the account name and number and the sort code to which the monies are to be sent so that the promoter can arrange the bank transfer.

The promoter may insert a clause into the agreement giving the performer, for example, one year from receipt of the accounts to object to their accuracy. The performer should not accept any attempt by the promoter to reduce the six-year contractual limitation period to object to the accounts. The agreement should also contain an audit clause which will allow the perfomer or his professionally qualified accountant to inspect, audit and take copies of the promoter's books and records to determine the accuracy of the accounts. The clause will usually require the performer to give notice of his intention to carry out the audit, and will limit the inspection to one inspection a year at the performer's expense. In addition, the clause will usually provide that the audit will take place at the promoter's registered office or main place of business and will take place during the promoter's normal business hours. There may be an additional restriction that the accountant carrying out the audit for the performer is not presently engaged on another audit of the promoter on behalf of another performer.

The agreement should provide that where the performer has been underpaid by a specified sum, *e.g.* he has been underpaid by at least £5,000, or he has been underpaid by a specified percentage, 10%, whichever is greater, that the cost of the audit will be paid for by the promoter. Where the performer has been underpaid, the agreement should provide for the promoter to account to the performer for the underpayment. The performer should ensure the clause is drafted so that the promoter accounts for any underpayment immediately and that the promoter pays interest on any underpaid sum at 3 or 4% above a stated bank's base rate from time to time in force.

The audit clause should contain a provision confirming that the information disclosed to the performer and/or his accountant is confidential information and will not be disclosed to anybody except the performer's professional advisers. The promoter will usually require a copy of the performer's final audit report to be sent to him.

The agreement should restrict the promoter and the venue owners from selling any type of tour merchandise at the venue and should provide that the performer or his appointed merchandising licensee has the exclusive right to sell tour merchandise. The performer will require the promoter and the venue owner to help stop merchandisers selling unlicensed tour merchandise either inside or outside the venue. The promoter will be required to print a notice on the concert tickets that licensed tour merchandise is available for purchase only inside the concert venue and that the public should not buy tour merchandise from people outside the venue as this merchandise is not licensed. To try and prevent unlicensed merchandise being sold outside the concert venues the promoter should ensure that the local police and trading standards authority are informed of the potential problem and ask them to send officials to deal with the problem before and after the concert. The performer should also inform his solicitors of the concert dates and ask them to be present outside the venue before and after the concert to deal with the sale of unlicensed merchandise with the police and local trading standards officials.

Where the performer or his licensee wants to sell tour merchandise at the venue, the tour agreement should provide that the promoter will ensure that designated areas within the venue will be available for the performer or his licensee to do so. The tour agreement should also contain a provision requiring the promoter to ensure that delivery vans will be able to park at the venue before, during and after the concert to deliver, unload and reload the merchandise, and that the performer's staff or his licensee's staff will be allowed into the venue to set up the merchandise stall, to man it during the concert, and to dismantle it afterwards. The promoter should also be required to ensure that any necessary passes are obtained for the delivery vans to park in the venue's car park and for the performer's staff or his licensee's staff to enter the venue to set up and dismantle the stall and to man it during the concert. It should be noted (see below) that the venue owner may want to use his own staff to sell tour merchandise rather than allow the performer's staff or his licensee's staff to do so. Because of this, the promoter should ensure that the tour agreement provides that he will arrange for the performer's staff or his licensee's staff to be allowed into the venues to sell tour merchandise subject to the venue owner agreeing to it. There should also be a provision in the agreement requiring the promoter, where a concert will be held at a venue for two or more consecutive nights, to arrange with the venue owner for any unsold merchandise to be stored in a safe area within the venue overnight.

The agreement should require the promoter to obtain consent from the venue owner to enable the performer or his licensee to sell tour merchandise at the venue. The promoter may, and the venue owner will charge the performer a fee to allow him to sell tour merchandise at the venue. Where the promoter charges a fee this should be set out in the tour agreement. The venue owner's fee will be set out in the licence which the venue owner will grant to the performer or his licensee allowing the venue to be used to sell tour merchandise. The venue owner's licence fee will usually be in the region of 35–40% of the gross sales of the tour merchandise on the evening of the concert. Whether the venue owner will use his own staff to sell the merchandise or whether the performer or his licensee will be allowed to bring in his own staff to sell the merchandise at the venue will need to be negotiated between the parties. Most venue owners want to use their own staff as this will enable them to keep an eye on how much merchandise is sold, and so ensure that the correct licence fee is paid. (See also Chapter 11 Merchandising, Merchandise licensing, The royalty.)

The tour agreement will require the promoter to supply food and drink for the performer and their guests before and after the concert. The agreement will contain a detailed list of the food and drink which the performer expects the promoter to supply. The food and drink requirements are frequently very specific, for example, one band was known to list amongst their requirements that the promoter would have to supply Smarties, but only the red coloured ones!

Touring abroad

Where the performer is touring abroad the tour agreement may need to deal with the following:

Entry visas and work permits

Where it is proposed that the performer will tour abroad, the tour agreement for the foreign dates of the tour should be conditional upon the performer being granted, where required, an entry visa and a work permit. Some countries will not grant the performer an entry visa or a work permit where he has a criminal conviction. The issuing of relevant permits should not be taken for granted. What may be regarded by many as a comparatively innocuous conviction for an offence committed 20 years ago by the performer, *e.g.* a fine for possession of cannabis, may mean that the performer will be barred from entering certain countries.

In addition to the permits for the performer, permits will need to be obtained for the performer's tour crew and other personnnel involved in the tour.

The promoter should liaise with the tour agent and the performer's manager to obtain the relevant permits for the tour. The promoter will not usually be responsible for obtaining them, but where he is, the tour agreement should make it clear that it is his responsibility.

(It should also be remembered that a foreign performer who is performing in this country may need an entry visa and a work permit.)

Equipment and instruments

Where the performer is performing abroad he will usually take his own instruments with him and will frequently use his own sound and lighting and other special effects equipment. A carnet should be arranged so that the performer's equipment can be imported into foreign countries for the concert without any liability for import tax. There will be a liability to pay import tax in each of the countries which the equipment passes through where a carnet is not obtained or where the equipment was taken into a country covered by the carnet but was not taken out of the country after the concert. The performer's manager will usually be responsible for obtaining the carnet. In the unlikely event that the promoter is responsible for obtaining the carnet, the tour agreement should contain a clause providing for this.

Tax

In certain countries withholding tax may have to be deducted from the ticket sale proceeds. The tour agreement should provide that the promoter will pay the tax due and obtain a tax deduction certificate from the relevant tax authority.

Termination, suspension and other clauses

For details about the termination, suspension and other clauses which should be included in a tour agreement *see* Chapter 3 Music Industry Contracts, Chapter 5 The Legal Status of Band and Solo Artist, Chapter 6 The Management Agreement, Chapter 7 The Publishing Agreement and Chapter 8 Recording Agreements.

The additional clauses which should be in a tour agreement include:

(a) A termination clause.
(b) A suspension clause.
(c) A confidentiality clause.
(d) A clause which provides that the performer has been advised to obtain and has obtained independent legal advice on the contents of the agreement from a solicitor with experience of music agreements.
(e) A jurisdiction and choice of law clause. (*See* Chapter 3 Music Industry Contracts.)

(f) An invalidity clause. (*See* Chapter 3 Music Industry Contracts and Chapter 5 The Legal Status of Band and Solo Artist).

(g) A clause emphasising that the promoter has no rights to any of the performer's or his band's copyrights, moral rights or performer's rights, nor the right to use the performer's or his band's name, likeness, biographical details or any trade mark belonging to him or his band except where expressly authorised in the agreement.

(h) A clause providing that the tour agreement does not constitute a partnership, joint venture or employment relationship between the promoter and the performer.

(i) A clause making it clear that the promoter has the right to promote other performers.

(j) A clause confirming that the agreement reflects the whole of the agreement between the parties and replaces any earlier oral or written agreement.

(k) A non-waiver clause. (*See* Chapter 5 The Legal Status of Band and Solo Artist.)

(l) A *force majeure* clause. (*See* Chapter 3 Music Industry Contracts.)

(m) A notice clause. (*See* Chapter 5 The Legal Status of Band and Solo Artist.)

(n) A clause which provides that the performer and the promoter will sign any documentation which is necesssary to carry out the terms of the agreement. (*See* Chapter 7 The Publishing Agreement.)

(o) A clause confirming that the performer is free to enter into the agreement.

(p) An indemnity clause. (*See* Chapter 3 Music Industry Contracts and Chapter 6 The Management Agreement.)

(q) A clause dealing with the Contracts (Rights of Third Parties) Act 1999. (See Chapter 3 Music Industry Contracts.)

The performer should ensure the tour agreement contains a clause that the promoter cannot assign the agreement. The only variation on assignment that the performer may be prepared to accept would be to allow the agreement to be assigned to a company which is owned and controlled by the promoter. An assignment may be acceptable to the performer in this limited case if the agreement is varied to include a key man clause, if the assignee (i.e. the company) enters a direct covenant with the performer that it will comply with the terms of the tour agreement, and if the promoter provides the performer with a suitably worded side letter. (See Chapter 6 The Management Agreement, Appointment of the manager above for the key man clause and for the side letter.)

Tour agreement and sponsorship agreement

There is a certain amount of inter-relationship between the clauses in a tour agreement and a sponsorship agreement. The performer's solicitor should bear this in mind when negotiating the provisions of the tour agreement. Matters which will be dealt with in the sponsorship agreement and which need to be taken account of in the tour agreement include:

(a) insurance,
(b) that the concert venues comply with all relevant laws and regulations which apply to staging concerts,
(c) advertising,
(d) tickets,
(e) details of the tour dates and venues and of any changes to the tour itinerary.

Consideration of how these matters should be dealt with in the tour agreement are dealt with in Chapter 10 Tour Sponsorship.

Tour Sponsorship

Introduction

As mentioned earlier (*see* Chapter 9 Touring), touring is expensive and for many performers is a loss-making exercise which has to be subsidised by the performer's record company in the form of tour support.

Another way of bringing in money to help a performer defray the costs of, or to help increase the profits from a tour, is to seek a tour sponsor to sponsor the performer for either the whole tour or for individual tour dates, *e.g.* a manufacturer of a product may look to sponsor a performer's nationwide tour, whereas a local radio station may only sponsor the performer for those concerts he plays which are within its broadcast region.

For many performers tour sponsorship will not be an available option as sponsors want to achieve maximum publicity for their money and this is generally best achieved by sponsoring an established performer rather than someone who is relatively unknown.

Some sponsors prefer to sponsor a series of concerts at a particular venue rather than a performer's tour, *e.g.* a local business may decide to sponsor a town's local music concert festival at the town hall. Such sponsorship money will not be paid to the performer but to the venue which holds the concert series or to the organiser of the concert series.

Sponsorship must be distinguished from endorsement and merchandising. A sponsor is paying for the right to be associated with the performer's concert(s). The sponsor will use this association to promote one or more of its goods or services. Sponsorship is not a direct recommendation by the performer of the sponsor's goods or services although it may be seen as a discrete passive form of recommendation because a performer would not accept sponsorship from a company whose products he disliked, *e.g.* a vegan would not want his tour sponsored by a meat company, as, apart from sending out the signal he is a hypocrite, it would associate him with the acceptability of meat products. A sponsor will be allowed to use its firm's name and logo, and the relevant product(s) which are the subject matter of the sponsorship agreement on the performer's concert programme, concert advertising material and possibly on the concert stage.

Endorsement is a personal recommendation of a company's goods, *e.g.* a performer recommends and uses a particular make of guitar and guitar strings or a particular make of saxophone and saxophone reeds with the implication that these products are good and help make him the performer he is.

Merchandising is the selling of t-shirts, badges, postcards and other assorted paraphanelia which features the name, likeness and logo of the performer.

The tour sponsorship agreement

Use of intellectual property rights

For the sponsorship agreement to work properly the sponsor will need to be able to use the performer's intellectual property rights, *e.g.* it will need the right to use the performer's name and likeness, his biographical details and any trade mark belonging to him, and where he is in a band the right to use the band's name and likeness, the band's biographical details and any trade mark belonging to the band in order to advertise and promote its sponsorship. (In addition, where the sponsor wants to use the performer's recordings to advertise and promote its sponsorship it will need to obtain the right to use the sound recording copyrights which exist in the performer's recordings and the right to use the literary and musical copyrights which exist in the compositions which are comprised in the recordings. Permission to use these will have to be obtained from the relevant copyright owners.) The sponsor's intellectual property rights will also need to be used for the sponsorship agreement to work properly as the sponsor will want, for example, its name and logo to be included on the performer's promotional tour posters.

The sponsor and the performer will grant each other licences to use their respective intellectual property rights to carry out the terms of the agreement. It is important to provide that these rights will be only used within the terms of the agreement.

Where the promoter needs to use a sponsor's intellectual property rights, *e.g.* where the promoter needs to use the sponsor's name and logo on the tour advertising, the sponsor should licence the promoter to use these rights.

The agreement should also provide that whenever a party's intellectual property rights are used its ownership of these intellectual property rights will be acknowledged, *e.g.* a trade mark symbol will be included alongside the sponsor's logo on the tour posters.

The agreement should also provide that where one party is aware of an infringement of the other's intellectual property rights that party will undertake to inform the other of the infringement.

Parties

The parties to the agreement will be the performer and the sponsor. Where the performer contracts through a company the sponsor will require a side letter from the performer guaranteeing that he will personally honour the obligations of the sponsorship agreement in the event that his company does not do so. The performer should ensure where he is required to enter a side letter that there is a provision in the side letter that he will honour the contractural obligations provided the sponsor is not in breach of the contract.

Territory

The agreement will need to provide whether the sponsorship covers the whole of the tour or only a specific part of the tour. The venues, dates and times of each concert should be set out in the agreement.

Term

The term will frequently be defined to include a period of time both before and after the concerts which the sponsor is sponsoring. This will enable the sponsor to build up and wind down its advertising campaign around the sponsored concerts. (*See also* Sponsor's right to exclusivity below.) The definition of the term should also take account of:

(i) any postponed concerts which have been re-arranged to take place after the proposed sponsorship term, and

(ii) any extra concerts which have been added due to popular demand which will take place after the proposed sponsorship term.

Because the term may be open ended due to re-arranged or extra concerts being added after the proposed sponsorship term, the performer should require a long stop date which provides that notwithstanding (i) and (ii) above, the term will not run, for example, beyond six months after the proposed sponsorship term. In addition, as the term may be open ended the sponsor may for commercial reasons, *e.g.* because it has a new advertising campaign about to start, want to be able to give the performer notice terminating the agreement at the end of the proposed sponsorship term, notwithstanding any right it may have to sponsor any postponed or extra concerts which have been added to take place after the proposed sponsorship term. (*See also* Termination below).

The sponsor may want an option to extend the sponsorship agreement beyond the current tour and into the performer's next tour. If the performer is prepared to grant the sponsor an option to sponsor his next tour, the contractual terms relating to sponsoring the next tour should be set out in the sponsorship agreement. Probably the most important term which needs to be considered is the sponsorship fee payable upon the exercise of the option. The agreement might contain a formula which will be used to calculate how much the sponsor will have to pay the performer if it wants to exercise the option, or alternatively the agreement might provide that the performer can negotiate with other parties but will have to give the sponsor a matching right, i.e. give the sponsor a period of time to match an offer by another party. If the sponsor decides to match the offer, it has the right to sponsor the tour. If the sponsor does not want to match the offer the performer is free to enter a sponsorship agreement with the other party upon the terms offered to and rejected by the sponsor. The agreement should provide where the sponsor has a matching right whether the sponsor has to match all the terms offered by the other party or only specific key terms such as the sponsorship fee.

Sponsor's right to exclusivity

The sponsor will want the exclusive right during the term of the agreement to be the performer's sponsor for those types of goods/services which are the subject matter of the sponsorship agreement, *e.g.* if the performer is sponsored by a company which manufactures a cola drink the sponsor will not want the performer to be sponsored by another soft drinks company during the term of the agreement. (*See also* The sponsor's rights below.) The sponsor will require this because it wants its sponsorship and any related advertising campaign to have maximum impact. The sponsor might also try to restrict the performer from accepting:

(a) any other sponsorship for the term of the agreement,
(b) any endorsement for the term of the agreement for:
  (i) any goods/services which are similar to the sponsor's goods/services, or
  (ii) any goods/services.

The degree to which the performer is prepared to be restricted will depend upon negotiations between the parties and upon how much money the sponsor is providing. The more money provided by the sponsor, the more the performer may be prepared to be restricted. The minimum a sponsor will expect for its money is the right during the term of the agreement to be the exclusive sponsor for those types of goods/services which are the subject matter of the sponsorship agreement.

Sponsorship fee

The fee will be paid to the performer either upon signing the agreement or, which the sponsor will prefer, it will be paid in stages, *e.g.* a percentage will be paid on signing the agreement, on commencing the tour, and at the end of the agreement term. The agreement will usually provide that the sponsor's obligation to pay the fee will be subject to the performer complying with his contractual obligations.

The sponsor's rights

The most important right the sponsor requires is the right to publicise its sponsorship of the performer. In order for the sponsor to be able to publicise its association with the performer during the term of the sponsorship agreement, the performer will be required to grant the sponsor the right to use his name and likeness, his biographical details and any trade mark belonging to him together with the right to refer to the fact that it is the official tour sponsor in its advertising and promotional material. The sponsor will also want the right to refer to its sponsorship on the packaging of the goods which are the subject matter of the sponsorship agreement.

Where there is only one sponsor for the tour, the performer will grant the sponsor a non-exclusive right to use his name and likeness etc for the term of the agreement together with the exclusive right to be and to refer to the fact that it is the official tour sponsor. (Where there is more than one sponsor of the tour, the performer will grant each sponsor a non-exclusive right to use his name and likeness etc. a non-exclusive right to refer to the fact that it is a tour sponsor and an exclusive right to refer to the fact that it is the sponsor in a specified range of goods/services.)

The performer will want the right to approve any proposed use of his name and likeness etc by the sponsor in any proposed advertising and promotional material. The performer will also want the right to approve any proposed use of his name and likeness etc by the sponsor on the packaging of the goods which are the subject matter of the sponsorship agreement. The sponsor may only be prepared to agree to the performer having consultation rights. Where the sponsor is prepared to let the performer have approval rights the sponsor will usually only agree to the performer having qualified approval rights, *i.e.* that the performer's approval will not be unreasonably withheld.

The sponsor will want the right to have its name included on all the promotional tour posters, in all newspaper, radio and television advertisements for the tour, and on all the concert tickets. Different laws and regulations apply to different parts of the media and what may be acceptable in a newspaper advertisement may not be acceptable in a television advertisement. The agreement should provide that the sponsor's name will be included on all tour advertising provided its inclusion is not prohibited by law or by any regulatory authority's rules. The agreement should specify how the sponsorship will be referred to in the advertisements, *e.g.* "In Association With..." or "Sponsored By...", the size of the reference to the sponsor and where it is to be positioned in the advertisements. Before the performer can agree to these proposals, he must check that the tour agreement requires the promoter to include the proposed reference to the sponsor in all the tour advertising. (If the tour agreement does not contain a requirement for the promoter to refer to the sponsor in all the tour advertising, the sponsor will very possibly not proceed with its sponsorship of the performer unless the promoter confirms that the required references to the sponsor will be included on all the tour advertising). (*See also* Chapter 9 Touring, The tour agreement, Performer's warranties and obligations and Promoter's obligations.)

The sponsor will also want the right to put up advertising signs and other advertising material in prominent places at the concert venues. The performer should allow the sponsor to display advertising signs subject to the concert venues giving their consent. Where a concert is to be shown on television the right to put up advertising signs should also be subject to broadcasting regulations. (The sponsor should liaise with each concert venue to arrange when it can go into the concert venue to set up and take down advertising material.)

The sponsor may want the right to manufacture and give away its own promotional tour merchandise to promote its sponsorship of the performer. If the performer is prepared to agree to this he should check his merchandising agreement to see if he is prohibited from permitting promotional tour merchandise being manufactured and given away. Where the merchandising agreement enables the performer to let the sponsor manufacture and give away its own promotional tour merchandise and the performer is prepared to let the sponsor do this, the sponsorship agreement should list the type of merchandise products which the sponsor can manufacture and give away. The performer will want the right to approve the artwork, design and quality of each product the sponsor proposes to manufacture and give away. The sponsor will only want the performer to have at most qualified approval rights. *i.e.* the performer has the right of approval with such approval not to be unreasonably withheld. The performer will also want samples of each product to be sent to him throughout the term of the agreement so that he can ensure the quality is being maintained. In addition, the sponsor should be required to warrant that each product will conform to health and safety standards. Because some venues will not allow promotional tour merchandise to be given away, there should be a provision in the sponsorship agreement that the sponsor can only give away its promotional tour merchandise at those venues which allow it. (*See also* Performer's warranties and obligations and Sponsor's obligations below.)

A merchandising agreement will prohibit anyone else from making and selling tour merchandise. Because of this, the performer should ensure that there is a provision in the sponsorship agreement which expressly prohibits the sponsor from making and selling any tour merchandise. If the performer does not have a merchandising agreement, he should still prohibit the sponsor from making and selling any tour merchandise unless he is being paid an additional sum for merchandising rights by the sponsor. (For merchandising *see* Chapter 11 below.)

The sponsor may want the right to have its company name and logo and product name and logo incorporated on the performer's tour merchandise which is sold at the concerts, *e.g.* on t-shirts, sweatshirts, badges, baseball caps etc. The sponsor should ensure that the sponsorship agreement specifies the size, wording and positioning of any such reference on the tour merchandise and whether the reference is to be included on all or only some of the range of merchandise products. Before the performer can agree to this provision, he should check his merchandising agreement to see if there is a provision which requires the merchandiser to include a reference to the sponsor's company name and logo and to the sponsor's product name and logo on the tour merchandise. If there is such a requirement in the merchandising agreement, the performer should make sure that the provision in the sponsorship agreement dealing with the size, wording and positioning of the reference to the sponsor's company name and logo and its product name and logo corresponds to that provided for in the merchandising agreement. Obviously, if there is no such provision in the merchandising agreement then the performer cannot give the sponsor such a right in the sponsorship agreement.

The sponsor will usually want a free advertisement in the performer's souvenir tour programme and a reference to its sponsorship included on the front page of the programme. The agreement should specify the size and positioning of the advertisement the sponsor requires *e.g.* a full back page colour advertisement, and should also specify the wording, size and positioning of the reference to its sponsorship on the front page of the programme. The sponsor may also want the printing and all the other costs involved in making up the advertisement to be paid for by the performer. Normally, either the promoter or the tour merchandiser will have the right to produce the performer's souvenir tour programme. The performer should ensure that his agreement with whoever has the right to produce the souvenir tour programme contains a clause which allows the sponsor a free advertisement in the souvenir tour programme and a reference to its sponsorship on the front page of the programme as per the sponsor's requirements. The party with the right to produce the souvenir tour programme will not, however, agree to bear the printing and all the other costs involved in making up the advertisement in addition to providing a free advertisement to the sponsor. For this reason, although the performer may be prepared to let the sponsor have a free advertisement in the souvenir tour programme, he will require the sponsor to pay the considerable printing and other costs involved in making up the advertisement.

(As was mentioned earlier, *see* Use of intellectual property rights above, the sponsor will need to license the use of its intellectual property rights where it wants its company name and logo and/or its product name and logo used, for example, on the performer's tour advertising or incorporated on the performer's tour merchandise which is sold at the concerts.)

Performer's warranties and obligations.

As was mentioned earlier, (*see* Sponsor's rights above), the performer will be required to grant the sponsor the right to use his name and likeness, his biographical details and any trademark belonging to him. In addition, the performer will be required to warrant that he has the right to use his name and likeness etc and that any such use will not infringe any third party right.

The performer may be required to use his reasonable endeavours to get his record company to:

(a) let the sponsor have a specified number of the performer's records for free for the sponsor to use in any competition which it might run during the tour,

(b) grant the sponsor a licence for the term of the sponsorship agreement to use the artwork on the performer's records on the sponsor's advertising material,

(c) grant the sponsor a free licence to use extracts from the performer's records on the sponsor's radio or television adverts for the term of the sponsorship agreement. (A licence will also be needed from the composer/publisher to use the compositions which are comprised in the recordings. The performer may be required to use his reasonable endeavours to help obtain a free licence from the composer/publisher to enable the sponsor to use extracts from the compositions on the sponsor's radio or television advertisements for the term of the sponsorship agreement). In addition to the need for a licence to use the composition and to use the sound recording, the agreement should provide that the sponsor will be responsible for paying any PRS and PPL monies due for the public performance of the composition and the record on the radio or television advertisement.

The performer may be required to attend a press conference on a particular date to publicly unveil details of the sponsorship. The agreement should provide that any reasonable expenses incurred by the performer in attending the press conference will be paid for by the sponsor.

The sponsor will require the performer to be available on specified dates, or where no dates are specified the performer should be required to be available on a specified number of occasions subject to being given reasonable notice, and subject to his previous professional or personal engagements, to attend a photo shoot to enable the sponsor to take photographs for its advertising material. The agreement should provide that any reasonable expenses incurred by the performer in attending the photo shoot will be paid for by the sponsor. There should also be a provision in the agreement for the performer to be able to approve the photographs which the sponsor intends to use along with the right for him to approve the way they are used in any advertising material, although the agreement will provide that his approval should not be unreasonably withheld.

Some sponsors may require the performer to make a radio or television advertisement for them. Such a requirement may go beyond the realms of sponsorship and into the field of endorsement. If the advertisement primarily promotes the tour but also refers to the sponsor, *e.g.* the performer says he is on tour and you can see him at the following places and the tour is sponsored by the company, it is arguable that the advertisement is primarily promoting the performer not the sponsor and so is sponsorship not endorsement. If the advertisement sees the performer using the sponsor's products and appearing to recommend them with only a brief reference to his tour, this would be endorsement not sponsorship. If the sponsor wants the performer to make an advertisement for him and the performer is prepared to do so, the performer should require an extra fee for doing it on the basis that it is either direct or indirect endorsement of the sponsor's product, and that a requirement for a performer to make a radio or television advertisement for a sponsor is not a standard requirement in a sponsorship agreement.

The performer will be required to supply the sponsor with details of tour dates and venues and of any changes to the tour itinerary. The sponsor will also want details of when the tickets for each concert will be put of sale to the public. The name and address of the promoter should be given to the sponsor so that contact can be made between them as the need arises. (The tour agreement should contain a provision requiring the promoter to supply the tour itinerary to the sponsor and to inform the sponsor of any changes to the tour itinerary. In addition, the promoter should be required to supply the sponsor with details of when the tickets for each concert will be put of sale to the public.)

The performer will be required to warrant that all insurances required for the tour have been arranged and that he will produce evidence of all such insurance to the sponsor. The sponsor may also require the performer to ensure that its interest is noted on a third party's insurance policy. This is to protect any right which the sponsor may have to any of the proceeds arising out of a claim made on a third party's insurance policy. As it is the promoter's responsibility to arrange most of the insurance which is required for the tour (*see also* Chapter 9 Touring, The tour agreement), the performer must ensure before he gives an insurance warranty in the sponsorship agreement that the tour agreement deals adequately with insurance. Where the performer has a sponsorship agreement (or wants to obtain sponsorship), the performer must ensure that the tour agreement reflects the need for his sponsor to have evidence of insurance and for the sponsor's interest to be noted on any relevant insurance policy(ies).

The sponsor will require the promoter to warrant that the concert venues will comply with all the relevant laws and regulations which apply to the staging of concerts, e.g. that the venues will comply with all health and safety requirements. The performer should check that the tour agreement contains a requirement for the promoter to ensure that this is the case before agreeing to such a warranty in the sponsorship agreement. (*See* Chapter 9, Touring, The tour agreement, Promoter's obligations.)

The agreement will contain a morals clause requiring the performer not to do anything which will bring himself, the sponsor or the sponsor's products into disrepute. The performer will usually have to accept a morals clause in the agreement even though he may feel that it is unnecessary. In addition, the performer will be required to warrant that he will not change his usual musical style or image during the tour. This warranty is required because the sponsor has targeted the performer's particular musical style and image as suitable for it to be associated with, and the sponsor will be concerned that a change in the performer's musical style and image may not be suitable for it to be associated with. The performer will also be required to warrant that he will perform at the concert venues at the agreed times, and that his performances will be given to the best of his ability.

Using the sponsor's products

Depending upon what the products are, the sponsorship agreement should provide that the performer will use his best endeavours to be seen to be using the sponsor's products in concert. The sponsor will also want the performer's tour staff to use its products at the concert venue. The sponsor will be required to supply sufficient quantities of its products at its own expense for the performer and his tour staff to use.

The sponsor will often provide, at its own expense, the performer's tour staff with tour clothing to be worn at all the concert venues. This is a comparatively cheap and effective form of advertising for the sponsor. The agreement will often require the performer to use his reasonable endeavours to ensure the clothing is worn by his tour staff at all the concert venues.

The agreement will usually contain an obligation upon the performer to provide the sponsor with free tickets for each concert. The sponsor will want free tickets for the concert so that it can either give them away in promotional competitions or use them for its own purposes, e.g. to entertain valued clients. The agreement should specify the number of free tickets the sponsor will be entitled to for each concert and should also provide that the tickets will be for the best seats in the house. Although the tickets will be for the best seats in the house, the performer will probably not want the sponsor to have free tickets for the front ten or fifteen rows at the concert venues. This is to ensure that real fans can buy these tickets and so help generate a proper atmosphere for the performer and the rest of the audience at the concert. The agreement may provide for the tickets to be in designated areas such as box seats or areas for corporate hospitality. The sponsor may also want the right to buy a specified number of tickets for the concert(s) at a favourable price in addition to its free ticket allocation. Before agreeing to any such provision in the sponsorship agreement, the performer should check his tour agreement to ensure he is able to provide his sponsor with free tickets and that he can provide the sponsor with tickets at a favourable price. The sponsorship agreement should always prohibit the sponsor selling any tickets which it has been given or bought at a favourable price.

The performer may be required to let the sponsor and its guests go backstage before and/or after the concert so that guests can meet the performer. A sponsor's post concert party might require the performer's attendance. The agreement should require the sponsor to provide the promoter with a list of those people needing backstage passes not later than, say, 14 days before each event.

The reason why the performer is prepared to meet the sponsor and its guests is because he is obliged to do so. The performer may not wish to and indeed, may have little time to do so, if he has to move on to the next concert venue. The agreement should therefore provide a minimum amount of time the performer is required to spend after each concert with the sponsor and its guests. The agreement will also need to specify who provides and pays for hospitality food and drink — in most cases this will be the sponsor.

The sponsor may want the right for their guests and themselves to be able to park their cars at the venue's car park. The agreement should specify the number of car parking spaces required at the venue and a requirement for the sponsor to provide the promoter not later than, for example, 14 days before each concert, with a list of the people needing parking permits and their car registration numbers. Before agreeing to this provision the performer should check the tour agreement to ensure the promoter will make the necessary arrangements for the sponsor and their guests to park their cars at the venues.

The performer will be required to inform the sponsor as soon as he is aware of any illness or disability which will or might prevent him performing in concert. In addition, the sponsor will want the right for its doctor and/or its insurer's doctor to examine the performer where the sponsor has taken out cancellation insurance or where the sponsor has an interest in any cancellation insurance which has been take out by the performer or promoter.

Sponsor's obligations

The sponsor's obligations include that it will:

(a) Pay the sponsorship fee.
(b) Comply with all laws and regulations relating to advertising or promoting their sponsorship of the performer.
(c) Not do anything which might affect the performer's image or reputation.
(d) (Where it is allowed to produce its own promotional tour merchandise), supply the performer with samples so that he can approve the artwork, design and quality. In addition, the sponsor will be required to send the performer samples of the promotional tour merchandise throughout the term of the agreement so that the performer can check that the quality is being maintained. The sponsor should also warrant that each product will comply with all relevant safety legislation and that it will indemnify the performer for any such breach. Product liability insurance should also be arranged by the sponsor and the performer's interest should be noted on the policy. In addition, the sponsor will be required to ensure that the promotional tour merchandise, the packaging and any advertising and promotional material contains the appropriate copyright and trade mark notices along with a reference to the fact

that the promotional tour merchandise is made under licence from the performer. The sponsor will also be required to ensure that the promotional tour merchandise is labelled in such a way that it contains all the information which is required by the law. (*See also* Performer's warranties and obligations above and The sponsor's rights above.)

(e) send to the performer any proposed advertising or promotional material which uses his name and likeness, his biographical details, or any trade mark which belongs to him, for his approval. (Where the performer is in a band there will also be a similar obligation relating to the use of the band's intellectual property rights by the sponsor on any proposed advertising or promotional material.) (See also Use of intellectual property rights and Performer's warranties and obligations above.)

Termination, suspension and other clauses

For details about the termination, suspension and other clauses which should be included in a tour sponsorship agreement *see* Chapter 3 Music Industry Contracts, Chapter 5 The Legal Status of Band and Solo Artist, Chapter 6 The Management Agreement, Chapter 7 The Publishing Agreement and Chapter 8 Recording Agreements.)

The additional clauses which should be in a tour sponsorship agreement include:

(a) A termination clause. The agreement may provide that the sponsor can terminate the agreement at the end of the proposed sponsorship term, notwithstanding any right the sponsor may have to sponsor any postponed or extra concerts which have been added to take place after the proposed sponsorship term. (*See also* Term above.)

The agreement should also provide that termination will occur where legislation is brought in subsequent to the parties entering into the agreement which prohibits the sponsor sponsoring the tour because of the type of goods or services which are the subject matter of the sponsorship agreement.

The agreement may provide that if a certain number of concerts or specified key dates on the tour are postponed or cancelled the sponsor may terminate the agreement and be entitled to either a full refund or a proportionate refund of the sponsorship fee based upon either the actual number of performances given compared to the number which were supposed to be given, or based upon a formula set out in the agreement which is weighted in favour of the key tour dates.

(b) A suspension clause.

(c) A confidentiality clause.

(d) A jurisdiction and choice of law clause. (*See* Chapter 3 Music Industry Contracts.)

(e) An invalidity clause. (*See* Chapter 3 Music Industry Contracts and Chapter 5 The Legal Status of Band and Solo Artist.)

(f) A clause emphasising that the sponsor has no rights to any of the performer's or his band's copyrights, moral rights or performers' rights, nor the right to use the performer's or his band's name, likeness, biographical details or any trade mark belonging to him or his band except where expressly authorised in the agreement.

(g) A clause providing that the sponsorship agreement does not constitute a partnership, joint venture or employment relationship between the sponsor and the performer.

(h) A clause confirming that the agreement reflects the whole of the agreement between the parties and replaces any earlier oral or written agreement.

(i) A non-waiver clause. (*See* Chapter 5 The Legal Status of Band and Solo Artist.)

(j) A *force majeure* clause. (*See* Chapter 3 Music Industry Contracts.)

(k) A notice clause. (*See* Chapter 5 The Legal Status of Band and Solo Artist.)

(l) A clause which provides that the performer and the sponsor will sign any documentation which is necesssary to carry out the terms of the agreement. (*See* Chapter 7 The Publishing Agreement.)

(m) A clause confirming that the performer is free to enter the agreement.

(n) A clause prohibiting either party from assigning the agreement. Where assignment is permitted in certain circumstances and/or is permitted subject to certain conditions the clause should detail the relevant circumstances and conditions which apply.

(o) An indemnity clause. (*See* Chapter 3 Music Industry Contracts and Chapter 6 The Management Agreement.)

(p) A clause dealing with the Contracts (Rights of Third Parties) Act 1999. (See Chapter 3 Music Industry Contracts.)

Chapter 11

Merchandising

Introduction

It is only once a performer has achieved a certain level of popularity that merchandising may become an important source of income for him. The amount the performer can earn from merchandising depends upon the status of the performer and the type of music he performs. For example, a pop or heavy metal music audience is more likely to buy the souvenir tour programme, badges, t-shirt and baseball cap than a classical music audience.

There are two types of merchandise, namely retail merchandise and tour merchandise. Out of the two, tour merchandise is usually the more lucrative for the performer because the audience who are likely to be fans, and are therefore a captive audience to buy the tour merchandise which is usually only available to buy on the evening of the concert, will tend to spend money impulsively as they are wrapped up in the enjoyment of the evening and want to take home souvenirs of the concert. In addition, tour merchandise tends to have a more expensive range of products available to buy than retail merchandise. The potential value of retail merchandising should not, however, be underestimated, especially via the internet. There is a sizeable sum which can be made from sales of badges, t-shirts, postcards and authorised magazines on the performer in retail shops, from inserts in record sleeves advertising the performer's merchandise via mail order, and from merchandise sales through the performer's own website. Record companies are certainly aware of the value of a perfomer's website for all purposes including merchandising (*see* Chapter 8 Recording Agreements, Grant of rights by performer above for record companies trying to obtain the performer's merchandising rights, and for reference to a report in *Music Week* (1 May 1999) concerning a recording agreement which contained a clause giving the record company ownership and control of a band's website).

There is no personality right in English law which the performer can license to a merchandiser. Instead, the performer will license a combination of the copyrights, trade marks and other rights which he possesses which the merchandiser needs to enable the merchandise to be manufactured, distributed and sold.

Where an unauthorised merchandiser produces merchandise without the performer's permission, the performer's rights (if indeed he has any) against the unauthorised merchandiser will lie under one or more of an assortment of laws, *e.g.* under the law of copyright, trade mark, passing off, breach of confidence, defamation, malicious falsehood.

Frequently, often for tax reasons, a merchandising agreement will be entered into not by the performer in person but by a limited company which is owned and controlled by the performer. Where the performer's own company deals with his merchandising the performer should ensure that all the necessary copyrights, trade marks and other rights have been licensed or assigned by him to his company. The rest of this chapter is written on the basis that the performer will enter into any merchandising agreements in person and not through his own company.

Merchandising does not fall strictly within the scope of a book on music contracts. However, as a performer may earn sizeable sums from merchandising it is useful to briefly examine the role of the merchandising agent and some of the key clauses in a merchandising agent agreement and some of the key clauses in a merchandising licence agreement. (For a detailed examination of merchandising and merchandising agreements readers are advised to refer to specialist books on the subject.)

Endorsement is the personal recommendation by a performer of a product such as a make of guitar or microphone. Although there are some performers in the music business who endorse products the majority are not involved in endorsing products. (It should be noted that an examination of endorsement and endorsement agreements is beyond the scope of the book. Readers are advised to refer to specialist books on endorsement for details.)

Merchandising agents

A merchandising agent will use his contacts to help secure suitable merchandising licence deals for the performer. The merchandising agent will want to be appointed as the performer's sole and exclusive agent for merchandising and will want a commission in the region of 20% plus expenses. (The permitted expenses should be defined in the agreement. There should also be a provision in the agreement that the merchandising agent is required to produce receipts for the expenses for which he is seeking re-imbursement.)

The merchandising agent agreement should obviously set out all the terms and conditions needed for the appointment of the agent. Set out below are a list of some of the key clauses which need to be included in the agreement. These include that:

(a) The merchandising agent has no rights to any of the performer's copyrights, trade marks or any other rights which the performer has, nor will the merchandising agent claim any rights in them.

(b) The merchandising agent will not do anything or allow anything to be done which might infringe the performer's copyrights, trade marks or any other rights which the performer has.

(c) The merchandising agent will immediately inform the performer where he becomes aware of any infringement by a third party of the performer's copyrights, trade marks or any other rights which the performer has.

(d) The performer will supply the agent with artwork showing how his name and logo may be used on the merchandise, together with approved photographic negatives of himself and the artwork for other images such as his album cover sleeves which may be portrayed on the merchandise. (The performer should check that all the necessary property rights are vested in him so that these items can be used on the merchandise.)

(e) Only the artwork supplied by the performer is to be used on the merchandise, and no other artwork is to be used without the performer's consent. Where the performer consents to other artwork being used the agreement should provide that copyright in the work and the physical property on which the work was created will belong to the performer.

(f) Upon termination of the agreement the merchandising agent will return all the items in (d) and (e) above to the performer.

Where the performer is in a band (a) to (f) above will need to be amended to reflect this situation.

To ensure that the terms of each licence granted by the merchandising agent are consistent and will not place an unexpected burden upon the performer, there should be a schedule in the merchandising agent agreement setting out the standard terms and conditions which must be in each merchandising licence. The merchandising agent should not be allowed to grant licences on anything other than these standard terms and conditions. The merchandising agent may, however, need some freedom to deviate from the standard terms and conditions as some licensees may not be prepared to contract on the standard licence terms. To allow some degree of flexibility, the performer may allow the merchandising agent to grant a licence which does not comply with the standard licence provided it does not differ from the standard licence in a material way.

Merchandise licensing

The retail and tour merchandising agreements should obviously set out all the terms and conditions needed for the appointment of the merchandiser. Set out below are a list of some of the key clauses which need to be dealt with in these licence agreements. These include:

Term

The term of the agreement will be defined in such a way that it will last for a minimum period of time and will continue until any advance paid to the performer has been recouped, *e.g.* the term will run for one year or until the advance has been recouped, whichever is the longer. The merchandiser should be allowed a chance to at least recoup his advance but the performer will not want the term to be open ended. To ensure the agreement is not open ended the performer could either insert a long stop date, *i.e.* the term will be for one year or until the advance has been recouped, whichever is the longer, but in any event the term will not last less than one year nor for more than two years in total, or the performer could provide that the term will be for one year or until the advance has been recouped, whichever is the longer, but if after the first year the advance has not been recouped the performer can at any time thereafter pay the merchandiser the unrecouped amount.

The advance

A recoupable advance will be paid either in full on signing the agreement or in staged payments throughout the term. What is unusual with a merchandising advance is that the agreement will often be drafted to provide that the merchandiser will in certain circum-stances be entitled to a refund of the advance from the performer plus interest at a specified rate. (*See* Performance and audience attendance guarantees below for how the performer's solicitor's should deal with such a provision.)

Performance and audience attendance guarantees

This provision is only relevant in a tour merchandising agreement. The merchandiser will want to sell its merchandise in all the tour venues and will want the performer to play to as large an audience as possible. To enable the merchandiser to calculate the advance it is prepared to pay the performer it will need to have details of the venues the performer will perform at, the maximum audience capacity allowed at each venue, and an estimate of how many people the performer believes will attend each concert.

The merchandiser will often require a guarantee from the performer that he will perform at a minimum number of concerts on the tour and in addition that he will perform in front of a minimum number of people. The agreement will often further provide that the performer will refund the advance plus pay interest on the advance at a specified rate if he does not perform at the guaranteed minimum number of concerts or if he does not perform in front of at least the guaranteed minimum number of people. The performer's solicitor should try and remove any such clause from the proposed agreement. It is unlikely that the merchandiser will agree to remove such a clause from the agreement in which case the performer's solicitor should try and obtain an amended version of the clause. Firstly, the performer's solicitor should try and remove any provision which requires the performer to pay interest on the money which is refundable to the merchandiser, and secondly, the solicitor should try and replace the requirement for the performer to refund the whole of the advance with a formula which requires the performer to refund a sum which is less than the whole of the advance e.g. that only a pro-rata amount of any unrecouped advance will be refundable. If, for example, the performer is given a £100,000 advance and he guarantees that he will perform at least 10 concerts on the tour and that he will perform in front of at least 100,000 people on the tour but in fact he only performs in front of 75,000 people; if the agreement provides that the performer will refund the whole of the advance plus interest if he does not satisfy the guarantee, he will have to refund the £100,000 advance plus interest even if he has recouped, for example, £50,000 of the advance. If, however, the agreement contains a formula which provides that the maximum amount refundable will be the unrecouped balance of the advance limited to the percentage by which the actual number of people who attended the tour falls short of the minimum audience guarantee, using the figures in the above example, the performer would only have to refund £12,500 i.e. as the performer is £50,000 unrecouped and he has fallen 25% short of the minimum audience guarantee he will have to refund 25% of £50,000, namely £12,500.

A formula such as the one suggested above would in practice be considerably further refined. For example, if the merchandiser agrees to a formula it will only want those people who paid for tickets to be eligible to be counted towards the minimum audience guarantee. This is because people with free tickets frequently do not spend any money buying tour merchandise or spend considerably less on tour merchandise than those people who buy their tickets.

The royalty

The royalty may be for example:

(i)   a specified figure per item, *e.g.* 50 pence per badge, £2.50 per t-shirt, 20 pence per postcard, or

(ii) a percentage of the gross wholesale or retail sale price per item less VAT, *e.g.* 35% of the gross retail sale price less VAT for badges, 30% for t-shirts, 34% for postcards.

The agreement might also provide for the royalty rate for an item to be escalated where sales of the item exceed a certain amount, *e.g.* if sales of badges exceed a certain amount the badge royalty rate increases to 36%, if sales of t-shirts exceed a certain amount the t-shirt royalty rate increases to 31%, if sales of postcards exceed a certain amount the postcard royalty rate increases to 35%. It is also possible for the royalty rate to be escalated on sales at each venue rather than on sales for the whole tour, *e.g.* if the badge royalty rate was a basic 25%, if there were five concerts on the tour and one of them was at Wembley Stadium it might be that for all dates bar Wembley the badge royalty rate would increase to 26% for badge sales over a certain figure, but for Wembley where sales might be expected to be substantially higher than at the other concerts the royalty rate would increase to 26% for sales over a certain figure, and 27% for sales in excess of this figure.

The royalty rate for tour merchandise will usually be somewhere in the region of 25–40% of the gross retail sale price less VAT. With the exception of VAT there should be no other deductions from the gross retail sale price. Due to the production costs involved, the royalty rate for the souvenir tour programme will not be based on the gross retail sale price, but will instead be based on the net profit after the deduction from the gross retail sale price of all the costs involved in producing the souvenir tour programme.

As mentioned earlier, (*see* Chapter 9 Touring, The tour agreement, Promoter's obligations) the promoter may, and the venue owner will charge a fee to sell tour merchandise at the venue. The venue owner's licence fee (which will usually be negotiated by the performer's manager or his tour agent) will be in the region of 35–40% of the gross retail sale price of the concert merchandise sold on the evening of the concert. This should not be deducted by the merchandiser from the gross retail sale price when calculating the performer's merchandise royalties. As mentioned above, VAT is the only deduction which should be made from the gross retail sale price when calculating the performer's royalty. Because the venue owner's licence fee to sell merchandise at the concert venue is a substantial percentage of the gross sale receipts and is borne by the merchandiser, thereby reducing its profits, it will be concerned that the licence fee does not spiral out of control. In an attempt to keep some control on the size of the venue owner's licence fee the merchandiser may insert a clause in the tour merchandising agreement providing that if the licence fee charged exceeds a certain percentage, *e.g.* 40% of the gross retail sale price, the performer will bear the excess out of his merchandise royalties.

The royalty rate for retail merchandise will usually be somewhere in the region of 15% of the gross wholesale price less VAT. Where retail merchandise is sold through mail order, the royalty rate will be in the region of 25% of the gross retail sale price less VAT. Where a retail merchandiser does not manufacture certain specialist items of merchandise it will want to grant sub-licences to specialist companies to manufacture these items. The royalty payable to the performer for these items will be in the region of 75% of the money received by the merchandiser from the sub-licensee.

(To ensure the sub-licence terms are acceptable to the performer the retail merchandising licence may either contain a schedule setting out the standard terms and conditions upon which the retail merchandiser may grant a sub-licence (*see also* Merchandising agents above for further comments on such standard terms and conditions), or the merchandiser will be allowed to grant sub-licences subject to the approval of the performer which should not be unreasonably withheld.)

The agreement should also contain a provision as to when the royalty is payable, and a provision for the performer to receive a statement of account. In addition, there should be a provision for the performer or his professionally qualified accountant to inspect, audit and take copies of the merchandiser's books and records to determine the accuracy of the accounts. (For further details on these and other related points *see* Chapter 6 The Management Agreement.)

Rights granted to the merchandiser

Where a merchandiser is only appointed for certain territories throughout the world the performer should grant the merchandiser the following rights:

(i) A non-exclusive right to use his name and likeness, his biographical details and any trade mark belonging to him on the products, in the territory, for the term.
The agreement must define the products, the territory and the term. The grant of a non-exclusive right enables the performer to allow others, *e.g.* his record company and his sponsor to use his name and likeness etc. (Where the merchandising agreement relates to a band, the merchandiser should also be granted a non-exclusive right to use the band's name and likeness, the band's biographical details and any trade mark belonging to the band.)

(ii) A non-exclusive right to manufacture the products throughout the world for the term.
This will enable the merchandiser to manufacture the products anywhere in the world without objection from either the licensor (the performer) or licensees in other territories.

(iii) An exclusive right to distribute and sell the products in the territory for the term.
Both domestic and EC law should be considered very carefully when drafting the rights clause to ensure the agreement does not fall foul of competition law, or restricts the free movement of goods, or abuses a dominant position within the whole or a substantial part of the EU. For example, it is within the law for the licensor to draft the rights clause to prohibit the licensee from "actively" selling merchandise outside the defined territory, whereas it is against the law for the licensee to be prohibited from "passively" selling merchandise outside the defined territory. Active selling

occurs where, for example, the licensee whose defined territory is England sets up a base in France to sell the merchandise products. Passive selling occurs, where for example, a third party who knows the licensee has the right to sell merchandise in England, telephones the licensee off his own bat to place an order for goods to be sold to him in France. Passive selling also include selling on the internet. If there is a challenge to the agreement based on Article 81, it would be possible to apply to the commission for individual exemption which if granted would be backdated to the date of the agreement. However, the commission would not grant an exemption to an agreement which contained a ban on outside sales.

(iv) A non-exclusive right to sell off the goods for six months after the term.

The agreement should provide that throughout the term the merchandiser will only manufacture those amounts of merchandise which it reasonably believes are necessary to satisfy consumer demand. To avoid accidental or deliberate building up of stock, the agreement may actually restrict the amount of merchandise the merchandiser can manufacture towards the end of the agreement.

Notwithstanding any limitation which is placed on stock production, the merchandiser will usually be left with stock on his hands at the end of the term. The agreement will often provide that the performer will have a four-week period from the end of the term within which he can buy any left over stock at cost price, and if he decides not to buy the left over stock the merchandiser will have six months within which to sell the stock, and that after the six-month period any stock which has not been sold will be destroyed. The clause will often provide that where the performer buys the stock, either no royalty or a reduced royalty will be paid. In addition, there will usually be a provision that where the merchandiser sells off the stock during the six-month period, it cannot sell it at prices which might suggest that the goods are either seconds, fire damaged or a discontinued line.

Where the left over stock relates to tour merchandise, the agreement should allow the tour merchandiser to sell the left over stock through retail outlets. The royalty payable should then be based on the retail royalty rate.

Approval of products, quality control, labelling

The performer will want to ensure the merchandise is of good quality and complies with all relevant safety legislation. If the merchandise is sub-standard this may reflect badly on the performer because it is of poor quality or is unsafe the fans may blame him for this rather than the merchandiser.

As the merchandise will incorporate the performer's name and likeness etc, the performer will want the right to approve the artwork, the design and the packaging of each product before it is manufactured. The performer will also want to approve samples of the product and its packaging before it goes into production to ensure the product is of good quality. Samples should also be sent to the performer throughout the term of the agreement so he can check that the quality is being controlled. The merchandiser should warrant that the products will comply with all relevant safety legislation and that he will indemnify the performer for any such breach. Product liability insurance should be arranged by the merchandiser and the performer's interest should be noted on the policy.

The merchandise products, the packaging and any advertising or promotional material must contain the appropriate copyright and trade mark notices along with a reference to the fact that the products are made under licence from the performer. The merchandiser must also label the products in such a way that they contain all the information which is required by law.

As well as controlling the artwork, design, quality and packaging of the merchandise, the performer should ensure that he has the right to approve any advertising or promotional material produced by the merchandiser to help sell the merchandise products. The performer should also ensure that any copyright material prepared by or on behalf of the merchandiser is assigned to him. This will enable the performer to use such copyright material himself and will enable him to control its use by the merchandiser and by others.

It should be noted that although the performer will want approval rights, the merchandiser will only want the performer to have (at most) qualified approval rights, i.e. the performer has the right of approval, such approval not to be unreasonably withheld.

Protecting performer's intellectual property rights

The agreement should protect the performer's intellectual property and other rights which he has licensed to the merchandiser. The agreement should provide *inter alia* that the merchandiser:

(i) Confirms that it has been granted a licence to use the performer's copyrights, trade marks and other rights for specified purposes only.

(ii) Confirms that all copyrights, trade marks and other rights which have been licensed to it belong to the performer, that it has no proprietary right or interest in the performer's copyrights, trade marks and other rights and that it will not claim any right or interest in them.

(iii) Will not do anything or allow anything to be done which might infringe the performer's copyrights, trade marks or other rights.

(iv) Will immediately inform the performer where it becomes aware of any infringement or possible infringement by a third party of the performer's rights.

(Where the performer is in a band (i–v) above will need to be amended to reflect this).

The agreement should also deal with who is responsible for taking action where the performer's/band's rights have been infringed, and who is responsible for paying for the costs involved in taking such action.

Maximising sales of the merchandise

The agreement should contain clauses designed to help maximise sales of the merchandise, *e.g.* the performer will require the merchandiser to *inter alia*:

(i) Manufacture the merchandise throughout the term of the agreement.

(ii) Manufacture those amounts which it reasonably believes are necessary to satisfy consumer demand.

(iii) Make the merchandise available for the public to buy throughout the term of the agreement, *e.g.* for tour merchandise this means it will be on sale to the public at the concerts, and for retail merchandise it will be made available to the public through the usual retail channels.

(iv) Spend a minimum amount of money each year promoting and advertising the merchandise in the territory.

(v) Not sell any merchandise on sale or return.

Merchandising a band

Where the merchandising agreement relates to a band the agreement should deal with what happens if a member leaves or a new member joins the band. The merchandiser will want the agreement to continue subject to an option for it to be able to terminate the agreement if a specified key member(s) leaves the band, or the make up of the band alters so that it is substantially different to the band which originally signed the merchandising agreement.

The merchandising agreement should provide that where there have been personnel changes in the band and the merchandiser has not terminated the agreement, the merchandiser will continue to have the right to use the band's name and likeness etc on the band merchandise until the merchandising agreement terminates. The merchandiser will also want a provision in the merchandising agreement that the band will require any new member to be bound by the terms of the merchandising agreement and that the band will require any new member to sign a document with the merchandiser agreeing to be bound by the terms of the merchandising agreement.

The agreement should contain a provision requiring the merchandiser not to manufacture any merchandise featuring the name or likeness of a member of the band on the band merchandise after he has left the band. The merchandiser should not be prohibited from selling stock which has already been manufactured which contains the name or likeness of a member who has left the band.

The merchandiser will want a clause in the agreement requiring a leaving member to give him proper notice of his intention to leave the band. This should help the merchandiser to avoid manufacturing a new batch of stock featuring a band member on or about the time he decides to leave the band and thus prevent the merchandiser being left with new supplies of outdated stock.

Where a band member decides to pursue a solo career and either remains with or leaves the band, the merchandiser will want the option to produce merchandise relating to that member's solo career. In addition, where a member leaves to join another band the merchandiser will want the option to merchandise the leaving member individually and to merchandise the band he is joining. Whether this is possible will to a large extent depend on whether the new band has its own merchandising deal.

Merchandising agreement and tour sponsorship agreement

As was mentioned earlier (*see* Chapter 10 Tour Sponsorship, The tour sponsorship agreement, The sponsor's rights), the tour sponsor will usually want the right to manufacture and give away his own promotional tour merchandise at the concerts. The merchandising agreement should be checked by the performer to see if he is prohibited from permitting the tour sponsor giving away his own promotional tour merchandise at the concerts. Even if there is no provision in the merchandising agreement which prohibits this, there will usually be a provision in the merchandising agreement which prohibits the performer from allowing his sponsor to sell his own promotional tour merchandise at the concerts.

Chapter 12

The Future

As the Bob Dylan song says "The Times They Are A-Changin'". The music industry is facing a massive threat from, and is having to adapt rapidly to massive developments in technology, and in particular from the existence and growing popularity of the internet.

The internet may in time change the face of the music industry. It is estimated that by 2004 10% of all music sold will be via the internet. It is now possible to buy a top selling CD on-line. Some recordings are not available for purchase in retail shops and only can be bought on-line. Merchandise can be bought through a performer's website. Live concerts by major perfomers can be heard on the internet, for example, Netaid broadcast live performances from Wembley, Geneva and New York and included performances by David Bowie, George Michael and Robbie Williams among others. Sir Paul McCartney's 1999 Cavern concert which was broadcast on the web attracted 50 million hits worldwide. Performers are readily embracing the internet as a medium for selling records, for example, David Bowie released his album "hours..." in North America for downloading onto a computer a week or so before it was released on conventional formats. (The user had to pay a fee to download the album which was encrypted so that it could only be played back on the computer to which it was downloaded.)

New developments in the delivery of music continue at a rapid pace. For example, MP3.com have recently established a service called my.mp3.com which allows a person to listen to his own CD music collection from anywhere in the world via an MPEG player connected to the web. (The way the service works is that a person uploads his own CDs to MP3.com. The contents are checked along with a check that he owns the CDs whereupon details of the CDs are stored in his own personal database. By using an MPEG player connected to the web he can listen to the music. In fact he is not listening to the tracks which are on his CDs but to the same tracks which are stored in MP3.com's music library.) In response to this Sony, Universal, EMI, BMG and Warners took legal action in the United States against MP3.com. In April 2000 the United States District Judge Rakoff held that the my.mp3.com database of recordings was an infringement of copyright. It should also be noted that judgements have been made in the United States against Napster.com concerning the sharing of music between computer users via MPEG3 files.

Internet record companies now exist. An internet record company will have its own website and will act as a distributor for unsigned bands who have recorded their own music. The internet record company may play 30 seconds snatches of each track from the band's album on the website so that the listener can hear what the album is like before purchasing. In addition, some performers allow the internet record company to offer a whole track to be made available for it to be freely downloaded by the listener to an MPEG3 file. The listener can then, if he wishes, either order the whole album on CD from the internet record company or can download the whole album for free onto a MPEG3 file.

Internet record companies generally offer the performer a royalty in the region of 50–75% of the gross receipts less VAT and distribution costs, such as postage and packing where this is not paid for by the purchaser. As with conventional recording agreements there should be no deduction for the internet record company's normal business expenses, *e.g.* there should be no deduction for the internet record company's office rent, business rates, staff salaries etc. Generally, the performer not the internet record company will own the copyright in the sound recordings. The agreement term is often only for one year and continues until either party gives the other notice of termination.

The distribution of music via the internet is still in its infancy. Indeed in the not too distant future it will be possible to access music from the net on mobile phones, car stereos, hi-fi systems and even from watches. As the internet has no territorial boundaries anyone anywhere in the world with a computer and appropriate software can log on and download music from a website. Many thousands of music websites exist. Many are legal, but equally as many are unauthorised. It is possible to find albums by top performers posted out in cyber space before they have been officially released which people can illegally download onto MPEG 3 files. Music industry associations are fully aware of these problems and are quite correctly acting to close down sites which offer material which infringes copyright.

Some people believe the problem with the internet is not so much a copyright law problem but an access right problem. Encrypting the music which can be downloaded will doubtless help protect the relevant rights owner's interests. Encryption software does exist for music which can be downloaded to a computer see, *e.g.* David Bowie's "hours…" album which could be downloaded but was encrypted to stop copying. The real problems lie in stopping unauthorised people putting a performer's music on the internet without it being encrypted so that it can be freely downloaded with CD quality sound by anyone with a computer and appropriate software.

Like it or not the internet is here to stay and the use of music on the internet will evolve. The industry will evolve and adapt as it always has done since the days of Thomas Eddison. Record and publishing companies rather than performers and composers own the majority of the existing literary, musical and sound recording copyright material. With such a substantial back catalogue in their possession the big music companies will still continue to thrive or even expand for some considerable time as the internet can be used by them as another way of exploiting their copyright material. Indeed at the time of writing, EMI and Warner Music have announced a proposed £12 billion merger at the same time that Time Warner, the parent of Warner Music, is being taken over by America On-Line. One of the reasons for the proposed merger is the huge potential for music sales via the internet. One potential threat is that very successful performers may when they are out of contract decide not to sign another recording agreement but instead finance the recordings themselves and sell them on the internet through their own website. Whether this will in fact happen remains to be seen.

This last chapter could have been named after Kraftwerk's 1981 album "Computer World" or after Radiohead's 1997 album "OK Computer". Computers are here to stay and may well be the future for music distribution. Music publishers and record companies will continue to exist and will obviously adapt their businesses to take on board the changes which will occur in the music industry brought about by the internet, as can be seen by the proposed merger between EMI and Warner Music. Most importantly, performers will continue to provide us with their creative talents which we can listen to on radio, LP, CD, Cassette, Mini Disc, DVD, MPEG 3 or whatever format their recordings may come out on in the future. The music lawyer will still be there negotiating and litigating in one of the most exciting areas of the law. As for the future of this book, hopefully there will be enough developments over the next few years in the music business to require an updated second edition!

Useful Addresses

The Performing Right Society Limited
The Head Office of PRS is at:
29/33 Berners Street
London W1P 4AA
Tel. 020 7580 5544
Fax. 020 7306 4455
E-mail. info@prs.co.uk
Web Site. http: //www.prs.co.uk

Mechanical-Copyright Protection Society Limited
29/33 Berners Street
London W1P 4AA
Tel. 020 8664 4400
Fax. 020 8769 8792
E-mail. info@mcps.co.uk
Web Site. http: //www.mcps.co.uk

British Music Rights Limited
British Music House
26 Berners Street
London W1P 3DB
Tel. 020 7306 4446
Fax. 020 7306 4449
E-mail. britishmusic@bmr.org

Association Of United Recording Artists Limited
Membership Office
11 Stoney Common
Stansted
Essex CM24 8NF
Tel. 01279 647201
Fax. 01279 647205
E-mail. auraartistuk@aol.com

Phonographic Performance Limited
1 Upper James Street
London W1R 3HG
Tel. 020 7534 1000
Fax. 020 7534 1111

The British Phonographic Industry Limited
25 Savile Row
London W1X 1AA
Tel. 020 7287 4422
Fax. 020 7287 2252
E-mail. general@bpi.co.uk
Web Site. http: //www.bpi.co.uk

The Musicians' Union
National Office
60/62 Clapham Road
London SW9 0JJ
Tel. 020 7582 5566
Fax. 020 7582 9805
Web Site.
www.musiciansunion.org.uk

Performing Artists' Media Rights Association
161 Borough High Street
London SE1 1HR
Tel. 020 7940 0400
Fax. 020 7407 2008
E-mail. office@pamra.org.uk
Web Site. www.pamra.org.uk

The Band Register
65 George Street
Oxford OX1 2BE
Tel. 01865 798795
Fax. 01865 798796
E-mail. nbr@bandreg.co.uk
Web Site. http:
//www.bandreg.com

The Music Publishers'
Association
3rd Floor
Strandgate
18/20 York Buildings
London WC2N 6JU
Tel. 020 7839 7779
Fax. 020 7839 7776
E-mail. mpa@mcps.co.uk

The International Managers
Forum
1 Glenthorne Mews
115A Glenthorne Road
London W6 0LJ
Tel. 020 8741 2555
Fax. 020 8741 4856
E-mail. office@imf-uk.org
Web Site. http: //imf-uk.org

British Association of Record
Dealers
Colonnade House
1st Floor
2 Westover Road
Bournemouth
Dorset BH1 2BY
Tel. 01202 292063
Fax. 01202 292067

Index